Around the World
with
Mark Twain

AROUND THE WORLD
WITH
MARK TWAIN

ROBERT COOPER

Arcade Publishing • New York

FIRST EDITION

Excerpts from *Mark Twain's Notebook* by Mark Twain. Copyright © 1935 by The Mark Twain Company. Copyright © renewed 1963 by Louise Paine Moore. Reprinted by permission of HarperCollins Publishers, Inc.

Excerpts from *Mark Twain's Correspondence with Henry Huttleston Rogers, 1893-1903*. Edited by Lewis Leary. Copyright © 1969 by University of California Press. Reprinted with permission.

Library of Congress Cataloging-in-Publication Data
  Cooper, Robert, 1931–
    Around the world with Mark Twain / Robert Cooper
      p. cm.
    Includes bibliographical references and index.
    ISBN 1-55970-522-1
    1. Twain, Mark, 1835–1910—Journeys. 2. Authors, American—
  19th century—Biography. 3. Voyages around the world—History—
  19th century. 4. Storytelling—History—19th century. I. Title
  PS1334.C66 2000
  818'.409—dc21
  [B]   00-25045

Published in the United States by Arcade Publishing, Inc., New York
Distributed by Time Warner Trade Publishing

Visit our Web site at www.arcadepub.com

10 9 8 7 6 5 4 3 2 1

EB

Designed by API

PRINTED IN THE UNITED STATES OF AMERICA

For Alice

CONTENTS

Around the World
with
Mark Twain

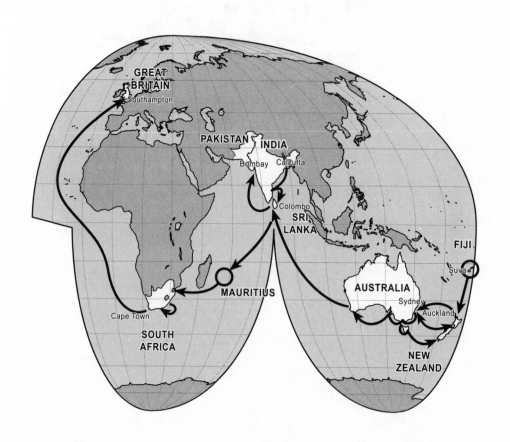

Ports of Call

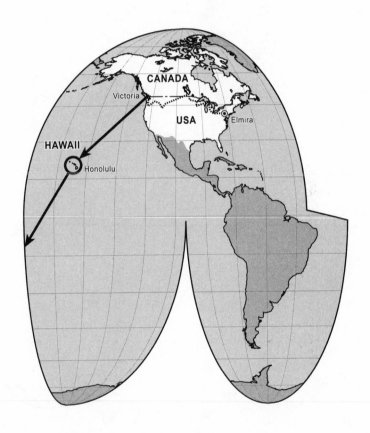

World Tour

Prologue

OLD, SICK, BROKE, AND DEPRESSED, Samuel Langhorne Clemens boarded a night train from Elmira to Cleveland on Sunday, July 14, 1895. He was five months short of his sixtieth birthday, an advanced age in those days. He had been bedridden for weeks, suffering from an immense carbuncle on his leg. The publishing firm of which he was principal partner had collapsed the year before, leaving huge unpaid debts and casting him into bankruptcy. Because he had failed as a businessman, he felt he had failed as a father and husband as well.

To his wife, Olivia Langdon Clemens, business failure meant disgrace. She urged him to pay the firm's debts in full, although he was not obliged to do so. He received the same counsel from a surprising source, his friend and admirer Henry Huttleston Rogers, a piratical, monstrously rich director of the Standard Oil trust. If, as many supposed, trusts were satanic, Rogers sported two horns and a tail. As a businessman he was ruthless, rapacious, and unscrupulous. But he was a loyal, generous, and sensitive friend. He took the Clemenses' financial affairs in hand, negotiated with creditors and publishers, and saved the Clemenses from ruin without injuring their pride. Clemens, who revered and loved him, listened when Rogers told him that an author could afford to be poor in money but not in character.

So Clemens was returning to the lecture circuit. When he had left it ten years before, he'd thought that he would never again suffer the noisy, dusty, bone-shaking trains, missed connections, and boring small towns associated with an interminable succession of one-night stands. But a lecture tour was still his quickest means for raising money. Not only was he the international celebrity Mark Twain, constantly interviewed and photographed, whose mop of bushy hair, tufted eyebrows, and swooping mustache made

him instantly recognizable, he was also a superb platform entertainer.

Cleveland was to be the first stop in a year-long tour that took
him, his wife, and their second daughter, Clara, to the Pacific
Northwest, Fiji, Australia, New Zealand, India, Ceylon, Mauritius,
and South Africa. One hundred years later to the day, I set out from
Elmira to follow them.

As a recently retired academic, I'd been craving a long journey.
Like Huck Finn, "all I wanted was to go somewheres; all I wanted
was a change, I warn't particular." Paul Theroux set the direction of
this change. In the introduction to a selection from his travel writings, he listed *Following the Equator*, Mark Twain's account of his
world lecture tour, as one of the few travel books he likes.

Almost as soon as I began to read it, I found a personal connection to the book. My wife's grandmother once met Mark Twain,
probably in 1901, when she was eighteen years old. A photograph
from that period shows her looking at you over her shoulder, half
smiling, half flirting, standing slim and erect in a long white gown.
Years later she would tell her grandchildren what she had said to the
great man when she was introduced: "Mr. Clemens, I'm not *a bit*
embarrassed. Are you?" This so delighted him, she would say, that
he kept her with him for several minutes to chat. She never
explained why the old man was pleased.

In the second chapter of *Following the Equator*, Clemens told
about having been introduced, years before, to a taciturn President
Grant. The president took his hand, dropped it, and then stood
silent.

"There was an awkward pause, a dreary pause, a horrible pause.
Then I thought of something, and looked up into that unyielding
face, and said timidly:

" 'Mr. President, I — I am embarrassed. Are you?'

"His face broke — just a little — a wee glimmer, the momen-
tary flicker of a summer-lightning smile . . . and I was out and gone
as soon as *it* was."

Ten years later he was again introduced to Grant. Before
Clemens could think of an appropriate remark, the general said,
"Mr. Clemens, I am not embarrassed. Are you?"

Although this anecdote solved a family mystery, it meant more to me than that. Suddenly the historical figure, Samuel Clemens, became human, a man pleased by the subtle flattery of a pretty young woman. Suddenly the last turn of the century seemed not impossibly distant. Could I come closer to him and his times by following the Clemenses, one hundred years later, along the route of Mark Twain's lecture tour? I wanted to try. I hoped to leave Elmira on July 14 and complete the journey in Cape Town on July 15 of the next year, as he did, traveling by surface transportation wherever possible.

This vision did not enchant Alice, my wife. She was not eager to rattle around the world for a year, changing accommodations every third day, boarding trains at five in the morning, and wearing the same two blouses and skirts month after month. On the other hand, neither of us wanted a long separation. We finally agreed that I would travel alone along the Clemenses' North American route during the summer of 1995 and that she would join me on the West Coast in late August and accompany me for the rest of the journey. But with one condition: we would return twice to our home in Jerusalem, for about a month each time, during the year-long project. Before she could change her mind, I flew to New York and from there found my way to Elmira.

1

NORTH AMERICA

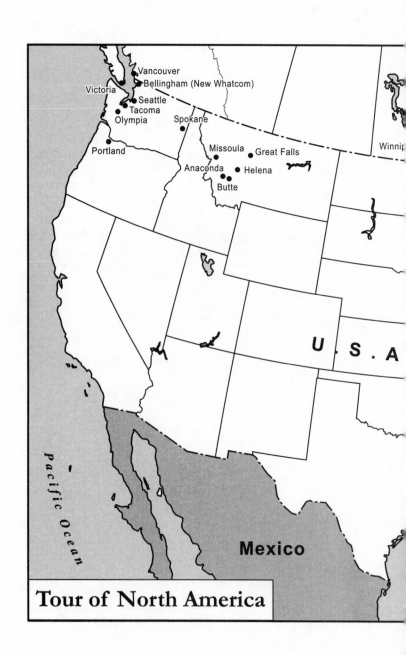

Tour of North America

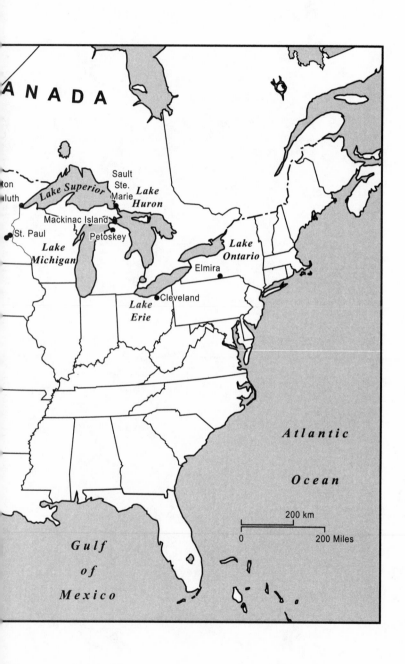

Chapter One

*E*LMIRA, THE SEAT OF CHEMUNG COUNTY, is a small town in New York State, about ten miles from the Pennsylvania line. Now, one hundred years after the Clemenses embarked on their tour, the Huck Finn Little League Ball Park adjoins Elmira's Holiday Inn, where Weight Watchers meet in the Becky Thatcher Room. You can walk from the hotel to the Mark Twain Riverfront Park, which follows the meandering Chemung River. Turning north, you will find the Samuel L. Clemens Performing Arts Center. Nearby is a tall red brick structure, the Connecticut Yankee Building, from which you can catch a bus to the Mark Twain Motel, formerly the Tom Sawyer Motel. The phone number at the Chemung County Chamber of Commerce, in downtown Elmira, is 800-MARK-TWAIN. If you call, you will hear the receptionist answer, "Hello, Mark Twain Country."

Elmira's attachment to Mark Twain stems from his summer visits. During the 1870s and 1880s, Sam and Olivia Clemens spent most summers at Quarry Farm, the home of Olivia Clemens's sister and brother-in-law, Susan and Theodore Crane.

In 1874, the Clemenses' second summer in Elmira, the Cranes surprised their brother-in-law with a study that they had created for him. It stood above their house on a knoll about 100 yards away. A small octagonal room built of oak, with a peaked roof and a window on each of its eight sides, it suggested the pilot house of a Mississippi steamboat, offering its occupant splendid views in all directions. From this hideaway, Clemens could look down at the distant town and its river and across at the blue hills beyond.

After a steak breakfast, he would climb the hill to his study and write without a break until late afternoon. There, undisturbed by domestic life, he composed much of *The Adventures of Tom Sawyer,*

The Adventures of Huckleberry Finn, Life on the Mississippi, The Prince and the Pauper, and *A Connecticut Yankee in King Arthur's Court.*

"It is a cozy nest," he wrote to friends, "with just room in it for a sofa and a table and three or four chairs — and when the storms sweep down the remote valley and the lightning flashes above the hills beyond, and the rain beats upon the roof over my head, imagine the luxury of it!" Clemens viewed his summers at Quarry Farm as "a foretaste of Heaven."

"The city in the valley is purple with shade, as seen from up here at the study," he wrote to his brother's wife on a summer Sunday in 1885. "The Cranes are reading and loafing in the canvas-curtained summer-house, fifty yards away, on a higher (the highest) point; the cats are loafing over at Ellerslie, which is the children's estate and dwelling-house in their own private grounds (by deed from Susie Crane), a hundred yards from the study, among the clover and young oaks and willows. Livy is down at the house, but I shall now go and bring her up to the Cranes to help us occupy the lounges and hammocks, whence a great panorama of distant hills and valley and city is seeable. The children have gone on a lark through the neighboring hills . . . with the coachman for comrade and assistant at need. It is a perfect day indeed."

Clemens was a familiar figure in Elmira, a booming and progressive industrial community. When he walked into town in his white linen suit and wide-brimmed straw hat, played billiards at the Century Club, gossiped with reporters at the *Elmira Daily Advertiser,* or spun yarns within the marble and walnut sanctum of Klapproth's Saloon, he was recognized not only as Mark Twain but also as a relative of the Langdons, one of the town's richest and most distinguished families. His father-in-law, Jervis Langdon, began his career as a country storekeeper, but he amassed a fortune from the mining and transport of coal. Although a flint-eyed businessman, he was a model of civic responsibility, a philanthropist who supported numerous progressive causes, including the education of blacks and women.

Today you can still walk from downtown Elmira to Quarry Farm on East Hill, two and a half miles away, as Clemens often used to do. One hundred years ago, you would have found four stone watering troughs, which the Clemenses had installed along the steep ascent, for the benefit of the horses that labored up to the house. Each trough was inscribed with the name of one of the Clemenses' children. Two of the troughs, in which flowers are now planted, stand near the house today.

The wooden, two-storied, gabled and dormered structure that the Clemenses knew, with its deep, arcaded and trellised front porch, is still recognizable, although the house was later enlarged and its exterior trim changed. Quarry Farm was a refuge for both of the Clemenses. It gave him uninterrupted time to write. It gave her a welcome respite from constant entertaining and from managing a household so elaborate it required the services of six full-time servants.

Quarry Farm, which Olivia Clemens's great-nephew presented to Elmira College, is not open to the public, but Gretchen Sharlow, director of the college's Center for Mark Twain Studies, has kindly invited me to see it. She has shown me the house and taken me up to the knoll where the study once stood. We have returned to the front porch, where Clemens's family would gather to hear him read from his day's work. The upholstered chairs and the patterned and fringed carpet that once furnished the porch are gone, but a few simple rocking chairs relieve the bareness.

Ms. Sharlow has left me alone for a moment. I look out at "the great panorama of distant hills and valley and city" and listen to the silence. It is about four-thirty in the afternoon. Just about now, Clemens would be descending the stone steps from his study, a sheaf of completed pages in one hand, a fresh cigar in the other.

When you go back to town, you can visit his study, which was moved to the campus of Elmira College more than forty years ago. Clemens's father-in-law was a founder and trustee of the institution, which was established as Elmira Female College, the first academy in America to offer a B.A. degree to women. His son-in-law's study now overlooks trim lawns, fountains, Georgian Revival and Gothic Revival buildings, and the black iron fence that once surrounded the Langdons' home and garden.

That stately house, a landmark for almost one hundred years, was demolished in 1939. On the site where Clemens courted Miss Langdon, where their first daughter was born, where Clemens and Rudyard Kipling met, and where one by one five Clemenses were eulogized, you can now buy a pizza at Picnic Pizza, mail a package at Mail Boxes Etc., or negotiate a loan at American General Finance. This complex is called Langdon Plaza.

Across the street stands the church that Langdon's money built. This is the Park Congregational Church, a massive, lofty fieldstone structure with tower and dome. Its founders, Langdon among them, had left the First Presbyterian Church to protest that congregation's refusal to condemn slavery. Like Elmira College, the breakaway church was a pioneering institution, a "church home," perhaps the first church in America to provide parlors, kitchen, playroom, library, and employment service. Now an important issue confronts the congregation: whether to adopt an "open and affirming" policy toward homosexuals.

Another progressive institution of the Clemenses' day, which also still exists, is the New York State Reformatory. Opened in 1877 as the Elmira Reformatory, the prison offered early release to young first offenders if they took classes in academic subjects or in industrial arts. The superintendent, a friend of Clemens's, would invite well-known speakers to address the inmates. Clemens tried out his material on them the night he embarked on his world tour. It was, he reported to Rogers, a "roaring success."

When the Clemenses returned to Elmira in May, after living abroad for several years to reduce their household expenses, Clemens had intended to prepare three programs, or "readings" as he called them, before setting out for Cleveland. During the North American segment of his world tour, he would be performing only once in each town except for Winnipeg, where he would appear twice. But in each of the larger towns of Australasia, India, and South Africa, he planned multiple performances. Because he preferred not to repeat himself in the same town, he would need several programs, which he hoped to prepare in Elmira.

But the carbuncle on his leg kept him bedridden. "My project of preparing and familiarizing myself with *three* readings, is knocked in the head," he wrote to Rogers in early June. "To do that with *one* reading is the most that I can do." Three weeks later he was still in bed. "My gracious," he wrote to Rogers, "it looks as if I've got to go on the platform only half prepared!" In his letter to Rogers the next day, he groused, "I'll go to Cleveland on a stretcher, sure." Almost two weeks later he complained to Rogers, "I shan't be able to stand on a platform before we   start west . . . I've got to *stand*. I can't *sit* and talk to a house — and how in the nation am I going to do it? Land of Goshen, it's *this night week!* Pray for me."

A carbuncle, he wrote on the first page of *Following the Equator,* "elected" to accompany him on his world tour. "The dictionary," he continued, "says a carbuncle is a kind of jewel. Humor is out of place in a dictionary." The infection on his leg may have been as red as a ruby, but that was its only resemblance to a jewel.

A carbuncle's redness and burning pain explain its name, from the Latin for "small coal." Like a boil, it produces an acute inflammation under the skin, but it covers a larger area and is more severe. In the days before antibiotics, it caused great suffering, often prostrating the patient, as in Clemens's case. If bacteria from pus pockets seep into the bloodstream, death can ensue. It was thought that persons who were depressed or worried were particularly susceptible to the disease.

The Clemenses' night train to Cleveland left from the Erie Railroad Depot, a bandbox of a station house. It was an ivy-clad brick structure of two stories, with striped awnings, a clock tower, a statue of an Indian at one side, and a file of horse-drawn carriages awaiting incoming passengers. One hundred years later, a PRIVATE PROPERTY, NO TRESPASSING sign marks the building, its arched windows and doors boarded up, its ivy, awnings, tower, and statue gone. A hideous railroad viaduct, built during the Great Depression and still scarring the town, disfigures its upper story. Traces of old trolley-car tracks, removed years before, stamp the brick street in front of the entrance, which faces the stray yellow flowers of a vacant lot. In place of a line of carriages stands a lone parked car. Most of the surviving buildings across the street are derelict, their slate sidewalks cracked, broken, and askew.

From the Erie Depot it's a short walk downtown, where vacant storefronts are common, new construction is rare, and the few new buildings are drab. No recent downtown structure reflects the supreme self-confidence of the sumptuous Italian Renaissance Town Hall, erected the year of the Clemenses' tour.

The last passenger train left the Erie station in 1970. Just as one can no longer ship anthracite from the coal mines of

Pennsylvania to Chicago entirely by water (Jervis Langdon was the first to do so, sending barges through canals in Pennsylvania and New York and through Lake Seneca and the Great Lakes), one can no longer travel from Elmira to Cleveland, or indeed to any other place, by rail.

You cannot follow the Clemenses' North American itinerary as they did, by trains and Great Lakes steamers. Like Elmira, many of the North American towns that they visited are no longer served by passenger trains, and the Great Lakes steamers disappeared long ago. Even the Great Lakes freighters no longer take passengers.

With the help of a few ferry rides, you can visit all the towns on the Clemenses' North American itinerary by bus, although you will have to double back between towns a few times. But if you are put off by the prospect of waiting for buses in stations as dismal as Elmira's, your only alternative is to drive. So, on July 14, exactly one hundred years after the Clemenses boarded the train in Elmira, I leave for Cleveland in a small white car.

Chapter Two

WHEN THE CLEMENSES ARRIVED IN CLEVELAND, they repaired to Stillman House, where Clemens, nervous and weak, his leg still painful, went immediately to bed. He cheered up in the afternoon, when reporters from all the morning and evening papers called on him for an interview, the first of scores that he would grant during the course of his world tour.

Despite having to answer the same questions over and over, Clemens willingly submitted to interviews, even when he was tired or ill, as a means of promoting his performances. But promotion was not the whole story. Reporters helped Clemens learn about the local scene, and they served as sounding boards for his impressions. He liked reporters, he could talk to them as an insider, and he relished his interaction with them.

In this first interview, the reporters asked him if he was the author of *Joan of Arc*, which Clemens had wanted published anonymously for fear it would otherwise not be taken seriously. It was then being serialized in *Harper's Magazine*.

"I have been asked that question several times," he replied. "I have always considered it wise, however, to leave an unclaimed piece of literary property alone, until time has shown that no one is going to claim it. Then it is safe to acknowledge that you wrote that whether you did or not. It is in this way that I have become recognized, and respected, as the author of 'Beautiful Snow,' 'Rocked in the Cradle of the Deep,' and other literary gems."

His performance that evening began late, because the enthusiastic friends and relations of a newly married couple, who preceded him with a program of flute and violin solos, demanded and received encores. Even worse, because the performance benefited a newsboys' home, five hundred newsboys sat along a high tier of benches on the platform, "which made them," as he wrote to Rogers the next day, "the most conspicuous object in the house. And there was nobody to watch them or keep them quiet. Why, with their scuf-flings and horse-play and noise, it was just a menagerie . . . They flowed past my back in clattering shoals, some leaving the house, others returning for more skylarking!"

Nonetheless, he told Rogers, "I got *started* magnificently." After hobbling onto the stage of the beastly hot Music Hall, the largest auditorium in Cleveland ("4,200 people present at prices ranging from 25 cents to $1.00," noted his manager), he introduced a scheme for the regeneration of the human race. "I was solicited to go around the world on a lecture tour by a man in Australia. I asked him what they wanted to be lectured on. He wrote back that those people . . . would like something solid, something in the way of edu-cation, something gigantic; and he proposed that I prepare about three or four lectures at any rate, on just morals, any kind of morals, but just morals, and I liked that idea. I liked it very much, and was perfectly willing to engage in that kind of work, and I should like to teach morals . . . I do not like to have them taught to me, and I do not know of any duller entertainment than that, but I know I can produce a quality of goods that will satisfy those people."

He would, he continued, illustrate his lecture on moral prin-ciples with examples of actual transgressions. Crimes, he asserted slowly and solemnly, are "not given to you to be thrown away but for a great purpose." If you impress upon your mind the lesson from each crime you commit, you will never commit that crime again, which will enable you to "lay up in that way, course by course, the edifice of a personally perfect moral character." There are 462 crimes, he said, a number which he changed from performance to performance. "When you have committed your 462 you are released of every other possibility and have ascended the staircase of fault-less creation, and you finally stand with your 462 complete with absolute moral perfection, and I am more than two-thirds up there. It is immense inspiration to find yourself climbing that way, and have not much further to go."

The stories that followed were offered as elaborations on this theme. He told about the first time he stole a watermelon. When he opened it, he found it green. "Now then, I began to reflect . . . and I said to myself, I have done wrong; it was wrong in me to steal that watermelon." When he decided to restore it to its rightful owner, as a "right-minded and right-intentioned boy" should do, he "felt that electrical moral uplift which becomes a victory over wrongdoing." He upbraided the farmer for selling a green watermelon to a trusting customer. The farmer was ashamed; "he said he would never do it again, and I believe that I did that man a good turn, as well as one for myself . . . I restored the watermelon and made him give me a ripe one. I morally helped him, and I have no doubt that I helped myself at the same time, for that was a lesson which remained with me for my perfection. Ever since that day to this I never stole another one — like that."

According to one reviewer, the audience was "convulsed" by his scheme for moral regeneration, but Clemens reported that within a half hour "the scuffling boys had the audience's maddened attention and I saw it was a gone case; so I skipped a third of my program and quit. The newspapers are kind, but between you and me it was a defeat."

But it was not long before he hit his stride. Less than a week later he wrote to Rogers from Mackinac, Michigan, that "at Sault Ste. Marie and here . . . they say I satisfied my houses. As to satisfying myself, that is quite another matter." A few days later he wrote to Rogers from Minneapolis: "I am getting into good platform condition at last. It went well, went to *suit* me, here last night."

In Cleveland he used the morals theme as a thread with which to piece together his stories. At some other performances during the world tour there was no common thread at all, but the transitions between stories were always so natural that the unrelated yarns he spun seemed to form a coherent whole. Occasionally his memory would fail him. But he was such a master of his craft that he could segue from the middle of one story to the middle of another without anyone in the audience detecting the slip, not even Olivia Clemens, who knew the stories as well as he did.

When you read verbatim accounts of his performances in newspaper reviews, you wonder why his material elicited such uncontrollable hilarity. Why would his listeners scream with laughter at a simple story that he strung out for ten minutes? They would, for example, find uproarious the story of a christening at which a minister extols the fine baby before him, foresees the infant as an upstanding young man, predicts a glorious career for him as a poet, soldier, or captain of industry, and learns, when he asks for the child's name, that it is Mary Ann.

According to Clemens, there are many kinds of stories, but the humorous story is the one most difficult to tell. "The humorous story is strictly a work of art — high and delicate art — and only an artist can tell it; but no artist is necessary in telling the comic and the witty story; anybody can do it." Unlike the comic and the witty story, whose effect depends upon their content, the effect of the humorous story depends upon the manner of its telling. "The humorous story is told gravely; the teller does his best to conceal the fact that he even dimly suspects that there is anything funny about it." If the humorous story ends with a punchline — a nub, point, or snapper as he called it — "in many cases the teller will divert attention from that nub by dropping it in a carefully casual and indifferent way, with the pretence that he does not know it is a nub." Critics often commented on his deadpan style. "From the time of his stepping out before the footlights to his leaving," wrote a reviewer in Melbourne, "the lecturer is never guilty of even the ghost of a smile — he is as solemn all the time as a wart on an under-taker's horse."

He took enormous pains to memorize his material and to rehearse its delivery, modifying both in accordance with his audiences' reactions. Dressed in white tie, starched shirtfront, and tails, he told his stories in a conversational style, as if he were chatting with his hearers. Although he took most of these stories from his writings, he did not recite them verbatim, because even stories written in a vernacular style sound literary when spoken. Rather, he reworked his routines so that their oral delivery would create the illusion of spontaneity. In fact, his delivery was no more spontaneous than the lines spoken by actors impersonating Othello or Hamlet. He memorized his material, utterance by utterance, not only the words themselves but also the manner of their presentation down to the last stammering repetition, hesitation, misplaced emphasis, side remark, and pause, fooling some reviewers into thinking that his performances were impromptu. His seeming naturalness on stage contrasted with the melodramatic theatrical performances and bombastic oratory of the day. Perhaps his most masterful acting lay in his impersonation of Mark Twain, the amiable, even-tempered, and insightful humorist and moralist.

His listeners' laughter was sometimes so unrelieved as to be painful to them. Soon after his Cleveland performance, he accepted his wife's suggestion that he insert serious or poignant material — such as the scene in which Huck decides not to betray Jim — to give his listeners a chance to catch their breath. He had done this successfully in earlier tours, which may explain his readiness to do so again.

His effectiveness depended in part upon the strategic pause. "The performer," he wrote, "must vary the length of the pause to suit the shades of difference between audiences. These variations of measurement are so slight, so delicate that they may almost be compared with the shadings achieved by Pratt and Whitney's ingenious machine which measures the five-millionth part of an inch. An audience is that machine's twin; it can measure a pause down to that vanishing fraction." To determine the proper pause, the performer must watch his listeners, which even the most skillful reader cannot do. This is one reason that Clemens quickly abandoned the dramatic readings with which he had experimented ten years before. He wanted to keep his eyes on the audience.

Perhaps his most spectacular use of the pause was in a story without a grain of humor, the "Golden Arm." He heard it from Uncle Dan, a slave on his maternal aunt and uncle's farm near Florida, Missouri, where he spent part of every year as a child.

On a snowy night, a man goes to his wife's grave, digs up her body, and takes her arm, solid gold from the shoulder down. On his way home from the graveyard, as he trudges through the snow, he hears a voice. "W-h-o — g-o-t — m-y — g-o-l-d-e-n — *arm?*" Shivering and shaking, he continues home. The voice follows him. "W-h-o — g-o-t — m-y — g-o-l-d-e-n — *arm?*" He reaches his home, races up the stairs, throws himself into his bed, and pulls the covers over his head. He hears the stairs creak. He hears the door latch open. He feels something cold by his head. Almost dead from fright, he can hardly breathe. Then the voice says, right at his ear, "W-h-o — g-o-t — m-y — g-o-l-d-e-n — *arm?*"

After this last quavering, sepulchral question, Clemens would pause. Then he would leap into the air, point at that person who seemed to be following the story most intently, and, with a blood-curdling cry, shout, *"You've got it!"*

If the pause was right, the effect was electrifying. But, according to Clemens, "you *must* get the pause right; and you will find it the most troublesome and aggravating and uncertain thing you ever undertook."

He once reminisced about hearing the story as a child. "I know the look of Uncle Dan'l's kitchen as it was on privileged nights, when I was a child, and I can see the white and black children grouped on the hearth, with the firelight playing on their faces and the shadows flickering upon the walls, clear back toward the cavernous gloom of the rear, and I can hear Uncle Dan'l telling the immortal tales which Uncle Remus Harris was to gather into his books and charm the world with, by and by; and I can feel again the creepy joy which quivered through me when the time for the ghost-story of the 'Golden Arm' was reached — and the sense of regret, too, which came over me, for it was always the last story of the evening, and there was nothing between it and the unwelcome bed."

Clemens's biographer Justin Kaplan suggests that the "Golden Arm" resonated subconsciously for its illustrious teller. As Clemens's business affairs declined, he relied more and more upon his wife's fortune, which derived in large part from coal, dug up from the ground. Further, as Clemens told Joel Chandler Harris, the "Golden Arm" was a parable about a man willing "to risk his soul and his nightly peace forever" to become rich.

Clemens was no stranger to the destruction of nightly peace. His bankruptcy stemmed from his continuing investment in a ravishingly seductive mechanical typesetter, so complicated that it could not be kept working for long. After its failure was clear, it was presented to a museum in a college of engineering, where it was exhibited as the most expensive piece of machinery, for its size, ever built. Its inventor, James W. Paige, who combined mechanical ingenuity and perfectionism with the eloquence of a snake-oil salesman, continually assured Clemens that the typesetter could be completed with just a few more infusions of cash. "He could persuade a fish to come out and take a walk with him," Clemens confided to his journal. "When he is present I always believe him — I cannot help it." A century before black holes became known to the world, Clemens, his wife, and his publishing company, whose assets he raided for the typesetter, saw their money sucked into one. Had he heeded the story he told so well, he would have cut his losses years earlier. But the machine obsessed him. The prospect of becoming a tycoon seemed always around the next corner, until the Panic of 1893 pushed his overextended publishing company into collapse. Now, in an effort to repay his creditors, he was galvanizing audiences around the world with the tale of the "Golden Arm."

Neither Stillman House, to which Clemens returned after his performance, nor the Music Hall now stands. One hundred years later a brick office building occupies the ground of the former, giving no hint of the spacious lawn that fronted the hotel. As for the auditorium, where thousands climbed its steep stairs to the uncomfortable balconies, it burned down three years after Clemens's performance.

Disappointed to find no physical reminders of Clemens's visit, I take a taxi back to my hotel. The rain that has been threatening all day begins to fall. I tell the pleasant, middle-aged cabbie about my quest for Mark Twain.

"It's a shame," he says, "that schools ban some of his books."

"Why do you say that?"

"Because he represents the best of America."

Chapter Three

*M*AJOR JAMES B. POND AND HIS WIFE MARTHA accompanied the Clemenses along the North American leg of their journey. Pond, one of America's top lecture agents, began his career by managing the speaking tour of Ann Eliza Young, Brigham Young's mutinous nineteenth wife. In 1884–85 he had managed Clemens's successful joint tour with George Washington Cable, the New Orleans writer. Now, ten years later, he was administering the North American portion of Clemens's world tour.

Like many veterans of the Civil War, Major Pond kept his military title. In 1863–64, as commander of a small force in Baxter Springs, Arkansas, he repulsed an attack by Confederate guerrillas who were disguised as Union soldiers. One of a handful of survivors, he was commended for gallantry by his superior officers. Thirty-two years later, in coping with a tired, sick, and irascible Samuel Clemens, he needed not only bravery but skill.

Pond left a remarkable record of the 1895 North American tour. Not only did he publish a lively account of the journey, but he also photographed it. Both his journal entries, which were the basis for his published account, and his snapshots were published in 1992 by the Center for Mark Twain Studies at Quarry Farm.

The snapshots, taken with an 1888 Kodak box camera ("You press the button, we do the rest"), show the party traveling and sightseeing across the northern tier of states, with forays into Canada. We see them on board the SS *Northland*, a luxurious Great Lakes steamship, which took them from Cleveland to Sault Ste. Marie. Clemens, in a dark three-piece suit and thin bow tie, wears a visored flat-topped cap, from which his grayish white curls escape, cascading down the sides and back of his head. A watch chain loops across his vest. Holding a pipe in his left hand, he sits with his back against a wall. He is looking up at a smiling Mrs. Clemens, who bends toward him, speaking. According to Pond, she is urging her husband, who is susceptible to bronchitis, to wear his overcoat on this cold day on the lake. She herself has donned a short cape. The thinnest of veils, attached to a confection of ribbons and artificial flowers atop her head, covers her face, which is viewed here in profile. At forty-nine, ten years younger than Clemens, she is still a good-looking woman.

In another photo, she is seated next to her husband. The twenty-one-year-old Clara stands between them, her head slightly bowed, apparently speaking. Shading her heart-shaped face is a dark straw boater. Her leg-of-mutton sleeves sheath her lower arms from elbow to wrist and meet the tops of her shiny leather gloves. Around her tiny waist hangs a leather purse. The photograph does not show to advantage her "ink-black hair" or her "large dark eyes," features that a Sydney newspaper was to mention in September. Her hat covers most of her hair. Her eyes are lowered. Even so, she is enchanting. Pond wrote that she was the loveliest girl he ever saw.

The three Clemenses, with their dark clothes and sober expressions, might have been waiting for a funeral to begin. Theirs was not a pleasure excursion. They had recently parted from Clara's two sisters, who had been left under their aunt's care at Quarry Hill and whom they could not see again for at least a year. A creditor had threatened to seize their luggage in Cleveland. Clemens was dissatisfied with his debut. His wife faced a more formidable job than usual of soothing, encouraging, and protecting him.

Still, Clemens was pleased that Pond had arranged an itinerary that would take them by steamers and ferries to towns along the Great Lakes before they headed out by train for the rest of the North American tour. The Great Lakes steamers were like oceangoing vessels, which Clemens, perhaps the most traveled writer of his generation, enjoyed. The *Northland*, for example, with its spacious promenade decks, boasted its own ice plant, producing five tons of ice daily. "I have seen no boat in Europe," he wrote in his journal, "that wasn't a garbage barge by comparison."

On the second day out, when he appeared on deck for the first time, many passengers made excuses to speak to him. One young man asked him if he had ever seen a shaving stone and then handed him one. It was, reports Pond, "a small, peculiar, fine-grained sandstone, the size of a miniature grindstone, and about the size of an ordinary watch." The young man explained that if you rubbed it along your face, you would become clean shaven.

Clemens moved it along his unshaven cheek, expressed astonishment at the result, and transferred it to his pocket. "The Madam," Pond reported Clemens as saying, "will have no cause to complain of my never being ready in time for church because it takes so long to shave. I will put this into my vest pocket on Sunday. Then, when I get to church, I'll pull the thing out and enjoy a quiet shave in my pew during the long prayer." At this time the city of Elmira was enforcing a state law prohibiting barbers from operating on Sunday. "A man may, indeed, shave himself," wrote a local paper that summer, "but unless he has practiced the art in youth, it is a fearful task, and for a middle-aged gentleman whose beard on a Sunday shows like a stubble field, there is no hope." This was several years before the introduction of Gillette's safety razor with its replaceable, double-edged blades.

When the *Northland* approached Port Huron, it sailed through a narrow passage with a row of summer cottages on one side. In his journal Clemens described the ship's progress through the corridor, with "groups of summer-dressed young people all along, waving flags and handkerchiefs, and firing cannon — our boat replying with four toots of the whistle and now and then a cannon and meeting steamers in the narrow way, and once the stately sister-ship of the line crowded with summer-dressed people waving — the rich browns and greens of the rush-grown far-reaching flat lands, with little glimpses of water away on the further edges, the sinking sun throwing a crinkled broad carpet of gold on the water — well, it is the perfection of voyaging."

Clemens did not mention that the warm greeting was for himself, his presence on the vessel having been announced. The waving and cannon were a salute to his courage and gallantry in setting out upon a world tour in order to pay his debts, an intention well reported in the press. He was an inspiration during that period of depression, one of the worst in American history.

Following the Panic of 1893, scores of railroads, hundreds of banks, and almost 16,000 businesses failed, and more than two million workers lost their jobs. The Sunday, July 14, 1895, edition of *The*

New-York Times contained only four notices in the "Help Wanted — Male" column, compared to sixteen times that number in the "Situations Wanted — Male" column. For women, no "Help Wanted" notices appeared at all, whereas more than ninety notices for "Situations Wanted — Female" were listed. (Women then represented about twenty percent of the labor force outside the home.)

Most of the positions in the situations-wanted columns were for domestic work, particularly as coachmen, butlers, cooks, and chambermaids. A "young girl, lately landed," sought housework or upstairs work. An "elderly lady, good housekeeper" sought "any light work," giving an address that was good for two days.

The average annual wage of a manufacturing worker at the turn of the century was $435. Female sweatshop workers took home four dollars a week. Young girls tending a textile loom made as little as two dollars a week.

Postage for a first-class letter cost two cents, *The New-York Times* three cents (to be reduced to a penny three years later), a ride on an electric tram five cents, and a vaudeville ticket twenty-five cents. In Elmira, during the week in which the Clemenses left for Cleveland, Hyland and Brown offered men's sweaters for twelve and a half cents; Coykendall carried summer corsets for thirty-three cents; and Elmira Crockery sold one-hundred-dish dinner sets for $4.50.

It is with these incomes and prices in mind that we must view Clemens's debt. He could pay his firm's creditors fifty cents on the dollar after the assets of the defunct firm were sold. If he was to repay his firm's obligations in full — to banks, printers, binders, and dealers in various publishing materials — he would have to raise another $70,000. Rogers reported Clemens's reaction upon learning how much money was involved: "I need not dream of paying it. I never could manage it." But, said Rogers, "he stuck to it."

In 1995 dollars, $70,000 would be equivalent to about $1,280,000. This is a formidable sum to most of us, but relatively small change to a handful of superstars, who earn millions per year. None of them is more celebrated or more successful than was Mark Twain in his day, yet his debt was anything but trivial. Although his books were best-sellers around the world, in English and in translation, the market for them was smaller than it would be today, both in the number of readers and in their buying power, and the means for promoting them were less powerful, so they earned relatively less than they would now. Movie and television rights were, of course, years away. As for his performances, none could be attended by more than a few thousand souls, whereas audiences of millions are available today. Consequently his value as a writer, performer, and celebrity was less than it would be today, when he could promote huge book and product sales, advertising revenues, and box-office receipts.

Were Clemens alive today, he could settle a debt of one or two million dollars with relative ease. On the other hand, given his passion for sudden wealth and given the investment opportunities available to a star of his wattage, he is likely to have made a proportionally devastating plunge. Be that as it may, both he and his contemporaries viewed his net debt of $70,000, the debt remaining after all the assets of his firm had been sold, as catastrophic. This was the debt that motivated his world tour.

Chapter Four

MOST OF THE HOTELS that hosted the Clemenses during their world tour and most of the auditoriums in which Clemens performed have been destroyed, either by fire or by the wrecking ball. The great majority of these were in city centers, where real estate often became too expensive to justify the low-density structures of one hundred years ago. Even when this was not the case, it was often cheaper to raze a building and construct a new one than to modernize the old one. Among the handful of exceptions is Michigan's Grand Hotel, on Mackinac Island.

The Clemenses arrived at the island on July 19, by means of an Arnold Line ferry, five days after leaving Elmira. Clemens had performed the night before at the Grand Opera House in Sault Ste. Marie, where a woman in the audience suffered a heart attack, brought on, perhaps, from convulsive laughing. Today the same line that ferried the Clemens party, now the Arnold Transit Company, brings you to the island. One hundred feet above Lake Huron, the huge, white, colonnaded hotel, built of pine and topped by a cupola, is still the island's most prominent landmark.

Most of the island is a state park. Neither in the park itself nor on the remainder of the island are automobiles permitted, save a few government vehicles. When the ferry docks, an emissary of the hotel takes your bag and places it on a horse-drawn wagon. If you are too feeble or tired for the ten-minute walk up the gentle hill to the hotel, a horse-drawn bus will transport you. The Victorian horse-drawn wagons are romantic, but you have to watch your step. One horse produces five tons of manure a year. A squad of young men is kept busy sweeping up.

At the time of the Clemenses' visit, the hotel dining room was two stories high. From a balcony a twelve-piece orchestra played

Victor Herbert's latest compositions. The tables, covered with fine Irish linen, supported heavy silverware and the best European glass and china. In 1895, when physical amplitude was admired, the guests ate three full, leisurely meals a day, and the best chefs were employed to encourage them to do so. Those chefs would have been surprised if not horrified by the low-fat cottage cheese, salt and butter substitutes, and vegetable plate that are offered by the hotel today.

Today's dining room no longer soars, its ceiling having been lowered to accommodate additional guest rooms. A five-piece combo has replaced the twelve-piece orchestra. But grandeur has not vanished entirely. You can find it in the dining room staff, stately, physically impressive men, who serve you deftly and who speak softly to each other in Jamaican creole. This evening, on my first visit to the dining room, their clientele is exclusively white.

The hotel was once a watering place for the rich, those who could afford three to five dollars per night for the room alone and who would often stay for weeks. The guests are still prosperous, or so it seems as they parade into the dining room. Everyone obeys the hotel's evening dress code: for men, jackets and ties; for women, what the hotel calls "one's best clothes." Most of the men wear blazers and slacks. The women favor street-length dresses, many in flowered silk, and loose pantsuits. No evening gowns. No gorgeous fabrics. No decolletage. No spectacular jewels.

One hundred years ago, a female guest would have had to bring many changes of clothing to be properly attired. At Grand Hotel (the hotel insists on dropping the article from its name), women brought outfits for morning promenades as well as changes for lunch, afternoon tea, and dinner. They required hats. They required gloves. They required the several detachable collars and cuffs that were made for each dress. And, because Victorian women avoided tanning in deference to the ideal of a peaches-and-cream complexion, they required parasols.

The Clemens women required, in addition, ball gowns. At a September ball given at Government House in Sydney, for example, Clara would wear a gown of buttercup satin, with cream lace, while her mother would wear one of white figured silk. They also had to pack sets of extensive undergarments, including corsets, camisoles, and petticoats.

One advantage of the large amount of clothing that women wore in those days was that it prevented sweat from penetrating beyond the layer next to the skin. Most grime on clothing was external, caused by street filth and air pollution. Horse-drawn vehicles splashed clothes with mud. Horse droppings, which were hard to avoid, and the dirt and mud of the streets, then mostly unpaved, soiled trouser cuffs or the hems of long dresses. Coal smoke, from cooking and heating as well as from industrial uses, smudged clothes as well. So the Victorian custom of changing for the evening meal was not an affectation. When you came home you had to remove your external garments, brush off the dirt, and then put them aside if you could not clean them right away.

When washing or cleaning a dress, it was common practice to open up the seams, even elaborate garments with forty to fifty yards of fabric, lay out all the sections on a clean table, smooth out the creases, scrub each side with soapy water and then rinse (or, if the dress could not be washed, apply a cleaning agent such as gin), before sewing the sections back together. Since cleaning was often time-consuming, travelers had to pack enough garments so that they could wear clean clothes while dirt was being removed from the soiled ones. Indeed, the Clemenses and Ponds traveled with an impressive amount of baggage: sixteen pieces of hand luggage and a multitude of vast steamer trunks.

The summer of 1895 was a hot one. Pond complained that in Cleveland the temperature reached ninety degrees in the shade at seven-thirty in the morning. He recorded ninety-eight degrees on board the SS *Northland*, on the Great Lakes. When he and Clemens left the women on Mackinac Island, on Saturday, July 20, for an engagement on the mainland in Petoskey, a small resort town, they found forest fires on both sides of the track. According to Pond, the smoke was "so thick as to be almost stifling."

In Petoskey, a reporter for *The Daily Resorter* wrote an account of an interview with Clemens that included a fabrication. The reporter put words into Clemens's mouth in order to ridicule a plan for a volunteer newspaper, organized by a schoolmaster named Hall, as a means for teaching journalism. "The scheme to get people to do reportorial work under the fond delusion that they are 'learning journalism' struck [Clemens] as going one better than the scheme by which one of his juvenile heroes got the other boys to whitewash his fence."

The next day, after he had returned to Mackinac Island and read the interview, Clemens sent a note to Pond: "This is too bad. Here for the first time since I started from the east language is manufactured for me. I have said not a single word about Dr. Hall's paper. I don't like being used as a waste pipe for the delivery of another man's bile." Pond immediately forwarded the note to Hall, who relayed it to *The Daily Resorter*'s rival, *The Petoskey Record*. The *Record* published it along with the offending interview and a defense of Hall's scheme.

The Clemenses and the Ponds left the island on Sunday, July 21, sailing on the SS *Northwest*, and arrived in Duluth at nine the following evening, late for Clemens's performance. Their vessel had been delayed at the locks between Lakes Huron and Superior, where Pond observed hundreds of sailing boats and steamers waiting their turn. Clemens, already dressed for his performance, was the first passenger off the ship. His driver rushed him to the First Methodist Church, where 1,250 ticket buyers had been been seated for more than an hour in hundred-degree heat. "I am very glad, indeed," he drawled, "that my strenuous efforts did succeed in getting me here just in time." Clemens did not like to perform in churches, where audiences, he thought, were reluctant to laugh.

After his performance in Duluth, Clemens appeared in Minneapolis, St. Paul, and Winnipeg. By the time he reached Winnipeg he felt secure about his first program and was ready to try out his second. He found it thirty-five minutes too long. At the end of an hour and a half, the length of his typical performance, he offered to stop, but the audience urged him to continue, and so he did. "Thus far," he wrote to Rogers the day after he left Winnipeg, "I have had more people in three opera houses than they've ever had in them before, winter or summer; and they swelter there with admirable patience; they all stay and see me through."

One of his auditors in Winnipeg was the young Stephen Leacock. He told Clemens that he had always wanted to have a brief word with him. "Why, why?" asked Clemens. The young man replied, "for what you said about the owl from Nova Scotia." Leacock was referring to "Jim Baker's Bluejay," a yarn from *A Tramp Abroad* and one of the staples in Clemens's platform appearances. The story tells of a bluejay who tried to fill a deserted shack with acorns, dumping them through a knothole in the roof. For three years birds came from all over the United States to laugh at this performance. But an owl from Nova Scotia, who dropped in on his way home from Yosemite, saw nothing funny in it. Yosemite disappointed him, too. In response to Leacock, Clemens laughed and said, "I'll move that owl to Montana to-morrow."

It was in Winnipeg that Clemens added his name to a petition urging clemency for Maria Barbella, a young Italian immigrant who had been sentenced to death. "I have read all about the case," he wrote along with his signature, "and hold it a privilege to be allowed to sign the petition." Barbella was the first woman in New York to be condemned to death after the state introduced the electric chair seven years before. She was to be executed during the week of August 19.

Maria Barbella had been been convicted of murdering her lover, Domenico Cataldo, who had promised to marry her but had repeatedly reneged. Shortly before she killed him, she learned that he had a wife in Italy. Nonetheless, on the day of the murder, she went to a bar where he was playing cards and demanded that he marry her.

"Only hogs marry," he said.

Slowly she walked behind his chair, brought her arms up around his neck as if to embrace him, pulled back his head, and cut his throat. She had been carrying an old razor in her hand.

The defense claimed that her life had been blameless until she met Cataldo, that his brutal behavior had goaded her to desperation, and that she had been unable to control her fiery temper. After a two-day trial, which began the week before the Clemenses left Elmira, the jurors accepted the prosecution's claim that the killing was premeditated. They deliberated for an hour and a half. When the judge imposed the mandatory death penalty, he told Barbella, through an interpreter, that "the evidence produced, mainly undisputed, was overwhelming in proof of your guilt."

Immediately thereafter, prominent Italian Americans went to work on her behalf. Thousands of people, including Lillian Russell as well as Clemens, signed a petition for pardon. Activists on Barbella's behalf organized mass meetings and parlor meetings. Letters and telegrams pleading for mercy poured into the Governor's office. A prominent clergyman preached a sermon in her support, referring to an incident in the Gospels in which a sinful woman is told to "go and sin no more." He said that Barbella ought to be exonerated "because what she did the public believes was excusable."

The New-York Times thundered against efforts to secure a pardon: "For Gov. Morton to pardon the murderess would be to violate his oath of office . . . The facts in the case are self-evident to all not mentally blind. A savage murder was committed to avenge a wrong . . . There is absolutely nothing more to the case than that." The governor's private secretary accused those who signed the petition of being ignorant of the facts. "All that is apparent is a sensational craze pervading the whole country . . . on behalf of the prisoner."

The assistant district attorney who prosecuted Barbella issued a statement in response to the public agitation. He claimed to possess evidence — which he had not introduced in court because, he said, he had not wanted to make her look even worse — that Maria Barbella went willingly to live with her lover on the basis of a financial arrangement. The lover had promised, according to the prosecutor, to give her half of the $825 deposited in his savings account, and when he later refused to give her $400, she became enraged and threatened to kill him.

A new defense attorney took on the case pro bono, filed an appeal, and won a new trial. At Barbella's second trial, he argued that she had inherited "psychical epilepsy," which allowed her to commit an act unconsciously, even though she could recall it later. After less than an hour's deliberation, the jury acquitted her, delighting the women in the crowded courtroom. In broken English, Maria Barbella thanked each juror. They returned her greeting, reported *The New-York Times*, "as though it had been a pleasure to acquit her."

After the weekend in which he signed the petition, Clemens and his party left Winnipeg and traveled to Crookston, Minnesota, where they stayed at the new Hotel Crookston. The town was proud of the hotel, which it considered the finest in the Northwest. The party arrived two nights before the hotel's gala opening, so they were its first guests and, that night, its only ones. True, they had to wait several hours before an electrician persuaded the lights to work, but this did not bother Clemens, who went to bed immediately. The hotel, built to last one hundred years, the first in the area with hot and cold running water and electric lights, was knocked down in the 1960s.

The Grand Opera House, where Clemens performed and elephants once appeared on the stage, burned down in the 1980s. It had not been used as an auditorium since 1912, when new fire laws prohibited the operation of a theater entered from an upper story. Nonetheless, its site is still called the Opera Block.

Although these buildings have disappeared, the memory of Mark Twain's visit remains. In 1994, Ed Melby, chief curator of the Polk County Historical Society, impersonated Twain in the town's annual Ox Cart Days Festival. A tall man of about seventy, with a full head of white hair and a firm, cleft chin, he dressed in his father's white suit, stuck a drooping white cotton mustache onto his upper lip, and rode through town on a float in the Torchlight Parade. He won a prize for the best historical entry. Mark Twain's performance, Mr. Melby tells me, was such an important event that special trains were run. Some of the sleeping cars were left on the sidings to save passengers the cost of a hotel.

On the day of his Crookston performance, Clemens wrote to Rogers that he hoped his audience would allow him to lengthen his program by adding a new piece that he hoped to try out. "But I won't without their consent, for a special train-load of them are coming 180 miles and I must not tire them."

It was a small town then, with only 3,992 persons. The count probably overlooked residents such as "the servant girl and the hired man," according to the Crookston *Daily Times*. The paper would have liked "to see the record increased beyond the 4,000 mark at least, if for no other reason than to gratify the pride of the people." As to municipal services, a horse and wagon picked up the garbage, and twice a week a team pulling a wooden, barrel-like tank of water on wheels flushed down the streets, unpaved until the twentieth century. Fires were fought by a volunteer force. Its ladders were chained and padlocked to a large tree in front of the Merchant's National Bank, so that the firemen would not have to hunt up the housepainter during a fire call.

The *Daily Times* told its readers that "this is the first and will probably be the last opportunity the people of the Northwest will have of seeing the man who stands today as perhaps the most popular author in the world . . . no one who can possibly afford it should allow it to be said that they neglected to see this celebrated man." Later the paper gave his performance a rave review, which declared that "the close attention he received must have been very gratifying. Of course there were a few who had gone with the idea of hearing something on the negro minstrel order and these were disappointed."

From Crookston, Clemens wrote to Rogers: "I'm stealing a moment to scribble this line. I have to *steal* my odd moments, for I am at work *all* the time on my lectures, on board the trains and everywhere." He was practicing and testing new material, introducing about twenty new items during the North American segment of his tour.

The morning after the Crookston performance, the Clemenses and Ponds rose at three-thirty in order to catch the 4:00 A.M. train. When they arrived at the station five minutes before their scheduled departure, they found a notice on the bulletin board that the Pacific Mail was one hour and twenty minutes late. The morning was chilly and the waiting room dismal, so they walked up and down the platform. Clemens grumbled and griped. He insisted that he had contracted with Pond to travel and not to wait around railroad stations at five in the morning. Mrs. Clemens suggested that he was not entirely reasonable. No, he said, standing next to a baggage truck, he was entirely reasonable. Pond should fulfill his contract by wheeling him about on the baggage truck. "He insisted on traveling," wrote Pond, "so he got aboard the baggage truck and I *travelled* him up and down the platform."

As the sun rose at five, Clara snapped the scene: Pond, in an overcoat and straw boater, trundles Clemens, who faces him. Clemens's overcoat collar is drawn up to his ears, and his feet dangle over the cart. Olivia Clemens, her hand shielding her eyes from the rising sun, looks out at her daughter, whose long shadow appears on the print. Martha Pond, in white boater and veil, is half hidden behind a great pile of trunks.

The train took them west, through the prairies of North Dakota, the fields green with wheat just ripening, then onward across the Missouri River. The next day, at seven-thirty in the morning, the train deposited the Clemenses and Ponds in Great Falls, Montana, where Pond complained that "the extortions from porters, baggagemen, and bellboys surpass anything I know of. The smallest money is two bits here — absurd."

Clemens noted in his journal that he changed his watch for the third time. He probably meant twice, since Great Falls, as today, was only two zones away from New York. Standard time zones were only twelve years old, having been determined not by the government but by an association of railroad managers in 1883. The time zones did not become federal law until 1918.

Great Falls was the first town in which Clemens felt well enough to walk outside. Pond photographed him sitting in front of a tarpaper shack on the outskirts of town and holding two kittens to his chest. Clemens, who was fond of cats, is trying to buy them from the kittens' owner, a small, barefoot girl in a white bonnet and long-sleeved dress, who looks apprehensively at the camera. Pond reported that after she tearfully refused to part with them, Clemens restored her good humor by telling her a story. Her frowning, frowzy, tired-looking young mother, in long-sleeved blouse and long skirt, stands next to her, holding the hand of a younger daughter. A third girl, a towhead in high buttoned shoes and dotted, long-sleeved dress, stands within reach of the great man.

Paris Gibson, founder of Great Falls, and his brother took the Clemenses and Ponds to the Giant Springs, one of the world's largest freshwater springs, and to Rainbow Falls. Lewis and Clark noted the deep blue-green color of the springs seething out of the ground on the banks of the Missouri, a color that both Pond and Clemens mentioned in their journals. On the way, the party saw a young cowboy, who was showing off, thrown over his horse's head. The horse was injured and Clemens would likely not have been sorry if the cowboy had been, too.

A few years after the Clemenses' visit, the Rainbow Falls were diminished by the construction of a dam at the site. But as for the springs, even today its color is as beautiful as ever, as it flows into the Missouri, creating a ribbon, several hundred feet long, within the river. The site, now a state park, with well-kept lawns and mature shade trees, provides a luxurious setting quite unlike the rough, treeless scrub that forms the background of a photo of Sam and Olivia Clemens, Martha Pond, and Paris Gibson at the springs.

The excursion, a long ride from town, tired everyone, particularly Clemens. His act that night at the Opera House (which became a venue for wrestling matches before it was torn down in 1955) was not his best. This almost broke his heart, according to Pond. The next day, while they traveled from Great Falls to Butte, Clemens brooded about his disappointing performance.

But he more than made up for it that night in Butte. Pond "escorted Mrs. Clemens and Clara to a box in the theatre, expecting to return immediately to the hotel, but I found myself listening, and sat through the lecture, enjoying every word . . . I had never known him to be quite so good. He was great. The house was full and very responsive."

Clemens found a sophisticated audience, "intellectual and dressed in perfect taste," he noted in his journal, a "London-Parisian-New York audience out in the mines." The audience probably included, along with their families, the owners and managers of mines, smelters, and reduction works, their senior technicians, and the principals and senior employees of the banking, freighting, and merchandising enterprises that had arisen to serve the town.

After the lecture, Clemens and Pond went to what the latter described as "a fine club, where champagne and stories blended until twelve." This was probably the Silver Bow Club, which survives to this day, although in different quarters. Clemens, whose preferred nightcap, according to Pond, was "hot Scotch, winter and summer, without any sugar, and never before 11 P.M.," did not drink the champagne.

The elegance of the club contrasted with the rawness and

bleakness of the town. Butte arose as a mining camp in the 1860s, with first gold, then silver, and finally copper dominating its economy. Demand for copper, an ideal medium for electrical conduction, had grown enormously with the development of electric lights, street railways, and telephones. When the Clemenses visited Butte, it was one of the largest and rowdiest mining towns of the period, with almost three hundred saloons (open twenty-four hours a day, seven days a week), as well as a suitable complement of whorehouses, gambling parlors, and dance halls. Its red-light district was one of the largest in the country.

Open dumps of roasting ore, which the local Indians called "stink pits," released clouds of sulphur and arsenic fumes, settling over the town in a pall so dense that streetlights sometimes burned during the day. The town was grim. Mining magnates built lavish mansions, but they could not front them with lawns. Grass would not grow. The leaves of houseplants left near an open window would yellow and wither, and the plant would die. The town was a wasteland of smelters, roasting ovens, cranes, and smoke stacks, a black and yellow industrial splotch upon a landscape of wildflowers, foothills, and canyons.

The mines that ran beneath the town, some sunk to the depth of almost a mile, were exceedingly dangerous. Many miners were killed in work accidents. They fell down shafts. They were blown up by premature explosions. They were mangled by machinery. They were crushed by falling rock. In the words of a song from western Ireland, from which many of the miners came, the streets of Butte were paved with Irish bones.

Working conditions in the mines were nightmarish. The great depth made ventilation difficult. Carbon dioxide levels were twenty times that of country air, ten times that of Butte air. It was so hot and humid that although the miners drank gallons of water (delivered in open wooden barrels and thus a source of typhoid), many had no need to urinate during a full ten-hour shift; they sweated all the water out. If they were not killed or mutilated, or disabled by tuberculosis, which spread in the close quarters of rooming houses, the work-life expectancy of Butte miners was about fifteen years.

But the pay was good and the work steady. By the time of the Clemenses' visit, underground miners earned $100 per month, almost three times the average for industrial workers nationwide, enough to permit home ownership. Also enough for a ticket to Clemens's performance, if they had the energy to attend it after ten hours of brutal labor.

Although Butte was rowdy, barren, and grim, it offered some of the amenities of cosmopolitan high culture besides theaters, including literary societies and lessons in dancing, singing, and French. Modistes traveled to Paris every year to buy gowns and select designs, so that rich Butte women could wear the latest French fashions.

Today, the smelters and reduction works gone, Butte is not the environmental disaster it was one hundred years ago. But it is, to be kind, a dump. It remains a casualty of the drop in copper prices about twenty years ago, which forced the Anaconda Copper Mining Company to abandon first its deep mining near the center of town, which had become more and more costly as the veins played out, and then its open-pit mining in the eastern part of town.

My motel stands in the "historic uptown," which occupies a steep slope looking out at flatlands and the snowy peaks beyond. At the top of the slope stand derelict rigs or headframes. These supported cables that lowered miners, dynamite, timbers, ore cars, and, in Clemens's day, mules, into the mines. Scattered among the frames, which stand on terraces of yellow waste, are disused workshops that once serviced the mines.

Nearby on Broadway, many upper stories are vacant, with gray rotted curtains hanging in those windows that are not boarded or bricked up. Faded slogans painted on the sides of buildings, such as "Creamery Cafe, Booths for Ladies," or "National Trunk Factory," serve as tombstones for dead businesses.

With little economic incentive to replace them, dozens of turn-of-the-century buildings remain. A few opulent mansions now serve as down-at-heel B&Bs or funeral homes. The Dumas, built in 1890 as a "parlor house" or brothel, once employing one hundred women in three daily shifts, operated for almost one hundred years, closing in 1982. But it has opened again. As a museum.

Maguire's Grand Opera House, where Clemens performed, did not survive, but next to its site stands a three-story structure built in 1891 by the Independent Order of Good Templars, a temperance organization. A plaque affixed to the building cites the Templar ethic: "Never cease until the last vestige of that fearful vice . . . is driven from our land." The building now houses a saloon.

Anaconda, twenty-six miles to the west, was the site of Clemens's next performance. Anaconda, where an alert vendor was advertising "Mark Twain cigars," was even more hideous than Butte. Its immense smelter, constructed in the 1880s, sent into the atmosphere clouds of noxious smoke seen from thirty miles away, producing air pollution so horrific that nothing could grow even on the hills nearby. It also created enormous black heaps of slag, which greet you today at the entrance to town. Part of these, when decontaminated under the supervision of the Environmental Protection Agency, will form sand traps in a new golf course. Behind the course, on land that lay bare for one hundred years, grass now grows. Nothing remains of the smelter today except its 585-foot smoke-stack, built in 1918, said to be the world's tallest free-standing brick structure. Now the nearby hills are becoming green. Schoolchildren plant trees there once a year.

Marcus Daly, who discovered and developed the rich copper deposits in Butte, where he founded the Anaconda Copper Company, built the smelter, and established and ran the town. One of eleven children born to a poor Irish family in County Cavan, he left home for America when he was fifteen, without a day of formal schooling. He started his mining career in 1865, after he had been in the country for nine years, when he became a common laborer in the Nevada Territory, at Virginia City's Comstock silver mine.

This was a year after Clemens had left Virginia City, where he had worked as a reporter for the *Territorial Enterprise.* So the claim by Daly's biographer that Daly not only met Clemens in Virginia City but knew him well enough "that he could have had a hand in the fake holdup perpetrated on the great writer" is unlikely to be true.

Almost thirty years before his performance in Butte, Clemens was the victim of an elaborate practical joke in Virginia City. Denis McCarthy, a former co-owner of the *Enterprise,* organized the stunt along with Steve Gillis, a friend and former *Enterprise* colleague of Clemens's. After a Clemens performance at Gold Hill, he and McCarthy were walking back to Virginia City. At the lonely Gold

Hill Divide, a place notorious for its holdups, masked men confronted them with six-shooters. With silver dollars at the sides of their tongues to disguise their speech, they told Clemens and McCarthy to put up their hands. According to Gillis, who described the event about forty years later, Clemens "wasn't a bit scared or excited. He talked to the robbers in his regular fashion . . . He was cool all the time." When Clemens started to lower his hands to comply with the bandits' demand that he turn over his gold watch and the receipts from his performance, they told him to stick them up again. How could he give them his valuables, he asked, without his hands? His treasure, he said, did not lie in heaven.

When Clemens learned that the robbery had been a hoax, he was, according to Gillis, "mad clear through." He canceled the extra performance he had scheduled in Virginia City, where he had planned to tell about the holdup, and decamped for San Francisco.

Whether or not he ever met Clemens, Daly became a great tycoon, one of Montana's Copper Kings. To promote Anaconda as a potential state capital, he built the lavish brick Montana Hotel in 1889. Special trains ran from Helena, Butte, and Great Falls to transport 1,500 guests to the hotel's opening ball, at which the wife of one copper magnate wore a necklace of diamonds and rubies. Clemens and Pond, who had left the women behind in Butte, spent the night there.

A few blocks from the hotel stood the Evans Opera House, where Clemens performed. The manager, who had known him thirty years before, was eager to bring him to Anaconda. But the town was too small to support the expectations of the manager, who was unable to produce what he had contracted to pay. "The manager was short about sixty dollars," reported Pond. "I took what he had, and *all* he had." When Clemens learned of this, he disapproved. "And you took the last cent that poor fellow had! Send him a hundred dollars, and if you can't afford to stand your share, charge it all to me. I'm not going around robbing poor men who are disappointed in their calculations as to my commercial value. I'm poor . . . but I don't want to get money in that way."

Chapter Five

*C*LEMENS REACHED HELENA, his next stop, on August 3, 1895, almost three weeks after leaving Elmira. Today the green, well-tended town seems heavenly after Butte and Anaconda. Grassy hills studded with ponderosa pine roll into the tree-shaded town. Downtown, the Montana Club stands on the piers of the original club, a magnificent Gothic Revival building in which the town's millionaires entertained Clemens after his performance.

In 1885, when the club was founded, Helena was enjoying a skyrocketing boom, fueled by its position as capital of the state, its proximity to gold fields and silver and lead deposits, and the arrival two years before of the Northern Pacific Railway, which soon quadrupled the population and substantially increased the traffic of goods into and out of the town. By 1888 the town was crawling with millionaires, fifty in all, about one for every 250 people. But by the time the Clemenses arrived, the town was less opulent. The Panic of 1893 had destroyed the boom, and Helena never regained its once fabulous prosperity.

The Montana Club was among the first of the dozens of men's clubs that were to honor Clemens during his world tour. Such dinners were formal, stag affairs offering numerous courses and plenty of wine. Champagne would accompany each of the eight or so scheduled toasts. In response to the obligatory toast in his honor, Clemens would give an extemporaneous talk, which usually caused the club members to explode with laughter.

On the night the club entertained Clemens, a few guests had come from Virginia City, Nevada, in order to see the man they had known thirty years before. One of them, now very rich, interrupted the toast to Clemens. "Hold on a minute," Pond recorded him as saying. "Before we go further I want to say to you, Sam Clemens, that you did me a dirty trick over there in Silver City, and I've come here to have a settlement with you." After a dreadful silence, Clemens drawled, "Let's see. That — was — before — I — reformed — wasn't — it?" One of the guests, former U. S. Senator Wilbur Fisk Sanders, defused the tension by suggesting that since the man from Silver City had never reformed, Clemens and all the others should forgive him and drink together. Clemens told stories until after midnight and then walked back with Pond to their hotel, "up quite a mountain," according to Pond, who observed that Clemens was getting strong. This was Clemens's first hard walk since leaving Elmira.

It was in Missoula, the Clemenses' next stop, that Pond saw "the first sign of the decadence of the horse: a man riding a bicycle . . . leading a horse to a nearby blacksmith shop." Pond photographed the scene at Clemens's suggestion. They were riding in a horse-drawn bus to the Florence Hotel, which offered all modcons including steam heat, electric lights, and electric bells. When the hotel was rebuilt in 1941, having burned down twice before, it included a parking garage, for automobiles, not bicycles.

By 1895, when automobiles or horseless carriages were merely a rich man's toy, bicycles had become such a craze that commentators predicted the death of the horse. Livery stable owners complained bitterly about declining business. The danger of colliding with cyclists induced some timid souls to give up their carriages, while others, particularly the younger set, preferred the bicycle to the horse. Merchants in Chicago claimed that no one had any extra cash because everyone was either saving money for a bicycle or buying one on the installment plan. Buyers were found even among those who figured their expenses so closely that a day's outing with their friends meant that they could not afford a streetcar fare for several weeks. Still, according to an article in *The New-York Times*, "the cycle will stay; progression is the law, and events do not move backward."

The bicycle is unlikely to have become popular if it had remained in its earlier form, the high "ordinary," with its huge front wheel and tiny rear one, derisively known as the "penny-farthing," after the largest and smallest British copper coins in circulation. The small back wheel set up an uncomfortable vibration, the rider had to pedal very quickly in order to maintain a decent speed, and, with the seat placed next to the handlebar above the tall front wheel, the rider was often pitched overboard when the tire encountered a small obstacle. (The expression "to take a header" is said to derive from the consequence of your front wheel's stopping suddenly.) In Hartford, during the mid-1880s, Clemens hired a young man to teach him to ride the penny-farthing. "Mr. Clemens," the young man said, "it's remarkable — you can fall off a bicycle more different ways than the man that invented it." In an essay burlesquing his difficulties in learning to ride, Clemens advised his readers to get a bicycle. "You will not regret it, if you live."

The bicycle that supplanted the penny-farthing, and the one Pond saw in Missoula, was the modern, rear-driven "safety," with wheels of equal or nearly equal size. After pneumatic tires were introduced in 1888, bicycles became hugely popular. Within two years, the safety monopolized the field. The postal service, the army, and the police used it. Delivery and messenger boys used it. Rich and poor used it both for exercise and for transportation.

Bicycle schools sprang up all over the world. Ten days after the Clemenses reached Australia, the premier of Victoria joined a class held in a gloomy, circular arena in downtown Melbourne. A reporter from the *Argus* recorded the scene. The premier "grasps the handles, and fixing his eyes about fifteen feet in front (as instructed), just the distance of the front Opposition bench, swamps the tiny seat, and . . . announces that he is 'ready to begin!' The teacher catches hold of all he can find of the saddle, and with a few preliminary wobbles, jactitation of legs commences. Slowly and gravely, almost painfully, the stately figure, with its supporting attendant, moves away into the heavy shadows, the white shirt-sleeved arms, like teapot handles, being the last portion of the citizen swallowed up in the darkness."

Although the hire of horses and light wagons declined, the horse was by no means dead. Well into the twentieth century, hitching posts and mounting blocks lined the streets of American towns. Just as filling stations, car dealerships, and auto accessory shops mark the modern urban landscape, so livery stables, feed barns, blacksmiths, and wagon and harness shops were everyday features of late-nineteenth-century towns. So was manure swarming with flies. New York City's horses were said to deposit two and a half million pounds of manure and sixty thousand gallons of urine per day.

It was a wagon fitted with seats and drawn by four mules that transported Clemens to Fort Missoula, four miles from town, the day after his performance at Missoula's Bennett Opera House, where the audience was composed mainly of officers from the fort and their families. The commander, Lieutenant Colonel Burt, had invited the whole party to lunch. Clemens had decided to walk slowly to the fort by himself — he thought it would do him good — but had taken the wrong road and did not discover his mistake until he had walked five or six miles. He was retracing his steps when Major Pond, who was being driven out to the fort, having been preceded by Olivia and Clara Clemens and Mrs. Pond, sighted him and picked him up. Clemens was "too tired to express disgust."

The fort was staffed by seven companies of the Twenty-fifth U.S. Colored Regiment. (Military segregation, abolished only after the Second World War, meant that white and black enlisted men served in separate units. Officers of black units were usually white.) When Clemens stepped out of the wagon, he was met by a sergeant who told him he was under arrest. The soldier marched him unprotesting across the parade ground to the guardhouse, where Colonel Burt met him and apologized for the practical joke. It was an old gag, which Clemens recognized.

The Clemenses and the Ponds heard a thirty-piece band, "one of the finest military bands in America," according to Pond, and watched a military drill. Clemens confessed to his journal that during the trooping of the colors, he had to be reminded to remove his hat and then to dispose of his cigar.

Pond reported learning that "colored soldiers were more subordinate and submissive to rigid drill and discipline than white men," and were less prone to desertion. Clemens noted in his journal that the soldiers looked like gentlemen, that the younger ones, educated in the public schools, could perform clerical duties, and that the black chaplain was saluted just like any other officer. Thirty years after the conclusion of the Civil War, most Americans viewed the second-class citizenship of blacks as an acceptable fact of life. Booker T. Washington, regarded by whites as the leader of the Negro race, declared in 1895 that the Southern white man was the Negro's best friend. The status of black American citizens had reached its nadir.

The night before the Clemenses left for Cleveland, a mob of seventy-five white men removed two black prisoners from an Arkansas jail. The two had been accused of murdering a white man. The horde took them to a nearby forest, gave them a moment to pray, and hanged them. The lynchers made no effort to conceal their identities.

The 1890s averaged more than 150 lynchings per year. Most of the victims were black, and most were killed in the South, where, a few years after the end of the Civil War, it had become an unwritten rule to lynch every black charged with assault, rape, or murder of a white person. Lynch victims were hanged, shot, even burned at the stake. Respectable, churchgoing citizens defended such practices as an unfortunate but necessary deterrent. Whether or not lynching performed this function, it could serve other purposes: in 1893, white pioneers in Oklahoma bragged about frightening away black land claimants by threats of lynching. "That's right," their neighbors told them, "we don't want any niggers in this country."

The 1890s witnessed the heaviest toll of lynchings in American history, as well as an increase in Jim Crow laws. Lynching so outraged Clemens that, moved by an atrocity in Missouri a few years after the conclusion of his tour, he proposed to his publisher an encyclopedia of American lynching. He even wrote an introduction, "The United States of lyncherdom," an essay that bitterly castigated the moral cowardice of the majority of American citizens, North and South, who opposed such barbarism but were afraid to speak out against it.

The day before I left Elmira for Cleveland, I submitted myself to a barber. He asked me what I was doing in Elmira. After I told him, he said that he remembered a tailor who had once served Mark Twain. The tailor had described him as "overbearing and demanding." "Of course I didn't know Mark Twain," continued the barber, "but I did know Ernie Davis." Ernie Davis was another local hero, the first black recipient of the Heisman Trophy.

"What was he like?"

"He was a nice guy. He knew his place."

"What do you mean?"

"He always came to the back door."

Chapter Six

*F*ORT MISSOULA HAD BEEN ESTABLISHED less than twenty years before the Clemenses' visit, as a defense against the Nez Percé Indians. During the summer of 1895, trouble with the Bannock Indians in Wyoming's Jackson Hole region, about three hundred miles southeast of Missoula, was providing sensational copy for newspaper readers.

For the previous two years the Jackson Hole settlers had been complaining about the Bannocks. The Indians, according to the settlers, were killing large numbers of elk in violation of the Wyoming fish and game laws, which had established closed seasons for hunting. The settlers claimed that the Indians took only the hides, littering the hillsides and ravines with skinned corpses. When the settlers arrived at these scenes of carnage, they said, motherless calves would follow their horses. In fact, the Indians killed game for meat, to supplement their rations on the reservation, whereas the Jackson Hole settlers, who killed twice as many animals, also out of season, often took the head and horns alone. Many of the settlers were only nominally ranchers and made their living from guiding big-game hunters from back East and abroad. The Bannocks interfered with their livelihood.

A federal treaty, however, had given the Bannocks the right to hunt on unoccupied government land "so long as peace subsists among the whites and Indians, on the borders of the mining district." Many white settlers resented granting special privileges to Indians, whom they despised as savages. Senator Fred Thomas Dubois of Idaho described the Bannocks as "among the laziest and most worthless redskins to be found on a Government reservation," and said that if whites may not kill game out of season, the Indians should not be allowed to do so either. "The extermination of the whole lazy, shiftless, non-supporting Bannocks would not be any great loss." Wyoming's governor also backed the settlers, claiming that Wyoming's laws superseded the treaty's provisions. The issue had not yet been brought to court. In the meantime, settlers were doing their best to encourage an Indian uprising, so as to justify the Bannocks' expulsion from one of the best big-game hunting regions in the country.

In pursuit of this scheme, a Wyoming constable, along with twenty-six deputies, set forth to arrest some Indian hunters. Four days later, on the day the Clemenses left for Cleveland, the posse surrounded a camp of Indians and arrested nine men and thirteen women, along with five babies. With the mounted band under guard, the whites and Indians started out for Marysville, Idaho. On the way, the deputies treated their captives harshly. They told them to expect execution, by hanging or shooting, as soon as the town was reached. After an all-day journey, as they were riding through a stand of timber, the whites loaded their guns. The women shrieked. The Bannock men, certain that they were about to be killed, fled into the woods. Earlier the constable had instructed his deputies to shoot any Indian who tried to escape. Now, with no warning, the posse shot at the fleeing men, hitting six. The maximum penalty for violating the game laws was a ten-dollar fine and three months in jail.

One man, shot four times in the back, was left to bleed to death. He was old and almost blind. His rifle, in the opinion of one observer, was "not fit to kill anything." A twenty-year-old lay on the ground, wounded. He remained there for ten days, surviving on the dried meat he had brought with him. Then he crawled, during three successive nights, to the home of a rancher sympathetic to Indians. The rancher nursed him back to health. In the tumult following the shooting, two infants fell from their horses. Mormon settlers found one and cared for him. The other child was never found.

The settlers then promoted a war scare, claiming that the Bannocks were bent on revenge. As the Clemens party sailed to Duluth across Lake Superior on the SS *Northwest*, newspapers reported that a team of Princeton students, on a geological expedition, were traveling through Bannock territory. Fears were expressed that the Indians had captured them.

While the Clemens party was in Minneapolis and St. Paul, the papers reported that Indians were gathering near Jackson Hole and that the Wyoming militia had been ordered to ready themselves to move into the area. Then word came that the Bannocks had killed three settlers — a mother, father, and child — and that a posse pursued the Indians, killing "10 or 15" of them in a battle fifty miles from Jackson Hole. *The New-York Times* fulminated about "the backward Bannocks . . . this particularly stubborn tribe," which seemed impervious to the influence of civilization.

By the time the Clemens party reached Winnipeg, the papers reported that the Bannocks had murdered all the settlers in Jackson Hole and had torched every house and cabin. But when the Clemens party arrived in Helena, the Indian scare was over. With the encouragement of Bannock chiefs, who had accompanied the first battalion of the U.S. Ninth Cavalry en route to Jackson Hole, the Bannocks were leaving the area for their reservation in Idaho. There had been no battle between whites and Indians. The Princeton students had never been in danger. In fact they reported that the Indians were frightened of the settlers, who seemed eager to pick a fight with them. The story of settlers massacred at Jackson Hole was either a fabrication or a fantasy. Nor was it true that Indians had killed a white family. Nor was it true that they were massing for an attack. After the whites had begun to shoot any Indian in sight, the Bannocks gathered together in order to defend themselves. Now, with federal troops in the area, they were going home.

A few months later, a U.S. grand jury for Wyoming failed to indict the marshal or any his deputies for the unprovoked shooting of the six Indians and the killing of one.

It would be pleasant to report that the courts eventually agreed with the Bannocks' claim that their treaty with the government transcended Wyoming law. But less than a year after the troubles, the U.S. Supreme Court found in favor of the state. In a dissenting opinion, one judge wrote that while preservation of Wyoming's game was important, it was "far more important to maintain the faith of the Nation, even with the despised Indians."

A few years later, in return for $75,000, the Bannocks agreed to relinquish their treaty rights to hunt on public land. The formerly nomadic Bannocks, proud of their tradition as hunters and warriors, could no longer leave their reservation in order to hunt.

Clemens, who was an avid newspaper reader, must have known about the Bannock war scare. Inasmuch as he and his party would be traveling no closer to Jackson Hole than two hundred miles, the alleged uprising posed no personal threat. A greater danger was that of armed holdups of trains, several of which were reported that summer. In any case, Clemens did not refer to the Bannocks in his journal or in his letters. Had he done so, it is not clear what he would have said about them.

On the one hand, Clemens had disliked Indians since his first encounter with them, in 1861, in the Nevada Territory. There he saw them snatching carrion from buzzards and coyotes. He saw them sifting through the town refuse. He saw them begging. His romantic view of the noble savage, based on his boyhood reading of James Fenimore Cooper, turned to repulsion and disgust. Later, in several of his works, he would portray Indians as treacherous and vicious.

On the other hand, he was dismayed by the shameful treatment of Indians by government officials and private citizens. He came to understand that white settlers had destroyed Indian livelihoods by stealing their land, and he was revolted by the continued killing of Indians for the benefit of settlers and speculators eager for still more land. In 1885 he wrote to President Cleveland urging him to protect the Indians in the West.

Ambivalent attitudes toward Indians may seem a strange characteristic for the author of perhaps America's greatest antiracist novel. He had grown up in a slave state, where his parents and his maternal aunt and uncle were slaveholders, where slavery seemed to him entirely natural and unremarkable, and where abolitionists were despised. Despite such an upbringing, Clemens was later to defend not only blacks but other despised or subjugated peoples, including Chinese immigrants, Jews, and Australian aboriginals. Perhaps it is more remarkable that he overcame most of the racial prejudices of the day than that he remained influenced by one of them.

When Clemens reached Spokane, the next town on his itinerary, he was gaining in strength, and Pond reported him as "enjoying everything," including the reporters who were waiting for him at his hotel. One reporter observed an upcountry miner approach Clemens and claim that they once were good friends. The miner referred to an essay Clemens had just published about James Fenimore Cooper's literary style.

"Clements," said the miner, misprouncing the name, "I didn't think it was in you. Did you really write it? Now, honest, did you do it yourself?"

"Well, I got the money for it."

Pond and Clemens were impressed by Spokane's "asphalt streets, electric lights, nine-story telegraph poles, and commercial blocks that would do credit to any Eastern city." Pond noted buildings ten stories high. The nine top floors, however, were often empty, and "to rent" signs could be seen on "many fine stores with great plate-glass fronts." The whole party, taken for an open carriage ride, was shown some of the town's mansions, including those of the receivers of failed companies. Clemens commented that if he had a son to send West, he would train him to become a receiver. "It seems to be about the only thriving industry."

While Clemens remained in his room, Pond dined with the three women in the great dining hall of Spokane House, the largest hotel Pond had ever seen. As they passed out of the room into an enormous parlor, Clara sat down at the piano and started to play a Chopin nocturne. Pond described the scene: "Stealthily guests came in from dinner and sat breathlessly in remote parts of the boundless room listening to a performance that would have done credit to any great pianist. Never did I witness a more beautiful sight than this sweet brunette unconsciously holding a large audience of charmed listeners. If it was not one of the supreme moments of her mother's life, who saw and heard her, then I have guessed wrong."

The night before, Clemens performed at the magnificent Spokane opera house, which boasted the largest theater stage in the United States and lobby corridors fitted out with brilliantly colored leaded glass. A shopping center now occupies the site.

I'm dining at a restaurant one block away. First the waiter and then the proprietor notice the book on my table, Jeffrey Steinbrink's *Getting to Be Mark Twain*. The waiter says that he devoted his fourth grade "research project" to Mark Twain, and that he illustrated it with a large crayola drawing of a Mississippi riverboat. The proprietor leafs through the book itself. When I ask him if he's a Mark Twain buff, he says he is not, but that it seems to him that half the

aphorisms in the world are attributed either to Oscar Wilde or to
Mark Twain. When the Clemenses were in Spokane, Wilde was confined to Wandsworth Prison, where he was employed "picking
oakum," scraping hard rope into fine shreds with his fingernails.

To travel from Spokane to Tacoma, the Clemens party went first
to Seattle, where they transferred to the *Flyer,* said to be the fastest
steamboat in the world, which was to take them down Puget Sound
to their destination. As they watched the "baggage-smashers"
remove the party's trunks from the train to a baggage wagon,
Clemens said, "Oh, how I do wish one of those trunks were filled
with dynamite and that all the baggage-destroyers on earth were
gathered about it, and I just far enough off to see them hurled into
Kingdom Come!" At his vituperative best all morning, he swore he
would never travel in America again.

Tacoma was "another overgrown metropolis," wrote Pond. "We
can't see it or anything else owing to the dense smoke everywhere."
After an unbroken drought, the virgin forests of the Olympic
Peninsula — the northwestern Pacific coast of Washington State,
over one hundred miles away — were ablaze, producing smoke as
thick as fog, sometimes obscuring the sun, smoke that reached 750
miles south to San Francisco. "Really, your scenery is wonderful,"
Clemens told a reporter. "It is quite out of sight."

Clemens next performed in Portland, Oregon, and Olympia,
Washington, while the women stayed behind in Tacoma. When
Clemens's nephew, Samuel E. Moffett, of the *San Francisco
Examiner,* met him in Portland, Clemens complained about the journey and its annoyances, cursing and blaspheming as he did so,
although he admitted, in the end, that the arrangements could not
have been better had they been made by the Almighty. But after all,
he said, he was not traveling for pleasure. Perhaps his outburst
helped his performance that night. At any rate, the next day Pond
wrote that "each time it seemed as though his entertainment had
reached perfection, but last night surpassed all."

A Portland reporter asked Clemens if there was any truth to the
story that Tom Sawyer was named after a bartender in San
Francisco, who claimed to have met Clemens in that town long ago.
"That story," he answered, "lacks a good deal in the way of facts."
In the same interview, Clemens suggested that Portland pave all its

streets and pay for the work by commandeering all the bicycles and renting them out. There is no need to be alarmed, he continued: If a city can give away a trolley franchise, why can't it operate a monopoly itself?

At Olympia, where he arrived on August 10, almost four weeks after leaving Elmira, a delegation of distinguished citizens met his train. Their spokesman apologized for the smoke. Clemens said that he was accustomed to smoke: "I am a perpetual smoker myself."

He returned to Tacoma, where, at a party given him by the Tacoma Press Club, he said that he had once felt like cursing fate for burdening him with a large debt so late in life. But now he felt it a privilege to lecture again, to meet so many people who wished him well. Pond remarked that Clemens had "found his friends by the loss of his fortune." Strangers, young and old alike, kept telling him of the pleasure his writing had given them.

The next day, a reporter observed Clemens "vigorously puffing a cigar" in the smoking car of the train to Seattle. Dressed in a plain dark suit, he sat quietly, attracting no notice, until he removed his blue traveling cap. With his bushy gray hair exposed, he looked as he did in his photographs, so that his fellow passengers whispered up and down the aisle, "That is Mark Twain."

In Seattle, even a successful run of *H.M.S. Pinafore* did not keep Clemens from attracting a large audience. His performance was sold out, with standing room only. The smoke may have contributed to his hoarseness that evening, but it did not affect his wit. When he began his discourse on the German language, a rough voice from the gallery cried out, "Haf you been to Heidelberg?" "Yes," he responded, "I studied German there, and I learned many other things also, among them how to drink beer." One critic characterized his performance that night as "one of those strange medleys of humor and philosophy which have so much the sound of a great literary improvisation."

In Seattle he was asked about an article about him that had appeared in the *Washington City Post*, by a reporter who falsely claimed to have interviewed him. "Well," he said, "a fellow oughtn't to be too severe on a man that's as hard up for an interview as that."

Clemens and Pond, leaving the women behind in Seattle, went

north to Fairhaven, where they spent the night at the Fairhaven Hotel. The theater was in the adjoining town of New Whatcom, to which Clemens and Pond rode on a trolley. (The two towns formed a single agglomeration, and nine years later they combined to create the new town of Bellingham.) Neither he nor Pond recorded the fact that their venue, the Lighthouse Theater, was on the fourth floor of a building with no fire escapes. This should have worried them, as well as the audience, inasmuch as the forest fires were so close that householders in town kept ladders on their roofs and buckets of water handy.

Pond reported that Clemens was in a foul mood the whole day. His hoarseness in Seattle proved to be from a cold, which was getting worse. Now he was so hoarse he could hardly speak. When the audience kept filing in long after his performance began, he left the stage. Pond, thinking he was ill, rushed to him, only to find him white with rage. "You'll never play a trick like this on me again. Look at that d—— audience. It isn't half in yet." When Pond explained that the trolleys ran only every half hour, he was mollified, returned to the stage, and captivated the audience, which, at the conclusion of his performance, demanded an additional story.

Pond's local agent had failed to provide refreshments for Clemens after the performance. All public places were closed. No lights were burning, even in the Fairhaven Hotel. So a few members of the Cascade Club took him back to their club rooms. These had been furnished during the boom times of the 1880s, when one hundred men contributed $100 apiece for leather chairs, solid mahogany reading tables, and other amenities. An English steward, a veteran of the Crimean War, had presided over this magnificence. But two years after the crash of 1893, the club could afford no servants. Thus the members were embarrassed when Clemens asked for a hot whiskey. One of the members dashed down two flights of stairs, sprinted down the street, persuaded a restaurant owner to make a fire and heat some water, and returned with it, breathless. Although by this time the water was tepid, Clemens claimed it was hot enough and even insisted on a second drink, "no doubt to make us feel better," according to the member who chronicled the event. Clemens coughed a great deal.

If New Whatcom and Fairhaven were dead at night, with no

lights showing even in the Fairhaven Hotel, their successor town, Bellingham, was judged by *Swing Magazine* one hundred years later as the best town in America for singles to live. The criteria for the editors' selection were three: availability of jobs, accessibility to nature, and the liveliness of night life.

On August 15, when the Clemenses were traveling north from New Whatcom on their way to Canada, Clemens commented in his journal that they had traversed "a stretch of 18 miles in which there is not a single place named Victoria . . . This shows that we are not under the British flag." Although in 1895 Canada was self-governing, it was still an imperial dominion, its formal relations with other countries conducted solely through the British foreign office.

In Vancouver, Clemens complained to reporters that in western hotels, "electric light is only turned on at a certain hour in the evening, and no matter how dark or foggy the day — maybe so dark that even those who dwelt in Egyptian darkness would find it impossible to see . . . you cannot obtain artificial light."

If smoke-induced darkness during the day was not quite Egyptian, it was nonetheless notable. "There is a rumor afloat," wrote Pond in Vancouver, "that the country about us is beautiful, but we can't see it, for there is smoke, smoke, everywhere, and no relief." The smoke was no help for Clemens's hoarseness. He had to struggle to make himself heard in the crowded auditorium. "He is," wrote Pond, "a thoroughbred — a great man, with wonderful will power, or he would have succumbed." The audience, which Pond characterized as "very English," was, according to one critic, "convulsed at times to the point of incoherence."

Chapter Seven

*T*HE SMOKE IS SO DENSE all over this upper coast," wrote Clemens to Rogers from Vancouver, "that you can't see a cathedral at 800 yards." The Clemenses learned in Vancouver that the departure of the SS *Warrimoo*, on which they were to sail from Victoria to Sydney, had been delayed. It was to have sailed on August 16, the day after Clemens's performance in Vancouver. But before it reached Victoria, it ran aground in the fog and smoke as it entered the Juan de Fuca Strait, the hundred-mile passage that connects the Pacific Ocean to the town, and so had to be repaired. This ill wind brought at least two benefits. It gave Clemens a chance to recover from his cold — he stayed in bed most of the time during his extra four days in Vancouver — and it provided Pond with an opportunity to arrange a performance in Victoria.

The day after Clemens's Vancouver performance, a doctor examined him and announced that he was not seriously ill. Nonetheless, Mrs. Clemens was worried. "I was very anxious about him," she wrote to Rogers, "fearing an attack of bronchitis or lung fever. We have kept him in bed now for two days and he seems better."

"Mrs. Clemens is curing him," noted Pond. "The more I see of this lady the greater and more wonderful she appears to be. There are few women that could manage and absolutely rule such a nature as 'Mark's.' She knows the gentle and smooth way over every obstruction he meets, and makes everything lovely." During the last years of his life, when Clemens was dictating his autobiographical notes, he said that meeting Olivia Langdon had "made the fortune of my life — not in dollars, I am not thinking of dollars; it made the real fortune of my life in that it made the happiness of my life."

When they left Vancouver for Victoria on August 20, the smoke was denser than ever. The slight rain that was falling could not disperse it. Clemens was still weak, his voice still hoarse. He was, according to Pond, downhearted in spite of his tremendous success on the platform, perhaps because of unfavorable reports of the *Warrimoo* and his wife's dread of the long Pacific crossing.

He may have been depressed, but he managed to sound cheerful in a letter he gave to the *San Francisco Examiner*, the paper for which his nephew worked. "Lecturing," he said, "is gymnastics, chest-expander, medicine, mind-healer, blues-destroyer, all in one. I am twice as well as I was when I started out. I have gained nine pounds in twenty-eight days, and expect to weigh six hundred before January."

The next day, he wrote in a similarly ebullient fashion to Kipling about his forthcoming visit to India: "I shall arrive next January, and you must be ready. I shall come riding my Ayah, with his tusks adorned with silver bells and ribbons, and escorted by a troop of native Howdahs, richly clad and mounted upon a herd of wild bungalows, and you must be on hand with a few bottles of ghee, for I shall be thirsty."

Before they left Vancouver for Victoria, Clemens gave a statement to *The New-York Times* about his debts. He wanted to scotch the rumor that he was lecturing for his own benefit and not for that of his creditors. "The law recognizes no mortgage on a man's brain, and a merchant who has given up all he has may take advantage of the rules of insolvency and start free again for himself; but I am not a business man, and honor is a harder master than the law. It cannot compromise for less than a hundred cents on the dollar." He explained that his wife was the firm's principal creditor, to whom he had assigned his copyrights until his debt to her should be paid. "The present situation is that the wreckage of the firm, together with what money I can scrape together with my wife's aid, will enable me to pay the other creditors about 50 per cent. of their claims. It is my intention to ask them to accept that as a legal discharge, and trust to my honor to pay the other 50 per cent. as fast as I can earn it."

From his reception thus far on his lecturing tour, he said, he was confident that if he lived he could pay off his debts within four years, when, at the age of sixty-four, he could start life anew. "In my preliminary run through the smaller cities on the northern route, I have found a reception the cordiality of which has touched my heart and made me feel how small a thing money is in comparison with friendship.

"I meant, when I began, to give my creditors all the benefit of this, but I begin to feel that I am gaining something from it, too, and that my dividends, if not available for banking purposes, may be even more satisfactory than theirs."

By the time he reached British Columbia, Clemens had earned $5,000. He sent it to Rogers to hold for the firm's creditors.

The *Charmer*, which was to convey the Clemenses and Ponds on a long southwest slant down the Strait of Georgia to Victoria, arrived in Vancouver at one in the afternoon, half an hour late. After the Clemenses and the Ponds had rushed to the vessel, the captain informed them that the departure would be delayed to enable him to unload 180 tons of freight. They would have to postpone and reschedule Clemens's peformance. After the women had gone aboard, wrote Pond, Clemens told the captain, "in very plain and unpious language, his opinion of a passenger-carrying company that, for a few dollars extra, would violate their contract and obligations to the public." The captain's face reddened, but he said nothing. After Clemens joined the women, who apparently had overheard his outburst, he asked Pond to approach the captain and apologize for his abuse. Pond obliged, establishing amicable relations between the captain and his famous passenger.

The Victoria *Times* stopped its presses to insert a note informing ticketholders that Mark Twain's performance was postponed; all telephone subscribers were notified; handbills were distributed. Nonetheless, many ticket holders appeared at the theater only to be disappointed, particularly those who came from across the straits on the Olympic Peninsula and could not remain to hear him the next night.

The *Charmer*'s delay was the only occasion during the North American leg of the world tour that forced the postponement of a performance. Considering the enormous sweep of territory that the Clemenses covered in North America, the number of trains and steamers on which they traveled, the forest fire through which the train carrying Clemens and Pond sped in Michigan, and the dense smoke through which they all traveled in the Pacific Northwest, their delays were remarkably few.

Still, they needed to be flexible. When they arrived in Duluth, for example, they learned that their agents in New York had forgotten about that night's transfer to Minneapolis. Pond had to attend to it himself, although the party was in Duluth for only a few hours. More than a week later, when Clemens and Pond were traveling from their hotel in Butte to the train station (the women stayed behind), their electric trolley stopped dead after only three blocks. The power had failed. No cab was in sight. When the owner of a grocery wagon demanded ten dollars to take them to the station, Pond told him to go to hell and offered the driver of a nearby wagon "any price" to reach the train. Clemens and Pond mounted the seat next to the driver, who lashed his two horses and arrived at the station in record time. The driver asked for one dollar. Pond handed him two. The train was moving as Clemens and Pond jumped on.

Although they slept in more than twenty different hotels, in no case was the party unexpected (of course, it's not every day that an international celebrity and his entourage arrive at your hotel). And of the twenty-two North American theaters in which Clemens performed, Major Pond complained of insufficient arrangements in only two instances, and in only one did he accuse the manager of trying to avoid his contract. The only real muddle was in Cleveland, where Clemens was delayed by two soloists and undermined by five hundred newsboys. All in all, the travel and theater arrangements worked well. So the sentiments that Clemens inscribed in a presentation copy of *Roughing It*, which he gave to Major Pond in Vancouver, seem entirely appropriate: "Here ends one of the smoothest and pleasantest trips across the continent that any group of five has ever made."

Nonetheless, Clemens was dissatisfied. On board the *Warrimoo*, he wrote to Rogers that Pond, three years younger than himself, was "superannuated," without gumption, intelligence, or judgment. "I must make no contract with him to platform me through America next year if I can do better." And from India, in February, he told Rogers, "I mean to write my book (or books) before I decide on an American lecture season. I don't see how I can stand Pond, he is such an idiot. Yet I know no other American lecture agent."

Perhaps, as Mrs. Clemens had gently suggested at the Crookston railway station, Clemens was not entirely reasonable. Perfection itself was unlikely to have pleased him during his North American run, during that hot summer of fire and smoke, when he was plagued by hoarseness, a cold, and a hole in his leg, when he was forced to compose and memorize new routines as he traveled from one engagement to the next, when he had to change hotels more than twenty times within a forty-day period, and when, in spite of the brave face he showed to *The New-York Times*, he did not know if he could ever pay his debts in full.

The *Charmer* carried the Clemens party from Vancouver to Victoria in about six hours. Today the ferry takes about an hour and a half. The ride is steady and, during the last half hour, beautiful, as you sail between heavily wooded islands flecked with summer cottages. As you approach the dock, seagulls drift in a lazy ellipse above the water.

The house was full for Clemens's performance in Victoria. Governor-General and Lady Aberdeen, with their small son in Highland kilts, came to hear him. When they entered fifteen minutes late, to the strains of "God Save the Queen," the audience rose. Clemens wished that the Queen's representatives would always attend his performances because it was not permissible to start before they arrived, and by that time the latecomers had found their seats. During his performance, the audience laughed when a kitten walked across the stage behind him. It was not until after the show that he learned why they laughed in the wrong place.

The SS *Warrimoo*, on which the Clemenses sailed to Sydney, was one of the two new vessels that made up the Canadian-Australian Royal Mail Steamship Company, established in 1893. Most of the passengers who had arrived with the *Warrimoo* in Victoria were bound for other cities, for the line provided the most direct available route from Australasia to North America.

The accident that delayed the *Warrimoo*'s departure would have been a disaster had the wind and sea not been calm at the time. Heavy fog at the entrance to the Juan de Fuca Strait, one of the most treacherous places to navigate on the northern Pacific coast, caused the vessel to proceed at half steam, with frequent soundings. When the captain heard breakers ahead, he shut down the engines. The vessel had almost stopped when it ran onto the Sea Lion reef, in water that navigators usually avoided. The *Warrimoo*'s crew pumped water ballast from the vessel's forward compartments and then, using a nearby rock as a fulcrum, swung the steamer clear of the ledge. This, however, pushed her onto rocks, from which she was ultimately lifted by the rising tide and the efforts of her crew, who then took her to a safe anchorage in deep water.

A few fishermen visited the vessel while it was stranded. They were reported to have informed the passengers that the woods on Vancouver Island, visible from the vessel, were full of ferocious panthers as large as tigers. The passengers were said to have conscientiously recorded this information in their notebooks and diaries.

A maritime inquiry concluded that although fog had caused the accident, a chart with unreliable soundings contributed to the mishap. The vessel's chart, which did not mark the reef, was based on soundings taken forty years before and now incorrect. Later measurements were more reliable, but these were unavailable in Sydney at the time of sailing. While the board of inquiry reported that the captain exercised due caution in steering the course and in taking frequent soundings, and while it praised him for good seamanship in getting the ship off the reef, it criticized him for not taking into account the stage of the tide and the set of the current, although the latter was of unknown quantity. Taking all factors into consideration, however, it recommended that his certificate not be revoked.

The captain was R. E. Arundell, who had been the vessel's first mate and was now substituting for the regular captain, who was on holiday. This was Arundell's first command. He must have been a charming fellow, if we can trust the passengers' letter to him at the conclusion of their voyage to Victoria. They asserted that he was not to blame for the accident, expressed admiration for the "masterful way" in which he extricated the ship from its hazardous position, and thanked him for his "uniform courtesy and untiring care," which "converted what might have been a monotonous voyage into a pleasant trip."

Clemens's description of him in *Following the Equator* is an encomium. "Our young captain was a very handsome man, tall and perfectly formed, the very figure to show up a smart uniform's finest effects . . . The captain, with his gentle nature, his polish, his sweetness, his moral and verbal purity, seemed pathetically out of place in his rude and autocratic vocation. It seemed another instance of the irony of fate." The passengers, Clemens wrote, were all sorry for the captain, who was going home under a cloud, despite the maritime board's recommendation not to revoke his license. Everyone feared that the steamship company would dismiss him.

When the ship reached Auckland, the damage was found to be much greater than had been thought. Thirty or forty plates on the vessel's bottom had been crumpled out of shape. One plate was so badly dented that at its joint with the next plate a gap appeared. The money spent to repair the vessel was almost one-third as much as the initial cost of building it. Had the Clemenses realized how unsafe it was, they might have waited for another ship. When the repaired *Warrimoo* sailed back to Victoria, Arundell was not on board. The regular captain had returned to his post and under him served a new first mate.

On Friday, August 23, the day the *Warrimoo* left Victoria, Clemens and Pond spent the morning buying books, cigars, and tobacco. Pond reports that Clemens bought 3,000 manila cheroots and four pounds of Durham smoking tobacco. "If perpetual smoking ever kills a man," wrote Pond, "I don't see how 'Mark Twain' can expect to escape." Clemens, who said he "came into the world asking for a light," claimed that it was always his rule "never to smoke when asleep, and never to refrain when awake." The manuscript on which *Following the Equator* is based, now held by the New York Public Library, smells faintly of cigar smoke.

The Ponds and the Clemenses boarded the *Warrimoo* and lunched together for the last time. Olivia Clemens told Pond she was disappointed by the ship, but that she intended to "brave it through." Pond photographed the three Clemenses standing at the *Warrimoo*'s rail, shortly before departure. Clemens is sucking on a long-stemmed pipe, the bowl of which rests in his left hand. Mrs. Clemens, wearing a pince-nez, her arms akimbo, smiles gamely. Between her parents stands Clara, arms on the rail, holding a white handkerchief in her right hand. Affixed to the rail is a large notice that all stowaways will be prosecuted at Honolulu and brought back to Victoria. Honolulu was to be the vessel's first port of call.

A subsequent snapshot shows the *Warrimoo* on its way, issuing an enormous plume of coal smoke from its single stack. The Ponds and the Clemenses waved good-bye until they vanished from each other's sight.

2

AUSTRALIA

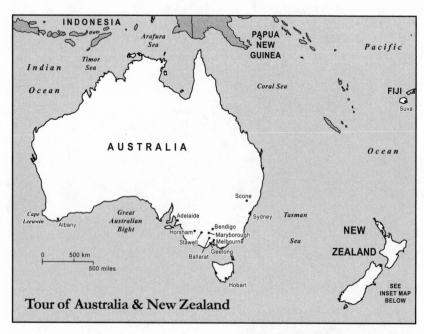

INDONESIA

Arafura Sea

PAPUA NEW GUINEA

Pacific

Timor Sea

Indian Ocean

Coral Sea

FIJI

Suva

AUSTRALIA

Ocean

Scone

Cape Leeuwin

Albany

Great Australian Bight

Adelaide

Sydney

Tasman

NEW

Horsham

Bendigo
Maryborough

Sea

ZEALAND

Stawell

Melbourne

Ballarat

Geelong

0   500 km

500 miles

Hobart

SEE INSET MAP BELOW

Tour of Australia & New Zealand

0   200 km

200 miles

NORTH ISLAND

Auckland

Gisborne

New Plymouth

Hawera

Napier

Wanganui

Palmerston North

Nelson

Wellington

SOUTH ISLAND

Christchurch

Timaru

Oamaru

Invercargill

Dunedin

Bluff

INSET MAP

Chapter Eight

ONE WEEK AFTER QUITTING THE SMOKE of Victoria, the *Warrimoo* sailed past Diamond Head, dropped anchor near Honolulu, and waited for the pilot to board. It was night. The vessel lay one mile from the shore, close enough that passengers could see the glimmering lights of the town.

Almost thirty years before, Clemens had spent four months in the islands as a reporter for the *Sacramento Union*, which had engaged him to write a series of travel letters. Although he found the native Hawaiians in a degraded state, their numbers decimated by European diseases and their culture vitiated by missionaries, and although he suffered for weeks from saddle sores after riding from plantation to plantation, he remembered the islands as a paradise. For years he had longed to see them again. Now he would have an opportunity to do so, when he performed in Honolulu.

The small boat that approached the *Warrimoo* that Friday night did not bring the pilot, as everyone expected, but a notice that cholera had broken out. Five deaths had been reported that day. Neither passengers nor freight would be taken on, nor fresh produce for the kitchen, nor even the mails. Those passengers who disembarked would not be taken back. They might have to wait for months before the quarantine was lifted. Two Bostonians, an elderly woman and her son, who had gone to the Finger Lakes region of western New York for a holiday and gradually worked their way west, now found themselves sailing home via Sydney and London. A couple who had expected to spend a month in Honolulu, leaving three small children in Canada, also stayed with the ship, unable to inform anyone at home. Mail from Honolulu was embargoed. No cable had yet been laid between Hawaii and California. To send a cable, they would have to wait until they reached Auckland, a journey of close to two weeks. The cargo for Honolulu was offloaded onto freighters without any help from longshoremen, who were forbidden to board. Clemens had to cancel his performance and refund $500 in advance sales.

Let us hope that he missed the report, published in Sydney a few days after he arrived there, that the deaths in Honolulu were due not to cholera but to the consumption of poisoned fish. In fact, as was reported later, the scare was fully justified. Within a month after the first case was reported, sixty-two victims had died of cholera, most of them native Hawaiians.

The next day, while the offloading proceeded, Clemens could only sit under a canopy and gaze at the shore, "just as silky and velvety and lovely as ever." Paine, his authorized biographer, likened Clemens's banishment to Moses' exclusion from the Promised Land. But Clemens, of course, had been there before. "If I might I would go ashore and never leave."

The paradise from which Clemens was excluded, the Sandwich Islands, was no longer the kingdom which he had known, when it was ruled by Kamehameha V. It was now a republic. Two years before, settlers from Europe and America had toppled the reigning monarch, Queen Liliuokalani, who had alarmed them by her efforts to expand the powers of the monarchy and by her view, strenuously expressed, that Hawaii belonged to the Hawaiians. President Cleveland, to whom she had appealed for help, ordered the queen restored, but the president of the new republic refused, asserting that the United States had no standing in the matter. Seven months before the Clemenses' visit, the queen had inspired a royalist insurrection. When it failed, she was forced to abdicate in order to win the release of her supporters from prison.

"The old imitation pomps, the fuss and feathers, have departed, and the royal trade-mark — that is about all that one could miss, I suppose," wrote Clemens about the new republic. "That imitation monarchy was grotesque enough, in my time; if it had held on another thirty years it would have been a monarchy without subjects of the king's race."

Clemens adored sea voyages. He found the languid vacancies, the "eternal monotonies" restorative. After a forced march of one-night stands across the sweltering North American continent, he welcomed a three-week sea voyage. "We had the whole Pacific

Ocean in front of us," he wrote in *Following the Equator,* "with nothing to do but do nothing and be comfortable."

The *Warrimoo,* like other transoceanic passenger liners of the day, offered most of the comforts of a good hotel. As with other such vessels, its appointments were modest, for the transformation of liners from hotel to floating palace was only just beginning. So the *Warrimoo* boasted no grand staircases, no opulent staterooms, no orchestras, no palm courts, no salons lavished with mahagony and sandalwood. The Clemenses were too early for that.

The *Warrimoo*'s cabins were outfitted with flush toilets and electric lights, but it is unlikely that the passengers enjoyed hot running water, which was not provided as a matter of course until well into the twentieth century.

If the *Warrimoo*'s passengers had nothing to do but be comfortable, a large staff worked hard to make them so. Both saloon-class and second-class passengers had their own bedroom stewards and salon stewards. Of the more than eighty officers and men, only about fifty-five were devoted solely to the management of the vessel and its freight, including engineers, greasers, firemen, trimmers, able-bodied seamen, and a "donkeyman," who operated a small "donkey engine" used to power a winch.

The *Warrimoo* was a liner, a passenger-carrying vessel that sailed a fixed route and followed a fixed time table. Today, trans-oceanic liners, like the Great Lakes steamers, are extinct. Nowadays vessels that convey passengers across the ocean are either cruise ships, offering casinos, nightclubs, and organized activities to amuse their hundreds of passengers, or freighters, whose revenue is derived primarily from cargo. Most freighters carry no passengers, but those that do usually carry no more than twelve, the maximum allowed by international maritime regulations for vessels with no physician on board.

Among the ten passengers who are sailing with me from California to New Zealand and Australia is my wife, Alice, who joined me in Oakland, where we embarked for Sydney, one hundred years and two days after the Clemenses sailed from Victoria. Like the *Warrimoo,* our freighter will take about three weeks to reach Sydney. (Although the speed of our vessel is probably a bit greater than that of the *Warrimoo,* our route is longer, inasmuch as we will sail down the coast of California before setting out across the Pacific. We average about 17.5 knots per day compared to the minimum of fourteen knots required by the *Warrimoo*'s contract with the Canadian mails, a speed that it "easily ran.")

Unlike the *Warrimoo*, which derived a substantial proportion of its revenue from passenger fares, our vessel earns relatively little from its passengers. A single one-way fare equals the revenue from merely one of the many hundreds of freight containers on board. The allocation of functions among the crew reflects the relative unimportance of the passengers. Of the twenty-five or so employees, there are only three stewards and two cooks, who serve the crew as well as us. Of course, we don't need much done for us. The self-service kitchen in which we can prepare our own snacks contains a washing machine, drying closet, iron, and ironing board.

Heaps of luggage accompanied the *Warrimoo*'s passengers. Stickers announcing "not wanted on the voyage" were pasted on immense, brass-bound trunks that would be kept in the hold until their owners reached their destination. In contrast, we and our fellow passengers, who have taken very little on board, keep all our luggage in our rooms.

Unlike the *Warrimoo*, which was staffed by British officers and men, our freighter, owned by a British firm, employs only two British officers, the captain and the chief engineer. The junior officers and crew are from the Philippines. While the crewmen's wages are low by British standards, they are luxurious in comparison to the average Philippine wage, so the crew are keen to keep their jobs, even though they can spend little time at home. They receive only six weeks' leave after nine months at sea. From each port they call home, using reduced-rate telephone cards that they purchase from seamen's associations.

The officers have a better deal, with three months on shore after six months at sea, an arrangement that would have been unworkable one hundred years ago, when it might require one month just to sail home. The British chief engineer on the vessel that took the Clemenses to Ceylon told Clemens that in thirty-three years, spent mainly in the tropics, he was home for Christmas three times.

The *Warrimoo*'s passengers amused themselves in much the

same ways as we do on our freighter. They read; they played cards; they napped; they gazed at the sea and the enormous sky and the changing shapes of clouds; they watched the occasional albatross and pod of dolphins accompany the ship; they pointed out to one another the flying fish, which Clemens likened to "a flight of silver fruit-knives," as the creatures leaped out of the vessel's path.

Unlike us, the *Warrimoo*'s passengers engaged in what Clemens termed the "violent exercise" of shuffleboard, a deck game that required both skill and strategy, and, owing to the ship's random rolling and pitching, left something to chance as well. Our freighter's decks, devoted mainly to containers, have no room for shuffleboard, but we play a miniature version indoors after supper, using quarters as counters, which we hit with the edge of our hands.

Towards the end of the *Warrimoo*'s voyage, Clemens partici-pated in the ship's shuffleboard playoffs. In *Following the Equator*, he reported losing the final game through a series of moves so improb-ably bad that in retrospect he was proud of his performance. "It will take a century to produce another man," he wrote, who could lose in so spectacular a fashion. But in fact, as he reported to Rogers, he won the game, becoming "Champion of the South Seas."

Although he told Rogers, in a letter written a few days before landing in Sydney, that the voyage was "charming," elsewhere Clemens recorded numerous gripes: rats and cockroaches infested the ship; the food was terrible ("furnished by the Deity and cooked by the devil"); seamen in the early morning would douse the decks, along with passengers sleeping near open portholes; and, although the vessel was going into drydock when it reached Australia, the crew were forever painting exterior surfaces, staining the passen-gers' clothes. When the Clemenses' bathroom flooded, their com-plaints produced no results. When a passenger requested ice for his sick wife, he was told that he would have to wait two hours, even though Clemens was convinced that ice was readily available. He worried about the absence of a watch at the rear of the vessel: what would happen if someone at the stern fell overboard?

The regular captain's pet dog, who had remained on board while his master stayed in Sydney, would decorate the decks. So when a notice appeared reminding passengers that ship rules for-bade smoking in the cabins and the main reception rooms, Clemens took the doctor aside, showed him a turd, and told him that as long as the animal was allowed to roam freely, the captain should keep quiet about breaking the rules.

Anxiety may have colored his view of the *Warrimoo*. After about two weeks at sea, Olivia Clemens wrote to her sister that Clemens "is pretty cheerful — in fact he appears entirely cheerful — but underneath he has a steady, unceasing feeling that he is never going to be able to pay his debts."

One evening, shortly before sunset, our captain shows us the navigation bridge and its array of instruments, one of which receives satellite readings of the ship's exact location. Why, then, I ask the captain, does one of the junior officers take readings with a sextant? The captain explains that if officers practice their skills with a sextant, they can be independent of the fancy equipment, which may occasionally fail. Ability to read the sextant is a requirement for the young man's promotion to the next grade.

I ask if the watch uses radar to avoid collisions at sea. "No," says the captain, "they use their eyes." By and large, then, the officers on this vessel could navigate it by means of last century's maritime methods, and to some extent still do.

I told the captain that Clemens, who believed that vermin were an inevitable accompaniment of a South Seas voyage, complained about the excess number of rats and cockroaches on the *Warrimoo*. The captain said that to avoid rats, you must keep the decks clean, because rats on the wharves can smell food on deck. In addition, you must coat the lines that tie a vessel to the wharf with an antirodent substance. Our vessel was certified rat-free when it tied up in Los Angeles. As for cockroaches, the vessel is sprayed every two weeks with a poisonous liquid that becomes a powder, which the cockroaches track into their nests. After about two weeks on board, we've seen no evidence of either rats or cockroaches.

In addition to playing shuffleboard, reading, card playing, and staring vacantly at the sea and sky, the *Warrimoo*'s passengers told each other stories. Clemens wrote in *Following the Equator* that "we have come far from the snake liar and the fish liar, and there was rest and peace in the thought; but now we have reached the realm of the boomerang liar, and sorrow is with us once more." He related several of the boomerang stories he heard, including that of the

Australian passenger who said that his brother saw a boomerang kill a bird and bring it to the thrower.

Clemens was no slouch as a teller of tales that lacked, as he said in Portland, "a good deal in the way of facts." In *Following the Equator*, he informed us that "an enormously rich brewer" on board the *Warrimoo* had promised to give $10,000 to an infant due to be born in steerage class if the child arrived on the rich man's birthday. The baby emerged at the exact moment that the vessel was crossing the International Date Line. The doctor thought he was born on Tuesday and the nurse thought he was born on Sunday. Monday, the day that dropped from the calendar, was the brewer's birthday. One needn't check the records to suspect that the story is too implausible to be true.

One evening, Alice and I are talking to the captain over a postprandial coffee. The conversation turns to stowaways. After he tells us of his experiences with them, I describe the sign on the *Warrimoo* that promised to return unauthorized passengers to Victoria, where they would be prosecuted. I ask him what will be done in Suva, which we reach tomorrow, to discourage stowaways from boarding the vessel.

"Wait and see," he says.

Chapter Nine

*M*ORE THAN A WEEK OUT OF HONOLULU, the *Warrimoo* reached Suva. It was midafternoon. Clemens, lucky to visit on a sunny day, wrote in *Following the Equator* that the small, reef-protected harbor was a "brilliant blue and green." Suva is the capital of Fiji, a sparsely inhabited group of about three hundred islands strewn over hundreds of miles of the southwestern Pacific. When our vessel docked in Suva, the harbor and sky were gray, the hills filigreed by mist. It has been raining intermittently ever since. This is the dry season.

Clemens did not invent his sunny day — the sun does shine in Suva. I saw it myself, now and then, during a four-day stay a few years ago, when the weather was mainly as it is today — soft rain, alternating with the threat of rain.

Suva's rain once caused an unusual problem. In 1872, Louie, a Filipino cook on a visiting schooner, knifed and killed a fellow crew member. This was two years before the official cession of Fiji to Britain, but after the British had begun to impose their judicial system. Condemned to death by hanging, Louie escaped execution on the appointed date because the sheriff, owing to his wife's illness, had been delayed.

Louie then appealed to the court to release him, on the grounds that the date specified by the sentence had passed. The court, rejecting this argument, set a new date for hanging.

The day came, Louie mounted the scaffold, stood while the noose was placed around his neck, and dropped when the trapdoor opened beneath his feet. The rope, which had been prepared the night before and left outdoors, was so swollen with rain it could not run in the noose, which caught Louie on the chin but did not tighten around his neck. Stunned by the fall, he hung for about ten minutes before he regained consciousness and began to struggle. He begged bystanders to shoot him. The Chief of Police cut the rope and returned him to his cell.

The King of Fiji commuted Louie's sentence. Louie was now destitute, having given away all his earthly possessions in anticipation of death. He was provided with funds and allowed to leave the country.

The king who commuted Louie's sentence was Cakobau. In *Following the Equator*, Clemens described an interchange between a British official and the king when the latter ceded his islands to the Crown. The official, whom Clemens claimed was trying to comfort the king, described the cession as "a sort of hermit-crab formality, you know." To which the king replied, "Yes, but with this difference — the crab moves into an unoccupied shell, but mine isn't." Clemens commented that this was "a neat retort, and with a touch of pathos in it, too."

The king's career may have been tragic, but it was not pathetic. Contemporary sources described him as extremely handsome, well built, and athletic, as well as cruel, cunning, and arrogant, a man who devoted himself principally to women and war. He is said to have clubbed to death a vassal who was slow in paying tribute and to have eaten a rebel's tongue, joking all the while, in the presence of his victim. Such cruelty was characteristic of the semi-divine chiefs of his day. A chief would crush his enemies under the new foundation posts of buildings; he would eat them at feasts; he would force them to serve in place of logs, as rollers for a giant war canoe as it was brought down to the sea.

Cakobau inspired such fear that he became the most important of the Fijian chiefs. But his power eroded in the wake of European settlement. Threatened by both colonial and native dissidents, unable to reconcile the competing interests of Europeans and Fijians, and powerless to prevent imminent bloodshed and anarchy, he ceded Fiji to Britain. "The whites who have come to Fiji," he said, "are a bad lot . . . if we do not cede Fiji, the white stalkers of the beach, the cormorants will open their maws and swallow us."

When the Clemenses visited Fiji twenty-one years later, they stood before a memorial to the fearsome chief, a cut-stone monument set in an enclosure in the middle of Suva. Alice and I, here for half a day like the Clemenses, look for the "notable monument" that

Clemens described. The historical marker in the center of town does not mention the king. But farther along the main street, Victoria Parade, on the grounds of the massive, gray government buildings, stands a stone monument to Cakobau. The inscriptions are in Fijian, so we can understand only the dates, all in the nineteenth century. At the top of the stone column is a bronze bust of the great man, presented in 1980 by his great-grandson, Sir George Cakobau, who was then governor general.

The chief's family is still politically active. The day before our visit, Ada Samanunu Cakobau was confirmed as candidate for a by-election later in the month, after an objection to her candidacy had been thrown out. A challenge to a member of a chiefly family would have been unthinkable a few decades ago, according to an editorial in the day's *Fiji Times*.

Not far from the monument is the Fiji Museum, which is approached through Thurston Gardens, named for a British civil servant, Sir John Bates Thurston, an amateur botanist who founded the gardens. He is remembered today not for his botanical interests but for his role in the development of Fiji as a Crown Colony. As Cakobau's chief secretary and minister of foreign affairs, he negotiated the cession of the islands to the Crown and later became governor of the colony and High Commissioner of the Western Pacific. He was a champion of Fijian rights, as he saw them, and established such a distinguished local reputation that when Cakobau was dying, the king installed Thurston as chief of all the Fijians. Sir John was governor of Fiji when the Clemenses visited Suva.

A few days before the Clemenses arrived, Sir John wrote to *The Times* of London in response to criticism of his administration. "In order to protect themselves against the superior ability and energy of the white man," he wrote, "[the Fijians] ceded their islands to her Majesty the Queen . . . There is perfect confidence between the natives and the Government. The Fijian knows his protector and friend."

In *Following the Equator*, Clemens reported that he drove out of town to meet the head of state. This was not, in fact, Thurston, then in England on medical leave, but rather the acting governor. Clemens admired the "noble and beautiful view of ocean and islands and castellated peaks from the governor's high-placed house." That house, near the Thurston Gardens on the edge of town, survived until 1921, when it burned to the ground after lightning struck it.

Thurston Gardens, soggy from rain, boast glorious hibiscus, which Clemens described as red enough to make one blink. It is still intensely red, but yellow and pink varieties abound as well.

Having traversed the gardens, we enter the Fiji Museum and stroll over to a case containing implements for the consumption of human flesh. A Fijian is passing through the room. "Don't look at that!" he says with a laugh. Before sustained European contact and Christianization in the nineteenth century, cannibalism was a fundamental feature of Fijian life, sanctified by religion, practiced for millennia, and taken utterly for granted. Victims were usually enemies killed or captured in battle. Eating your foe disgraced him and, in an ancestor-conscious society, insulted his family. When an enemy of high rank was slain, bits of his body would be distributed throughout the district, and sometimes his skull would be used as a ceremonial drinking cup. We gaze at a log with the bones of victims stuffed into the crevices.

It is time to leave the museum and make our way back to the harbor. We return through the damp garden to Victoria Parade, which we follow into town. As we walk, we admire the Fijians. They are, as Clemens noted, a pleasure to look at, tall, graceful, and magnificently built. Clemens admired not only their majestic physique but also their mental acuity. They were, he recorded in *Following the Equator*, "a fine race . . . with brains in their heads and an inquiring turn of mind." As for the benefits of Western civilization, he noted that "only sixty years ago they were sunk in darkness; now they have the bicycle."

Clara Clemens recalled that the huge, carved wooden club of a Fijian policeman delighted her father, who tried to buy it. The policeman declined, although the offer greatly amused him. As Alice and I return to our vessel, we are approached by a Fijian who holds out his hand to shake ours, asks us where we are from and what we think of Suva, and then offers to sell us a carved wooden paddle.

Clemens did not mention the Indians, who now make up about half the population, because they were then not so numerous, the importation of indentured Indian laborers having begun only sixteen years before his visit. Besides, most of them would have been found on plantations in the countryside. The Fijians were reluctant to work for the plantation owners, and in any case, Fiji's first resident governor, Sir Arthur Gordon, set up a system of taxation that discouraged them from doing so. (He also halved the Europeans' land claims, leaving the overwhelming bulk of the land under Fijian control, with the land communally held.) It was the first governor, Gordon, who proposed the importation of Indian indentured laborers, a solution that was, in the words of one historian, "a British substitute for the slavery they had abolished in 1833."

Poor, uneducated Indian workers were willing to accept the harsh conditions of foreign plantation labor. At least some were. Unscrupulous recruiters misled many and kidnapped others. Once in Fiji, the laborers were required to work for five years. After another five years, they could return to India, their passage paid, or remain in Fiji. Inasmuch as nonagricultural work was initially limited, they often had to spend their second five years under contract again if they did not wish to return to India.

As plantation laborers, they were fed, housed, and cared for at a level of adequacy appropriate for farm animals. Three single men, for example, would share a room a bit smaller than ten by seven feet. But their appalling living conditions were not so different from what they could expect to find as factory or plantation hands in India. And once they had served their time and saved a bit of money, they could exploit opportunities that would have been undreamed of in their own country, where they would have been bound by caste restrictions. In Fiji, where the trauma of transportation and resettlement had weakened such constraints, they began to work for themselves, opening shops and renting land to cultivate sugar or raise livestock. As they increased in numbers and prosperity, they came to dominate the economy.

For many years after independence in 1970, Fiji appeared to be a model of intercommunal harmony. But racial tension surfaced after the fifth election, in 1987, when the political party dominated by indigenous Fijians lost the power it had held since independence. Two other parties, one dominated by Indians, the other by trade union leaders, formed a governing coalition. Fijian chiefs, fearful of losing influence, inflamed their followers, asserting that Indians would take control of the country, annul Fijian land rights, and stifle Fijian culture.

That year, following two bloodless coups, a Fijian lieutenant colonel declared Fiji a republic, severed its ties to Britain, and ordered a new constitution guaranteeing political dominance to Fijians. The Indians, about as numerous as the Fijians, have lived in Fiji for four or five generations, have promoted its economic development, and have no other home. Even the language they speak among themselves, a variety of Hindi influenced by Fijian, English, and the numerous languages the immigrants brought with them, is spoken only in Fiji. Yet the law now restricts them to fewer than one-third of the seats in Parliament, where a majority of seats, as well as the posts of president, prime minister, chief of police, and civil service commissioner, are reserved for Fijians.

Whatever smoke may be rising from smoldering racial fires, casual tourists, in Suva for half a day, do not detect it. The Indians, however, must be exquisitely sensitive to intercommunal tension. Remembering the expulsion of their brethren from Uganda, shuddering at the occasional threat by a Fijian back bencher to evict them, and mindful of this century's frightful record of violence, the Indians are unlikely to feel as calm as they appear to the outsider.

Alice and I return to the harbor and climb the gangway to our ship. All the entrances to the accommodation block are locked except for one, next to which a seaman stands guard. A sign on the vessel's side announces the next port of call: Vladivostok.

Whether or not that sign fooled anyone, no stowaways are with us now, one day out of Suva, as we sail to Auckland. We journey southwest through boisterous seas, our first day of rough weather. If we were on the *Warrimoo* this morning, the staff might be roping fast the furniture in the lounges and fitting the dining tables with higher wooden edges or "fiddles," perhaps adding wooden covers with cutouts for dishes and glasses. Our freighter's great size — its carrying capacity, over 17,000 gross tons, is almost five times that of the *Warrimoo*'s — keeps it reasonably stable. The mild rolling disturbs no one. It proves to be our only day of rough weather.

The *Warrimoo* also experienced but one day of rough weather, en route from Auckland to Sydney. "Atlantic seas on to-day," Clemens wrote to Rogers, "the first we have had. And yet not *really* rough. Satchels keep their places and do not go browsing around." He added that Clara lost her balance on a piano stool, while playing hymns at Sunday services.

Because of the smaller ships, passengers were more likely to suffer from seasickness than they are today. This was well before Dramamine made life bearable at sea for those susceptible to motion sickness. Many remedies were recommended for seasickness, including bismuth, opium, a little soup with cayenne, a pint of sea water swallowed in one gulp, and small doses of tincture of iodine. But according to John Brinnin, a social historian of the Atlantic crossing, "the most time-honored method of treating seasickness was entirely verbal: you simply told the victim — in a tone of voice implying that some slackening of moral fiber was involved — that it was all in his mind." Brinnin quotes Mark Twain: "We all like to see people seasick when we are not, ourselves."

A few days after our patch of rough weather, we pass small islands, each with sheer cliffs and a dark green cap, each with its own cloud, like the character in the *L'il Abner* comic strip with the unpronounceable name. Here and there a beach, a village, a harbor, a few boats.

It is evening. Soon we will reach Auckland. An extraordinary sunset heralds our approach: glowing bands of yellow, orange, and magenta melt into a purple sky. Yellow lights, scattered across hills above the harbor, punctuate the blackness. Our 17,000-ton vessel weaves between channel buoys, red at port, green at starboard, and touches its berth as lightly as a kiss.

Two days later our Pacific voyage is almost over. The absence of four passengers who debarked at Auckland reminds us of change and loss. At its bow, the ship creates great arcs of spray, on our last full day of open sea. Tomorrow, September 16, three weeks after our departure from Oakland, we will land in Sydney, one hundred years to the day after the Clemenses did so.

Chapter Ten

*T*HE CLEMENSES WERE AT BREAKFAST when the *Warrimoo* tied up at Circular Quay in Sydney Harbor on September 16, 1895. Before they had risen from the table, a reporter approached Clemens and requested an interview. Like most visitors, Clemens praised the harbor. It is, he was to write in *Following the Equator,* "the darling of Sydney and the wonder of the world." Sydneysiders continue to be proud of their harbor, which they offer to show you from several points of view, including the deck of a ferry.

Striking postmodern structures, like the glass tube that soars skyward from a concrete sheath, dwarf Sydney's surviving "towers and spires and other architectural dignities and grandeurs" that Clemens described. New architectural dignities and grandeurs have arisen, including a complex that has become an Australian icon, the performing arts center known as the Sydney Opera House, poised at the harbor's edge. With its great white roofs billowing like the sails of a clipper ship, it rivals the harbor itself as the darling of Sydney and the wonder of the world.

Clemens's interview that morning was not his first in Sydney. The night before, while the *Warrimoo* was anchored offshore in Watson's Bay, the journalist Herbert Low spoke to him. Low had come out to the *Warrimoo* in a launch. As it bobbed up and down, he hollered up to Clemens, who leaned over the *Warrimoo*'s rail to respond.

According to an account of the interview, which appeared the next day, Low asked Clemens his ideas about Australia. "I don't know," he said. "I'm ready to adopt any that seem handy. I don't believe in going outside accepted views." Noise submerged his next remarks, but then he said he was going to start his book about Australia right away, because "you know so much more of a country when you haven't seen it than when you have."

Low reported that Clemens was unwilling to fight Max O'Rell, who had challenged him to a duel. Max O'Rell was the pseudonym of the French humorist Léon Paul Blouet, whose books, translated into English, were widely read in the English-speaking world and whose lecture tour of Australia, a few years earlier, was a happy memory in the minds of Low's readers.

Clemens had recently aroused O'Rell's ire by publishing an unfavorable review of an American travelogue written by Paul Bourget, an influential French novelist and critic. Clemens wrote the review after he and his family had left their beloved Hartford home to live in France in order to economize and while he was half-mad with worry about his finances. This state of affairs, along with his dislike of the French, may have sharpened his irritation with the book, which made sweeping, negative generalizations about American life based on a brief and biased exposure to it. Clemens claimed in his review that if a foreigner wanted to learn about a country, he should read that country's novels. When Clemens went to France, he said, he took along a copy of *La Terre*. This remark particularly infuriated O'Rell, inasmuch as Zola's novel is a grim, repulsive portrait of French peasant life.

O'Rell was so enraged that he published a mean-spirited personal attack on Clemens, whom he unjustly accused of having "settled his fortune on his wife in order to avoid meeting his creditors." O'Rell's article appeared in March of 1895, only four months before the Clemenses embarked on their world tour.

Now, when asked about the proposed duel, Clemens was reported to have dismissed it. "I can disgrace myself nearer home, if I felt so inclined, than by going out to have a row with a Frenchman. The fact of the matter is I think Max O'Rell wanted an advertisement, and thought the best way to get it was to draw me. But I'm far too old a soldier for that sort of thing."

He continued jabbing at O'Rell the next morning, when he told the reporter who interviewed him on board the *Warrimoo* that Max O'Rell's challenge was nothing but "twaddle." Unlike Bourget, whom Clemens characterized as "a man of great literary reputation and capacity," O'Rell as a writer had "no rank whatever." Before he could continue, Mrs. Clemens placed "a delicate hand" over her husband's mouth.

As for the interview the night before, during which Clemens was quoted as having called out, "Don't forget my soulful eyes and deeply intelligent expression," it is possible that most of his comments were invented. Thirteen years later, in 1908, Low wrote that the interview was largely imagined. "After a few attempts at questions, I gave it up — I could neither be heard nor hear. I bawled out, 'Mr. Twain, I'll have to imagine this interview,' to which he screamed in a lull of the winch, 'Go ahead, my boy; I've been there myself!' . . . Well, I imagined an interview, which, although not true, ought to have been; and no one was more pleased than Twain."

Clemens presumably told him so when he met him the next day. Before Low's launch returned to shore, Clemens called out, "I'll meet you at the Australia to-morrow at eleven o'clock."

The Australia, where the Clemenses were staying, was Sydney's premier hotel, a palatial structure of seven stories, with marble columns supporting the ceilings of its public rooms. According to its handbook, the bar offered a "display of glass unrivalled in the colonies," and its "experienced male dispensers of liquid refreshments" presided over a counter forty feet long.

It was at the Australia's bar that a reporter spotted Clemens at about noon of the day of his arrival, drinking a whiskey cocktail with two men. It is likely that the reporter, who was then a freelancer and probably supplying several papers with reports of his interviews with Clemens, was Low.

Clemens, due to be photographed at a studio, invited the reporter to accompany him. Because Clemens's agent had posted pictures of Mark Twain on every flat surface in town, he was instantly recognizable. Thirteen years later Low claimed that as he and Clemens walked about, they were "blocked by a veritable race of genteel cadgers . . . Men would pause, in affected abruptness, as Twain approached, then rush up to him, shake hands enthusiastically, saying something like this: 'You are Mark Twain; I know it. Sir, it is the glory of my life to have shaken hands with you.' " Then they would take him aside and ask for money. These interruptions became so frequent that Clemens invented a remedy. "Approached by an enthusiastic literary admirer with a borrowing eye, he did not disclaim his identity, but after acknowledging it he would say rapidly, 'Yes, indeed, I am Mark Twain; but I regret to say after all my labors in the literary vineyard I have arrived here in very distressed circumstances. Could you oblige me with half-a-crown till I get back to the States.' It was a complete cure." If this was not true, it ought to have been.

The article that appeared the next day got Clemens into trouble on several fronts. At the photographer's studio, Clemens was shown a portrait of Sir Henry Parkes, the grand old man of Australian politics, five times premier of New South Wales, at that time a separate colony. "Mr. Clemens was delighted with the work," wrote the reporter, "and, commenting upon the subject, said that Sir Henry had a truly splendid head, and that it was hard to believe that he could make the bitter speeches that he had heard attributed to him." Clemens had unknowingly stepped into a line of political fire.

That summer, in a general election, Parkes had contested the seat for one of Sydney's electoral districts. His opponent was George Reid, premier of the outgoing government. The contest was particularly bitter and marked by the grossest personal abuse. Parkes, who had long supported free trade, now advocated protectionism, the erection of customs tariffs in order to defend local agricultural and industrial interests. Reid, who championed free trade, won the seat by a tiny margin, but his party attained an overwhelming majority.

Asked his opinion about free trade, Clemens innocently said that his instinct told him that protectionism was wrong. "Surely it is wrong that on the [West Coast of the United States] they should be compelled to bring their iron from the east when they might get it landed at a much lower price direct from foreign ships at their own door." His chapter on free trade in *A Connecticut Yankee*, he said, was written at a time "when one of the New York papers was publishing a great deal about the progress of New South Wales under free trade."

One hundred years later, it is the conventional wisdom that free trade stimulates economic development, at least in the short run, and Australia's ruling Liberal Party subscribes to this view. But even today the controversy is not dead. John Howard, the opposition leader, charges that in its enthusiasm for integration with the global economy, the government is costing Australia its soul. Local icons such as Arnotts Biscuits and the Speedo swimsuit are now owned by American companies. If Clemens's judgment is to be trusted, it is perhaps a bit late in the day to worry about foreign influence. "The Australians did not seem to me to differ noticeably from Americans, either in dress, carriage, ways, pronunciation, inflections, or general appearance," he was to write in *Following the Equator*.

Having advocated free trade, Clemens stumbled again by commenting on land use. He said that the proposal to "let the Government own the land, and lease it to people who would work it, and not leave it lying idle" had in principle "a measure of justice. But I do not see how so prodigious a revolution like that could be brought about without stopping dead and starting again; and to do that would mean a sort of revolution that is not to be brought about in this world except by bloodshed." Some readers construed his remarks as supporting Reid's proposed land tax, which aimed not only at replacing revenue from customs duties, which the government wanted to reduce, but also at breaking up the great land monopolies.

Perhaps sensing that he had blundered, Clemens told the reporter that "having thoroughly established my reputation for humour by talking of politics seriously, I shall stop." If Clemens had been in any doubt as to the propriety of discussing political matters, the *Australian Star*, Sydney's protectionist paper, put him straight the next day in an infuriated editorial, which suggested that he ask the premier to preside at his first lecture. Alluding to Clemens's advocacy of international copyright law, the paper noted that "he wants plenty of protection for his own books."

Clemens, awake to the folly of alienating potential ticket buyers, became more cautious in his statements to the press. Thereafter, all he was willing to say publically about politicians was that "it is easy to see that they are able men, and remarkable men, or they would not be in these positions."

If Clemens's remarks on Parkes, protectionism, and land use dumped him into simmering water, his comments on his fellow American writer Bret Harte turned up the flame. Little read today except for a few well-anthologized short stories, Harte was then a major figure. Asked his opinion about Harte, Clemens said he detested him because his work was shoddy. "His forte is pathos, but there should be no pathos which does not come out of a man's heart. He has no heart, except his name, and I consider he has produced nothing that is genuine. He is artificial. That opinion, however, must be taken with some allowance, for . . . I do not care for the man."

Clemens's hostility to Harte was an abiding passion. They had become friends in San Francisco in 1864, when Clemens was twenty-eight and Harte a year younger. At the time Clemens was a wild journalist from Nevada, whereas Harte was the leader of the city's young writers, the editor of a distinguished literary magazine, and the city's foremost literary critic and arbiter of taste. According to Clemens, Harte helped him revise *The Innocents Abroad*, his irreverent account of a European and Holy Land tour, a book that became one of the great best-sellers of the nineteenth century, and the one that made Clemens's reputation. "Harte read all the MS of the 'Innocents' & told me what passages, paragraphs & *chapters* to leave out — & I followed orders strictly," Clemens wrote toward the end of 1870. And if his letter of a few months later is to be believed, Harte influenced him more generally. Harte "trimmed & trained & schooled me patiently until he changed me from an awkward utterer of coarse grotesquenesses to a writer of paragraphs & chapters that have found a certain favor in the eyes of even some of the very decentest people in the land."

In the early years of their friendship, Clemens admired Harte's work. When annotating a collection of Harte's stories about frontier life, Clemens wrote that "The Luck of Roaring Camp" was "nearly blemishless." In 1871, after that collection became a best-seller and Harte's poem "Plain Language from Truthful James," better known as "The Heathen Chinee," created a sensation, *The Atlantic Monthly* offered Harte the unprecedented sum of $10,000 to write a series of pieces over a one-year period. He moved to the East in a princely progress.

By this time both men were famous, but the Eastern literary establishment, from which Clemens sought approval, took Harte's work more seriously than his own. At those literary luncheons and dinners in and around Boston that both men attended in 1871, Clemens was merely another guest, whereas Harte was the star. In that year Clemens wrote to his brother that "I will 'top' Bret Harte again or bust."

Five years later Harte proposed to Clemens that they collaborate on a play that would serve as a vehicle for Ah Sin, the Chinese laundryman from Harte's "The Heathen Chinee." Harte's play, *Two Men from Sandy Bar*, had contained a small part for a Chinese man, and although the play had failed, the actor Charles Parsloe, who performed the Chinese character, won acclaim in that role. Perhaps Parsloe could be persuaded to impersonate Ah Sin. Harte, chronically in debt and desperate for money, saw a collaboration with Clemens as a quick solution to his financial woes. Clemens, although a best-selling author and the husband of an heiress, was living beyond his means and felt poor. As always, he was attracted by a fast-money scheme. Besides, a few months earlier, his creative tank dry, he had abandoned work on *Huckleberry Finn* and was now in the literary doldrums. Remembering the success of "The Heathen Chinee," mindful of Parsloe's triumph, and anticipating public interest in the collaboration of two leading writers on a play that featured a famous character, he agreed.

It was during their collaboration, during the fall and winter of 1876, or shortly thereafter, that the relationship between the two men ruptured byond repair. Each man angered the other. Harte may have offended Mrs. Clemens during a visit in December 1876. "Tell Mrs. Clemens," he wrote after his visit, "that she must forgive me for my heterodoxy — that until she does I shall wear sackcloth (fashionably cut), and that I would put ashes on my forehead but that Nature has anticipated me." During that stay, Harte asked for a loan, which Clemens refused on the grounds of poverty. Harte, who already owed Clemens a considerable sum, felt hurt when he learned that Clemens subsequently loaned the same amount to Parsloe. Harte was insulted by Clemens's offer of twenty-five dollars a week plus room and board to collaborate on a second play. They disagreed about revisions to *Ah Sin*. Earlier, at Clemens's urging, Harte had submitted a novel to Elisha Bliss, Clemens's publisher, and when it sold poorly, Harte accused Clemens of conspiring with Bliss to promote *Tom Sawyer* at the expense of the other books on the list. Harte was right. Clemens, a director of the firm, had urged Bliss to do so. By the time *Ah Sin* opened in New York, in the summer of 1877, the two men were no longer speaking to each other. In view of their troubled collaboration, it is perhaps no wonder that the play failed.

"The holy passion of Friendship," wrote Clemens, "is of so

sweet and steady and loyal and enduring a nature that it will last through a whole lifetime, if not asked to lend money." Unpaid debts have ruined many a friendship, but it is unlikely that this was the primary cause of the break. It is more likely that Clemens was envious of Harte's critical success, resented being called a follower of Harte (whose stories of frontier life had stimulated public interest in the West, which Clemens exploited in *Roughing It*), disliked being in Harte's debt for having "trimmed and trained and schooled" him, and was irritated by what he viewed as Harte's condescension, now that a teacher-pupil relationship was no longer appropriate. His feelings finally erupted, burying in boiling lava his admiration for Harte's work and his affection for the man.

When the reporter in Sydney asked Clemens his opinion of Harte, Mrs. Clemens was not present to prevent the fusillade of invective that followed. (A few days later, when she walked into a room in which he was being interviewed, she said, "I think it would be better if your wife saw your interviews in print before they were published.") Perhaps Clemens did not know that in Australia, Harte's work was popular and critically admired, or that, off and on for twenty years, plays based on Harte's stories had been performed in Sydney and Melbourne. The newspapers' report of Clemens's outburst was followed for several days by editorials and letters to the editor vigorously defending Harte.

One reader, possibly in a sly allusion to Max O'Rell, suggested that Clemens had sought "a mild . . . form of advertising" in lambasting Harte. He thought it likely that Clemens and Harte would probably "go around the corner . . . and over gin cocktails or some other equally abominable American invention, have 'some laughs.'"

The storm aroused by Clemens's remarks about Harte helped to keep Mark Twain's name before the public, and may even have stimulated ticket sales. For a performer, unfavorable publicity is better than no publicity at all. Sydney's Protestant Hall, seating at least 2,000, was "crammed from floor to ceiling" at his first *At Home*, as his performances were called, and the hall was equally jammed during his subsequent appearances.

It is perhaps ironic that *At Home* should have described performances so far from home. But whether he himself or his manager

Robert Sparrow Smythe proposed it, the term suggested perfectly the unstudied informality, spontaneity, and ease which he strove to project. His audiences helped him to produce this illusion. They felt, according to one reviewer, "that an old friend — a personal friend, who had been speaking words of wit and wisdom to them from away back — had come to town."

His first appearance elicited a roar of welcome when he walked quietly onto the stage. The *Australian Star,* which, a few days before, had chided him bitterly, reported "such an ovation, such an outburst of uncontrollable enthusiasm as but rarely comes within the experience of the average man. The man's work and the feeling of it was evidently in the hearts of his audience, who not only cheered but waved hats and handkerchiefs as he stepped out behind the Stars and Stripes."

Protestant Hall, the scene of Clemens's triumph, survives today, gray, dilapidated, and boarded up. According to a fireman at the brick firehouse across the street, Protestant Hall closed about ten years ago, after serving as headquarters for the Australian Workers' Union. The firehouse was built in 1888. Above its central door, a sculpted bust of Queen Victoria still contemplates the scene. One hundred years ago, the queen gazed at theatergoers crowding in to see Mark Twain. Their roars of welcome and applause were loud enough for even a head of stone to note.

One hundred years later, Alice and I wait for Mark Twain to appear on stage at Sydney's Lookout Theatre. The auditorium is tiny, holding not 2,000 but thirty, although every seat is taken. Polite applause greets the performer, a middle-aged South African actor who is impersonating the master in one of his *At Home*s. His head encased in a white wig, a mustache fitted under his nose, he is dressed not in the white tie and formal black evening suit that Clemens wore for his performances, but in a white suit with a cream vest. (Clemens became famous for his white suits, but it was not for another ten years that he extended their use beyond the summer. According to his longtime servant Katy Leary, "he made up his mind, when he was seventy he could do as he darned pleased and nobody would dare say anything to him. So he was going to wear white for the rest of his life.")

Tonight the actor takes his pieces from Clemens's writings and autobiographical dictations. We recognize one item that Clemens used in his performances, the story from *The Innocents Abroad* in which the young Clemens, spending the night in his father's office, gradually becomes aware of a corpse lying on the floor. "I went out at the window, and I carried the sash along with me; I did not need the sash, but it was handier to take it than it was to leave it, and so I took it." The audience chuckles half-heartedly.

In *Following the Equator*, Clemens tells of "lecture-doubles" who, pretending to be Mark Twain, performed before unsuspecting American audiences. He even heard of another impostor operating in Australia. In 1881, on the day President Garfield was shot, Mrs. Clemens received a letter from Melbourne. The writer hoped that her grief would be assuaged by the knowledge that her husband's Australian lecture tour had been a great success and that the whole population mourned his untimely death, as she would have already learned from the newspapers. Although the writer had not arrived in Melbourne in time to view the body, he did have the unhappy privilege of serving as a pallbearer.

According to *Following the Equator*, when Clemens arrived in Sydney fourteen years later, he asked journalists about the swindle. He was curious because "if the people should say that I was a dull, poor thing compared to what I was before I died, it would have a bad effect on business." But to Clemens's surprise, the journalists had never heard of the impostor. Neither, he claimed, had the journalists in Melbourne. The reader is kept in suspense for several chapters before the "mystery" is resolved.

In fact Clemens invented most of the mystery himself, although there was a kernel of truth to it. The 1881 letter of condolence was from Reginald Cholmondeley, who had entertained the Clemenses eight years before at Condover, his splendid Elizabethan house near Shrewsbury, and who was yachting around the world for pleasure when he wrote that letter to Mrs. Clemens as a practical joke. Clemens wrote back to Cholmondeley: "Being dead I might be excused from writing letters, but I am not that kind of a corpse."

The South African actor, at any rate, is quite alive. Influenced by the tradition of modern standup comics, he sprinkles his routines with fillers such as "you know" and "seriously." He makes no effort to approach Mark Twain's technique, the deadpan expression, the slow delivery, the delicate pause. His performance, at best mildly amusing, reminds us that Clemens's stupendous effect depended not upon the content of his stories but upon the manner of their telling.

Chapter Eleven

*T*HE SUNDAY ON WHICH THE *WARRIMOO* ANCHORED OFFSHORE was a "day of public humiliation and prayer," proclaimed by the Government of New South Wales. The colony was enduring its worst drought in memory. No doubt, argued one editorial writer, periods of drought followed fixed laws. "So far, however, [Man] hasn't learned them, partly, perhaps, because he devotes so much time to football, cricket, horse-racing, organising Chinese missions, arguing about creeds, splitting hairs of theology, drinking and other unintellectual pursuits."

One hundred years later, football, cricket, and horseracing are as popular as ever in Australia, where per capita beer consumption is perhaps the third highest in the world, and if Australians no longer send missions to China, there are churches in Australia that cater to Chinese immigrants. The Central Baptist Church near Sydney's Chinatown offers services in Cantonese.

On that Sunday of public humiliation and prayer, Canon Taylor, preaching at Sydney's St. Andrew's Cathedral, declared that the drought was divine punishment that could be removed only by national repentance. The next day, September 16, 1895, when the Clemenses set foot on Australian soil, rain fell in various parts of the colony. Pipes from the roof of the Colonial Secretary's buildings overflowed, converting the secretary's long room into a reservoir and deluging the office of the Railway Department's cashier. The best part of the rain, however, fell in the adjoining colony of Victoria, whose residents were enjoined by a newspaper editorial not to feel self-righteous on that account, "for the Scriptures tell us that rain, when it does descend, descends equally upon the just and the unjust."

Like the Clemenses, we arrived on a day when rain first fell after months of drought. But a few days later the sky is blue, as Alice and I walk to the New South Wales State Archives. We're looking for references to Captain Arundell. Did he sail again with his steamship company, or did the directors sack him, as Clemens feared?

We find the *Warrimoo*'s inward passenger list. Passengers are listed for saloon class and second class only, so Clemens's story about a child born in steerage at the International Date Line, on its face a tall tale, is confirmed as just that. We find fifteen passengers listed in saloon class, including three Clemenses and a Mr. Smith. In *Following the Equator*, Clemens tells us that "the brightest passenger in the ship, and the most interesting and felicitous talker," was a young Canadian. He was the scion of a rich and powerful family who would have helped him pursue a distinguished career if only he could stay sober. Instead, they were dispatching him to the end of the earth, where he was less likely to disgrace them and where they would send him a small monthly allowance. He would become what was called at the time a "remittance man." In a journal entry from Melbourne, Clemens mentions seeing many such unfortunates and then refers to one by name, Smith. Here he is, listed with the Clemenses and Mr. and Mrs. Chase, the Bostonian mother and son whose trip to the Finger Lakes took them around the world.

Captain Arundell has signed the manifest in a large, confident, well-formed hand, a signature as handsome as his person. If he is under a cloud, his writing does not betray it. But his name does not appear on the lists of incoming vessels for the first four months of 1896. Perhaps he took a long leave, or perhaps I missed his name.

Leaving the archives, we savor the flash and dazzle of downtown Sydney. Skyscrapers, set at unexpected angles to one another along the narrow, winding streets, reflect one another in their glass façades. They also reflect massive brownstone buildings from Clemens's day. The Australia Hotel no longer survives even as a reflection, but a librarian told us that its bar counter was salvaged and now stands in the Marble Bar of the Hilton Hotel. Alas, even librarians make mistakes. The Marble Bar, according to a plaque, comes from the Adams Hotel, which occupied the site on which the Hilton now stands. So the Australia's forty-foot counter and its

unrivaled display of glass have gone forever. They have joined the
experienced bartenders as well as their patrons who, like Clemens,
once drank whiskey cocktails there at noon.

It was probably whiskey that Clemens drank at the Athenaeum
Club on September 18, 1895, two days after he had stepped off the
Warrimoo. One hundred members of the club entertained him at
dinner. In response to a toast in his honor, Clemens gave a speech
that concluded with the sentiment, "Advance Australia." This slo-
gan, referring to the proposed federation of Australasian colonies,
was associated with Sir Henry Parkes, a principal promoter of federation. Among those who responded to Clemens's speech was Sir
Henry, who presented Clemens with his book of poems, published
that year.

Sir Henry seemed not at all disturbed by the controversy
aroused by Clemens's endorsement of free trade. Later he entertained the three Clemenses at lunch. Mrs. Clemens, writing to her
sister Mrs. Crane, reported that he had lost his second wife about
three months before. That wife was not received by society because
she had been Parkes's mistress. Upon his second marriage, his
daughters from his first wife left home, but they returned to care for
their eighty-year-old father and his young children after their step-
mother died. Mrs. Clemens guessed that the oldest daughter was
fifty and that the small child who was brought into the drawing room
was about two and a half. At first she thought it was the old man's
grandchild, but it turned out to be his child.

A little more than a month after the Athenaeum Club dinner,
Sir Henry horrified many Australians and amused others by marry-
ing his twenty-two-year-old housemaid. "He said he could have
married more advantageously from a worldly point of view," Mrs.
Clemens informed her sister, "but he preferred to marry for love."
His middle-aged daughters once again flounced out of their father's
house.

Henry Parkes's career exemplifies the major issues that New
South Wales confronted during the nineteenth century, the enormous changes the colony experienced during that time, and the
great opportunities it offered to an able man of obscure background.
He was born in 1815, a few weeks before the Battle of Waterloo. The
son of a fieldworker on the Warwickshire estate of an English

grandee, he became premier of New South Wales under the gover-
norship of that nobleman's son-in-law. When he arrived in Australia
in 1839, the interior of the country was largely unknown, and few
settlers were brave enough to live far from the coast. In that year,
free workers in New South Wales, resentful at competition, succeeded in halting the practice of assigning convicts to settlers, a
modified form of slavery. A year later Britain abolished the transportation of convicts.

In a classic example of the law of unintended consequences,
these measures created a financial disaster. Britain stopped its sub-
sidies, which had been justified by the colony's status as a penal
settlement, and cheap labor vanished. The Bank of Australia failed.
Land values plummeted. Sheep sold at a shilling apiece. The sheep
farmers, who constituted the only important industry and who were
faced with ruin, agitated for the return of convict transportation and
labor. But when these practices were revived in 1849, the fury of the
free workers quickly stopped them. Parkes was active in the successful agitation.

But the issue of competition from convict labor would in any
case have become unimportant after the discovery of gold two years
later. As gold seekers swarmed into the country, convicts became a
small proportion of the white population. The new immigrants,
mostly energetic, independent men, forwarded the movement for
self-government, in which Parkes was active. When a committee of
the old legislative council proposed the creation of a hereditary
nobility, from which the upper house of the new legislature would
be formed, Parkes was a prominent leader of the furious opposition
that quashed the plan. First elected to office in 1854, he continued
to serve, almost without interruption, as representative, minister, or
premier until his defeat in the summer of 1895. By then he had out-
lived nearly all his colleagues.

Like Clemens, he was a self-made man from the margins of
society. Like Clemens, he was both a writer and a master of excoriation. And like Clemens, he was a poor businessman. But unlike
Clemens, he neither smoked nor drank nor gambled, nor talked for
the sake of talk. One of Parkes's admirers wrote that "his whole time
was so sacredly devoted to the public service that he hesitated even
to speak with persons unknown to him, his theory being that it was

sheer waste of time to converse with nine men out of ten." And unlike Clemens, he did not seek wealth. Parkes died a poor man. The Clemenses could not know, as they sat around his table at lunch, that he would be dead in seven months.

In addition to Parkes, other eminent persons entertained the Clemenses in Sydney. The commander of the Australian Naval Station, Admiral Bridge, asked them to tea aboard the warship *Orlando*, and Lieutenant Governor and Lady Darley invited them to a ball at Government House. A few days later, Clara and Mrs. Clemens attended a luncheon party aboard the admiral's flagship, which was "gaily decorated with flags and evergreens," and on which a naval band played for dancing until six in the evening.

So many admirers in Sydney sent flowers to the Clemenses that Clara thought the bouquets seemed to suggest condolence rather than welcome. She remembered that she and her mother worked hard answering the mail, which at times overwhelmed them. Clemens wrote to Rogers from Sydney that he hadn't a moment's time that was his own since he arrived. "I don't know what would become of me but for Mrs. Clemens and Clara; they slave away answering letters for me half the day and night and paying not only their own calls but as many of mine as can be brought within their jurisdiction." He was, he said, spending as much time as possible perfecting his performances.

Perhaps it was during his first days in Sydney that he created a routine in which he told of his persistent efforts to compose a poem about Australian fauna. "Land of the Ornithorhyncus / Land of the kangaroo / Old ties of heredity link us," he would begin, and then stop, seemingly stuck. He would start anew, "Land of the fruitful rabbit / Land of the boomerang," and would falter, confounded again. He would then recite twenty lines of verse, which he had composed while still in British Columbia (in *Following the Equator* he attributes the poem to a fellow passenger, a learned "naturalist") — "Come forth from thy oozy couch, / O Ornithorhyncus dear! . . ." — and would predict that if he could persevere and if his inspiration did not desert him, he would probably complete his masterpiece in another year. He introduced this routine during his third performance in Sydney, two days before he wrote to Rogers. It became such a popular item in his repertoire that advertisements for his performances sometimes noted it.

He wrote to Rogers in bed, "with what seems to be a new carbuncle" halfway between his left knee and ankle. The Clemenses were leaving that afternoon for Melbourne. "We have had a darling time here for a week," he told Rogers, "and really I am almost in love with the platform again."

Chapter Twelve

AT ABOUT FOUR-THIRTY on Wednesday afternoon, September 25, the Clemenses left the Australia Hotel for the railroad station, where they boarded their train to Melbourne. Accompanying them was Robert Sparrow Smythe, one of Australia's most experienced and best-known theatrical managers. He styled himself "the much-travelled." He had conducted Australian performers to India, Japan, South Africa, and America, and had brought to Australia numerous foreign artists, including Max O'Rell. Among his clients was the journalist and African explorer Henry M. Stanley. It was Stanley who recommended him to Clemens, who then signed with Smythe for a tour of the Sandwich Islands, Australia, New Zealand, India, Ceylon, Mauritius, and South Africa.

Writing to Rogers from Paris at the beginning of February 1895, Clemens said that he had discussed his world lecture tour with Stanley. "I have to-day written his lecture-agent in Melbourne and asked him to make me a proposition and send duplicate (signed) contracts for consideration, together with his guess as to how much my profits might exceed my expenses." Shortly thereafter he wrote to Rogers again: "More Mental Telegraphy . . . I wrote Smythe nine days ago — *and got a letter from him from Melbourne last night answering my questions!* There — how's that! It is true that his letter left Melbourne Dec. 17 and went to America and then back to Paris — still it was odd that he should take a notion to write me just about the time that I was going to write him. I hadn't thought of Australia away back there in December; so I conclude that his mind telegraphed the idea into mine across the ocean."

The brief article about the incident that Clemens wrote for *Harper's Magazine* was reprinted in various Australian newspapers to promote his tour, as part of the publicity that Smythe mounted for him. A blitz of posters, advertisements, and news releases preceded Clemens's entry into each of the towns in which he performed.

The train at Sydney into which the Clemenses and Smythe stepped was "clean and fine and new," according to Clemens in *Following the Equator,* although he complained about having to pay extra weight for his baggage. He was impressed by the Blue Mountains, which he saw through the train's windows. "They are of a blueness not to be paralleled in the world," he told a reporter, and in *Following the Equator* he wrote that they were "a wonderful color — just divine."

He added that a local resident informed him that what seemed to be mountains were really piles of dead rabbits. "Long exposure and the over-ripe condition of the rabbits," the local told him, "was what made them look so blue." Clemens commented that the stranger may have been right, but experience had taught him to be wary of information supplied to travelers. "The rabbit-plague has indeed been very bad in Australia, and it could account for one mountain, but not for a mountain range, it seems to me. It is too large an order."

The animals that Europeans introduced to Australia — among them cattle, sheep, cats, rats, foxes, and rabbits — have, in conjunction with the settlers' technology, created in two centuries more harm to the environment than was created by the Aborigines in fifty millennia. As a fitting punishment, perhaps, the rabbits soon threatened the settlers' livelihoods, eating up the pastures meant for sheep and cattle. When, in 1881, a member of the New South Wales legislature expressed regret that the government's program did not include a proposal for dealing with the rabbits, he was laughed down. Another member said that "they might as well propose a Bill for the extermination of fleas." The next few years did, in fact, see governmental intervention, but with little success. For example, in a year in which the government paid for 27 million rabbit skins, there were more rabbits at the end of the year than at the beginning. By the time the Clemenses reached Sydney, New South Wales had spent huge sums in its war against the rabbit, including the erection of 15,000 miles of supposedly rabbitproof netting. Even so, rabbits had forced ranchers to abandon more than 7 million acres.

At one time, New South Wales employed 3,000 men to hunt rabbits. The hunters would settle down in a thickly infested area and work there until it was no longer easy to kill rabbits. Then, fearing to destroy their own employment, the men would move on to the next area and allow the previous location to become reinfested. By 1895, Australians regarded the rabbit as ineradicable.

Poison is not an advisable weapon because it also exterminates birds, which control an even greater pest, the grasshopper. About forty years ago, Australians resorted to biological warfare, infecting rabbits with a virus that is usually fatal. This killed most of the rabbits exposed to it, but left enough survivors to repopulate the country with descendants naturally resistant to the virus. Today enormous numbers of rabbits are dying from an even deadlier virus, which recently escaped from an island off the southern coast of Australia, where it was undergoing quarantined field trials. Apparently the virus kills only rabbits. It remains to be seen whether a strain of rabbit will develop resistance to it. In the meantime, Clemens's joke about a mountain of dead rabbits captures the degree of rabbit devastation that Australian ranchers now hope to see.

The color of the Blue Mountains may have seemed a wonder to Clemens, but "the oddest thing, the strangest thing, the most baffling and unaccountable marvel that Australasia can show," he wrote, was made not by the Almighty but by people. At Albury, on the frontier between New South Wales and Victoria, all the passengers were routed out of their warm beds and, by lantern light, forced to change trains in the cold of the early morning. From Sydney to Albury, the rails were narrow gauge; from Albury to Melbourne, a broader one. "Think of the paralysis of intellect that gave that idea birth," stormed Clemens. "The two governments were the builders of the road and are the owners of it. One or two reasons are given for this curious state of things. One is, that it represents the jealousy existing between the colonies — the two most important colonies of Australasia. What the other one is, I have forgotten. But it is of no consequence. It could be but another effort to explain the inexplicable."

"I believe in early rising — for everyone but myself," Clemens told a reporter, possibly Herbert Low, after the change in gauges. Clemens talked to him about railroad travel in America, where coach seats were no longer covered with buffalo skin. "There are no buffaloes in America now, except Buffalo Bill . . . I can remember the time when I was a boy, when buffaloes were plentiful in America. You had only to step off the road to meet a buffalo. But now they have all been killed off. Great pity it is so. I don't like to see the distinctive animals of a country killed off."

When Clemens heard that kangaroos were disappearing, he said he hadn't seen one, but that he had seen a native Australian bird, the kookaburra or "laughing jackass," when he was in New South Wales. "It sat on a tree, and I stood looking at it. But it wouldn't laugh for me. I tried to make it laugh; indeed I did, but it respectfully declined." Mrs. Clemens, who was sitting in the opposite corner, said, "Probably it didn't think you were funny." Clemens agreed. "Probably not, but I did my best."

The sleek, stainless-steel coach in which Alice and I are riding from Sydney to Melbourne is, like the Clemenses' train, clean and fine and new. The toilet and shower room that we share with an adjoining roomette is a miracle of streamlined compactness, only slightly larger than a telephone booth. Unlike the Clemenses, we did not have to weigh our luggage. More important, we need not change trains, since a single gauge now connects the two cities. As we approach Melbourne, fields of silvery green, turning pale yellow at the western horizon, appear through our large window. The train slows as we pass the port, with its containers and cranes. Finally the skyscrapers of central Melbourne appear, their upper stories covered by cloud. The train stops. We have reached Melbourne's Spencer Street Station, where the Clemenses and Smythe stepped out one hundred years ago.

About two hundred people met them. The greeting party included the American consul, members of the Institute of Journalists, the owner of the Melbourne *Herald*, and John Lamont Dow, a former Minister of Lands and Agriculture and now editor of an agricultural weekly. Dow, a weaver's son who was born in Scotland, had fallen into bankruptcy a few years before. At that time, many Victorians saw their savings wiped out as land values collapsed along with banks that had squandered depositors' funds in unsound mortgages. Clemens may not have known of Dow's bankruptcy, but everyone else on the platform did. They also knew of Clemens's gallant effort to pay his creditors, a struggle that was probably greeted with special sympathy in Victoria.

That afternoon, in a parlor at his hotel, he talked with a reporter from Melbourne's *The Age*. Enveloped by "clouds of tobacco smoke," he complimented Australia for its tall city buildings, which the rapid hydraulic lift, he said, made possible. America used them too, he said, but in Europe "they still stick to the old slow going lift that carries two people and a half, and you arrive at old age on your trip to the sixth floor." Clemens, who had not slept well on the train and whose new carbuncle was bothering him, was resting up for his first performance in Melbourne, scheduled for the next evening.

Demand for tickets was so great that "to prevent crushing and inconvenience," reported one journalist, "the management resorted to the expedient of distributing numbers . . . Half an hour after the first seat was marked off the greater portion of the dress-circle and nearly the whole of the stalls had been reserved, and the cry was 'Still they come.'" The theater was not the largest in Melbourne, with the result that some people had to sit on the stage, three rows deep, around the back and sides.

During his first performance in Melbourne, a voice from the gallery called out twice, "Is he dead, Mark?" The caller was referring to a running joke in *The Innocents Abroad*, in which Clemens, his roommate, and the ship's surgeon, who had left the vessel for a month-long tour of Italy, would torment their guides by feigning simplicity and asking moronic questions. "The doctor asks the questions, generally, because he can keep his countenance, and look more like an inspired idiot, and throw more imbecility into the tone of his voice than any man that lives." Shown a bust of Christopher Columbus, the doctor asks the Genoan guide, "Is — is — he dead?" In Rome, he asks the same question about a mummy. Now, decades after his Italian ramble, Clemens did not catch the gallery shouter's reference. It was only after the performance, when he inquired, that the sally became clear.

Many clergymen attended the first show. "That gentleman in the higher stage-box," wrote one reviewer, "who laughed till his face was scarlet and banged the end of his walking-stick on the floor, was an archdeacon, and close to him was a rural dean, backed by a number of the minor clergy, all cackling like schoolboys."

Some parishioners may have thought Mark Twain's *At Home*s were unsuitable for clergymen, because the next week both the Catholic and the Anglican papers defended the entertainments. The Protestant writer wondered why people with no sense of humor attended the performances. He reported overhearing two old ladies criticizing the *At Home*s. They agreed that Twain's lying was pernicious: "The young men of Australia were inclined to go astray quite fast enough without wickedness being made attractive to them." As for the ornithorhynchus, "that was only another of his fairy tales."

The Catholic critic reported that he had sat next to "a stolid Englishman, who listened impatiently" to the "Mean Man" story, in which an employer docks a worker's pay for the time that the latter, blown into the air by an explosion, has been aloft. The Englishman turned to the critic and said, "Well, that is about the most barefaced lie I ever heard. If he expects us to believe that he must take us for gulls."

After Clemens's second appearance, Melbourne's professional and literary elite entertained him at a club supper, welcoming him, according to one journalist, "with a storm of applause." He expressed his appreciation of the warmth with which he had been received in Sydney and Melbourne, "although he modestly admitted that it was thoroughly deserved." In a long speech, mainly about his experiences on the Mississippi River, he asserted the unity of the English-speaking peoples.

He could not have foreseen that one hundred years later, Australia would be home to large numbers of immigrants from non-English-speaking countries. Changes in Australian immigration policy, during the 1970s and 1980s, have allowed into the country large numbers of immigrants who formerly would have been excluded, including Asians. The Melbourne telephone directory lists more than nine pages of Nguyens. In Victoria, immigrants who do not speak English receive a card that they may present to public service providers to request an interpreter. In Sydney almost a quarter of the population speaks a language other than English at home, and,

under every second skyscraper, food courts offer a selection of ethnic cuisines unimaginable a generation ago.

From Friday, September 27, through Wednesday, October 2,
1895, Clemens gave five performances in Melbourne, with only one
day off, on Sunday. At his fifth show, added in response to the colossal demand for tickets, the theater had to turn away disappointed
theatergoers. Clemens's schedule in Melbourne was more tiring
than in Sydney, where he appeared four times over a six-day period.
Moreover, in Melbourne his carbuncle was plaguing him. At the
club supper there in his honor he remarked that the carbuncle
"reminds me of its company occasionally. I have a greater respect for
it than for any other possession I have."

Clemens was impressed by Melbourne's Collins Street, whose
buildings, he said, compared favorably with those on Regent Street.
A remarkable number of those structures still stand. One of them, a
Gothic Revival building, looks as if it had been built as a church
when in fact it was built as a bank and continues to serve as a bank,
dedicated to another god entirely. Some of the ornate façades of
buildings that were razed have been incorporated into tall, modern
structures. The surviving Victorian buildings and façades reflect
enormous exuberance, from a time when Melbourne was one of the
richest cities in the world's greatest empire. Today this broad tree-
lined boulevard, laid out at about the time that Baron Haussmann
was rebuilding and modernizing Paris, has borrowed the current
American practice of illuminating tree branches at night with tiny
white lights.

Clemens had planned to leave Melbourne on Thursday,
October 3, to perform for two nights at Bendigo, a town in central
Victoria. But by this time his carbuncle was so painful that performing, even traveling, was out of the question. Smythe canceled
the Bendigo performances, placing a notice in the Bendigo evening
paper and distributing handbills to ticketholders arriving at the theater. Mrs. Clemens and Clara must have been planning to stay in
Melbourne while Clemens was in Bendigo, because on the day he
was to have left town, they were the guests of honor at a "tea and
chatter party." Clara, according to a Melbourne paper, "charmed
everyone with her two well-executed pianoforte solos."

The next day, Dr. Thomas Fitzgerald, the leading Australian

surgeon of the day and the first Australian to be knighted for eminence in medicine, attended Clemens. The doctor froze and lanced Clemens's carbuncle, gave him an injection of opium, and prescribed plasters, which Mrs. Clemens conscientiously applied. Clemens remained quietly in Melbourne for almost a week. "The study of wall-paper patterns, even if they are various," he was to say about this period of enforced idleness, "is not hilarious enjoyment." He stayed out of public view. He read the papers, received callers, and went to at least one dinner party ("the table, table-ware & decorations beautiful & in perfect taste," he noted in his journal. "No disposition to put the host's millions on display.") Among his visitors was Justice William Windeyer, whom he had met at the Athenaeum Club supper in Sydney and who was staying in the same hotel on his way to Adelaide.

In *Following the Equator*, Clemens wrote that a judge from New South Wales, "who was going out on circuit, and was going to hold court at Broken Hill," accompanied the Clemenses on the train from Melbourne to Adelaide. Broken Hill was in New South Wales, seven hundred miles northwest of Sydney, but the judge told him that in order to reach Broken Hill, he would have to travel in a great arc of about 2,000 miles, first southwest to Melbourne, then northwest to Adelaide, and finally northeast to Broken Hill. Clemens explained that Adelaide, the capital of South Australia, was close to Broken Hill. After enormous deposits of silver were discovered there, "Adelaide threw a short railway across the border before Sydney had time to arrange for a long one," thus capturing the Broken Hill trade.

The judge to whom Clemens was referring was Mr. Justice Windeyer, but he was not on the train with Clemens, who, writing more than a year later, either misremembered or placed him there for the sake of the anecdote. In fact, while Clemens was on his way to the train, Windeyer was already in Adelaide, a guest of the lieutenant governor at Government House, a regency mansion that still stands.

Chapter Thirteen

*I*F CLEMENS READ THE PAPERS when he arrived in Adelaide, he might have noted an editorial greeting Mark Twain. The editorial, which referred to the writer's drawl as a Yankee accent, remarked that "an increase of public curiosity as to the personal appearance and private life of public favorites is admittedly one of the marked characteristics of this age."

Adelaide's papers, assisted by promotional pieces from Smythe, had been writing about Clemens since his arrival in Australia. Adelaide's satirical weekly *Quiz and Lantern* threatened reprisals if Mark Twain was not funny enough. South Australians "will hand him over to the tender mercies of Max O'Rell, who is very anxious to fight a duel."

Even merchants promoted Mark Twain. Shopkeepers displayed photographs of Clemens, distributed by Smythe, in their windows. Charlick Brothers published an advertisement suggesting that the lecturer would exclaim "Innocents at Home," while sipping a cup of their pure blend teas.

The crowd that gathered at the Adelaide train station to greet Clemens was disappointed when the train arrived without him. After leaving the train at Aldgate, he and his party drove to town in an open carriage, with the American consul, C. A. Murphy. A few days later Clemens remarked that if the rest of South Australia or even a small part of it were as beautiful as the drive from Aldgate to Adelaide, it was a fortunate country. Everything he saw on the drive was unfamiliar, he said, except the grass, which he had seen before. "The trees, shrubs, plants, and flowers were all new, and so they would have remained" had he not been riding with his fellow American, Mr. Murphy, "who, though knowing nothing whatever about them, described every one accurately." As a stranger in a strange land, Clemens asserted, what he longed for was information about that country. It did not matter whether the information was correct. The ride down from Aldgate ended at the South Australian Club Hotel, where the consul's two young daughters presented flowers to Mrs. Clemens and Clara.

Shortly thereafter, Clemens met reporters, to whom he confided that he had smuggled his carbuncle past the customs officers. One journalist, impressed by Clemens's drawl, called it "a constant protest against the hurry and worry of the nineteenth century." Clemens thought that Australians were more American than English: "There is a frankness, a bluntness, and an absence of self-consciousness about them." He defended American newspapers from the accusation that they are corrupt, a charge that he compared to the belief that all Americans carry revolvers and are quick to shoot one another, especially in the South. Communities in the South, he said, are as "religious and peaceable" as those in the North. That may be so, but in Clemens's day the nation's highest murder rate was found in the South, a distinction that the region continues to maintain.

When asked about racial feeling in America, Clemens replied that "much of the talk is exaggerated by windy agitators and stump orators, and does not represent the real feeling. Away back there was talk of deporting the negroes to Africa, and of disfranchising a large number, but you do not hear much of it now." As for the Chinese, they are "poor, hardworking, industrious . . . always busy and always sober." Even so, he said, the Chinese are friendless and not wanted in America. "But America is a place for all people, it seems."

One of the reporters talked to Clara, whom he described as "a lively, self-possessed, frank, chatty young lady." She asked him if South Australians did much riding. "I do so love a good horse," she said. The reporter reckoned that South Australians "also loved a good horse and knew its points and paces to perfection," but the bicycle might make horses extinct. Clara said that she preferred horses to bicycles.

That night, with His Excellency the lieutenant governor in attendance and about forty standees in a semicircle at the rear of the stage, Clemens gave the first of four performances at the Theatre Royal. When he appeared, wrote one reviewer, "a great roar of applause, recognition, and welcome" burst forth and continued for several minutes, slackening only after he had bowed many times. Such a greeting, Clemens said, made a stranger doubt if he was a stranger at all.

"The doctor says I am on the verge of being a sick man," he said, alluding to his carbuncle. "Well, that may be true enough while I am lying abed all day trying to persuade his cantankerous, rebellious medicines to agree with each other; but when I come out at night and get a welcome like this I feel as young and healthy as anybody, and as to being on the verge of being a sick man I don't take any stock in that. I have been on the verge of being an angel all my life, but it's never happened yet." He took the pretty bouquet of flowers from the table next to him and said he "presumed they were intended for him, but whether they were or not made no difference, for he accepted them very kindly just the same."

Just as Clemens walked onto the Theatre Royal's canted stage, the Mayor of Adelaide was switching on an electric light at a major downtown intersection. The mayor was implementing the City Council's resolution to experiment with "electric-lighting in the Streets of Adelaide." The current was supplied by the same company that at the moment was illuminating the Theatre Royal and the South Australian Club Hotel, where Clemens retired after a late-night supper hosted by the town's literary lights. According to one report, a number of tedious postprandial speeches "bored poor Mark Twain almost to death."

The Theatre Royal and the South Australian Club Hotel survived for most of the twentieth century. The destruction of the theater, whose 1914 reconstruction probably retained only the original walls, did not create as much controversy as the razing of the hotel. The "South," as it was affectionately called, was for almost one hundred years a venue for elegant lunches, teas, dinners, and receptions. When that genteel reminder of the colonial past fell, the public clamored to buy its bricks as souvenirs.

Alice and I step into the Intercontinental Hotel, which stands on the site of the old South Australian Club Hotel. The bell captain, a short young man with blue eyes, tells us that the old hotel hosted Pavlova, Nureyev, and the Beatles. When we inform him that Mark Twain stayed there too, he seems pleased. He points out a bronze plaque that bears a relief of the gracious colonial building, complete with three-story veranda. Its successor, about twenty stories high, is inoffensive enough, but scarcely distinguished. Still, if it stands for one hundred years, the memories it begets and the nostalgia it creates will transform it into beauty.

Not far from the Intercontinental and the ghosts of the South Australian Club Hotel stands the Playhouse of the Adelaide Festival Centre. From its balcony you can see St. Peter's Cathedral, built in 1869, dramatically spotlit against the night sky. We are sitting inside the playhouse, watching Tom Stoppard's *Arcadia*, set in the drawing room of an eighteenth-century country house. The action occurs first in the early nineteenth century, then in the late twentieth century, and finally in both centuries simultaneously, as the characters from each era walk about and speak, in parallel worlds, oblivious of each other.

Chapter Fourteen

*T*HE ADDITIONAL WEEK spent in Melbourne waiting for his carbuncle to heal forced Clemens to reverse his route. Instead of traveling from Melbourne to Adelaide via small towns in Victoria and then returning to Melbourne directly from Adelaide, he returned to Melbourne through the Victorian country towns. The first of these was Horsham.

Horsham, in the center of endless wheatfields, was one of the smallest venues in which Clemens performed during his world tour. Smythe would probably have skipped this town of 3,000 souls if its citizens, led by an enthusiastic secretary of the Mechanics' Institute, had not underwritten the performance. They guaranteed Smythe thirty-five pounds, about $3,200 in today's terms. In effect, Horsham's citizens, on their own responsibility, invited Mark Twain to entertain them.

The Clemenses stepped onto the Horsham platform at two-thirty in the morning. The secretary of the Mechanics' Institute and another young man met them and drove them to the White Hart Hotel, gorgeous with cast-iron verandas. In its day the best hotel in town, known for its lofty ceilings and the best stable facilities out-side Melbourne, it still operates, although neither stables nor veran-das remain. A blown-up page from a history of Horsham, with a photograph of the hotel circa 1895, adorns an inside wall. The text notes that Mark Twain slept there, although if he were to see it today, he might choose more comfortable accommodations in one of the town's motels, as we have. "Mark Twain?" asks the proprietor of our motel, as if trying to remember where she had heard the name. "Oh yes," she says, "they named a boat after him at Disneyland."

Across the way from the Clemenses' hotel, in front of the London Bank of Australia, was what Clemens described as "a very

handsome cottonwood . . . in opulent leaf, and every leaf perfect."
Today the Commonwealth Bank of Australia stands across the
street, shaded by a eucalyptus, neither handsome nor opulent, but
large in relation to the other trees on Firebrace Street, still the town's
main drag. The street is broad and brightened by flowers and flowering shrubs, and many handsome turn-of-the-century buildings
remain. But those old structures that have escaped fire and the
wrecking ball have been remodeled without concern for their original design. A cantilevered portico juts out over the street, breaking
the vertical line of a building; only one shop in a row of four pre-
serves the columned cornice that once unified them all; false fronts
proliferate above the second story. Architectural mutants and nondescript modern structures have combined to produce an unpleas-
ing streetscape.

At about noon, on a windless, cloudless day of brilliant sun-
shine, the Clemenses rode out in an open wagon to Longerenong
Agricultural College, about eight miles away. "The air was fine and
pure and exhilarating," wrote Clemens about the journey. "If the
drive had lasted half a day I think we should not have felt any discomfort, or grown silent or droopy or tired."

Thomas Kirkland Dow, the principal, drove them out to the
college. He was the brother of John Lamont Dow, the former
Minister of Lands and Agriculture who had greeted the Clemenses
upon their arrival in Melbourne. Like his brother, the college principal was born in Scotland, and like his brother he had fallen into
bankruptcy, having speculated unsuccessfully in mining shares. He
took over the college in 1890, a year after land prices had collapsed,
wool and wheat prices had plummeted, and foreign investment had
ebbed. The depression reduced the college's income from the state
and from its agricultural tenants, many of whom were unable to pay
their rents. The calamitous drought at the time of the Clemenses'
visit contributed to the distress of the college, which within two
years would be forced to close until the middle of the next decade.

Those woes did not prevent Mr. and Mrs. Dow from entertaining the Clemenses at tea, or from presenting candy to Clara and
flowers to both women. Clemens toured the college, inspecting the
nurseries, which had demonstrated that "all manner of fruits" could
be grown in the region, and observing a sophomore class in sheep

shearing. Sometimes the students "clipped off a sample of the sheep," he wrote, "but that is customary with shearers, and they don't mind it; they don't even mind it as much as the sheep."

About forty students were in residence at the time of the Clemenses' visit. Most were sixteen years old or younger, and most were from urban middle-class homes. Clemens thought it "a strange thing that an agricultural college should have an attraction for city-bred youths, but such is the fact." Most farmers during the depression were struggling, unable to afford the school's fees, modest as these were. Large landholders sent their sons to private schools and could teach them to manage properties by means of on-site training. About one-fifth of the pupils came from homes headed by women, who perhaps saw the school as a means for providing a relatively inexpensive, respectable, masculine environment for sons who were hard to control.

It was an environment that represented to Australians of the day the "real" Australia, far from the corrupting influence of the coastal cities where, even then, the overwhelming majority of Australians lived. It is still widely accepted in Australia that farms and ranches and small towns preserve the essential character of this intensely urban country. This is so even though agriculture represents a smaller and smaller component of the nation's output. Farm incomes are falling, farm debt is rising, rural populations are declining, small-town businesses are collapsing, and government services to rural areas are contracting. Nonetheless, an annual agricultural exhibition, the Royal Melbourne Show, advertises itself this year as the place "where the real Australia comes to town."

For most of its history, the Longerenong college was essentially a boys' boarding school. Today it is a tertiary institution, part of the Victorian College of Agriculture and Horticulture, affiliated with the University of Melbourne. Although its students still learn from practical work on the farm, the college has seen some impressive changes. A graduate, returning in the 1920s, commented that by introducing electricity and hot water, the college was spoiling its students for living on the farm, where they would never find such conveniences. In his day, pupils had studied by candlelight. When the first tractor was introduced in the 1920s, at a time when Clydesdales provided most of the nation's motive power, students were not permitted to use it without supervision. In later years, they could not take out horses without supervision. But even at the time of the college's founding, the agricultural and pastoral industries of Victoria had seen great changes. Fifty years before, there were no shearing, reaping, or binding machines, but "only the shear in the shed and the sickle in the field," according to an editorial that appeared in another Victorian town, a month before the Clemenses' visit to Horsham.

The Clemenses drove away from the college through the long avenue of gums and pepper trees that the first students had planted, and onto the road to Horsham, where that night Clemens gave one of his best performances to date. He had recovered from his carbuncle, and the townspeople themselves had invited him. Mrs. Clemens, writing to her daughter Susy, commented that he had "never talked to a more enthusiastic audience." The young man who sat next to her "began to pound his sides as if troubled with stitches in them and turning to me said, 'Well if it is all as funny as this I shall die!' "

Chapter Fifteen

*F*ROM HORSHAM THEY TOOK THE TRAIN to Stawell (pronounced "Stall"), about forty miles to the southeast. Mrs. Clemens and Clara went directly to the Commercial Hotel while Clemens proceeded to Town Hall, where he was welcomed by a delegation of dignitaries, and where later that night he performed.

Today the Hall Keeper, Mr. Graham Rickard, a handsome, middle-aged man with a trimmed beard and a military posture, shows us what's left of the upstairs auditorium where Clemens performed. Now, with its ceiling lowered, the great room has been converted into offices, and there is no long view to the wooden stage, slightly canted toward the audience, to which Mr. Rickard guides us. Clemens would have been accustomed to a "raked" stage, though it was unnecessary for his solo performances. The angled platform helped those watching from a level floor to see players in the rear. By the time of his tour, flat stages had already begun replacing raked ones, to facilitate the use of free-standing, three-dimensional props, so Clemens probably performed on both kinds. Even today, especially in London, performers can experience the challenge of adjusting to an angled stage — more of an issue for dancers than for actors — and set designers can confront the problem of making props that stand on a slanted floor appear level.

It was probably in Stawell, before her father's performance that evening, that Clara took a walk in the country and found a sheep lying on its side. Convinced it was dying, she walked back to town, where she bought ether and learned how to use it to put the creature out of its misery. Fortunately, on her way back, she met the owner of the sheep, who explained that once a sheep falls down at this time of year, it cannot rise by itself because its wool is too heavy. After he hauled the sheep to its feet, she reported, it "toddled off, contented with the world."

The next day the Clemenses visited the nearby Great Western winery. Holding lighted candles, they descended into the underground cellars, where, by flickering light, they saw 120,000 bottles of champagne in various stages of maturation. The cellars, hacked out of granite by out-of-work gold miners, provided a constant, perfect temperature of fifteen degrees centigrade. The winery, still in operation, has become the world's second-largest producer of champagne (the largest is in Spain). Its tunnels or "drives," greatly extended since the Clemenses' visit, now hold two million bottles of premium champagne. Like the Clemenses, you can descend from the heat of the day into the cool cellars, see the hewers' pickax marks, and learn about the *méthode champenoise*. But unless you are a distinguished visitor, you are unlikely to be accompanied by an entourage like that of the Clemenses', which included the Minister of Mines, the Mayor of Stawell, other local politicos, and the winery's proprietors, Mr. and Mrs. Hans Irvine. Today, even distinguished visitors will not be guided by the owner, now a public corporation.

On their way back to Stawell, the Clemenses stopped at a clump of about twenty huge, rounded boulders in a grove of gum trees. These rocks or tors, formed eons ago by the erosion of a granite mass, are called the Sisters or the Three Sisters. They were probably named for the three daughters of the Levi family, early settlers who once made their home near the rocks. It is said that the sisters' descendants still live in Stawell.

The Clemenses would be surprised if they could see the boulders today. The rocks now display a psychedelically bright palimpsest of spray-painted names and slogans. Mr. Rickard's father, Donald Rickard, a seventy-eight-year-old local historian, tells us that the rocks have been painted as long as he can remember, although the spray-painting is relatively new. According to a contemporary photograph, the rocks were still unmarked at the time of the Clemenses' visit.

Another rock painting can now be seen in the area. The Clemenses did not inspect it because it was unknown to Europeans. There were only rumors that Aboriginal paintings could be found near Stawell. It was not until 1957 that members of the Stawell Field Naturalists Club discovered, on a hill about seven miles southwest of town, a crude white drawing of Bunjil, an ancestor-god venerated by Aboriginal peoples from northwestern and central Victoria. Known as a good spirit who never hurt a human or an animal, he created the land, brought it rain, grass, and roots, and conveyed to the people their laws and customs. When he completed his work, he left the earth to live in the sky as a star. His image, next to the figure of two dogs, smiles inside the hollow of a great granite boulder. Most of the graffiti that appeared there after Europeans learned of the picture's existence have been removed. A wire grill now protects the drawing.

The boulder sits with others on a rise. If you stand with your back to the hollow you can see the gum trees that dot the hill's slope and, beyond, the plain and the mountains. In the late afternoon of a warm spring day, with the low, slanting light casting shadows on the daisy-spangled grass, you will hear nothing but birdsong and the susurration of leaves.

The Djab Wurrung people once hunted, fished, and gathered from the lakes, swamps, and land below, obtaining an abundant, nutritious diet without too much effort. But their way of life had vanished by the time of the Clemenses' visit in 1895. About fifty years before, Europeans began to move enormous flocks and herds into the area, displacing the kangaroo and emu hunted by the Djab Wurrung. The original inhabitants fought the intruders as long as they could. Those Aborigines who survived the settlers' harsh reprisals were forced into missions, where they lived a generally degraded existence. Unable to pursue their ancient way of life, they lost much of their traditional skills and knowledge.

It is a pity that the Clemenses could not have visited the Bunjil Cave. They met no Aborigines while they were in Australia, but Clemens seemed fascinated by what he heard and read about these "marvelously interesting creatures," as he called them. The Aborigine's "place in art," he wrote in *Following the Equator*, "is not to be classified with savage art at all, but on a plane two degrees above it and one degree above the lowest plane of civilized art. To be exact, his place in art is between Botticelli and Du Maurier." The latter was a contemporary British illustrator of books and a satiric caricaturist for *Punch;* he is perhaps best known today as the author of *Trilby.* "That is to say, [the Aborigine] could not draw as well as Du

Maurier, but better than Botticelli." Clemens might have elevated Aboriginal art to an even higher plane had he foreseen the high prices that their work fetches today and the flourishing market in fakes that such prices and the naïveté of collectors have stimulated. Today's Aboriginal art includes work based on traditional motifs and designs as well as work reflecting nontraditional influences.

If Aboriginal drawing impressed Clemens, other Aboriginal abilities amazed him. He was astounded by their storied feats of tracking humans and game and by their skill in throwing the boomerang and the weet-weet, a two-ounce "fat wooden cigar with its butt-end fastened to a flexible twig," which is flung under-handed onto the ground, on which it skips repeatedly, "like the flat stone which a boy sends skating over the water."

Aborigines could not have been "such unapproachable track-ers and boomerangers and weet-weeters," he wrote in *Following the Equator*, were there not "a large distribution of acuteness" among them. He blamed "race-aversion" for "the low-rate intellectual rep-utation which they bear and have borne this long time in the world's estimation of them." During the Clemenses' first week in Australia, a newspaper article claimed that an Aborigine had applied for a job as a reporter with a Sydney newspaper. According to the report, the applicant was "so smart and generally competent" that the manager would have hired him had he not feared a revolt from his staff.

If Clemens respected the skills and intelligence of "those naked, skinny aboriginals," he nonetheless criticized them. "They were lazy — always lazy. Perhaps that was their trouble. It is a killing defect. Surely they could have invented and built a competent house, but they didn't. And they could have invented and devel-oped the agricultural arts, but they didn't. They went naked and houseless, and lived on fish and grubs and worms and wild fruits, and were just plain savages, for all their smartness."

Today we admire what Clemens and his contemporaries viewed as laziness: the ability to live harmoniously with nature and to maintain health with a minimum of work. It was typical of Aborigines, as with many other Stone Age peoples, to spend no more than four or five hours a day on average in gathering, hunting, and preparing food, fashioning tools, securing and maintaining shelters, and performing the other tasks required for their subsistence. They had ample time for recreation, spiritual pursuits, and the transmission of their skills, complex rituals, and rich mythology.

For 50,000 years, Australian Aborigines maintained their ways of life, until the first British settlements at the end of the eighteenth century. In the Australia that the Clemenses found, these ways of life had, for the most part, been destroyed or diluted. The number of Aborigines had been markedly reduced by the theft of their land, by exposure to European diseases and to alcohol, by heartbreak and humiliation, and by outright murder.

Although Clemens saw the Aborigines as "lazy," he saw the settlers' treatment of them as abominable. In *Following the Equator* he cited the story of a settler who feared an attack from Aborigines who had surrounded his property. The settler negotiated with them and offered them a "Christmas pudding" that all could eat and which would satisfy the hunger of all. He distributed the pudding, laced with sugar and arsenic, and the Aborigines ate it. "There are many humorous things in the world," Clemens wrote, "among them the white man's notion that he is less savage than the other savages."

Chapter Sixteen

THE CLEMENSES ARRIVED IN BALLARAT, about seventy-five miles southeast of Stawell, on Saturday, October 19, 1895. The next day they received letters from home, the first since mid-August. Their letter carrier was Carlyle Greenwood Smythe, the son and partner of their agent, Robert S. Smythe, who had sailed to Melbourne the day of Clemens's last performance in Adelaide. Smythe senior had intended to arrange a farewell matinee in Melbourne and then rejoin the Clemenses in one of the Victorian country towns. Now the Clemenses learned from his son that the old man was languishing in ship's quarantine. When his ship, the *Cuzco*, arrived at Melbourne two days before, medical inspectors found a crewman infected with smallpox. Instead of disembarking at Melbourne to remain in quarantine, he elected to sail on to Sydney, in the hope that the inspectors there would give a different diagnosis. Instead they found three more cases. "Until last week," wrote one newspaper, "there were two places on this globe which Mr. Smythe had not visited — quarantine and the North Pole — both considered unsuitable for lectures. Now there is only one." He could at least congratulate himself, as another newspaper pointed out, "that his lecturer did not travel by the *Cuzco* too."

His son replaced him as the Clemenses' shepherd. Carlyle Greenwood Smythe, "the more travelled," as he styled himself, in contrast to his father's sobriquet "the much travelled," was born thirty years before in the Himalayan foothills, when his mother, a popular Melbourne soprano, was touring with a musical company that his father was managing. Before joining his father in lecture management, he worked briefly as a journalist in Australia and Europe. Now he was to guide the Clemenses through the remainder of their Australian tour and through New Zealand, India, Ceylon, Mauritius, and South Africa.

Ballarat was the site of Australia's first great gold strike, its alluvial goldfields proving to be among the richest in the world. It was also the site of what Clemens called "the finest thing in Australasian history," the Eureka Stockade Rebellion. The good guys in this story, from the Australian point of view, were the prospectors, or "diggers," as they were called, who had neither the vote nor representation in the appointed legislative council. The baddies were the Victorian government, which imposed exorbitant licensing fees for the privilege of prospecting for gold that might never be found and, to make matters worse, employed brutal methods to discover tax evaders.

The diggers' grievances came to a head in 1854, three years after the discovery of gold. A digger was murdered in front of a hotel, and the hotel's owner, whom the diggers blamed for the murder, was acquitted by a government board of inquiry. In the rioting that followed, diggers burned down the alleged killer's hotel, and when the government punished the ringleaders, the diggers formed a league that pressed for prompt reform. Unable to obtain immediate satisfaction, many of the diggers burned their licenses, formed military companies, and built a timber stockade, which was named for the Eureka claim on which it stood. After government soldiers surrounded the garrison and demanded that the diggers put down their arms and leave the stockade, the rebels opened fire on the troops. The ensuing battle lasted fifteen or twenty minutes, during which the garrison was dispersed and about thirty people killed, most of them diggers. Stunned by the bloodshed, the public supported the reforms that speedily followed.

Although this celebrated rebellion had little effect in the long run — Australia would have become a liberal democracy in any case — for Australians it symbolizes resistance to government tyranny. An icon of this resistance is a flag sewn with the five stars of the Southern Cross, put together by the diggers' wives, from such odds and ends as their petticoats, and flown by the diggers as a symbol of solidarity. The soldiers who captured the flag allowed people to take souvenir snippets, but what's left of it can be seen hanging at the Ballarat Art Gallery, an opulent, well-maintained building from 1890.

Three survivors of the gold-boom era, members of pioneer societies, met Clemens at his hotel Sunday afternoon, October 20, to invite him to an afternoon social hour in his honor. He was unable to accept their hospitality, he said, because of a full schedule — he was to perform on each of the following two evenings — and because he was again unwell, suffering from a new boil. His visitors found him "stretched out at full length on a comfortable couch, his head propped up with a pillow," smoking alternately a pipe and a cigar. His indisposition did not prevent him from entertaining his visitors with about an hour of drollery, in which he meandered from one topic to another, told funny stories, and recounted his experiences in Australia. He complimented Australians as "a warm-hearted, genial, sympathetic, and appreciative people." Most of what he'd seen of Australia, he said, was from a railroad car. He'd done little besides lecture, except study wallpapers. "Every kind of wall-paper you possess in Australia has come under my purview, and if I fail as a lecturer, I shall write a book on Australian wall-papers, for I don't intend to be swindled out of everything by a carbuncle."

Bendigo, another great gold-mining center, about seventy-five miles northeast of Ballarat, was Clemens's next venue. According to a generally accepted story, the city owes its name to a local shepherd. The fellow admired a contemporary English prizefighter, William "Bendigo" Thompson, and thus, like his hero, became known as Bendigo. The shepherd's nickname was applied not only to his hut but also to the nearby creek where gold was found in 1851. Perhaps the authorities considered "Bendigo" an insufficiently stately name for the city that was growing up around the creek. Eighteen months after gold was found, the Chief Commissioner of the Goldfields suggested the name of Sandhurst, where he had been a cadet. The name lasted only thirty-eight years, until 1891, four years before the Clemenses' arrival, when Sandhurst became Bendigo again. It was not nostalgia that motivated the reversion, but the desire to identify the city, in the minds of British investors, with the Bendigo gold region.

The Clemenses stayed at the Shamrock Hotel, where, according to legend, the gold dust tracked in by miners' boots was regularly collected from the floor washings. The tracked-in gold dust must have been fairly meager by the time of the Clemenses' visit, because by then the gold boom was over, although gold mining continued. By that time, quartz mining was more important. Clemens complained to his journal that this hotel, like the others he had visited in the Victorian country towns, provided no wastebaskets in the rooms, that one of a pair of gas jets was plugged up, and that one of the beds was impossibly uncomfortable. He groused that hotel practices were determined by dolts: in Victorian country hotels you needed a ladder to reach your clothes, whereas in American hotels you had to bend down to see yourself in a mirror.

It was at this hotel, Clemens tells us in *Following the Equator*, that a middle-aged man called on him. "He was an Irishman; an educated gentleman; grave, and kindly, and courteous; a bachelor, and about forty-five or possibly fifty years old, apparently."

The Irish gentleman, who displayed an "amazing familiarity" with the work of Mark Twain, proved to have been president of the Mark Twain Club of Corrigan Castle, Ireland. He used to send Clemens reports of the club's monthly meetings, with summaries of discussions, along with quotations from the most brilliant of the speeches, particularly those made by five of the members, each of whom spoke in a distinctive fashion. "I could always tell which of them was talking without looking for his name," Clemens tells us. These reports were long, averaging 15,000 words each, but they were "absorbingly entertaining." Unfortunately, they were accompanied by requests that Clemens answer various questions about his work. In addition, the club asked for his reactions to the quarterly reports by the treasurer, auditor, and president. "By and by I came to dread those things; and this dread grew and grew and grew; grew until I got to anticipating them with a cold horror." Nonetheless, he would answer the club's questions. "I got along fairly well the first year; but for the succeeding four years the Mark Twain Club of Corrigan Castle was my curse, my nightmare, the grief and misery of my life." Finally, Clemens tells us, he rose up in revolt and burned the club's letters as soon as they arrived. Eventually they stopped.

Clemens now learned that neither the Mark Twain Club of Corrigan Castle nor Corrigan Castle itself had ever existed. The club's "president" was a rich man who had become bored with life but found, in the invention and elaboration of the club, more than an amusing way to pass the time. "The work gave him pleasure and kept him alive and willing to be alive. It was a bitter blow to him when the Club died."

The story as Clemens tells it, like his performances, combines humor with poignancy. Still, when I first read it I felt that "if he expects us to believe that he must take us for gulls." So it was with considerable surprise that I later read Clemens's journal entry from Bendigo, which noted his meeting the man from the Mark Twain Club of Ireland. There must have been, then, at least a kernel of truth to the story.

In *Following the Equator*, Clemens combined the story of his Irish admirer, "Mr. Blank," and that of Reginald Cholmondeley, who had written to Mrs. Clemens from Melbourne in 1881, offering condolences for her husband's death. In Clemens's narrative, it was "Blank" who not only founded the club but also wrote the letter of condolence. "Blank," wrote Clemens, confessed that he sent the letter "without stopping to think," had regretted it ever since, and begged Clemens's forgiveness. "So the mystery was cleared up," wrote Clemens in concluding the tale, "after so many, many years."

Today's Shamrock Hotel, restored to its original magnificence, stands on the site of the hotel Clemens knew, but it was built two years later, in 1897. Perhaps the defects he complained about stemmed from the management's unwillingness to invest in a structure about to be rebuilt. But the sumptuous Italian Renaissance post office across the street, complete with clock tower, dates from Clemens's time. You can still buy postage stamps there at its long oak counter, which seems to rest on the heads of seated lions.

Clemens complained about the post office clock, which woke him at six in the morning. "All Australia," he was to write in *Following the Equator*, "is simply bedamned with bells. On every quarter-hour, night and day, they jingle a tiresome chime of half a dozen notes — all the clocks in town at once, all the clocks in Australasia at once, and all the *very same* notes." According to legend, Nellie Melba successfully ordered the clock stopped to enable her to sleep, when she stayed at the Shamrock six years later.

Clemens had good reason to be annoyed by the post office clock in Bendigo. His performances and the club suppers or other entertainments that often followed them kept him up late, so it is understandable that he preferred not to rise early.

He performed twice at Bendigo's Royal Princess Theatre, opulent with crimson brocade and gilt. "The prices of admission were not so popular as 'Mark Twain,' and the result was but a moderate attendance," according to a local paper reviewing the first performance. Prices were lowered for the next night's show, which was fully attended.

Alice and I ask about the theater at the town library, where we learn that it became a cinema before it was demolished in 1963. A volunteer at the city's tourist information bureau even remembers going to the movies at the Royal Princess Theatre. We ask her how to reach Lone Tree Hill, which the Clemenses visited in the company of John Gregory Edwards, editor of Bendigo's *Independent*, and Mrs. Edwards. Either Clemens misremembered the name when he was writing *Following the Equator*, or the name has changed, because the volunteer tells us we're looking for One Tree Hill. Whatever its name, we drive out to it in the late afternoon.

From the top of the hill you see a carpet of trees. In one direction they stretch to the foothills of the Continental Divide. In the other, they lead to the town. It is indeed a fine view, but Clemens's comment to his hosts that it was "one of the finest panoramas he had ever seen, and it was typically American in its distance" seems to have been overly generous.

When the Clemenses were about to leave the Edwardses, Mr. Edwards asked Clemens for a memento. Years later the Edwardses' daughter reported that in response to the request, Clemens looked at his hosts for a moment and then took from his pocket a bit of paper, wrote something on it, and handed it to her father. It read, "Let us endeavor to so live, that when we die, even the undertaker will be sorry." It was dated and signed "Mark Twain." The maxim was one of many in *The Tragedy of Pudd'nhead Wilson*, which had been published the year before.

The next day, the Clemenses took a train to Maryborough, about forty miles southwest of Bendigo, where a delegation of leading citizens met them at the station. The five-year-old brick and limestone station, comically grand in view of the small town for which it was built, was the pride of Maryborough. It is said that the Minister for Railways selected the architectural plans from those submitted for the Spencer Street Station in Melbourne, which was built at about the same time but is not nearly so beautiful.

"Any town that has a good many votes and wants a fine station, gets it," Clemens was to write in *Following the Equator*, using the Maryborough station as an example. "You can put the whole population of Maryborough into it, and give them a sofa apiece, and have room for more. You haven't fifteen stations in America that are as big, and you probably haven't five that are half as fine." At the Town Hall reception for him, when asked what he thought of the railroad station, he said he had noticed its spaciousness, beauty, and sumptuousness. "It might be a little behind the average American city," he said, but that was as much as he was prepared to say: he didn't want to be accused of criticizing his own country.

The mayor complained that the station's tower lacked a clock, owing to a change of government, and he asked Clemens to publicize the station so that funds could be attracted to install a clock on the tower. Clemens, according to a newspaper account, hoped it would be chimeless. Both the mayor and Clemens got their wish: a silent clock was installed in 1914, but by then both men were dead.

The day Alice and I arrive at the station, the clock is slow, not yet reset following a power outage earlier in the day. After passenger train service was discontinued last year, the building became a tourist center, with shops selling antiques, books, furniture, and arts and crafts. It offers a restaurant called Twain's. Across the street, a half-dozen boys play on the high school lawn, oblivious of the seedpods raining upon them from the elm trees above. The yellow-green pods, thin as onion skin, float through the station's open doors and onto its wooden floor.

The magnificent Town Hall, in which Clemens performed on the evening of his arrival in Maryborough, was built in 1887, Queen Victoria's jubilee year. The building still stands. One of the town's commissioners, a pleasant middle-aged man dressed in a suit and tie, offers to show us the theater, which is on the ground floor opposite the main entrance. The auditorium, with its raked stage in place, is unchanged except for the false ceiling and its absence of chandeliers. The commissioner tells us that the authorities plan to remove the false ceiling, renovate the vaulted and painted original, detach the skylight cover, and bring back the original chandeliers, which someone had the foresight to save. He does not mention the next show, which we've seen advertised by a poster in town: an all-male review, presented by the Top Notch Strippers.

Chapter Seventeen

*T*HE CLEMENSES LEFT MARYBOROUGH the next morning on the five o'clock train, traveling first to Castlemaine, twelve miles away, and then to Melbourne. They could have taken the 7:15, but that train would have traveled through Ballarat and added two hours to their journey. Although their routing through Castlemaine was more direct, they found that their round-trip tickets did not include this twelve miles of road. They were told they could not buy extra tickets on the train; such business could be conducted only in the station. They would have to leave the train, and they would miss Clemens's matinee in Melbourne. In the end, however, they remained on board, helped, according to an entry in Clemens's journal, by a friend who intervened.

A columnist for the Sydney *Bulletin* reported the affair fifteen years later, in 1910. "A man who was travelling with [Clemens] on that train has a very vivid remembrance of one incident. It was at a junction from which it was possible to go to Melbourne *via* Ballarat or *via* Castlemaine. A ticket-collector rummaged the carriage. 'You're in the wrong train, sir.' 'Wrong train? Doesn't this go to Melbourne?' 'Yes, but your ticket is *via* Ballarat — this train goes *via* Castlemaine.' 'But,' said Mr. Clemens, 'I don't care *how* I go so long as it's the shortest way to Melbourne.' The ticket-collector kept to a pig-headed statement. 'Can't go on this train — you must go *round*.' Mark laid himself out for enjoyment. He lay back and refused to budge. A higher official joined the fray. 'Gerrout of here — I say — gerrout!' No movement from Mark Twain, but a pained drawl. At last arrived the Potentate, the Stationmaster, in red-faced fuss and much gold braid. 'Here, you — out of this!' Then Mr. Clemens leaned forward with his most ingratiating manner. 'My dear sir,' he said, 'put me out. Just put your hand on my shoulder and *put me out* — you'd make me *so* happy.' He grew confidential.

'I've got to lecture in Melbourne to-night and, old man, I *don't want to*. You put me out and I'll escape the lecture. It would suit me fine. I'd get more money out of your miserable railroad than I would out of the lecture.' "

Clemens vented his displeasure in *Following the Equator*, where he wrote that the Victorian "government chooses to do its railway business in its own way, and it doesn't know as much about it as the French. In the beginning they tried idiots; then they imported the French — which was going backward, you see; now it runs the roads itself — which is going backward again, you see." The government, having built a station "wherever anybody wants it — anybody that owns two sheep and a dog," and having constructed a lot of "palace-stations" as at Maryborough, all at a loss, economizes on the rolling stock. The coaches on the train from Maryborough are "passenger-kennels; cheap, poor, shabby, slovenly; no drinking-water, no sanitary arrangements, every imaginable inconvenience; and slow? — oh, the gait of cold molasses; no air-brake, no springs, and they'll jolt your head off every time they start or stop . . . They spend tons of money to house you palatially while you wait fifteen minutes for a train, then degrade you to six hours' convict-transportation to get the foolish outlay back."

No wonder Clemens was tired when the train pulled into Spencer Street Station later that morning. But that was just the beginning of his day. At three in the afternoon, he performed at the Athenaeum Hall; in the early evening he attended the first half of a piano recital, his entrance into the hall occasioning a round of applause that continued until he bowed to the audience; and later he was guest of honor at a dinner hosted by the Australian Institute of Journalists, which made him an honorary life member.

At the dinner, John Lamont Dow, the former government minister and now editor of an agricultural weekly, who had met Clemens at his first arrival in Melbourne, proposed Clemens's health. Dow joked that Mark Twain's comic essay, "How I edited an agricultural paper," had turned him from sheep ranching to agricultural journalism. In reply, Clemens said, "I recognize that in lifting Mr. Dow out of the sheep run, I have conferred a benefit upon the human race — and also upon the sheep."

After accepting a basket of flowers for his wife and daughter, who were, he observed, "thoroughly well qualified to appreciate" them, Clemens said that while he was technically the head of his family, "the real authority rests on the other side of the house. It is placed there by a beneficent Providence, who foresaw before I was born, or, if he did not, he has found it out since — that I am not in any way qualified to travel alone." On second thought, he said that his experience with Providence "has not been of a nature to give me great confidence in his judgment, and I consider that my wife crept in while his attention was occupied elsewhere."

When he thanked his hosts for his honorary membership, he referred to his sixtieth birthday, scarcely more than a month away: "I have detested old age from my infancy, and anything that removes from me even for a few moments the consciousness that I am old is gratifying to me. For the two or three hours that I have been here tonight . . . I have been young again." He may have considered himself old, but he displayed amazing stamina. After boarding the five o'clock train, giving a performance and attending one, and making several speeches at a dinner in his honor, he lingered to talk to friends, and then, as they accompanied him to his hotel, searched vainly for a street vendor of hot saveloys, highly seasoned dried sausages. "I reckon hot saveloys are the most sobering things on earth," he said, according to one reporter, who commented that "success has not spoiled him in the least degree. He confesses that he would rather meet a company of convivial friends — penmen for preference — and finish with a saveloy impromptu supper on the kerbstone, than dine with the great off silver dishes!"

He was to dine with the rich the next day, when the Clemenses were the overnight guests of Mr. and Mrs. John Wagner. In a letter to her sister, Mrs. Clemens wrote that they stayed at a "superb house looking on a most beautiful view." Their bedroom, she wrote, was at least thirty feet square. The front hall, she reported after a return visit in December, was twice the size of their hall in Hartford and arranged in such a way that one could sit there without being seen from the entrance. "Yesterday we had our four o'clock tea there."

John Wagner was sixty-eight when he met the Clemenses in 1895. A Canadian who had come to Australia more than forty years earlier, he was a founding partner of the Victorian branch of Cobb and Company, which almost monopolized the coaching and mail business of North Central and North Western Victoria, and which even built its own coaches. Wagner had expanded his interests into gold mining, manufacturing, and real estate, including great pastoral properties. Rich as he was, he seems never to have entered the Establishment, his name never appearing on the governors' guest lists.

The house that so impressed Mrs. Clemens was an enormous pile of forty rooms, built in 1890. The Wagners lived there for little more than ten years. Mrs. Wagner died three years after entertaining the Clemenses, and Mr. Wagner followed her a few years later. For the next thirty years it was the residence of the governors of Victoria, who would not have socialized with its former owner were he still alive. The house, now on the Toorak campus of Deakin University, is about to be restored, after a varied career that included service as a Red Cross convalescent home for wounded servicemen and women. In spite of its age and the many uses to which it has been put, much remains of its original grandeur. You can still find original oak paneling, star-patterned parquetry, and stained glass. The great entrance hall, two stories high, with its painted glass ceiling, is as impressive today as it was when Mrs. Clemens took tea there.

After leaving the Wagner mansion on Monday, October 28, Clemens traveled to Geelong, about forty miles southwest of Melbourne, where he performed that night. He seems to have offended some of the Germans in the audience by his discourse on the German language, normally a great crowd-pleaser. Mrs. Clemens and Clara stayed behind in Melbourne to attend a concert as the guests of Lord and Lady Brassey, the newly arrived governor of Victoria and his wife, whose landing three days before had been greeted by cannon salutes. Mrs. Clemens reported to her sister that at the concert she and Clara sat about two seats from the vice-regal couple. "It was all very interesting to see and be in."

The next day, Clemens performed at Prahan, near the Wagner mansion, in what is now a suburb of Melbourne. One thousand people crowded into the Prahan Town Hall, where Clemens pleased the audience with what one reviewer called his "inimitable drollery."

This was to be Clemens's last performance in Australia before sailing to New Zealand two days later, on October 31. From mid-September until the end of October, he had performed twenty-two times in ten different towns. In addition, he had submitted to numerous newspaper interviews and had given humorous talks at official receptions and club dinners, despite the onset of a boil in Melbourne and another in Bendigo. He deserved a rest.

Mrs. Clemens wrote to her sister that they were sorry to leave Melbourne, where they had met people they really liked. Many of their new friends came down to the steamer to see them off. The steamer was the Union Line's *Mararoa*. It carried them about 150 miles south to Hobart, the capital of Tasmania, where they spent a few hours, before it took them on a three-day voyage to Bluff, New Zealand.

Their visit to Hobart, Mrs. Clemens told her sister, was "pleasant but altogether too short." After breakfasting at the home of friends of friends, Mrs. Clemens and Clara took a carriage ride with an American woman, a Mrs. Walker, while Clemens went off with a former premier of Tasmania and his wife. Then Mrs. Clemens and Clara accepted Mrs. Walker's invitation for "a glass of wine & a piece of cake (or kike as the Australians say)." Mrs. Clemens reported that Mrs. Walker's home was "a bower," with the drawing room and dining room opening "onto a porch *covered* with roses, yellow and white, and looking off to the sea and mountains . . . a perfect mass of roses."

Clemens hoped to glimpse some of the convicts who had been transported to Tasmania. He found them at a Refuge for the Indigent, which contained, he reported in *Following the Equator,* "the oldest people I have ever seen." The average age at death, he wrote, was seventy-six. "Seventy is old enough," he commented. Once youth vanishes, there remains but "death in life; death without its privileges, death without its benefits." More than two hundred of the inmates were ex-convicts, he reported, "and could have told stirring tales, no doubt, if they had been minded to talk."

Clemens was sorry to see so little of Tasmania, whose beauty, he wrote in *Following the Equator,* contrasted with its horrifying history — its "wanton slaughter" of its Aboriginal population and its brutal use of convict labor. He liked Hobart, which he called "the neatest town that the sun shines on," a town in which "the modestest cottage looks combed and brushed, and has its vines, its flowers, its neat fence, its neat gate, its comely cat asleep on the window ledge."

Friends and relatives of people the Clemenses had met in Australia came to the *Mararoa* to see them off, and filled their cabin with flowers.On board, Clemens spoke to reporters before the ship's departure. Wearing a pilot's cap and smoking a cigar, he told them he was "downright sorry" to leave Australia, because "all my impressions of this country and of the people are of a pleasant sort, for the reason that it is the human element that makes a country beautiful or otherwise." Before a man approached with some prize kidney beans he wanted to show him, ending the interview, Clemens mentioned an earlier misconception about the distance between Australia and New Zealand. "I had an idea that there was probably a small ferry boat running eighteen or twenty times a day between Melbourne and New Zealand." Melbourne and Bluff, the nearest New Zealand port, are about 1,200 miles apart. The *Mararoa* left Hobart at 1:20 P.M., reaching Bluff on November 5, three days later.

Among the passengers was the New Zealand journalist Malcolm Ross, who was to describe Clemens's speech as a "slow Yankee drawl, with neither too much nor too little of the Yankee in it." During their chat, Ross mentioned *The Innocents Abroad*. "Yes," said Clemens, "that was a splendid trip. Everything was fresh and new then: everything is old now."

Another passenger was Michael Davitt, the one-armed nationalist politician from Ireland, who had been lecturing in Australia and would continue to do so in New Zealand. He had heard Clemens at the Athenaeum Club dinner in Sydney and now, on board the *Mararoa*, he presumably heard him again, inasmuch as Clemens was asked to entertain the passengers every night. It is unlikely that Clemens's compliance was hard to obtain. One of the great talkers of the age, he loved to talk; he could not, perhaps, help talking. Despite his occasional rages at the tedium, discomfort, and drudgery of the lecture circuit, he was drawn to the platform. He enjoyed dominating an audience, manipulating its responses, and sunning himself in its admiration and affection. His statement in Vancouver that "lecturing is gymnastics, chest-expander, medicine, mind-healer, blues-destroyer, all in one," expressed in exaggerated form an essential truth about him. After he abandoned his career as a platform entertainer, he would speak at important banquets for free. "I shan't retire from the gratis-platform," he told a friend at that point, "until after I am dead and courtesy requires me to keep still and not disturb the others."

3

NEW ZEALAND

Chapter Eighteen

*A*S YOU WALK THROUGH the ancient forest on Bluff Hill, you reach an opening, a rocky headland overlooking the sea. You are standing above Bluff, New Zealand's oldest European settlement and its southernmost town, on the south coast of the South Island. Only Stewart Island, a barely inhabited teardrop a few miles away, and a few wind-scoured islets lie between you and Antarctica. Below, you can see the harbor at which the *Mararoa* docked. You can also see, on a peninsula at the opposite side of the harbor, gray smoke spewing from one of the largest aluminum smelters in the world. An eyesore as well as the region's biggest employer, its fumes can be smelled from the little town of Bluff.

The *Mararoa* landed on Guy Fawkes Day, but if Clemens saw any of the traditional observances, he left no record of it. On that morning, at least in some of the larger towns, New Zealand school-children paraded through the streets with straw-headed effigies of Guy Fawkes capped with tattered hats, dressed in worn-out clothes, and stuffed with grass or newspaper. Thus armed, the children begged for pennies to buy firecrackers. That night they tossed the effigies onto bonfires as high as houses and set off their firecrackers as they watched the blaze. Fawkes had been dead for almost three hundred years.

Modern New Zealand, long independent of the English Houses of Parliament, continues to commemorate the failure of an ancient plot to blow them up. Although bonfires seem to have gone out of fashion on Guy Fawkes Day, fireworks are still set off, with municipalities often organizing official displays. Children no longer finance their firecrackers by begging, but, as was true at the turn of the century, a few are still badly burned every year.

From Bluff, Clemens and his party took a train to Invercargill, about seventeen miles north, where that night he was to make his

New Zealand debut. From the train windows he looked west at the Southern Alps, which run the length of the South Island. In his journal entry for that day he noted the country's natural beauty. His schedule, alas, was too crowded for a visit to the most spectacular region, the South Island's majestic west coast, with its glaciers, fjords, waterfalls, lakes, and mountains. Today a visiting celebrity could book a ride in a five-passenger ski plane, land on a glacier, and walk along the icy slopes, six thousand feet high, with other day trippers, and be back in time for an evening performance. As it was, Clemens had to be content with a distant view of the snowy mountains. He noted with ironic surprise that the grandest of these, Mount Cook, the loftiest peak in Australasia, was not yet named for Wellington or Victoria. Its Maori name, Aorangi, means "piercer of the clouds." He regretted the change.

On the day Clemens arrived in Invercargill, the New Zealand Railroad advertised a special train back to Bluff, leaving "15 minutes after Mark Twain closes his remarks to-night." The audience that greeted him in the Theatre Royal was one of the largest that Invercargill had ever seen, with many forced to stand. A local speculator was said to have profited handsomely by buying up the house. The Theatre Royal, whose cast-iron façade had been shipped out from Melbourne in the 1860s, burned down in 1983. Today a library and a multistory garage occupy its site.

Modern Invercargill's rectangular grid, parks, and wide streets date from the mid-nineteenth century, when a mile-square settlement was planned on what was then a dense forest. The city never grew large enough to justify the broadness of the principal streets, Dee and Tay, which today seem almost ludicrously wide in view of the low structures that line them and the sparseness of their traffic. In 1872, Anthony Trollope described Invercargill as a "small English town," but by the time the Clemenses arrived, its cultural amenities included the Invercargill Atheneum, which boasted a statue of Minerva on its roof. Inside, its shelves provided creeping space for a tuatara, a four-legged reptile with a crest of soft spines on its neck and back, thought to live as long as 150 years.

The tuatara ("spiny back" in Maori) became extinct throughout the world, along with the dinosaur, except in New Zealand. But now, after more than a thousand years of human settlement, the tuatara has almost disappeared from New Zealand as well. By Clemens's time it was no longer found in the wild on the South Island or the North Island, the two major land masses which form the country. A tuatara breeding program at Invercargill's Southland Museum and Art Gallery, a successor to the Invercargill Atheneum, displays several of the living creatures, including Henry, two and a half feet long. Henry is more than one hundred years old. He was alive, in other words, when Clemens performed at the Theatre Royal, and it may even have been Henry who gazed haughtily from the shelves of the old Atheneum while theatergoers rushed for places to hear Mark Twain. If not, at least one survivor reminds us of the earlier establishment. The Atheneum's helmeted statue of Minerva, which escaped conversion into scrap metal during the Second World War because not enough of it was salvageable, endures. Today, with a spear in one hand and a laurel wreath in the other, the goddess stands outside a huge white pyramid, the new home of the Southland Museum and Art Gallery. She now presides over Maori artifacts, natural history exhibits, and local arts and crafts displays, all housed within the largest pyramid in the southern hemisphere. And, as she did a hundred years ago, she guards a living tuatara.

The day after his New Zealand debut, Clemens and his party took the train to Dunedin, about sixty-five miles northeast of Invercargill, on the east coast. "A lovely summer morning; brilliant blue sky," he wrote in *Following the Equator*. "A few miles out from Invercargill, passed through vast level green expanses snowed over with sheep." Although new technology has increased productivity — for example, airplanes drop lime and fertilizer on the fields to keep them green all year round — the scene has changed little. As you travel from Invercargill to Dunedin, you pass more sheep than you could count in a lifetime of insomnia. Today, as one hundred years ago, the fields are a vivid coloring-book green, still threatened by gorse and broom, whose waterfall-spills of glorious yellow persist in delighting the nonfarmer. Lambs still cuddle against their mothers' flanks.

On the train to Dunedin, Clemens heard the results of the Melbourne Cup, a horse race run on Cup Day, which he characterized as "the Australasian National Day," the "supreme" day that "overshadows all other holidays and specialised days of whatever sort in that congeries of colonies," a day on which whoever can afford it goes to Melbourne, even from New Zealand. That year's winner, Auraria, won the Caulfield Cup as well, a feat accomplished by only ten or so horses since the Melbourne Cup was established in 1861. One hundred years after Auraria took both cups in 1895, another horse, Doriemus, did so as well.

Smythe later reported that "the Australian journals contended one against the other in making [Clemens] alluring offers to write a description of the 'Melbourne Cup,'" but he refused. Clemens, who was sorry to miss "a spectacle such as is never to be seen in Australasia elsewhere," told his journal that "everybody bet on the wrong horse." Maybe so, but a solicitor from Christchurch, New Zealand, won £13,500, almost a million and a quarter dollars in today's money, in a sweepstakes based on the Cup.

"The people are Scotch," wrote Clemens of Dunedin. "They stopped here on their way from home to heaven — thinking they had arrived." When the Otago Early Settlers Association adopted a new set of rules in 1898 to mark the province's fiftieth anniversary, it stipulated that Mark Twain's comment be adopted as colophon. Even today, perhaps thirty percent of Dunedin's population is of Scottish descent, with the Dunedin telephone directory listing page after page of surnames beginning with *Mac* or *Mc*.

Dunedin, whose name is based on the Scots Gaelic for Edinburgh, is often called "the Edinburgh of the South." Certainly Dunedin is reminiscent of Edinburgh, with its hilly site, Gothic Revival churches, stone buildings, and the lovely patchwork hills which surround it. Strengthening the resemblance is the frequency of rain and gray skies.

As in Edinburgh, good Scotch whiskey can be readily obtained, which was also true in Clemens's day, although, as he wrote in his journal, it was officially a dry town. "When men want drink," he had earlier told an interviewer in Australia, "they'll have it in spite of all the laws ever passed; when they don't want it, no drink will ever be sold." Sydney and Melbourne were officially dry on Sundays, he continued, but any stranger could see that "the most inveterate boozer can get all he wants while he is able to pay for it." Clemens argued that "what marriage is to morality a properly conducted licensed liquor traffic is to sobriety." He concluded the interview after looking at his watch. "Time is pressing; come let us solve the liquor problem in our own way. What are you going to have?"

Clemens arrived at Dunedin about an hour before his performance at eight. Greeting this apostle of liquor licensing were the members of New Zealand's Presbyterian Synod, all of whom appeared to be present. The clerics had concluded their annual session that afternoon. "Whether this was a case of cause and effect," one critic commented, "can of course be only a matter of conjecture . . . Certainly there could not have been a more merry audience," because "there was apparently only one serious person in the building, and that was the entertainer himself, who told his stories in a matter-of-fact way as if utterly unconscious of their drollery."

The next morning the three Clemenses visited Dr. and Mrs. Thomas Moreland Hocken on Moray Place. When introduced to the Hockens' eleven-year-old daughter, Gladys, Clemens joked, "My, how you've grown since I last saw you." Her father, born in England, had settled in Dunedin in 1862, the year after the discovery of gold in the region was transforming the settlement into a large town. His great energy, pleasing personality, and medical skills quickly made him one of Dunedin's most eminent practioners. During the gold rush of the 1860s, when typhoid and diphtheria raged through the hastily constructed and rapidly growing settlement, his earnings were high, enabling him to build, in 1871, the handsome two-story house, with gardens and greenhouses, that the Clemenses visited. This was "Ataharpara," after the Maori word for the first glimmerings of dawn.

Not only was he Otago Medical School's first lecturer in clinical medicine and not only did he serve as president of the Otago Medical Association, he also discovered, in a government basement buried in a pile of trash, the 1840 Treaty of Waitangi, now on display at the National Library in Wellington. The signing of this treaty, between Maori chiefs and the Crown, is regarded as the beginning of New Zealand's modern history and is commemorated every year as New Zealand's national day. An American's finding the original Declaration of Independence would be akin to Hocken's discovery. But it is neither his recovery of the Waitangi Treaty nor his medical career for which he is remembered. His name endures because of his superb collection of printed matter, manuscripts, photographs, paintings, and artifacts relating to New Zealand, Australia, and the Pacific. In 1897, two years after the Clemenses' visit, Hocken offered his collections to the nation. They are now housed in Dunedin at the Otago Museum and at the Hocken Library.

When the Clemenses came to call, Hocken — short, bearded, bespectacled, enthusiastic, and highly cultivated — introduced them to his treasures. Clemens admired the portraits of Maori chieftains. Unlike the Aborigines of Australia, he wrote in *Following the Equator*, "there is nothing of the savage in the faces; nothing could be finer than these men's features, nothing more intellectual than these faces, nothing more masculine, nothing nobler than their aspect." Their tattooing, he added, ought to make them look savage but it does not. "The designs are so flowing and graceful and beautiful that they are a most satisfactory decoration. It takes but fifteen minutes to get reconciled to the tattooing, and but fifteen more to perceive that it is just the thing."

Moko, or Maori tattooing, was a mark of rank, its absence indicating low social status. The untattooed face was ugly in Maori eyes, and indeed even to Clemens the undecorated European face seemed "unpleasant and ignoble." But beauty had its price. The process of tattooing was long and painful. Tiny bone chisels incised deep cuts to create the main lines, with a full-face tattoo requiring many sessions. While female facial tattooing was generally limited to the chin and lips, male faces were often fully decorated, with a large spiral on each cheek, smaller spirals on each side of the nose, and curving lines sweeping down from nose to chin and upward over the temples from between the brows. By the time the Clemenses reached New Zealand, facial tattooing was dying out, a casualty of westernization. It is now enjoying a modest revival, along with growing Maori assertiveness and self-confidence.

Hocken showed the Clemenses his Maori wood and jade carvings and gave them what Clemens described as "a ghastly curiosity — a lignified caterpillar with a plant growing out of the back of its neck — a plant with a slender stem four inches high." The oddity was a larva that had partially buried itself underground in preparation for becoming a ghost moth. Spores fell into soil on the caterpillar's neck and began to sprout. The plant sent roots through the creature and into the ground, sucking up the life of the worm, which slowly died as it turned to wood, its smallest features preserved. This happened not by accident, Clemens wrote, but by nature's design, another example, he noted in his journal, of "Nature's attitude toward all life," which is "profoundly vicious, treacherous and malignant." Hocken's lesson in natural history became the occasion for a bitter essay in his journal, about the malevolence of nature. He amplified this essay in his manuscript account of the world tour, an essay that was truncated in *Following the Equator* but preserved in the British version, *More Tramps Abroad*.

Today the Friends of the Hocken Collections hold an annual dinner; its theme this year is the centenary of Mark Twain's visit to Dunedin. The dinner's venue is the upstairs dining room of a hall built on the site of Ataharpara, the Hockens' home on Moray Place. The guests this night hear a talk about teaching *Huckleberry Finn* in America, listen to a drawling, deadpan Mark Twain impersonator deliver some of the master's one-liners, and examine a lignified caterpillar, loaned by the Otago Museum, which houses Hocken's enthnographic and natural history collections.

Too late for the dinner, Alice and I drop in on Anthony Harris at the Otago Museum and ask if we might see its lignified caterpillar. He enters a storeroom that emits the lovely aroma of cedar, extracts a specimen box, brings it out, and opens it. Inside are two such caterpillars, every feature and wrinkle distinct, with the remains of the plants that turned them to wood. Mr. Harris says that these date from Hocken's period and were likely present in the doctor's collection when the Clemenses visited him.

That evening Clemens gave his second Dunedin performance. He stepped onto the platform seemingly out of breath and claimed that he had been wandering about for the past forty-five minutes looking for the hall. That night he introduced a new item, which told how a Mrs. McWilliams, terrified by what she thought to be a thunderstorm, hid herself in a wardrobe and forced her husband to resort to various strategems to keep him from being struck by lightning. Following her frantic instructions, he donned a fireman's helmet, stood on a chair with its legs set in glass tumblers, and rang a large dinner bell for several minutes. The clamor attracted a crowd that

informed him that a cannon had been firing in celebration of
Garfield's nomination. Clemens's burlesque was inspired, perhaps,
by his wife's fear of lightning.

This performance was originally scheduled to be the last in
Dunedin, but demand justified a third appearance. Smythe scheduled the extra show for the following night at "popular prices,"
which meant a 25 percent reduction for the most expensive seats
and a 50 percent reduction for the cheapest. Like the first two *At
Home*s, it was well attended. Clemens wrote to his nephew that a
woman traveled for two hundred miles to hear him. One reviewer
commented that "the author of 'The Innocents Abroad' has neither
surprised nor disappointed his audiences: he simply satisfied them.
What higher tribute need be paid?"

The next day, before traveling north, he visited the Otago
Museum, the Dunedin Public Art Gallery, and the Otago Art
Society's nineteenth annual exhibition. William Mathew Hodgkins,
president of the Otago Art Society, was his guide. Hodgkins was a
principal founder of the Public Art Gallery (the first in New
Zealand), the driving force behind the Otago Art Society, and a
gifted landscape watercolorist. His daughter Frances was to become
New Zealand's most famous artist. If he was not the father of New
Zealand art, as his daughter claimed, he was the most prominent of
its three or four most important promoters during the second half of
the nineteenth century. He was a good friend of Dr. Hocken. Like
Hocken, he was born in England and arrived in Dunedin during the
gold rush. Unlike Hocken, he was born in modest circumstances,
but his emigration to the colonies enabled him to improve his social
and economic position. Starting as a clerk, he became a solicitor and
a much-loved, honored, and influential citizen.

Hodgkins attended the second of Clemens's *At Home*s and
sketched him twice as he told the watermelon story (according to
the artist's notation), a story told at that performance. In one of these
sketches, we see the performer in a characteristic pose, supporting
an elbow with one hand while pressing his cheek with the other, as
if, in the words of a Dunedin reporter, "suffering the agonies of an
80-horsepower, stump-jumping toothache."

Clemens was impressed by what Hodgkins showed him.
"Think of a town like this having two such collections as this, and a

Society of Artists," he wrote in *Following the Equator*. "It is so all over Australasia . . . pictures by famous European artists are bought for the public galleries by the state and by societies of citizens. Living citizens — not dead ones. They rob *themselves* to give, not their heirs."

He performed that evening at Timaru, a coastal town about 125 miles northeast of Dunedin. Mrs. Clemens and Clara had continued up to Christchurch, where Clemens would join them in a few days. His performance drew a mixed reception. A Timaru critic wrote that when Mark Twain speaks, "the moderate enjoyment of a reader becomes the unrestrainable delight of the listener." Still, he reported that many in the audience complained that "Mark Twain was not funny all the time." The critic explained that "such people must have been misinformed as to the character of the man. Mark Twain is not a mere 'funny' man. His humour is but the foam floating upon a deep stream of serious thought and of liquid wisdom." Clemens himself, during one of his first interviews in Sydney a few months earlier, had commented on the relationship between laughter and tears. "The two are as often as not simultaneous . . . Look at the poor fool in 'Lear'; look at Lamb, getting the quaintest, most spirit-moving effects with the tears just trembling on the verge of every jest; look at Thackeray and Dickens, and all the bright host who have gained niches in the gallery of the immortals. They have one thing always in their mind, no matter what parts they make their puppets play. Behind the broadest grins, the most exquisitely ludicrous situations, they know there is the grinning skull, and that all roads lead along the dusty road to death."

The day following his Timaru performance was a Sunday. After five consecutive *At Home*s, Clemens deserved a rest. He stayed in bed for part of the day, writing letters and attending to his journal. He decided not to watch an outdoor meeting of the Salvation Army in Timaru because his presence there would cause a stir and interrupt the Army's work, but he did drive five miles south of town to see the remains of a magnificent new three-masted steamer that had run aground on a reef a few years before and could not be refloated. Like the *Warrimoo*, it had been sailing with antiquated charts in dense fog.

Saturday was the birthday of the Prince of Wales, but in an early example of a long weekend, Monday was treated as a holiday as well. On that day Clemens retraced his steps, traveling from Timaru to Oamaru, about fifty miles southwest along the coast. His train, he wrote in *Following the Equator,* was scheduled to travel at twenty and a half miles an hour, "but it is fast enough, the outlook upon sea and land is so interesting, and the cars so comfortable . . . A narrow and railed porch along the side, where a person can walk up and down. A lavatory in each car. This is progress; this is nineteenth-century spirit."

In Oamaru, Smythe used the Monday holiday as an excuse to advertise lower ticket prices. Demand had been slack owing to competition from other shows and concerts that evening at lower tariffs. Even with lower prices, the theater was not filled. Dogs attended, however, and caused the only dogfight Clemens observed in his New Zealand venues. Although attendance was relatively sparse, Clemens's performance received an extremely favorable review.

When Clemens wrote that the New Zealand railroad displayed proper nineteenth-century spirit, he referred, of course, to technological advance and change. He might be surprised, were he to visit the town today, to see its efforts to preserve the nineteenth century. Oamaru boasts perhaps the most complete Victorian streetscape in New Zealand, with numerous nineteenth-century buildings standing one next to the other in a fairly good state of preservation. They survive in part because they are built of locally quarried, easily worked limestone. Had there been a ready supply of wood nearby, many of the buildings would have been lost to fire, as in other New Zealand towns. Another reason for their survival is that the town's commercial importance declined, as shipping shifted to larger ports. Oamaru port finally closed in 1970. There were few economic incentives to replace Victorian buildings with modern structures. When you walk through Oamaru's original business district alongside the harbor, you see opulent commercial structures — built as hotels, banks, offices, and grain and wool warehouses — fronted by elaborate neoclassical façades.

A civic trust is buying and renovating these empty structures with the aim of developing the historic area as a major tourist attraction. A few local businesses have already moved in. A bookbinder employs nineteenth-century methods. Through his window you can see a wooden screw for compressing pages. A restored hotel bar, open on Friday nights, sprinkles its floors with sawdust and offers beers brewed in the fashion of the late nineteenth century. A workshop produces penny-farthing cycles to order.

As we stand outside the cycle workshop, a red-haired young man rides toward us on a penny-farthing. He sees us gawking, dismounts gracefully, and tells us that it takes only ten minutes to learn to ride one. Perhaps, but remembering Clemens's humorous essay on the subject, we are doubtful. If it takes ten minutes to learn, it takes no time at all to fall off.

The splendid Victorian buildings and their period businesses are not alone in linking Oamaru to its past. As the dusk fades into night, blue penguins begin their nightly emergence from the sea. Oamaru was and remains a breeding colony for these birds, which, at about fourteen inches in height and weighing two pounds, are the world's smallest penguins. By the time of Clemens's visit, their breeding grounds had been degraded, after first becoming a quarry and then a dump, and the colony had declined. Nonetheless, the birds continued to repair to Oamaru for the breeding season, August to December, after seven months at sea, and as Clemens's audience was applauding his entrance, the penguins were tumbling onto the beach and braying to their chicks on the hill above.

Today the colony is protected and the flora of its breeding area has been restored. Two wooden bleachers enable you to watch the birds return from their day's foraging at sea. Their indigo backs glistening like wet fish, they waddle across the beach, shimmy up a steep bank, then huddle together at the top. When a critical mass of birds is achieved, they dash across an open space to their burrows in the rocky hill above, their bodies bent low over the ground. Their huddle, dash, and crouch protect them from avian predators found in other breeding sites but not in this one.

After watching the penguins race along their immemorial path, Alice and I return to our hotel, the Brydone. Clemens probably stayed there too — it was then the Queens Hotel — because it was, as it is today, the best hotel in town. We ascend its elegantly curving staircase to our room, grazing the ghost of Sam Clemens as he descends, cigar in hand, in search of a hot Scotch.

"It was Junior England all the way to Christchurch — in fact,

just a garden," Clemens wrote in *Following the Equator,* about his
140-mile journey northeast from Oamaru. This scenery, he told a
reporter, was "the most charming I have seen." One hundred years
later you can still admire the blue and green of the sea and "the
green fields and the trim hedges with the cottages nestling in a
clump of trees." But when you choose to drive, as we have, rather
than take a train or bus, it's harder to enjoy the view if you want to
avoid driving into a ditch. Unlike the modern driver, Clemens could
devote himself to the scenery.

On his arrival in Christchurch, the president and members of
the Savage Club welcomed him and escorted him to Coker's Hotel.
This grand hotel, once one of the most fashionable in New Zealand,
became a backpackers' lodge about a year and a half ago. Longtime
guests still arrive, to find not the doorman and bellboys they expect,
but a locked door that must be buzzed for admittance.

At the hotel, Clemens met interviewers. He was surprised by
the great cities of Australia, he said. Before his tour, he had never
talked to anyone who had been there. On a topic closer to home, he
said he saw no solution to "the negro problem," although he was
encouraged by the declining percentage of blacks to whites in the
South.

Asked how colonial audiences compared with American and
British ones, he said that "colonial audiences at once are friendly
with you. They encourage you to give your best. You feel as soon as
you step on the platform that they are your friends, that they wish
you to succeed, and that puts fire and mettle into you, and puts you
at once on terms with them." The same is true for English audiences. But the audiences in America are different. "They come prepared to demand that you give them the best you have got, and they
will therefore feel to you somewhat critical . . . They have made a
contract with you to give them something, and they hold you strictly
to your part of the bargain, and all the time they are watching to see
you don't go back on it." No audience could have demonstrated
their appreciation and affection more than the audience at his first
Christchurch *At Home.* At the conclusion of his performance, after
several minutes of stamping and cheering, they sang a rousing "For
He's a Jolly Good Fellow."

He concluded his third and final show by telling his audience that he had enjoyed himself in Christchurch, where "he left the crops flourishing and everybody prosperous, which was very satisfactory to him." Afterwards, the Savage Club gave him a late supper at the Canterbury Provincial Council Chamber, where the menu included Mayonnaise à Mons. Thomas Sawyer, Poudin à la tête de Wilson, and Gelée au vin Huckleberry. The members welcomed him with their war whoop "Ake, ake, ake, kia kaha!" and elected him an honorary member, the first in the club's history. The honor, he said, made him feel "as large as your great moa — and if I go on dissipating like this I shall be as extinct as your great moa." A few days earlier he had seen a skeleton of the extinct, giant bird.

He warned the members that if prohibition came to town, they could expect difficulties. He told them that in America, a few years before, a stranger came to a dry town and discovered that the only place he could get a drink was at a pharmacy. When he asked the pharmacist for a drink, he found he needed a doctor's prescription, except for snakebite. "The man said, 'Where's the snake?' So the apothecary gave him the snake's address, and he went off. Soon after, however, he came back and said, 'For goodness' sake, give me a drink. That snake is engaged for months ahead.' " "Christchurch is an English town," Clemens wrote in *Following the Equator,* "with an English-park annex, and a winding English brook just like the Avon — and named the Avon . . . Its grassy banks are bordered by the stateliest and most impressive weeping willows to be found in the world, I suppose . . . It is a settled old community, with all the serenities, the graces, the conveniences, and the comforts of the ideal home-life. If it had an Established Church and social inequality it would be England over again with hardly a lack."

The "settled old community" had been founded only forty-five years before, in 1850, when the first settlers arrived. The Church of England had planned the settlement, which was intended for English Anglicans, and its cathedral stands at the historic and geographic center of town. If the church was ever parochial, it is not so today. A new stained-glass window, devoted to the Pacific Islanders, portrays Jesus with a brown face (in an unfortunate slip, the hands and feet are white), and its book of prayer offers the liturgy not only in English but in Fijian, Maori, and Tongan as well.

Nearby stand the Canterbury Provincial Council Buildings, in whose Council Chamber the Savage Club entertained Clemens. Provincial councils administered New Zealand until 1876, when they were abolished. Their revenues arose from land sales, and inasmuch as few Maori lived in Canterbury, the provincial government there had much land to sell. The income paid for this splendid neo-Gothic complex on the banks of the Avon, the only council house to have survived.

In Christchurch, the Clemenses were befriended by the Joseph Kinseys, whose daughter May was about Clara's age. Although Kinsey, who was born and educated in England, had lived in New Zealand for only fifteen years when he met the Clemenses, he already headed his own shipping firm. Clemens found in the Kinsey home a copy of *Tom Sawyer*, which May had read so often it was in tatters. On the inside front cover, Clemens wrote her a note, in which he said that age is "disreputable" in a human, but "when an author observes the signs of it in a book of his own in another person's possession he recognizes that in *that* case age is a most pleasant & respectable thing."

The Kinseys took the Clemenses to the Botanical Gardens, which were founded in the middle of the last century, when the Albert Edward oak was planted to commemorate the wedding of the Prince of Wales to Princess Alexandra of Denmark. The great oak still stands. As you might expect, the lawns and colorful flower beds are beautifully tended. What is astonishing are the superb trees, so tall that you can't appreciate their height without human figures nearby — a stray boy from the adjoining Christ's Church School will serve as an unconscious yardstick for you as he walks by in his gray and black striped blazer.

Boys come from all over New Zealand to attend this boarding school, whose lawns are the sort that in England are said to require two hundred years to perfect. If you enter the quadrangle at the lunch break, you will see boys who have left the refectory relaxing in the shade of the cloisters, and if you hear them talking to one another, you will hear an accent that would not be out of place at Eton. They say that Christchurch is the most English town outside England.

On a rainy night, their last in Christchurch, the Clemenses and

Smythe boarded a train for Lyttleton, the port of Christchurch. They were scheduled to sail to Auckland, about 475 miles away on the North Island, via Wellington and New Plymouth. Mr. Kinsey and his daughter, who accompanied them to the port, gave them Maori artifacts and a stuffed platypus. In a thank-you note written from Auckland, Mrs. Clemens said that her husband held the creature himself when moving from train to ship to train. "He says it is his most treasured possession. He does not think even his wife beater surpasses it."

The Clemenses and Smythe boarded the Union Company's *Flora* on Saturday, November 16. This was Anniversary Day in Canterbury Province, with its race meetings and shows, which had attracted many people from the North Island. One of the two vessels that would ordinarily have taken them back to the North Island was removed from service, so passengers for two boats had to be jammed into one. The *Flora* had not been built to the same standard as most Union Company vessels; the company had recently bought it, along with seven sister ships, from a financially distressed line, and regarded it not as a "Company ship" but as inferior.

"The people who sailed in the *Flora* that night may forget some other things if they live a good while, but they will not live long enough to forget that," Clemens wrote in *Following the Equator*. The vessel was dangerously overcrowded. Had it gone down that night, he claimed, half the passengers would have perished. Mrs. Clemens and Clara and two other women shared a tiny room without towels, pillows, or bed linen, but they were better off than Clemens and Smythe, who slept in berths made up in the lounge. "I had a cattle-stall in the main stable," Clemens wrote, "a cavern" in which two long files of double-decker bunks, separated by a calico curtain, had been set out, with the males on one side and the females on the other. "The place was as dark as the soul of the Union Company." In her thank-you letter to Mr. Kinsey, Mrs. Clemens wrote that "we comfort ourselves now that if we should at any time be compelled to go steerage it could bring us little of experience that would be new."

"When the vessel got out into the heavy seas and began to pitch and wallow," Clemens wrote, "the cavern-prisoners became immediately sea-sick, and then the peculiar results that ensued laid all my previous experiences of the kind well away in the shade. And the wails, the groans, the cries, the shrieks, the strange ejaculations — it was wonderful."

Clemens's English publisher, probably fearful of a lawsuit, cut more than half the author's account of that voyage, with its colorful excoriation of both the Union Company and the *Flora*. The American edition gives a more complete version, in which we see a master of invective at work. The Union Company would remember his scalding condemnation for the next hundred years.

Chapter Nineteen

WHEN THE *FLORA* LANDED at Wellington the next afternoon, the Clemenses and Smythe debarked, along with other
disgusted passengers, rather than continuing on with her to New
Plymouth and Auckland. They soon found another vessel, the
Mahinapua, "a wee little bridal parlor of a boat," as Clemens
described her in *Following the Equator*, "clean and comfortable; good
service; good beds; good table, and no crowding. The seas danced
her about like a duck, but she was safe and capable." The vessel
would take them out of their way, to Nelson, on the South Island,
before transporting them north to Auckland.

The vessel's master, Captain W. J. Newton, took special pains
to give the famous author the best possible treatment, which may
explain Clemens's favorable impression of the ship. Twelve years
before, Newton had demonstrated exceptional ability by saving the
passengers of the SS *Niagara*, which he had encountered in flames
on the high seas. Despite a high swell, he managed to transfer its
passengers to his ship, earning the gratitude of the American people
along with a gold watch and chain awarded by the president.

Clemens experienced Newton's seamanship firsthand. After the
ship left Wellington, a terrible storm arose. The ship, wrote Clara
more than thirty years later, was "as helpless as a cork on the water."
Unable to remain vertical, the passengers staggered to their beds. She
recalled that her father came to her stateroom early in the evening to
ask if she was frightened. "But he couldn't stop to talk about it. For
the first time in his life he capitulated to the agitation of the waves
and lost his healthy digestion. 'If you want anything — .' But the door
slammed against him and he disappeared for good."

The seas calmed in the early hours of the morning. About forty
miles northwest of Nelson, the ship entered the French Pass, which
leads to the bay on which Nelson is situated. The pass, wrote

Clemens, seemed no wider than a street. "The current tore through there like a mill-race, and the boat darted through like a telegram." In the bay, "noble vast eddies swept grandly round and round in shoal-water, and I wondered what they would do with the little boat. They did as they pleased with her. They picked her up and flung her around like nothing and landed her gently on the solid smooth bottom of sand — so gently, indeed, that we barely felt her touch it, barely felt her quiver when she came to a standstill. The water was as clear as glass, the sand on the bottom was vividly distinct, and the fishes seemed to be swimming about in nothing."

Clara remembered the incident differently. After the storm subsided, she reported, it was possible to rest, which was so delightful that nothing could rouse her father, who slept through the ship's grounding. Passengers, many in their nightclothes, rushed to the lifeboats, but since the ship rested on a sandbank, there was no danger, and the captain ordered everyone back to their cabins. Clemens, his daughter wrote, "was disgusted to have missed the excitement."

After about a half hour on the sandbank, the captain extricated the *Mahinapua*, which then sailed on to Nelson, where Clemens was reported to have claimed that the French Pass was the "most 'tarnashun' place" he had ever been. Before returning in the late afternoon to the *Mahinapua*, which would take them to the North Island, the Clemenses spent the day in Nelson. There an interviewer found him holding a report of the Maungatapu Mountain murders, an atrocity committed about a dozen miles from Nelson almost thirty years before.

Maungatapu means "sacred mountain" in Maori. According to one account, a chief had prayed on its ridge before embarking on a successful surprise attack and then returned to the ridge to offer thanksgiving prayers. "Pass on," he told his followers, "and henceforth let no man set foot on the mountain, for it is *tapu*!" Alas, if the white population had ever heard the story, they paid it no attention. In 1866, on a narrow pass over the mountain, four armed men ambushed, robbed, and killed four unarmed travelers known to be carrying cash and gold. The victims — a Frenchman, two Englishmen, and a Yankee from New York State — were traveling from the nearby gold-mining camp of Deep Creek, where the takings had been declining. They were on their way to Nelson, from which they planned to sail to the more prosperous diggings on the west coast. Sixteen days later, a search party found their corpses on a steep hillside. Three had been shot, one strangled. A fifth body, covered by about a half-inch of earth and leaves, was discovered nearby a few days later. It was that of an old farm laborer who had unexpectedly happened upon the gang as they waited for the party from Deep Creek. They strangled him for his pittance in wages.

Richard Burgess, the gang's ringleader, confessed to the murders after one of his confederates, Joseph Sullivan, had turned state's evidence in the hope of a pardon. Burgess, enraged by this betrayal, sought not only to revenge himself on Sullivan, whom he hoped to send to the gallows, but also to save his other confederates by claiming they had left the scene of the crime before the murders took place.

In Clemens's account of the tragedy, he contrasted the arcadian town of Nelson with the nearby murder scene, a lonely track through a wild, primeval forest. Clemens, who quoted extensively from Burgess's narrative, noted its businesslike tone. "Any one who reads that confession," he observed, "will think that the man who wrote it was destitute of emotions, destitute of feeling. That is partly true. As regarded others he was plainly without feeling — utterly cold and pitiless; but as regarded himself the case was different. While he cared nothing for the future of the murdered men, he cared a great deal for his own." Clemens was appalled by Burgess's introductory remarks, which thanked a "faithful soldier of Christ" for helping him to see his "wretched and guilty state" and for assuring him that Jesus would receive him and cleanse him from sin. He died with classic highwayman bravura: unassisted, he ascended the steep flight to the gallows, selected the central noose, kissed it, and said that he regarded it as a "prelude to Heaven." Burgess, commented Clemens, "was as jubilantly happy on the gallows as ever was Christian martyr at the stake . . . We have to suppose that the murdered men are lost, and that Burgess is saved; but we cannot suppress our natural regrets."

Burgess insisted that he testifed in the interests of justice and religion, a claim that the trial judge characterized as a "fearful blasphemy." Before pronouncing sentence, the judge admonished Burgess that "if you have flattered yourself with the idea of becoming the hero of a life of crime; if you have flattered yourself that you shall depart from this world with some share of fame which shall remain behind you, and your name be spoken of among wicked men as that of one to be admired as a hero of crime, disabuse yourself of the idea at once. I trust and believe that there are few men in this world whose imaginations are so depraved as that they could look on such a life and such conduct as heroic, when it is only brutal."

Whether or not Clemens's account of the Maungatapu murders contributed to the Burgess gang's reputation, some share of fame has indeed remained behind them. At least two books about them have appeared within the second half of this century, an interest explained in part by their extraordinary trial, which saw two contradictory sworn confessions, both remarkably fluent and internally consistent, and in part by the puzzle of Burgess's character. Burgess was a charismatic leader, a steadfast companion to his criminal colleagues ("I have ever been a faithful comrade in sin"), and a gifted writer whose confession and subsequent autobiography display a powerful narrative drive. Nonetheless, he was utterly heartless toward his victims, butchering them with as little compunction as he would a stolen turkey.

The party from Deep Creek spent their last night at Pelorus Bridge, at an inn where a traveler warned them about four suspicious-looking men he had passed on the track. Pelorus Bridge was simply that, a bridge, not a settlement, and so it remains. In place of the nineteenth-century inn are a teahouse, cabins, and tent sites. From that spot a road leads to the Maungatapu trail. A bookseller in Christchurch told us that when he was a teenager, he and some mates, on a bicycle trip, traversed the trail, thinking it a shortcut. Perhaps it was, but it saved them no time. The trail proved so steep they were forced to dismount and walk, both uphill and down, for much of the track's five-mile length. His story inspired us to try to see the trail for ourselves.

At the teahouse, a worker informs us that a plaque set in stone marks the site of the Maungatapu murders and that it can be reached by a vehicle with four-wheel drive. Technicians who maintain the local power line use the track. Although we are driving a conventional car, we decide to travel along the trail as far as we can.

For much of the way, the valley on the left has been cleared for pastures, which are populated by sheep and deer, the latter molting, with velvet antlers. (The antlers will be harvested and sold to the Japanese, who view them as an aphrodisiac.) On the right is a forest planted in Monterrey pine. Soon the track takes us through a nat-ural forest, its overarching greenery filtering the light. Purple lupines border the track. Beyond it, on the other side of the lonely valley, loom distant, forested hills. We leave the car and listen to the silence, broken by occasional birdsong and by the crackling of twigs as we walk to the edge of the track. Far below, next to a swift river, three men and a woman prepare for white-water rafting. We cannot hear them, nor can they see us, as we inspect them through a screen of leaves, but they are close enough for a marksman to hit, one by one. We return to the car and continue slowly along the secluded track. It narrows, becomes rougher, and finally leads to a railless wooden bridge about the width of our car — perhaps we should attend to the long-ago Maori chief's ban on travel to the mountain. We turn around and head back to Pelorus Bridge.

Chapter Twenty

ON THE SECOND DAY of the voyage from Nelson to Auckland, the *Mahinapua* spent some hours in New Plymouth, on the west coast of the North Island, and on the third day, Wednesday, November 20, 1895, it arrived in Auckland. The Clemenses stayed at the Star Hotel, the best hotel in town. Its doorman was a "fine large Briton a little frosted with age," who had fought on the western front during the American Civil War, as Clemens claimed to have done during the first summer of the war, when he served as a second lieutenant in a Confederate militia organized in Hannibal, Missouri. Clemens ended his brief service, according to one account, after he sprained his ankle by jumping out of the burning barn in which his unit was sleeping.

An interviewer who found him at the hotel reported Clemens's comment that every writer contributes to stylistic change. "I was once idiot enough to ask the partner of Mr. Bell as to who was the inventor of the telephone. The reply I got was, Do you not know that 1500 men had been at work on the telephone for 5000 years — do you suppose that anyone could invent any such instrument in any one lifetime? It is the same with literature." The reporter said he supposed that Clemens would write a book about the people he met during his travels. Yes, he replied, particularly because he had not had time to see anything. "Travelling and lecturing are like oil and water; they don't mix. There are many fine sights in New Zealand that I haven't seen."

But Clemens did see something of Auckland. The town, situated on an isthmus between the Tasman Sea in the west and the Pacific Ocean in the east and extending over numerous extinct volcanoes, offers pleasing views of hills and water from many vantage points. The Clemenses, who stayed there for almost a week, enjoyed several scenic drives, including one to "the grassy crater-summit of Mount Eden."

From the peak of Mount Eden you can still see "the blue bays twinkling and sparkling away," but "the rolling green fields" he mentioned have been replaced by leafy streets, spreading in all directions from the Tasman Sea to the Pacific Ocean, the population having expanded from 60,000 at the turn of the century to 320,000 today, with another 600,000 in the suburbs. An elevated highway hums below.

The Maori call the mountain Maungawhau, after a shrub once valued for its corklike bark, useful as floats for fishing nets. They built a fortified settlement here hundreds of years ago, and you can still see the remains of their terraces and storage pits. After the last chief of the settlement was killed, the mountain became off-limits, another Maungatapu, never again the site of a village. Perhaps that explains its bucolic nature today. Alice and I, who have climbed the hill, find daisies clustering along the northern side of its grassy volcanic crater, as well as a herd of young black cows, white-faced and white-bellied, placidly grazing.

Before ascending Mount Eden, the Clemenses visited Auckland's library, which, along with an art gallery, occupied a French Renaissance palace, the newest and grandest of Auckland's public amenities. The building survives, but the library's space — a long, pretty white room with slender posts supporting a balcony — was taken over by the art gallery, among whose treasures is a collection of Gottfried Lindauer's Maori portraits. The artist began painting them in 1873 on his arrival from Bohemia. From the walls, chiefs and other aristocrats gaze at us with hauteur, their magnificence enhanced by jade pendants, earrings, and clubs, as well as by gorgeous tattooing. Many of the Maori visitors to the gallery are the descendants of Lindauer's subjects.

Diagonally across the street from the art gallery is the multistory present library. I rummage through a file of newspaper clippings about Mark Twain. Allan A. Kirk has written an article about some of the ships mentioned by Clemens in *Following the Equator*. Kirk traveled on the *Warrimoo* in 1904, after the vessel was bought by the Union Company. "I am prepared to swear on oath that if what

Twain said about the food was correct, there were different chefs in her nine years later. And I did not see any signs of cockroaches." Kirk suggested that Clemens exaggerated the vessel's failings for comic effect. (Actually, Clemens's description was based on his journal entries, which were even more critical than his book.) Kirk added that Clemens needn't have worried about the *Warrimoo*'s master, R. E. Arundell, because "the name of Arundell went down on the company's records as a most worthy fellow." I realize with some surprise that I too was worrying about that gentle, polished, handsome young man, whom Clemens thought "pathetically out of place in his rude and autocratic vocation." It's a relief to learn that he succeeded in that vocation after all.

After *At Home*s on Thursday and Friday, the Clemenses spent the weekend in Auckland, where they visited the American firm of Arnold, Cheney and Company, an exporter of kauri gum, a substance used mainly for making varnish and lacquer. The kauri tree, native to the northern half of the North Island, is a gigantic, straight-trunked conifer that lives for hundreds of years. Most of the gum was found in amberlike deposits, dug from the sites of earlier forests, but some of the gum was extracted by tapping the tree. The Maori found many uses for this substance, in both its soft and its semi-fossilized state, from chewing to producing pigment for tattoos, and they felled some of the trees for large carvings and canoes. With the arrival of Europeans, kauri wood became massively exploited, first for the masts and spars of sailing ships and then for houses, carts, church pews, and post-office counters. By Clemens's time the tree was being logged almost to extinction. Today the remaining trees are jealously preserved.

On Sunday Mrs. Clemens wrote to her sister that her husband seemed not to be as strong as she would like, and that he was discouraged by the possible onset of another carbuncle. She reported that they were being inundated with gifts, especially in Christchurch, where she "felt a little burdened, there was so much." She kept wondering if they would ever be able to pay their debts and live once again in their Hartford home. "Today it seems to me as if we never should. However, much of the time I believe we shall, but it is a long way." Her husband, she wrote, continued to attract large and enthusiastic audiences. For his last two performances,

2,172 people paid for their tickets. If only there were as many big cities in Australia and New Zealand as in America, she continued, he could earn much larger sums, "but the trouble is that there are so few cities, just a *very few* along the coast."

The Clemenses traveled along that coast again on Tuesday afternoon, November 26, the day after his third and last performance in Auckland. They sailed from Auckland's "vast and beautiful harbor" en route for Gisborne and Napier, on the east coast of the North Island. Clemens referred to the three-humped mountain in the harbor, "the mountain that 'has the same shape from *every* point of view.' That is the common belief in Auckland. And so it has — from every point of view except thirteen." Although he misremembered its name, calling it Tangariwa, an inland mountain farther south, instead of Rangitoto, he clearly meant the latter, inasmuch as he sketched its three humps in his notebook, where he indicated its location as Auckland Harbor. The myth of one hundred years ago survives. Friends who took us for a drive in Auckland pointed out Rangitoto and described it as the mountain that has the same shape from *every* point of view.

Chapter Twenty-one

*T*HEY REACHED GISBORNE the next day, but heavy seas prevented them from landing. Their vessel, the *Rotomahana*, anchored in Poverty Bay, a mile from shore, and waited for a launch to bring twenty-five passengers to the ship. The launch, wrote Clemens, "was an object of thrilling interest; she would climb to the summit of a billow, reel drunkenly there a moment, dim and gray in the driving storm of spindrift, then make a plunge like a diver, and remain out of sight until one had given her up, then up she would dart again, on a steep slant toward the sky, shedding Niagaras of water from her forecastle — and this she kept up, all the way out to us."

Passengers were transferred to the *Rotomahana* by means of a "primitive basket-chair," which was hoisted above the ship and then lowered onto the deck, "seldom nearer level than a ladder." A young seaman, in a sou'wester and a yellow waterproof suit, sat in the chair "to be a protection to the lady-comers," some of whom sat in his lap as he placed his arms around them. An illustration for *Following the Equator*, which appeared two years later, in 1897, shows the occupants of a basket-chair as it swings over the churning water: two pretty women, wearing hats and leg-of-mutton sleeves, holding tight to a smiling sailor.

Among the incoming passengers was a constable, along with four prisoners he was escorting to jail. When Clemens learned that one of the latter faced a year-long sentence, he said "I guess it ought to be shortened to six months after that trip in the tender."

The basket chair not only brought passengers from the tender to the *Rotomahana*, it also transferred passengers from the *Rotomahana* to the tender. Although the maneuver caused no injuries, Clara recalled years later that occasionally the basket landed upside down and that screams could be heard over the thunder of the sea. Clemens, viewing the transfer to shore as too dangerous, elected to stay on board. Smythe had to cancel the Gisborne performance.

Mrs. Clemens observed her fiftieth birthday that day. Her husband told her jokingly that she had either missed her birthday or that it had not yet occurred, because the anniversary exists as it does in America, "not here where we have flung out a day and closed up the vacancy." She was, perhaps, in need of cheering. To her sister she wrote, "I do not like it one single bit. Fifty years old — think of it; that seems very far on."

They reached Napier early the next morning and proceeded to their hotel, where three cages of canaries on a nearby porch so irritated Clemens that he had them removed. A canary's song, he told his journal, was "but the equivalent of scratching a nail on a window-pane. I wonder what sort of disease it is that enables a person to enjoy the canary." Perhaps the eruption of a new carbuncle contributed to his crankiness. Two physicians came to his room to examine him. After concluding that he ought to rest for a few days, they recommended that his appearance the following night be canceled. "We should have preferred that to-night's lecture had also been postponed," they wrote in a note to Smythe, "had it been possible to give timely notice to the public."

According to a critic who reviewed his performance that night, the audience was grateful to their visitor "for sacrificing himself on the altar of our curiosity." Among the audience were plenty of dogs. "At Napier," he told his journal, there was a "sign up, 'Dogs positively forbidden in the dress circle.' Tacit permission to fill up the rest of the house." Following his doctors' advice, he canceled the following night's show, disappointing ticketholders if not their dogs. "I wish I had been born with false teeth and a false liver and false carbuncles," he wrote in *Following the Equator*. "I should get along better."

The next day he wrote to his close friend, Joseph Twitchell, "one of the best of men," Clemens once said, "although a clergyman." Twitchell, handsome, athletic, and enthusiastic, who enjoyed Clemens's profanity and off-color jokes, was the pastor of an affluent congregation in Hartford (Clemens once called Twitchell's pulpit "the Church of the Holy Speculators"). He had co-officiated at the Clemenses' wedding in Elmira twenty-five years earlier, in 1870, and after the Clemenses moved to Hartford the next year, they saw him often. It was a conversation with Twitchell that stimulated Clemens to prepare the series of articles that eventually evolved into *Life on the Mississippi*, and it was Twitchell's companionship during a European ramble that enabled him to compose *A Tramp Abroad*.

Now Clemens was writing to him from a hotel bed in Napier. "I think it was a good stroke of luck that knocked me on my back here at Napier instead of in some hotel in the center of a noisy city. Here we have the smooth & placidly complaining sea at our door, with nothing between us & it but 20 yards of shingle — & hardly a suggestion of life in that space to mar it or make a noise. Away down here fifty-five degrees south of the equator this sea seems to murmur in an unfamiliar tongue — a foreign tongue — a tongue bred among the ice-fields of the antarctic — a murmur with a note of melancholy in it proper to the vast unvisited solitudes it has come from. It was very delicious and solacing to wake in the night & find it still pulsing there. I wish you were here — land, but it would be fine!" Twitchell would have cheered him up. "Day before yesterday was Livy's birthday (underworld time)," Clemens told him, "& tomorrow will be mine. I shall be 60 — no thanks for it!"

Clemens passed his birthday in Napier, which he left two days later, well in advance of the devastating earthquake and fire that destroyed the town in 1931. From Napier the Clemenses journeyed about ninety miles southwest by train to Palmerston North, where Clemens was to appear that night. Their journey was broken for a brief lunch at Waitukurau. In the restaurant Clemens mistook a framed picture to represent the death of Napoleon III's son, Lulu, in 1879. He broke into the conversation: "Do you remember when the news came to Paris —" Mrs. Clemens, whose back was to the picture, replied, "Of the killing of the prince?" "Yes," her husband asked her, "but *what* prince?" "Napoleon. Lulu." Her response convinced Clemens that he had "telegraphed" a thought to her. She ought to have mentioned some recent news, he argued later, because they had been living in Paris for a long stay that had ended only seven months previously. Instead she thought of an incident from a brief visit sixteen years ago. "Here was a clear case of mental telegraphy," he wrote in *Following the Equator*. "How do I know? Because I telegraphed an *error* . . . She had to get the error from my head — it existed nowhere else."

Their hotel in Palmerston North was, as Clemens noted in his journal, memorable. Its features included a "stunning Queen of Sheba style of barmaid," too dignified to perform any of the tasks he requested after she answered his bell; a red-faced, boorish manager who kept his hat on while talking to a lady; tiny rooms for which keys could not be found before midnight; and thin partitions that allowed him to hear an extraordinary piano concert early in the morning, "straight average of three right notes to four wrong ones, but played with eager zeal and gladness . . . and considering it was the cat — for it *must* have been the cat — it was really a marvelous performance."

The number of uncomfortable and inconvenient hotels the Clemenses encountered during their year-long journey was probably greater than those few about which Clemens complained. They did not expect palace hotels in small towns, and besides, they were not on a pleasure excursion. Their constant travel and attention to duty was in ironic contrast to the abundance of workingmen's holidays that Clemens noted in Australia and New Zealand.

From Wanganui, the next town on their itinerary, Mrs. Clemens wrote her daughter Susy that they had not stopped their work a single day for sightseeing. Imagine, she wrote, visiting Lucerne without traveling to Interlaken, especially if you knew that you would never again be so close to it. But they were traveling to pay their debts, she reminded Susy, and not to enjoy themselves. Even so, the trip was enjoyable and interesting.

The train ride to Wanganui, about sixty miles from Palmerston North, was slow, but the train itself was comfortable and "rationally devised." A passenger who was not contented by the well-designed cars and by the "charming scenery and the nearly constant absence of dust," Clemens wrote, "ought to get out and walk. That would change his spirit, perhaps; I think so. At the end of an hour you would find him waiting humbly beside the track, and glad to be taken aboard again."

In Wanganui, Clemens saw "lots of Maoris; the faces and bodies of the old ones very tastefully frescoed." Maoris were, he believed, "a superior breed of savages," as evidenced by their agriculture, carpentry, ornamental arts, fortresses, and military skill. "These ... modify their savagery to a semi-civilization — or at least to a quarter-civilization."

Since even the uncivilized have the right to defend their homes, Clemens was appalled by what he recalled as "a couple of curious war-monuments here at Wanganui." One of these was "in honor of white men 'who fell in defense of law and order against fanaticism and barbarism.' " How mischosen is the word fanaticism, he wrote. "Patriotism is Patriotism. Calling it Fanaticism cannot degrade it; nothing can degrade it ... It is right to praise these brave white men who fell in the Maori war — they deserve it; but the presence of that word detracts from the dignity of their cause and their deeds, and makes them appear to have spilled their blood in a conflict with ignoble men, men not worthy of that costly sacrifice. But the men *were* worthy. It was no shame to fight them. They fought for their homes, they fought for their country; they bravely fought and bravely fell; and it would take nothing from the honor of the brave Englishmen who lie under the monument, but *add* to it, to say that they died in defense of English laws and English homes against men worthy of the sacrifice — the Maori patriots."

The other monument, he wrote, is an invitation to treachery and disloyalty because it was "erected by white men to Maoris who fell fighting with the whites and *against their own people*." Nothing could rectify that memorial, he said, except dynamite.

The power of his rhetoric notwithstanding, Clemens remembered two monuments when there was but one. He saw it in Moutoa Gardens, a triangular two-acre park near the Wanganui River, where it stands today. The monument, a weeping woman carved in white marble, memorializes not English soldiers but Maori warriors and a Catholic lay brother, who were killed in the Battle of Moutoa Island in 1864.

Both parties to the conflict were Maori. The defenders of law and order were members of the Lower Wanganui tribe, who had established profitable trading links with the port of Wanganui, and members of other downriver tribes. The representatives of fanaticism and barbarism were members of a religious movement, Pai Marire (meaning "good and peaceful"), which arose from Maori bitterness over land confiscations. The religion, an amalgam of Christian, Jewish, and Maori doctrines combined with cannibalism, viewed the Maori as the new chosen people, whose immediate task was to expel the white invaders and regain ancestral lands. Adherents believed that shouting *"Pai Marire, Hau! Hau!"* in battle would shield them from the white man's bullets, a belief that not only led to the cult's popular name, Hauhauism, but also increased its warriors' boldness.

The movement was founded in 1864 by Te Ua, who reported that the archangel Gabriel had visited him, an event that so moved him that he sacrificed his son to atone for the sins of the Maori people. In that year Hauhaus from the Taranaki and Upper Wanganui tribes determined to attack Wanganui township and asked the Lower Wanganui for support. The latter, reluctant to abandon their profitable trade with the settlement, refused. When the Hauhaus nonetheless moved downriver, the Lower Wanganui mobilized other downriver tribes to resist the invasion.

Hauhaus and the downriver tribes met at Moutoa Island, in the middle of the Wanganui River. Both sides faced each other in the middle of a long field, like two football teams, while spectators lined both sides of the river to watch. After a brief and bloody battle, the downriver tribes repulsed the invaders. Forty corpses were left on the field, including Brother Euloge from the nearby Catholic mission. According to one account, he was shot dead while begging the combatants to stop fighting. His name and those of fifteen dead warriors from the downriver tribes appear on the monument.

The memorial was erected fifteen months later, in 1865, to express the European settlers' relief and gratitude. The battle of Moutoa Island, fifty miles north of their settlement, had saved them from slaughter, although the downriver tribes acted not to save the colonists' lives nor to defend law and order, but to preserve their own interests.

As Clemens well knew, when we fight for our interests, we call ourselves patriots. When our enemies do the same, we call them fanatics, and if their beliefs and practices are different from ours, we call them barbarians, too. If Clemens's depiction of patriotism seems old-fashioned today, when so few appeals to patriotism seem either honest or justifiable, there is nothing old-fashioned in what he wrote about the demonization of our enemies. He understood that it is hard to kill another when the victim seems no different from ourselves. War, he wrote in an essay published in 1885, is "the killing of strangers against whom you feel no personal animosity; strangers whom, in other circumstances, you would help if you found them in trouble, and who would help you if you needed it."

Chapter Twenty-two

*C*LEMENS AND SMYTHE LEFT WANGANUI for one-night stands in Hawera and New Plymouth, while Mrs. Clemens and Clara remained behind. In a letter to Susy, Mrs. Clemens justified her decision to stay in Wanganui: it was a pretty place, the hotel was reasonably comfortable, although not up to New York standards, and the traveling back and forth would have been strenuous. Clemens and Smythe returned to Wanganui for the weekend, and on Monday, December 9, 1895, they all traveled one hundred miles south to Wellington, the nation's capital. It was to be their last venue in New Zealand.

Clemens was scheduled to perform on Monday night, the night of his arrival in Wellington, but he and Smythe had misinterpreted the railroad schedule. They understood that an express train ran every day, not noticing the information in small type that limited the express to Tuesdays and Fridays only. The ten-hour journey by rail, Clemens told a reporter the next day, consisted of interminable stoppages at little stations and a "gentle, albeit sometimes jolty, ride from station to station, as though the train were out for an easy constitutional." He seems to have underplayed the ride's roughness, if his journal is to be trusted. There he noted that between New Plymouth and Stratford, a distance of about forty miles, "it was difficult to stay in your seat, so tremendously rough was the road." Since the region through which he was riding was rich in creameries and butter factories, he suggested that "they ought to put the milk in the train — that would churn it." The train arrived too late for Monday's performance, which was postponed to the next evening.

After a late supper, Clemens received a reporter "with the urbanity of a journalist and the courtesy of a man of the world," according to the interviewer. As Clemens paced back and forth, "shaking his vast head of wavy grey hair," he responded to the canard that *The Innocents Abroad* had been cobbled together from travel books and encyclopedias. "You see there's a Freemasonry about dealing with things you see yourself which can't be counterfeited. There is an ease and certainty of touch in describing what you see which you can't get artificially." When the interviewer mentioned Defoe as an exception, Clemens replied, "And how did Defoe write his plague of London? He knew London as well as you know the city of Wellington, every spot and corner of it. He had nothing in the way of local color to supply; it was all there before him. He got his details of the plague at first hand, from people who had seen. He made his studies in hospitals and by sick beds. What he saw he described; only changing here and there features of disease to suit the accounts of the plague. Defoe described what he saw, and added the equivalents which he had observed, and so he got his wonderful study. But to do a book of travel in that way, you would have know every city in the world as well as Defoe knew his London."

The next morning Clemens told a reporter that he was trying to observe colonial character, but that the urban population in New Zealand was much like the urban population elsewhere, "for travel is reducing the world to a terrible sameness." One of the most traveled men of his time, he was among the first to point out what has become a cliché.

Later that day Clemens called on the governor general, Lord David Glasgow, the only Australasian viceroy he met. "I was in Australasia three months and a half, and only saw one Governor," he wrote in *Following the Equator*. "The others were at home." The governors stay in England, he reported. "When they are appointed they come out from England and get inaugurated, and give a ball, and help pray for rain, and get aboard ship and go back home. And so the Lieutenant-Governor has to do all the work." In fact, Clemens's trip overlapped with the visits of two other governors general, Victoria's Lord Brassey, whom Mrs. Clemens and Clara met, and South Australia's Sir Thomas Buxton, whom he narrowly missed.

Lord David and the Countess of Glasgow attended Clemens's first *At Home*, at which Clemens made a faux pas by failing to acknowledge the governor's party as a prelude to his performance. "Didn't know it was custom," he later explained to his journal. In spite of this lapse, Wellington's *Evening Post* gave Clemens a glowing review, which praised his "quiet power of description, and facility for putting in local colour, local character, and local scenery in a few graphic touches." Still, he did not please everyone. A woman was overheard to remark after his performance, "Well, I didn't think much of it; it was all jokes!"

His second and last appearance in Wellington took place the following night, after which he was entertained at supper by a group of prominent Maoris, one of whom was the Honorable J. Carroll, the cabinet minister for Maori affairs. An editorial that appeared that day mentioned the minister's recent trip up the Wanganui River, on the occasion of the local Maoris' agreeing to remove their fishing weirs from the river at Pipiriki. "Natives of their own volition are entrusting 16,000 acres to the Government for settlement-land around the planned new town. Gradually but surely the Government is gaining the confidence of the Native people . . . It is evident that this Pipiriki incident is but part of a general advance towards the final settlement of Native affairs."

In Wellington, Clemens "spent the three days partly in walking about, partly in enjoying social privileges, and largely in idling around the magnificent garden at Hutt, a little distance away, around the shore." The garden, a noted beauty spot to which visitors to Wellington were usually taken, was operated by a Mrs. Ross, a young widow with many children, who bought the place in the 1890s and charged admission. There you could take tea, pick flowers, gaze at monkeys and squirrels, and ride on a miniature steam railway. Apparently you could amuse yourself in other ways as well, for Clemens and Smythe played billiards, a game to which Clemens was passionately devoted. A few years later, river floods ruined the gardens, which Mrs. Ross sold in the face of contrary advice, shortly before flood-control measures substantially increased the value of her land. Today, on a portion of the site, a hospice serves the terminally ill. The patients' families are permitted access to the grounds, to flowers and flowering shrubs, woodland paths, and a stream that flows below stately trees. The garden through which Clemens strolled gives comfort now to families of the dying.

The day after his visit to Mrs. Ross's garden, the Clemenses returned to Australia, where Clemens would perform for two weeks before sailing to Ceylon and India. "Our stay in New Zealand has been too brief," he wrote in *Following the Equator,* "still, we are not unthankful for the glimpse which we have had of it." The next afternoon they boarded the *Mararoa,* which had brought them to Bluff only thirty-nine days before.

Chapter Twenty-three

CLEMENS DESCRIBED THEIR VOYAGE to Sydney as "three days of paradise. Warm and sunny and smooth; the sea a luminous Mediterranean blue . . . One lolls in a long chair all day under deck-awnings, and reads and smokes, in measureless content." Perhaps his love of sailing mitigated the "swelling seas and cloudy skies" reported by the captain upon the ship's arrival in Sydney. The weather was threatening enough that Clemens could hope for a heavy storm as punishment for "the damnest menagerie of mannerless children I have ever gone to sea with."

The *Mararoa* arrived in Sydney at nine on Tuesday morning, December 17, 1895, after a "burster," a kind of hurricane from the south, had "knocked the mercury down 36 degrees in four hours," as Clemens observed in his journal. The reporters who met him at the ship disgusted him. "The interviewer," he told his journal, "is pathetically persistent in trying to worm out of you your 'impressions' of N.Z. & her people & audiences, & 'which city did I like best, there; & which audience; & are the audiences there as quick & bright as in Austral; & which do I think the most remarkable city, Syd or Melb; & which newspapers do I consider the best; but don't I think them *all* remarkable['] — & a dozen other questions of the same guilelessly idiotic sort, which only another idiot would answer." From his first interview in Cleveland, five months earlier, until he landed in Sydney for the second time, Clemens had responded to dozens of interviewers. It's hard to dream up original and interesting queries, especially in the presence of an incandescent celebrity, so it would not be surprising if by this time Clemens was fed up by his interviewers' repetitiveness. Here he seems to have been struck by the parochial rivalries that the reporters' questions suggested. "These towns & people are full of jealousies of each other, & perfectly ready to out with them in print or anywhere." But Clemens, who valued his good relations with the press, responded suavely. No, he said, he had gone through New Zealand so quickly that he had had no time to form an opinion of it. "I thought the people were particularly fortunate in living in a country with such a grand climate." To illustrate the hazards of jumping to conclusions about a country, he said that if he had left Timaru before the storm he remembered there had subsided, he would have thought Timaru a windy place. He saw no differences, he said, between audiences in New Zealand and those in Australia. As for New Zealand politics, "I have no impressions . . . if I had, they would just likely be erroneous ones. I don't think it is right to hurry through a place and form impressions. I have none — no publishable ones, anyway."

The day after they arrived, Mrs. Clemens and Clara made two calls and found, as Mrs. Clemens wrote her sister, that both families were about to leave town for long periods, both planning a visit " 'home,' as they all call England." But Justice William Windeyer was in town, and he invited the family to the Botanical Gardens, which Clemens praised in *Following the Equator* as "beautifully laid out and rich with the spoil of all the lands and all the climes of the world." Now overlooked by office towers, it continues to offer Sydneysiders "plenty of room for reposeful lazying and lounging" as well as the opportunity to enjoy splendid horticultural specimens from around the world.

It may have been on the day he visited the gardens that Clemens also saw one of the great Sydney beaches, where shark fishing was a popular amusement. The sharks, some of them monstrously long, were attracted by sewage spewed into the bay. Only ten days before, a shark had seized a boy swimming in the Parramatta River, which flows into the harbor, and mauled him so badly he died. Sharks were numerous enough to warrant a government bounty for their capture, which led sportsmen and others to try their luck. Clemens, persuaded to join the bounty hunters, reported in his journal that "I . . . caught [a shark] myself, but he thought he caught me — & as he was doing most of the pulling I conceded the argument & let go." Afterwards, a Sydney newspaper editor would enjoy telling the "story of his fishing expedition to Manly with Mark Twain, when an accomplice, planted among the rocks below, continually saw to it that the visiting American had a weighty schnapper on his hook."

In his journal, Clemens noted reports of items found in the stomachs of captured sharks, such as money, watches, and even prayer books. Although he was skeptical of these accounts, they probably inspired his fish story, in *Following the Equator*, about a young stranger in Sydney who made his first fortune by exploiting the financial pages of a London newspaper, which he found in the belly of a shark, before the paper arrived in its usual way to other Sydneysiders. The clever fellow, wrote Clemens, was Cecil Rhodes.

After two days in town, Clemens and Smythe traveled by train to Scone, a small inland town about 130 miles northwest of Sydney, for an *At Home* that evening. On the train Clemens read that two days earlier President Cleveland had sent to Congress an astonishing message with respect to a long-standing boundary dispute between Venezuela and British Guiana. The dispute, dormant for some time, erupted at the beginning of the year after a border incident. Cleveland, in a stupefying enlargement of the Monroe Doctrine, challenged the right of European powers to hold colonies in the western hemisphere and declared that "to-day the United States is practically sovereign on this continent, and its fiat is law." If Britain did not agree to submit its boundary dispute to arbitration, the United States would go to war. The American public, feverishly excited by Cleveland's appeal to patriotism, demonstrated volcanic support for his message. A telegraph survey of twenty-seven state governors representing both parties showed all but two in favor of Cleveland's policy. The patriotic lava flow engulfed even the violently anti-Cleveland New York *Sun*, which asserted in an editorial that "the American people will deal roughly with any Senator or any Representative who seeks to cripple the hand of the Executive, uplifted at this juncture in the discharge of an exalted message and in vindication of the nation's honour." The New York stock market collapsed, as English investors repatriated large amounts of capital.

The news must have troubled Clemens. On the one hand, he had long admired President Cleveland. On the other, he liked and respected England — although he had attacked or satirized some of its institutions in several of his books — and he was proud of his English ancestry (his mother's family claimed a connection to the earls of Durham and his father's to one of the commissioners who tried Charles I). He was sincere when, a few months earlier in Melbourne, he had told his hosts at a club supper that "when all is said and done, the Americans and the English, and their great out-flow in Canada and Australia are one . . . Oh yes! blood is thicker than water, and we are all related. If we do jaw and bawl at each other now and again, that is no matter at all. We do belong together, and we are parts of a great whole — the greatest whole this world has ever seen — a whole that, some day, will spread over this world, and, I hope, annihilate and abolish all other communities. It will be 'the survival of the fittest.' The English is the greatest race that ever was, and will prove itself so before it gets done — and I would like to be there to see it." Clemens hoped that war would be averted.

Clemens and Smythe spent the night in Scone and returned to Sydney the next day, arriving a half-hour late for the scheduled *At Home* there. Clemens apologized to his audience, according to one reporter, by explaining "that he had just arrived in Sydney after an eight-hours railway journey, and the train was 'only half an hour late.' Perhaps on the whole, he said, it was fortunate that he had arrived at night, since he had been compelled to change his clothes in the cab as it went through the streets."

Clemens exploited his late arrival to entertain his audience. "Whew! it was sweltering . . . I don't know where the other clothes are. They've gone in the cab. And I don't know where the cab is gone. It's probably melted. The only heat that I've experienced like this was what I once got in the Sandwich Islands. But there they don't trouble themselves much with superfluous clothing. The women wore — well, I don't remember what they wore. There wasn't enough of it. And the men — well, just on ordinary occasions they didn't wear anything. But on State occasions they did. They wore smiles, and they even smiled too much. If you in Australia have this kind of weather in the middle of December, what must you have in July?" The joke was not lost on his listeners, many of whom had emigrated from the northern hemisphere.

At the conclusion of his performance, Clemens walked to the edge of the stage and spoke about the threat of war. "In bidding his audience good night," the next day's *Sydney Morning Herald* reported, "he wished to express his belief, as well as his earnest hope, that the 'little war cloud' that had been lowering over England and America during the last few days would be quickly blown away under the influence of cooler and calmer counsels. (Loud cheers.) He trusted sincerely that the fruitful peace that had reigned between the two nations for 80 years would not be broken — (cheers) — and that the two great peoples would resume their march shoulder to shoulder, as before, in the van of the world's civilisation. (Prolonged cheering.)"

The following night, at the conclusion of an exceptionally rollicking *At Home* (one critic reported that as Clemens "gently waved his hand to amplify the points, to the accompaniment of wildly hilarious noises, it seemed as though he were conducting some maniacal orchestra"), he repeated his hopes for "an early removal of the friction which now prevails between his country and England. 'I hope,' he said, 'that we shall soon cease to be annoyed by all this unpleasant, unprofitable, and unbrotherly war talk.' "

Two days later, on Monday, December 23, 1895, the Clemenses boarded the P&O liner *Oceana*, bound for Ceylon via Melbourne and Adelaide. The Indian crew provided Clemens's first glimpse of the radiance, sumptuousness, and sensuousness of the East, an exoticism that was to captivate him in Ceylon and India. "A Lascar crew mans this ship — the first I have seen. White cotton petticoat and pants; barefoot; red shawl for belt; straw cap, brimless, on head, with red scarf wound around it; complexion a rich dark brown; short straight black hair; whiskers fine and silky; lustrous and intensely black."

On Christmas, the *Oceana* arrived in Melbourne, where the Clemenses were taken to the mansion of their rich friends the Wagners. Later that day they ate Christmas dinner with Smythe senior, who had been promoting the next two evenings' "farewell appearances." At both of these, delighted laughter greeted Clemens's Australian fauna poem, to which he had added verses not yet reported by the press.

Before reboarding the *Oceana*, Clemens responded to a reporter's question about the war scare. "He declares unmistakably," his interviewer wrote, "that the United States people are anxious to avoid war with any nation but particularly with England; and at the same time he declines to believe that the action of the

President was in any way an election move." Clemens said, nonetheless, that Cleveland's interpretation of the Monroe Doctrine was probably "strained."

By the time the Clemenses reached Adelaide, on December 30, the Anglo-American crisis had begun to subside. Congress had begun to worry that the president's threats usurped its right to declare war; the public, viewing with favor a conciliatory cable from the Prince of Wales and the Duke of York, had begun to awaken from its patriotic delirium; and the American press began to give the matter less attention.

Still, the war scare was in everyone's mind when Clemens, in the company of the American consul, C. A. Murphy, arrived late at an official luncheon, at the Glenelg Town Hall. Glenelg, a seaside resort near Adelaide, was the site at which the province of South Australia had been proclaimed, fifty-nine years before, in 1839. About two hundred people attended the luncheon, which the municipality organized as part of the celebrations commemorating the proclamation's signing. As the two Americans walked in, the guests stopped toying with their chicken and spontaneously applauded them.

The proceedings continued with a toast to the six attending "Old Colonists." Clemens reported in *Following the Equator* that "they showed signs of the blightings and blastings of time, in their outward aspect, but they were young within; young and cheerful, and ready to talk; ready to talk, and talk all you wanted; in their turn, and out of it. They were down for six speeches, and they made forty-two." His account of their deafness and senility is both amusing and touching, another example of his gift for combining the comic and pathetic, but it was fiction. Each of the six made only a brief speech.

The American-born Commissioner of Public Works proposed a toast to the navy, apologizing as he did so "for the absence of the Minister for War — (laughter) — . . . who was at present looking after the oyster-beds." As to the threatened Anglo-American war, he had "feared that the war-scare had led to the absence of Mr. Murphy, the American Consul, but he was glad to see that gentleman had ventured in under the guardianship of Mark Twain. (Laughter and cheers.)"

The president of the Legislative Council, when toasting the

visitors, alluded to a recent exchange of cables between London and New York. Clemens had recorded them earlier in his notebook: "The Board of Trade has cabled the N.Y. Chamber of Commerce: 'Pleasure boats will not be allowed to obstruct the movements of the British warships.' Reply of Chamber of Commerce: 'We hope your warships will be better than your yachts.' Nobody saw the first joke till the latter was cabled two days later, then there was a shout."

The jokes alluded to that September's running of the America's Cup between *Valkyrie III,* an English yacht commanded by Lord Dunraven, in his third attempt to win back the cup for England, and *Defender,* an American yacht owned by a syndicate whose principal was W. K. Vanderbilt. Dunraven withdrew from the third and final race after it had begun, complaining of a course swarming with pleasure boats, which had drawn near to permit their passengers to watch the race. The real cause of Dunraven's irritation was the Cup Committee's rejection of his complaint that in the second race *Defender* had not given *Valkyrie* enough room, and that crowding by excursion steamers prevented a fair course. Instead, the committee found that *Valkyrie* had broken the rules. Dunraven's withdrawal forced *Defender* to win on a technicality, much against the wishes of the Americans, who offered to sail all three races again, a proposal that the Cup Committee rejected. Shortly thereafter, Dunraven published a pamphlet accusing *Defender*'s yachtsmen of dishonesty, an assertion that was bitterly resented not only by the American sportsmen and by the New York Yacht Club, but also by the American public at large. If the incident contributed to the hostility to Britain invoked by Cleveland's threats of war, it also was the source of two good jokes that helped, perhaps, to defuse Anglo-American tension.

In response to a toast in his honor, Clemens deplored "any thought or suggestion of war between America and England — for certainly never in the history of mankind would any war or was any war so disastrous as this suggested war would be . . . It would certainly stand in the way of the progress and intelligence of the whole world for generations."

Because of Cleveland's bellicosity, England soon agreed to arbitration, thereby increasing America's prestige and facilitating its emergence as a colonial power over the next few years, not only in its own hemisphere, but in the Pacific and in Asia as well. In 1899 an international tribunal found against Venezuela and awarded most of the disputed territory to England.

On the last day of 1895, Clemens lunched with South Australia's lieutenant governor; called at Government House but missed the governor, who had asked him to spend the night, an invitation he was unable to accept; and visited the zoo, where he finally found a kookaburra that was willing to laugh at him.

The Clemenses reboarded the *Oceana* on New Year's Day, 1896. For three days they sailed west along Australia's southern coast, until they reached the harbor of port Albany, on King George Sound in Western Australia, where they anchored and spent most of the fourth day. In *Following the Equator*, Clemens reported seeing many ships arriving, transporting fortune seekers who were hurrying to the new goldfields.

He wrote that when the *Oceana* took up its anchor at sunset, he missed his dinner in order to watch "a little pilot in elaborately gold-laced uniform" advise the captain how to maneuver the large vessel, in the face of a strong wind, out of "a small deep puddle" into the narrow channel leading to the sea. "It was a fine piece of work," a display of seamanship that the old riverboat pilot could appreciate.

At nine in the morning, January 5, 1896, the *Oceana* passed Cape Leeuwin, at the extreme southwestern corner of Australia, and headed northwest for Ceylon, the Sri Lanka of today. As Clemens was leaving Australian waters, he noted in his journal some of his impressions of the country. "One must say it very softly, but the truth is that the native Australian is as vain of his unpretty country as if it were the final masterpiece of God, achieved by Him from designs by that Australian. He is as sensitive about her as men are of sacred things — can't bear to have critical things said about her." This unpleasant reflection is jolting after the many compliments Clemens paid Australia in his journal. He admired its climate, aspects of its landscape, the great parks and botanical gardens, the generosity of its citizens in funding public works, the openness and friendliness of ordinary Australians, and the gracious hospitality of some of its leading citizens.

Although he excluded his dig from *Following the Equator*, perhaps because later he thought it unreasonable or perhaps because he feared jeopardizing Australian sales, he did include his view of Australasian independence from Britain. Many on board, he wrote, favored independence and pointed to the United States as an example. He thought independence unwise and the two cases unlike. "Australasia governs herself wholly — there is no interference; and her commerce and manufactures are not oppressed in any way. If our case had been the same we should not have gone out when we did." (Today, pressure within Australia and New Zealand for a divorce from the Crown continues, and many local commentators view republican status as inevitable.) His journal's last word about Australasia was that "Australasia is the modern heaven — it is bossed absolutely by the workingman."

AN AWKWARD PAUSE.

"An Awkward Pause." Clemens meets a taciturn President Grant at the White House and struggles for something to say. *Illustration from* Following the Equator *(1897:39).*

Erie Depot, circa 1890. From this station in Elmira, New York, the Clemenses embarked on their year-long world tour. *Chemung County Historical Society, Elmira, New York.*

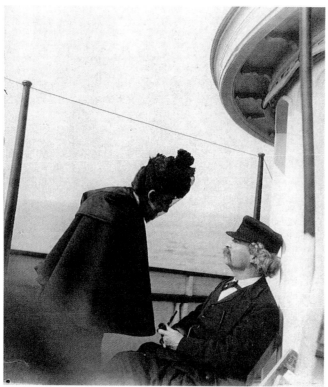

Clemens and Mrs. Clemens aboard the Great Lakes steamer *SS Northland*. Mrs. Clemens is urging her husband to put on his coat. *Courtesy of The Mark Twain Archives, Elmira College, Elmira, New York.*

The Clemens party waiting for a late train at Crookston, Minnesota, at a chilly five in the morning. Clemens irritably insisted that Pond fulfill his commitment for travel by "travelling" him on the baggage truck. The shadow is that of Clara, who snapped the scene. *Courtesy of The Mark Twain Archives, Elmira College, Elmira, New York.*

Wednesday Evening, Aug. 7

MARK
TWAIN

(SAMUEL L. CLEMENS)

WILL

LECTURE

Sale of Seats Tuesday, August 6th.

Advertisement for Mark Twain's performance at the Spokane Auditorium, Spokane, Washington. The theatre was so large it had never been even a quarter full. Nonetheless its manager was disappointed that Clemens did not fill it. *From the* Spokane Daily Review, *August 6, 1895.*

MING'S OPERA HOUSE
J. L. MING, MANAGER.

Positively One Night Only..

SATURDAY,
AUGUST 3.

The World Famous Author,

MARK TWAIN

(SAMUEL L. CLEMENS.)

In Talks and Readings From His
Own Rich Humor.

Sale of seats will begin Friday morning
at Lockwood's drug store.   Lower floor,
$1.00 ; gallery, 50c.

Advertisement for Mark Twain's performance at Ming's Opera House, Helena, Montana. After the show, he was entertained at the Montana Club, where one of the guests accused him of a "dirty trick" when both were young men in Silver City. *From the* Helena Daily Herald, *August 3, 1895.*

Henry Huttleston Rogers, the plutocrat who saved the Clemenses from financial ruin without injuring their pride. *Brown Brothers.*

Clemens in his hotel room, Olympia, Washington. He told the Olympia welcoming committee that he did not mind the dense smoke from the forest fires: "I am a perpetual smoker myself." *Courtesy of The Mark Twain Archives, Elmira College, Elmira, New York.*

Aboard the *SS Warrimoo* before its departure from Victoria. From left to right: Major Pond, Mrs. Clemens, Samuel Clemens, Clara Clemens, Mrs. Pond. *Courtesy of The Mark Twain Archives, Elmira College, Elmira, New York.*

Clemens aboard
the *SS Warrimoo*.
"We had the whole
Pacific Ocean in
front of us," he
wrote, "with
nothing to do but
do nothing and be
comfortable."
From Following
the Equator
(1897: frontispiece).

Mark Twain and a
"laughing jackass."
The frog in
Clemens's hand
alludes to his first
great success,
"The Celebrated
Jumping Frog of
Calaveras County."
Cartoon from the
Sydney Bulletin,
October 1895.
Reproduced in
Shillingsburg
(1995:cover).

THE WHITE MAN'S WORLD.

"The White Man's World." Throughout the account of his world tour, Clemens noted examples of colonial rapacity, cruelty, and hypocrisy. Commenting on an Australian settler who offered his Aboriginal neighbors a "Christmas pudding" laced with arsenic, Clemens wrote that "there are many humorous things in the world, among them the white man's notion that he is less savage than the other savages." *Illustration from* Following the Equator *(1897:187).*

Advertisement for Mark Twain's performance in Stawell, one of Australia's "country towns." It was probably at Stawell that Clara almost etherized a fallen sheep by mistake. *From* The Stawell News and Pleasant Creek Chronicle, *October 17, 1895.*

A sketch by William M. Hodgkins of Mark Twain performing in Dunedin, New Zealand. Clemens is captured here in a characteristic platform stance. *Alexander Turnbull Library, National Library of New Zealand, Te Puna Mātauranga o Aotearoa.*

Clemens and company in New Zealand. *From Carlyle G. Smythe, "'The Real' Mark Twain," in* The Pall Mall Magazine, *September 1898, 16 (65):33.*

Clemens with Carlyle Smythe, who managed the bulk of Clemens's world tour. *From Arthur Scott*, Mark Twain at Large *(1969).*

Mrs. Clemens and Clemens, photographed by Falk's Studio during their first day in Sydney. To a reporter who accompanied him to the session, Clemens made injudicious comments on local political issues and ill-tempered remarks about Bret Harte. A furious editorial and angry letters to the editor greeted him the next day. *From* Melbourne Punch, *September 26, 1895:199. La Trobe Collection, State Library of Victoria, Melbourne.*

4

INDIA

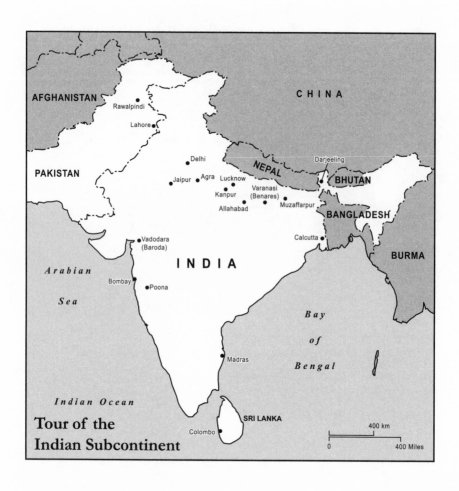

AFGHANISTAN

CHINA

Rawalpindi

Lahore

PAKISTAN

Delhi

NEPAL

Darjeeling

BHUTAN

Jaipur Agra Lucknow

Kanpur Varanasi
(Benares)

Allahabad Muzaffarpur

BANGLADESH

Calcutta

BURMA

Vadodara
(Baroda)

I N D I A

Arabian

Bombay Poona

Sea

Bay

of

Bengal

Madras

Indian Ocean

Tour of the
Indian Subcontinent

SRI LANKA

Colombo

400 km

0   400 Miles

Chapter Twenty-four

AS THE PALATIAL *OCEANA* STEAMED toward Ceylon, its passengers reclined on chaises longues, played deck games, and promenaded in the shade of canvas awnings. In the evening its passengers dressed for dinner. The women's colorful gowns were consistent, wrote Clemens in *Following the Equator,* with the elegance of the vessel and "the flooding brilliancies of the electric light." Clemens, who had not seen formal dress at sea before, attributed the custom to the calmness of the Indian Ocean. The sea was so smooth that games of cricket were played on the promenade deck, which was enclosed with netting to prevent the ball from escaping overboard.

"Peace, everlasting peace, and tranquillity," he wrote in his journal, a day after the vessel turned northwest toward Ceylon. By now America and Britain might have transformed the Australians on board into his enemies, but no matter. "A ship is a world of its own — one does not trouble himself about other worlds and their affairs."

Two days later he noted in his journal that it was "roasting hot," as each hour brought them closer to the equator. Nonetheless, this was "ideal sailing — long, slow, gentle rocking of the ship, soothing and lulling as a cradle motion, the atmosphere filled with peace and far-from-the-worldness — just enough breeze to keep your fat from melting and running down and greasing your clothes." That day the dining room began using punkahs, a kind of fan made by cloth strips hung above the tables and kept in motion by servants pulling ropes.

If there were few external irritations, other than "some ungoverned children," Clemens managed to irritate himself. Early one morning, in "the calm and holy dawn," as he told his journal, he resolved to swear no more. After bathing, dressing in white linen, and shaving, a "long, hot, troublesome job" that elicited no impieties, he remembered to take his tonic. As he was pouring out a second dose — he had dropped the first one — the ship lurched; the tumbler that he had placed on the washstand behind him crashed to the ground, and all but its bottom shattered into fragments; he picked up the bottom to toss it out the porthole; instead he threw out his measuring cup. "I released my voice. Mrs. C. behind me in the door: 'Don't reform any more, it isn't any improvement.' "

A few days later he had something more serious to complain about. "I am shut up in my cabin with another allfired cold on my chest," he wrote to Rogers, declaring that the toll of carbuncles and colds had left him "tired and disgusted and angry."

When the *Oceana* docked at Colombo a day later, on January 13, 1896, Clemens was still suffering from a bad cough. While Smythe supervised the transfer of trunks to the P&O liner *Rosetta*, on which the Clemens party would embark the next day for Bombay, Clemens stood at the ship's railing and observed the diving boys, the catamarans, and the outriggers. He told a reporter on board that "you only see things like this in places like Fiji and places of that sort, and even there they are different. Those boats and those dresses of the natives are quite novelties . . . I never saw anything like that anywhere." Soon surrounded by peddlers, he explained "that he was in no urgent need of a tortoise-shell shoehorn, a comb or a sapphire ring."

For once, Smythe's arrangements fell through. The influx of passengers from the *Oceana* strained the capacity of the Grand Oriental Hotel, which could not accommodate all the Clemenses. That afternoon Clemens was seen "with a tightly rolled umbrella and a hot weary look," searching for accommodations, which he found in the nearby Bristol Hotel. Exhausted by four in the afternoon, he went to bed, but not before a disquieting encounter. In *Following the Equator*, Clemens described his Sinhalese room servant, Brompy, as "an alert, gentle, smiling, winning young brown creature" who wore his "beautiful shining black hair combed back like a woman's, and knotted at the back of his head," the male Sinhalese style at the time, and clothed his "slender, shapely form" in a jacket under which flowed a beltless long white gown. "He and his outfit quite unmasculine. It was an embarrassment to undress before him."

Colombo overwhelmed Clemens. "I can see it to this day," he wrote in *Following the Equator,* about a drive along the shore, "that radiant panorama, that wilderness of rich color, that incomparable dissolving-view of harmonious tints, and lithe half-covered forms, and beautiful brown faces, and gracious and graceful gestures and attitudes and movements, free, unstudied, barren of stiffness and restraint." Into this romance marched a twin column of local schoolgirls, "dressed, to the last detail, as they would have been on a summer Sunday in an English or American village," in clothes "destitute of taste, destitute of grace, repulsive as a shroud." He looked at Mrs. Clemens's and Clara's clothes and then at his own, and was ashamed.

In today's Colombo, schoolchildren universally wear the "ugly, barbarous" clothes of the West. As for adults, the semi-nakedness and whirl of vivid color that intoxicated Clemens has been largely replaced, for the workaday world, by conventional Western dress. Colombo is still colorful, but its tints and hues derive mainly from tropical flowers and the aquamarine sea.

A hipless waiter in a spotless white jacket and ankle-length sarong serves coffee. We're sitting on the columned and balustraded veranda of the Galle Face Hotel, a grand Victorian establishment about a mile from the "Fort," the city center in which the Clemenses stayed. Sheltered by three sides of the building, we look out at the smooth lawn and at its stately coconut palms. Beyond lies the sea. We listen to the waves crashing against the lawn's stone retaining wall. On the roof of a nearby concrete tower, soldiers stand next to antiaircraft guns.

We linger over the coffee. Normally we would have left the hotel an hour ago in order to read microfilms at the town archives, or take notes at the town library, or inspect sites associated with the Clemenses' visit. But this morning, feeling slightly feverish, I've decided to stay put and write postcards. Alice plans to visit a bookstore downtown, where she hopes to find the reprint of a Victorian guide to Colombo, but I've persuaded her to stay a few more minutes to keep me company.

We are chatting about nothing in particular when a tremendous boom shocks us into silence. A second later, great slabs of glass crash down from the windows of the south wing, which faces the Fort. Waiters sprint onto the back lawn, disappear around the south wing, and return. A swimmer hauls himself from the pool and runs drip-ping across the lawn and into the hotel.

We enter the lobby to join confused, shocked staff and guests, including members of a wedding, the women in gorgeous gold-embroidered saris. Next to the front door, whose glass has been blown out, stand ornately wrapped presents. Fire engines, police cars, and ambulances, their sirens wailing, race toward a dense cloud of dirty smoke arising from the Fort. Hotel staff, worried about their family and friends in town, look helplessly toward the disaster. A half-hysterical British tourist asks a staff member, "Did my friends come back? Did my friends come back?"

We return to the veranda, as a dazed woman with a bloody face and arms is helped to a seat. She speaks with a Scottish accent. To the guests who wash and bandage her cuts, she explains that she was in her room at the Intercontinental Hotel, in the Fort, when she heard gunfire. She moved away from the window and dropped to the floor, just before a great blast blew the window frame into the room and shattered glass fragments and splinters all over her. She dashed down seven flights of stairs to the lobby, where water was gushing through a collapsed ceiling and blood-soaked victims were being carried out through a thick pall of smoke. She ran for a mile along the shore to our hotel. She has suffered only minor cuts.

The English-language radio station, which advertises itself as providing "uninterrupted news," ignores the explosion. We try to call each of our children in turn to tell them we are safe, but the out-going lines are jammed. Eventually we learn that a Tamil suicide squad drove an explosive-laden truck into the Central Bank, killing more than seventy people and wounding more than 1,200. The cen-tral business district is a shambles. In a decade of terrorist bombings in Colombo, this is the deadliest since 1987, when a car bomb killed more than one hundred people at the central bus station.

The Tamil Tigers, based in the north of the country, where Tamils form a majority, are fighting for a separate state in order to protect their people from Sinhalese domination. Tamils began emi-grating from southern India 1,000 years ago, and it is from this ancient community, rather than from the descendants of Tamil laborers imported during the nineteenth century, that the Tamil

Tigers are drawn. The conflict reflects the poisonous mixture of nationalism and religion: most of the Tamils are Hindu, whereas most of the Sinhalese are Buddhist.

The rivalry between Tamils and Sinhalese was not obvious in Clemens's day, at least not to the casual European or American visitor. Sectarian and interracial jealousies flared into violence only after independence, as a slowing economy intensified competition and as Sinhalese politicians preyed on their constituents' fears of being swamped by millions of Tamils from India.

When Clemens disembarked at Colombo, the only religious issue in the news concerned resentment at the dismissal of Mr. LeMesurier from the Colonial Service of Ceylon. This civil servant, after failing to obtain a divorce from his recalcitrant wife, converted to Islam and married, according to Muslim rites, an Englishwoman who had also converted to Islam. He was dismissed from his post on those grounds. The case was arousing considerable excitement, both in Ceylon and in India, because it violated the principle that the British should observe strict neutrality in matters of religion.

Among the news the Clemenses received when they arrived in Colombo was that an attempt two weeks earlier to foment revolution in Johannesburg had failed, and that war between America and Britain seemed less imminent. Clemens noted in his journal that America had asked Britain to protect American citizens in South Africa, and that this request was considered a sign of improved Anglo-American relations.

The Clemenses left Colombo the next day, on Tuesday, January 14, after only one night on the island. Their ship, the *Rosetta*, sailed too early to permit an *At Home* in Colombo, but Smythe hoped to arrange engagements several months hence, after the conclusion of the Indian tour, when the party would return en route for Mauritius.

On the day of their departure, *The Times of Ceylon* published a warm welcome "to one who is as well known in this British Colony as he is in the States . . . We may say without fear of contradiction that no community that we know of in the world claims a larger proportion of admirers of the great American humourist than that of the European residents of Ceylon." Before his departure, Clemens was taken on a tour of Colombo. Intoxicated by the town's radiant beauty and exoticism, he was shown, first of all, the new post office, much to his disgust.

Despite his guides' obtuseness, he was soon to tell a reporter in Bombay that his day in Colombo was "the most enchanting day I ever spent in my life. Everything was absolutely new — all that beautiful nakedness and colour, all those costumes which one hears of but never sees, and which if you see them on the stage you never believe in. It beggars all description: one simply laughs at the painter's brush; it is impossible for him to reproduce it."

Chapter Twenty-five

ACCORDING TO CLEMENS, the *Rosetta* was "a poor old ship, and ought to be insured and sunk." When its passengers dressed for dinner, he said, their finery brought the ship's shabbiness into disagreeable relief. He might have been less critical had he not recently completed a voyage on its sister ship, the opulent *Oceana*, and had he not been suffering from a bad cough, which confined him to bed for most of the voyage. The heat of the cabins, which drove Mrs. Clemens and Clara to sleep on deck, did not, however, seem to disturb him.

The *Rosetta* arrived in Bombay on Saturday, January 18, 1896, at about four in the afternoon, earlier than expected, forcing the cancellation of a formal reception that had been planned in Clemens's honor. He did receive a hearty welcome, however, from *The Times of India*: "The great humourist is with us, and he is going to lecture here; and if Bombay does not give him a royal reception she will not be doing herself any kind of justice."

The Clemenses stayed at Watson's Esplanade Hotel, in front rooms on a high floor, opposite the ranks of shade trees in the University Gardens. Each room on the first three floors had a bathroom, although he did not think much of his. Still, it was the best hotel in India. The building survives, converted into innumerable offices and stores. Tenants have added walls and windows to the balconies in an uncoordinated hodgepodge of materials and styles, the higgledy-piggledy accretions generating a structure so ugly that if Clemens were to return he would not recognize it.

The ugliness he saw was inside the hotel. When the Clemenses arrived, the thickset European manager visited their rooms with three servants in tow. After one of the servants began to repair or clean a balcony door, the manager cuffed him briskly on the jaw and then arrogantly told him how the work should be done. "It seemed such a shame to do that before us all," Clemens wrote in *Following the Equator*. "The native took it with meekness, saying nothing, and not showing in his face or manner any resentment. I had not seen the like of this for fifty years. It carried me back to my boyhood, and flashed upon me the forgotten fact that this was the *usual* way of explaining one's desire to a slave."

Clemens confined himself to his room to nurse his cold, attended by Dr. Sidney Smith, who visited him four times and then sent him a bill for 100 rupees, then about $27 or a little under $500 today. When Clemens learned that Dr. Smith charged other rich patients only 10 rupees a visit, he sent him a polite note enclosing 40 rupees and asking for an explanation for the additional charge.

Two days after his arrival, Clemens told his journal that he wished his "infernal cough" were in hell. In the meantime, he took all his meals in his room, where he was served "Irish stew under 14 different French names . . . I have been told that [the French chef's] name is O'Shaughnessy." He enjoyed ample opportunity to experience the hotel's noises, which began at about five in the morning, according to a journal entry. "Hindu servants yelling orders to each other from story to story. It is equal to a riot and insurrection for noise. And there are other noises — roofs falling in, windows smashing, persons being murdered, crows squawking, canaries screeching, fiendish bursts of laughter, explosions of dynamite. By seven o'clock one has suffered all the different kinds of shock there are and can never more be disturbed by them either isolated or in combination, then the noises all stop for hours."

While Clemens was convalescing, Mrs. Clemens and Clara embarked on a whirl of engagements. To her sister, Mrs. Clemens complained that she was so busy socializing and sightseeing that she had scarcely time to write to her about it, except to say that Bombay was without doubt "the *most* fascinating place" she had ever seen. For five days, from Sunday, January 19, through Thursday, January 23, Clemens stayed indoors, unwilling to accept invitations before his first performance, "lest my cough jump on me again." He even postponed an invitation to lunch at Government House with the Governor of Bombay Presidency, Lord Sandhurst. Nor did he accompany Mrs. Clemens and Clara to a brilliant evening reception for the prince of Palitana.

In the meantime, he spoke to interviewers. When asked about his methods of work, he replied that he was lazy in his preparation for a book, merely jotting down notes, which were, he claimed, inadequate. "However, there may be some advantage to the reader in this, since in the absence of notes imagination has often to supply the place of facts." (While many of his notes for *Following the Equator* were skeletal, others were full enough to be transferred, with few changes, to his book.) As for writing, he said he was not at all lazy. "I work very regularly when I work at all. I work every day and all day from after breakfast till late into the night until the work is finished. I never begin work before eleven in the morning, and I sit at it till they pull me away from table to dress for dinner at seven at night. They make me stop then for a while, as they think I might over-work myself, but I don't think there is any fear of that, for I don't consider the kind of writing I do is work in any way: it is no sense a labour with me." What he found most helpful in his work, he said, was tobacco. "I always smoke when at work: I couldn't do without it."

And did he prepare carefully for his lectures? "Yes, I am not for one moment going to pretend I do not. I don't believe that any public man has ever attained success as a lecturer to paid audiences (mark the qualification), who has not carefully prepared, and has not gone over every sentence again and again until the whole thing is fixed upon his memory . . . It is all very well to talk about not being prepared, and trusting to the spirit of the hour. But a man cannot go from one end of the world to the other, no matter how great his reputation may be, and stand before paid houses in various large cities without finding that his tongue is far less glib than it used to be. He might hold audiences spell bound with unpremeditated oratory in past days when nothing was charged to hear him, but he cannot rely on being able to do so when they have paid for their seats and require something for the money unless he thinks all out beforehand."

As for another genre that Clemens had mastered, the interview, he dismissed it as "mere fluff and foam." In most cases, he said, the interviewee has nothing to say worth printing. "In the first place there is nothing on the spur of the moment worth talking about, and in the second place there comes the question of phrasing, and it is phrasing that makes a piece of literature valuable. How are you going to do your phrasing unless you get time to think it over and get it ready? Phrasing is the difference between good literature and poor, commonplace literature." Perhaps his verdict applies to most interviews, but as for his own, they lacked neither substance nor style.

For the moment he entertained the public via interviews at his hotel. "I haven't seen anything yet," he complained to a reporter. "My wife and daughter overwhelm me with the fascinations of Bombay, and so make my imprisonment all the harder to put up with, but I hope to be released shortly, and then I shall see all that it is possible for me to see."

His imprisonment ended on Friday, January 24, when he performed at Bombay's domed Novelty Theatre, which could accommodate 1,400 persons. According to *The Times of India*, there had been an almost unprecedented demand for tickets, which were taken "by almost every prominent citizen of Bombay," including Lord Sandhurst, among a large party from Government House. The audience was mainly European, with perhaps one-third or one-quarter Indian. Wave after wave of loud and ardent applause hailed him as he stepped quietly onto the platform. "It is a rugged and even something of a romantic figure that Mark Twain presents upon the stage, with his masses of curly hair, now nearly white, his keen, kindly eyes looking out from great shaggy brows, and his strangely magnetic smile . . . nothing could have exceeded the eloquence or charm of his delivery." This in spite of occasional hoarseness, left him by his cold. The ninety minutes in which he spoke, according to *The Times of India*, were perhaps the most delightful ninety minutes of talk ever heard by that audience. The reviewer for *The Bombay Gazette*, who commented that "Mark Twain was there not as a stranger in a strange land, but as an old friend to well nigh everyone in the audience," observed that he "has the Virgilian sense of tears in human things, and he knows the acute sufferings of the soul."

Chapter Twenty-six

*B*OMBAY! A BEWITCHING PLACE, a bewildering place, an enchanting place — the Arabian Nights come again!" Clemens exclaimed in *Following the Equator*. Not blind to the destitution about him, he noted beggars, ragged children, multitudes of bundled forms asleep at the side of the road, and rats that ran along the street. But the collision of desperate poverty with opulence, pomp, and "barbaric gorgeousnesses" seemed to enhance the fairy-tale quality of his experience in India.

"Father," wrote Clara about Clemens in India, "seemed like a young boy in his enthusiasm over everything he saw. He kept reiterating: 'This wonderful land, this marvelous land! There can be no other like it.' He loved the heat, the punkahs, the bungalows, and the continuous opportunity to wear white clothes without attracting attention."

On Saturday, January 25, 1896, the day after his first performance in Bombay, Clemens began his exploration of India. In the company of Shri Virchand R. Gandhi, an authority on the Jains, the Clemenses visited a Jain temple. Gandhi reported that all three Clemenses appeared intensely interested and asked him numerous questions about the nature of Jain worship and philosophy. He told them that Jains have no priests, but only monks, and that believers must worship for themselves by reciting hymns and by contemplation, in hopes of attaining perfection as epitomized by the Jain prophets. Clemens, pointing to two small images set into a niche, asked about them. They were, Clemens was informed, representations of Yakshas, mortals who live within a celestial sphere, whose effigies are placed in the temple because they are thought to be devout followers of the Jain prophets.

Built of white sandstone, this was the most splendid of Bombay's Jain temples. It was located in Byculla, then an area of

elegant homes but today a lower-middle-class Muslim neighborhood. The view of Bombay, which Gandhi showed the Clemenses
from the top of the temple, is now blocked by taller structures,
mainly tenements. A few of the old mansions survive, broken up
into apartments or offices. Although it still operates, the Byculla
temple is now dilapidated and gray.

From the temple, the Clemenses went to the nearby palatial
residence of Mr. Seth Premchand Roychand, one of the founders of
the Bombay Stock Exchange (now the oldest and most active in
Asia), and a philanthropist whose munificence funded, among other
good works, the Rajabai Tower of the university library, which the
Clemenses could see from their hotel windows and which stands
today. Roychand was hosting one in a series of receptions organized
by the Jain community in honor of the Thakore Saheb, prince of
Palitana, on the occasion of the knighthood that the Queen-
Empress had recently conferred upon him. Mrs. Clemens and Clara
had already attended one of these receptions.

His Highness, entitled to a nine-gun salute, was the semi-
independent ruler of a petty principality, one of more than 550
Indian princely states that Britain governed indirectly. Although he
and most of his subjects were Hindu, his territory was important to
the Jains because of the celebrated Jain temples on Satrunjaya Hill,
above Palitana town, a place of annual pilgrimage from all parts of
India. Inasmuch as one of his first steps on ascending the throne, in
1885, was to resolve a dispute about the pilgrimage in a manner that
the Jains viewed as generous and reasonable, the Jain community of
Bombay was honoring him now with a congratulatory address.

"By and by, there was a burst of shouts and cheers outside,"
wrote Clemens in *Following the Equator*, "and the prince with his
train entered in fine dramatic style. He was a stately man, he was
ideally costumed, and fairly festooned with ropes of gems; some of
the ropes were of pearls, some were of uncut great emeralds —
emeralds renowned in Bombay for their quality and value." A few
young boys, splendidly dressed, sang songs specially composed for
the occasion; a congratulatory address, prepared on vellum, was read
aloud and then presented to the prince inside a carved silver casket;
His Highness responded in a brief speech of thanks; and a rich Jain
recited odes in his praise. The prince and many of the guests,

including the Clemenses, were decorated with garlands and presented with superb bouquets. Before the reception concluded, the
Clemenses were introduced to the prince.

When preparing his manuscript, Clemens described the prince
as wearing ropes of pearls and green rubies. Mrs. Clemens commented in a note that "perhaps you don't care, but whoever told you
that the Prince's green stones were rubies told you a lie, they were
superb emeralds. Those strings of pearls & emeralds were famous
all over Bombay. Perhaps you remember that his brother wore some
that were very much the same." Clemens responded to her note, "all
right, I'll make it emeralds, but it loses force. Green rubies is a
fresh thing. And besides, it was one of the Prince's own staff liars
that told me."

Five days after the reception, the Clemenses spent a few hours
at the prince's town residence on Malabar Hill. The prince, an athlete of commanding physical presence, was regarded by the British
as an able and conscientious administrator, who opened clinics and
schools in his territories and who employed educated and competent assistants. The owner of a famous stud of horses, an excellent
rider and polo player, and well regarded for his facility in English,
he lived up to his reputation for lavish hospitality when he received
the Clemenses. After refreshments had been served, he ordered
"bales of rich stuffs" brought in and opened, and then he invited the
Clemenses to select for themselves what they liked. In a thank-you
letter, Clemens told the prince that the visit "was our first glimpse
of the home of an Eastern Prince, & the charm of it, the grace &
beauty & dignity of it realized to us the pictures which we had long
ago gathered from books of travel & Oriental tales . . . We shall keep
always the portrait & the beautiful things you gave us; & as long as
we live a glance at them will bring your house and its life & its sumptuous belongings & rich harmonies of color instantly across the years
& the oceans, & we shall see them again, & how welcome they will
be!" The munificent prince had less than ten more years to enjoy
his sumptuous belongings. He died relatively young, in 1905, after
a long illness, and was succeeded by his five-year-old son.

The day after their first meeting with the prince, the
Clemenses rode along the seashore to Malabar Point, where they
lunched with Lord and Lady Sandhurst at Government House.

Lord Sandhurst, newly arrived in India, was governor of Bombay. Among the twelve Indian provinces subject to the Viceroy of India and his council in Calcutta, only two were headed by governors, Bombay and Madras, the other ten being managed by lesser officials. Lord Sandhurst administered a population greater than that of all the Australasian colonies combined. He remembered meeting Clemens about twenty years before, at the Garrick Club in London. Clemens commented that at least four of those present then were still alive, "not a bad average."

Among Lord Sandhurst's headaches at the time was the furious and outraged opposition of Bombay's mill owners and the local press, both native and European, to proposed changes in the customs and excise regulations. The government of India was about to lower the duties on cotton goods imported from Britain and to raise domestic taxes on cotton goods produced in India. These measures were intended to boost the depressed cotton manufacturers in Britain, based chiefly in Lancashire, at the expense of the Indian cotton mills, based chiefly in Bombay. Indian cotton mills would face greater competition at home, and the coarse cotton goods produced in India, purchased by the masses of India's poor, would rise in price. Comparatively few Indians could afford to buy the higher-quality goods imported from Britain, so the lowering of duties on those manufactures would benefit relatively few consumers. "Even in Lancashire," stormed *The Times of India*, "people can realise how much resentment would be awakened in England if some fine day the Chancellor of the Exchequer were to go down to the House of Commons with a proposal to take the duty off the rich man's champagne, and to increase the charge upon the poor man's beer." This exercise hardly supported Britain's pious claim that it ruled India in the latter's best interests. Lord Sandhurst probably did not discuss these troubles with the Clemenses over lunch.

"It is all color," Clemens wrote in *Following the Equator*, "bewitching color, enchanting color — everywhere — all around — all the way around the curving great opaline bay clear to Government House." Today they would have driven to Government House via Marine Drive, built in the 1930s, to the west of the old road, on land reclaimed from the bay. It is an eight-lane, palm-fringed road lined by flaking art deco apartment blocks on one side and a broad seaside promenade on the other. Although the carriages of the rich, "manned by a driver and three footmen in stunning oriental liveries," have been replaced by swarms of small black and yellow taxis and private cars, luscious color can be found in the jewellike costumes of women strollers, wearing saris and shalwar kameez. Gone, however, are the "rich-colored turbans" that delighted Clemens in their brilliance and diversity. At that time, a man's headwear identified his geographical origin and religious community. After the intercommunal violence which accompanied Independence and Partition in 1947, most men in Bombay have avoided advertising their religious identity, for fear of finding themselves in the wrong neighborhood by mistake. When the Clemenses drove up to Government House, they found "turbaned big native *chuprassies*" at the door "in their robes of fiery red." Today the orderlies wear khaki.

After lunch at Government House, the Clemenses drove up Malabar Hill to the Towers of Silence, where Sir Jivanji Jamsetji Modi, a distinguished scholar and teacher who was secretary of the Parsi Council Trust Funds, met them at the entrance. He explained the Parsi method of disposing of the dead, and showed them a model of the Towers. To avoid contaminating the sacred elements — earth, water, or fire — by contact with a dead body, the corpse is laid on a metal grill atop a tower, where vultures and other carrion birds pick it clean. After the skeleton has been exposed to the burning sun for a month, men with tongs cast it into a well, where it turns to dust. Clemens appeared very interested and asked several questions.

According to Smythe, someone in the party requested permission to photograph the Towers, but the authorities refused, for fear that Mark Twain would use the photos in order to poke fun at their method for disposing of the dead. If the story is true, Clemens's reputation as a humorist carried more weight than his behavior at the site, because the Towers strongly impressed him. "One marvels to see here," he wrote in the Council's book, "a perfect system for the protection of the living from contagion derivable from the dead — I mean one marvels to see this proof that modern science is behind the ancients in this so important matter." In *Following the Equator* he devoted several pages to a laudatory description of the method. "As a sanitary measure," he wrote, "their system seems to be about the equivalent of cremation, and as sure. We are drifting slowly — but hopefully — toward cremation in these days . . . When cremation becomes the rule we shall cease to shudder at it; we should shudder at burial if we allowed ourselves to think what goes on in the grave." One hundred years after Clemens's visit, Bombay's Parsis are considering a change to electric cremation, presumably because carrion birds occasionally let slip, onto the terraces and rooftops of Malabar Hill's fashionable apartment blocks, bits of flesh.

The exuberant tropical foliage that surrounded the Towers in Clemens's time continues today. Perhaps the trees are taller now, which would make it even more difficult to satisfy the curiosity of morbid voyeurs. If you stand across from the driveway leading to the entrance, you may see, through the shifting leaves, what might be a tiny portion of one tower. The Towers remain, as Clemens described them in *Following the Equator,* "remote from the world and its turmoil and noise," and the carrion birds still glide in slow ellipses overhead.

Chapter Twenty-seven

NEITHER IN AUSTRALASIA nor in India did the Clemenses manage without a servant. A maid accompanied them through Australia and New Zealand. When the family arrived at a station, she would take charge of the trunks and bags and ensure their safe arrival at the hotel. She would help with the constant packing and unpacking. Before a performance, she would brush and lay out Clemens's evening clothes, and place the buttons and studs in his clean shirt. The Clemenses did not take her to India because of the expense.

Even if you were not an international celebrity on tour, it was essential to hire a servant in India. Clemens wrote that "you hire him as soon as you touch Indian soil; for no matter what your sex is, you cannot do without him. He is messenger, valet, chambermaid, table-waiter, lady's maid, courier — he is everything." All three Clemenses commented on the custom of being waited on, at a hotel dining room, by one's own servants. British residents in India were accustomed to seeing at a dinner party not only their own household waiters but also their own crockery. Their host's steward would have organized both in advance.

Your servant, Clemens asserted, should be hired with care "because as long as he is in your employ he will be about as near to you as your clothes." The Clemens party of four traveled throughout India with two servants, who slept on the floor outside the party's rooms unless they were on a train, when the servants would find space in the third-class carriages.

According to Clemens's account in *Following the Equator*, the first servant they engaged proved to be slow, forgetful, inefficient, unskilled as a waiter, and incomprehensible and uncomprehending in English, so they dismissed him after a week's trial. His successor was fast, efficient, and bright. "All my heart, all my affection, all my admiration, went out spontaneously to this frisky little forked black thing, this compact and compressed incarnation of energy and force and promptness and celerity and confidence, this smart, smily, engaging, shiny-eyed little devil, feruled on his upper end by a gleaming fire-coal of a fez with a red-hot tassel dangling from it." Clemens considered the servant's name, Mousa, as "out of character; it was too soft, too quiet, too conservative; it didn't fit his splendid style." Clemens referred to him in his journal as Mousa or Mouza, although if we are to believe his account in *Following the Equator*, Clemens asked and received permission to call him "Satan." "He was always busy," Clemens reported in *Following the Equator*, "kept the rooms tidied up, the boots polished, the clothes brushed, the wash-basin full of clean water, my dress-clothes laid out and ready for the lecture-hall an hour ahead of time; and he dressed me from head to heel in spite of my determination to do it myself, according to my life-long custom."

He served them at table with great style, "in a swell hotel or in a private house — snow-white muslin from his chin to his bare feet, a crimson sash embroidered with gold thread around his waist, and on his head a great sea-green turban like to the turban of the Grand Turk."

At the railway terminal he would command the train of coolies who carried the Clemenses' luggage, and, once arrived at the sleeping car, would quickly arrange their belongings, make their beds, "then put his head out at a window and have a restful good time abusing his gang of coolies and disputing their bill until we arrived and made him pay them and stop his noise."

Clemens claimed that he loved Satan for his noise, "but the family detested him for it . . . As a rule, when we got within six hundred yards of one of those big railway-stations, a mighty racket of screaming and shrieking and shouting and storming would break upon us, and I would be happy to myself, and the family would say, with shame: 'There — that's Satan. Why *do* you keep him?' "

Finally, following a series of misadventures — the most serious of which was Satan's turning up drunk while they were guests in a private home — they dismissed him. "I loved him; I couldn't help it . . . To this day I regret his loss, and wish I had him back." His successor, who spoke with a low voice and moved about noiselessly, was "competent and satisfactory. But where he was, it seemed always Sunday. It was not so in Satan's time."

Early in Satan's tenure, he announced a visitor to Clemens: "God want to see you." Although Clemens may have invented the announcement, he did indeed receive a personage viewed by millions as a god. This was His Highness, Aga Khan III, spiritual leader of the Ismaili Muslims, a descendant of the Prophet, and a grandson of the Shah of Persia.

Clemens's visitor had received a religious education by Muslim clerics and a modern secular education by English tutors, who introduced him to English literature, in which he read widely and from which he could recite whole passages by heart. Also well read in the classical Persian poets, he knew French, German, Urdu, and Hindustani in addition to English and modern Persian. He became Imam when he was eight years old. By ten he was arbitrating religious disputes. By sixteen he had taken over the Imamate's practical administration. He was only eighteen when he called on Clemens, but such was his gravitas that Clemens remembered him as "not forty, perhaps not above thirty-five years old."

The Aga Khan became a pro-British mediating force between Muslims and Hindus, president of the All-India Muslim League, an important player in the London Round Table Conferences on Indian constitutional reform in the early 1930s, and president of the League of Nations. Today those of the general public old enough to remember him recall a stout, stupendously rich owner and breeder of racehorses (he won the Derby five times) and a religious leader whose followers weighed him in public, once on his golden jubilee (1936), when they gave him his weight in gold, and once on his diamond jubilee (1946), when they gave him his weight in diamonds. (He presented both gifts to charitable and public works.)

Clemens described him as "a most courteous and charming gentleman," who "wears his immense honors with tranquil grace, and with a dignity proper to his awful calling." His Highness, Clemens reported, mentioned the philosophy of Huck Finn and then "went luminously on with the construction of a compact and nicely discriminated literary verdict." He remained, Clemens recalled, a half hour.

Writing more than half a century later, the Aga Khan remembered spending a whole afternoon with Clemens and then dining with him at Watson's Hotel. "He had a pleasant, utterly unassuming charm," wrote the Aga Khan, "and a friendliness of manner which captivated the serious-minded lad that I was ... He seemed to me dear, gentle and saintly, sad and immensely modest for so great and famous a genius. He reminded me of one of those delicate white flowers, so sensitive that when you touch them they recoil and fold their clear, waxen petals, as if too shy and retiring to tolerate the slightest probe."

Among the fictions in *Following the Equator* is probably the question Clemens placed in his servant's mouth at the conclusion of the Aga Khan's visit: "Satan see God out?" To this question, "reverently" posed, Clemens allegedly answered "yes," and then "these mis-mated Beings passed from view — Satan in the lead and The Other following after."

The Clemenses paid Satan forty rupees a month, then about twelve dollars, today about $220. Because the employment was transient, he received far more than he would have earned from British residents, who paid only twenty rupees for servants such as butlers, cooks, and valets, and as little as four to seven rupees for menials such as sweepers and garden hands. On these stipends, servants were expected to keep themselves and their families. The Clemenses, who did not need to house or feed their Indian servants, paid in addition to salaries only the servants' transportation.

Clemens, appalled by the population's low per capita income, wrote that a farmhand supported his family on little more than one dollar a month, about eighteen dollars in today's terms. The farm family "live in a mud hut, hand-made, and, doubtless, rent-free," he said, "and they wear no clothes; at least nothing more than a rag. And not much of a rag at that, in the case of the males." Consider what these facts mean, Clemens asked his readers. India's "stupendous population consists of farm-laborers . . . India is one vast farm — one almost interminable stretch of fields with mud fences between. Think of the above facts; and consider what an incredible aggregate of poverty they place before you."

Although India during the past one hundred years has increased its average life expectancy, reduced its fertility rate, and improved its ability to feed itself, it is still a country of extreme poverty. One hundred dollars per month is a middle-class salary. Almost one-third of the population are classified as "food-insecure," only one failed monsoon away from starvation, and a great number are hungry, always hungry, hungry every day. People live on the streets, die from starvation on the streets, send their children — sometimes intentionally maimed — to beg on the streets.

Clemens did not need to leave Bombay to sample India's poverty. On Monday, January 27, he drove late at night to an opulent Hindu betrothal ceremony. He had already performed an *At Home* that evening, then spoken at the Bombay Club, whose members had conferred an honorary membership upon him and entertained him at supper, and finally had picked up Mrs. Clemens and Clara from a ball at the Royal Bombay Yacht Club, now the Atomic Energy Agency. After the Clemenses "had pierced deep into the native quarter and were threading its narrow dim lanes," the driver had to take care not to run over the hundreds of sleeping forms, wrapped in blankets and stretched out upon the ground. Occasionally, swarms of rats scurried across the horses' path. At both sides of the lane, petty merchants and their families slept motionless on the counters of their open booths or sheds, faintly lit by flickering oil lamps. The scene reminded Clemens of corpses, sepulchers, and death-lamps, "a prophetic dream, as it were," of the rat-borne plague that would soon devastate Bombay.

After driving along dim, narrow lanes strewn with sleeping forms, the Clemenses, according to *Following the Equator*, finally rounded a corner to find the home of a rich Hindu cotton merchant who had invited them to a marriage celebration. The house was "wrapped in a perfect conflagration of illuminations — mainly gaswork designs, gotten up specially for the occasion. Within was abundance of brilliancy — flames, costumes, colors, decorations, mirrors — it was another Aladdin show."

Clara remembered their traveling first to the bridegroom's house, where they were garlanded with flowers before walking in procession to the party for the bride. According to Clara, the bride was twelve years old and the groom, already a widower, was twenty. The bride's grandmother was only thirty-eight. Clemens was moved, reported his daughter, by the helplessness of the tiny bride.

Before the Clemenses left the festivities, they were approached by "a turbaned giant," who invited Clemens, on behalf of the Gaekwar of Baroda, to perform for His Highness. The Gaekwar, wrote Clemens in his journal, "is the stunningest of the Indian Princes except the Nizam."

The Arabian Nights splendor that captivated Clemens can still be glimpsed in Bombay. Many of the superb structures survive, including the prodigiously ornate Victoria Terminus, whose entrance is still guarded by a lion and a tiger. Women's garments still create "perfect flower-beds of brilliant color"; great crowds still form a "shining and shifting spectacle"; and burlap-shrouded figures still stretch out upon the sidewalks of the night.

Chapter Twenty-eight

*C*LEMENS'S PERFORMANCE IN POONA, on January 29, 1896, displeased the Bishop of Bombay. Forbidden fruit, Clemens said in a favorite routine, had always been as attractive to him as it had been to Adam. Everyone else likes it, too. Never in his travels had he found a place in which the apple Adam ate would have been safe — except Poona! The local reference, changed of course for each town, always raised a shout of laughter. Adam only ate the apple, Clemens continued, because it was forbidden, just as everyone else has been doing ever since. "The misfortune was that it wasn't the serpent that was forbidden, because then Adam would have eaten the serpent, and there would have been no more trouble." The Bishop of Bombay left the hall.

A listener who stayed to the end was the fourteen-year-old Miss J. M. Cursetjee, a member of an old and progressive Parsi family. Sixty-eight years later, in 1964, she told an interviewer what she remembered. The audience was mainly European, she said, and mainly male. Poona was an army town, and the hall was "splashed" by the red jackets of British soldiers. She didn't remember Mark Twain's physical appearance except that it was "insignificant," at least to an adolescent girl hoping to see someone handsome. The only unusual aspect of his looks was his "untidy" hair. In those days, she explained, people were taught the importance of tidiness. But once he began to talk, "you forgot about his untidy hair — and you were even apologetic about having had this first impression of him."

The native quarter of Poona, in which Miss Cursetjee presumably lived at the time of Clemens's performance, looked like "a village tenanted by people in very squalid circumstances," according to an Indian writer whose description was published in *The Times of India*. In contrast, the British residential quarters were characterized by "fine, wide, shaded roads, nice bungalows, and lovely gardens."

The British cantonment was no different from the native town, however, in its susceptibility to the flu, which was ravaging the Indians
and the British alike. According to one British resident, the epidemic was not an abnormal state of affairs "but a continuous and
ever-increasing evil." In addition, the town was noted for endemic
typhoid.

This insalubrious place, about eighty-five miles southeast of
Bombay, was the setting for the eleventh annual meeting of the
Indian National Congress, at the end of December, one month
before Clemens's appearance. The Congress had begun ten years
before as the representative of the new and minuscule middle class.
A modern education had given these men a common language —
English — and common values, attitudes, and interests, enabling
them to work with one another and to look at India as a whole. They
resented the government's manipulation of tariffs, the use of Indian
troops for imperial adventures, and the exclusion of Indians from
high office. They were outraged by the failure of a proposal to equal-
ize the mandates of Indian and European judges in Bengal, which
would have permitted Indian judges to try Europeans without a jury.
Resentment, outrage, and nascent nationalism led to the formation
of the Indian National Congress in 1885.

It began modestly, with only seventy delegates at its first session, which declared the Congress's loyalty and gratitude to the
Crown. But the Congress quickly spread all over India, and by the
end of the century it had become the government's chief opposition.
Sixteen hundred delegates and 4,000 observers attended the 1895
Poona conference, which, among numerous resolutions, demanded
that the government reduce its military and administrative
expenses, demanded that military expenses on the frontiers of India
be shared equally with Britain, demanded that the gag order on the
press in princely states be dropped, and protested the salt tax as a
regressive burden on the poor. The Congress in 1895, according to
its president, demanded "modest reforms," with the aims of assist-
ing rather than revolutionizing the government. Those aims were
soon to change. It was the Congress, under the leadership of Gandhi
and Nehru, that led India to independence.

At the end of his stay in India, a reporter asked Clemens if he
had heard of the Indian National Congress. "Well, I have read of it,

here a little and there a little, and all I can understand is that the men composing it, want a little more independence than they now have." He knew little of their aims, he said, but he was impressed by their proficiency in English. "There is, however, one good quality they lack as a nation — I believe they like to be called a 'nation' — and that is, inventive genius in the various practical arts."

Clemens showed little sympathy for the nationalist movement. No one, he told a reporter in Calcutta, "can deny the obvious advantages which the British have conferred on India. When one looks at the industrial and educational activity which has been set in motion all over the country, and when one considers its security and prosperity one cannot help coming to the conclusion that the British Government is the best for India, whether the Hindus or Mohamedans like it or not." One can argue, perhaps, that Clemens wanted to ingratiate himself with potential audiences, but later he said much the same thing in *Following the Equator*, where his attitude reflected the British point of view. For example, when discussing the great uprising of 1857, he called it a "mutiny," as the British did; he emphasized British heroism and Indian atrocities; and he ignored the appalling British reprisals. He wrote that India was lucky to be ruled by Britain: "When one considers what India was under her Hindu and Mohammedan rulers, and what she is now; when he remembers the miseries of her millions then and the protections and humanities which they enjoy now, he must concede that the most fortunate thing that has ever befallen that empire was the establishment of British supremacy there."

Clemens did not, however, believe in "the white man's burden," or in claims that colonization would "civilize" the ruled. "We are obliged to believe," he wrote in connection with the transportation of convicts to Australia, "that a nation that could look on, unmmoved, and see starving or freezing women hanged for stealing twenty-six cents' worth of bacon or rags, and boys snatched from their mothers, and men from their families, and sent to the other side of the world for long terms of years for similar trifling offenses, was a nation to whom the term 'civilized' could not in any large way be applied. And we must also believe that a nation that knew, during more than forty years, what was happening to those exiles and was still content with it, was not advancing in any showy way toward a higher grade of civilization." Nonetheless, he supported the Raj.

His support seems inconsistent with his contempt for claims of cultural superiority. It also appears inconsistent with the sympathy he expressed throughout *Following the Equator* for victims of colonial rapacity, cruelty, and hypocrisy: South Seas islanders, shanghaied and enslaved for work in the plantations of Queensland; Maoris and Australian aborigines, whose land was stolen from them; Tasmanian aborigines, who were exterminated; the Mashonas and Matabeles, who were robbed of their land and their cattle in Rhodesia; even the hotel servant in Bombay, cuffed by an arrogant manager. Where, then, was his sympathy for Indian independence?

Perhaps one reason Clemens showed no support for the Indian national movement was that it was still small, weak, and confined to a microscopic minority, whereas the British Empire was at its zenith, far too strong for such an unrepresentative minority to challenge it. As one Hindu commentator put it at the time, "appealing to the British nation at this stage of our political development is like steering a ship straight for a rock." Furthermore, European powers were continuing to seize territories in Africa, Asia, and Oceania, which may have made the partitioning of the globe among the powers of Europe seem inevitable. "In our day," wrote Clemens, "land-robbery, claim-jumping, is become a European governmental frenzy. Some have been hard at it in the borders of China, in Burma, in Siam, and the islands of the sea; and *all* have been at it in Africa. Africa has been as coolly divided up and portioned out among the gang as if they had bought it and paid for it." Clemens, who admired the English, probably believed that a target of imperialism was better off under British administration than it would be under that of a rival colonial power, particularly the French. In the case of Madagascar, for example, which the French invaded when the Clemenses were traveling around the world, Clemens scolded the British. England should have taken Madagascar from the French. "Without an effort she could have saved those harmless natives from the calamity of French civilization, and she did not do it. Now it is too late."

Although Britain ran the Indian empire for its own advantage, and although British civil servants in India were often serenely condescending, the administration was reasonably competent and honest, and the security of persons and property reasonably high. While the government's large-scale construction of roads, canals, and railroads benefited the British, these ambitious public works, especially the railroads, helped the local population as well. Except for repressing thuggee, the ritual strangulation of travelers by a murderous sect, and outlawing suttee, the self-immolation of Hindu widows upon their husbands' funeral pyres (Clemens wrote about both in *Following the Equator*), the British permitted the free exercise of religion. The mass of the population, ruled arbitrarily for millennia, often by foreign powers, accepted their yoke as they had always done, hoping that their overlords would maintain order and security and not levy taxes too hard to bear, criteria that the British satisfied as well as if not better than former rulers. Western notions of nationalism and representative government had not yet reached the Indian masses. In the meantime, if they had to be ruled by strangers, they could do worse than be ruled by the British, who placed all of India under a single administration for the first time in Indian history, and maintained security and stability.

Finally, Clemens may have viewed the congeries of peoples, languages, religions, and castes that constituted India as too diverse to work together for a common cause. Particularly striking was the animosity between Hindus and Muslims. An editorial in a Muslim paper, appearing shortly before Clemens's performance in Poona, declared that the two communities "live in a fever pitch of constant tension of feelings." A week later, a column in that paper accused the Congress of representing "only the Hindu element" and denied the possibility that Muslims and Hindus could unify their interests. "If the Hindus, who are so much better off, seek to enlist our cooperation, it must be because they think they can keep all the rewards to themselves." All things considered, Clemens's indifference toward Indian nationalism is understandable.

When Clemens was in India, in 1896, few could have foreseen that within only fifty-one years, within Clara's lifetime, the world's most powerful country would shrink to a second-class power and quit India; that India would be partitioned into Hindu India and Muslim Pakistan; that as a consequence millions of people would uproot themselves to flee from one state to the other; and that during their flight, tens of thousands would be raped and hundreds of thousands massacred, their corpses strewn along dirt roads and in bloodied railroad carriages. If those achievements and those horrors were hard to foresee, it was even harder to believe that it would be intangibles — the English language, the rule of law, a modern administration, and democratic political institutions — that would be the most important legacies of the British in India.

Chapter Twenty-nine

AFTER A HALF-DAY IN BOMBAY, the Clemenses took the night train to Baroda (now Vadodara), about 260 miles northeast. In *Following the Equator*, Clemens described the spectacle of the railway station, where it seemed to him "as if the whole world was present — half of it inside, the other half outside, and both halves, bearing mountainous head-loads of bedding and other freight, trying simultaneously to pass each other, in opposing floods, in one narrow door." The few Europeans he saw were accompanied by servants, each of whom "seemed to have put aside his natural gentleness for the time and invested himself with the white man's privilege of making a way for himself by promptly shoving all intervening black things out of it." Inside the station, "tides upon tides of rainbow-costumed natives swept along, this way and that, in massed and bewildering confusion," while in the midst of this commotion groups of travelers sat on "the bare stone floor . . . with their humble bundles and baskets and small household gear about them, and patiently waited." One hundred years later the scene is much the same, although white travelers are more likely to be walking in the space cleared for them by a travel agency's representative than by a personal servant, if a space has been cleared at all.

In addition to Satan, the Clemens party employed a second man, Barney. "We named him Barney for short; for we couldn't use his real name, there wasn't time." Like Satan, Barney helped with the party's luggage, including bedding. The party — probably Mrs. Clemens and Clara — had earlier attended to the purchase of blankets and pillows and bed linen, which they would need not only in the sleeping berths of trains, but in most of their hotels. Clemens explained, in *Following the Equator*, that the custom of traveling with your own bedding, even when visiting a private home, was a survival from the times before the construction of railroads and hotels, when travelers were obliged to carry their own bedding or do without it. Today you no longer have to travel with a bedroll, but if you want bed linen for your sleeping-car berth, you must reserve it when you book your ticket or before you board your train. However, you will find sheets, blankets, and pillows at your hotel.

The party had taken two connecting compartments, one for Mrs. Clemens and Clara, the other for Clemens and Smythe. Each compartment could sleep four — there was a wide leather-covered shelf that was folded up out of the way during the day, above each of two wide leather sofas — but according to Clemens the party generally traveled in India with only two persons to a compartment. A row of blue-tinted plate glass windows, which could be let down to encourage a breeze, ran along the length of each sofa. Although the compartment was "built of the plainest and cheapest partially smoothed boards, with a coating of dull paint on them," Clemens found it a "handsome, spacious, light, airy, homelike place," in which he could "walk up and down, or sit and write, or stretch out and read and smoke." He told a Calcutta reporter that "the American sleeping-car is a model of luxury and magnificence; in the Indian car there is not a suggestion of either, yet the Indian carriage is more comfortable."

The Clemenses' sleeping-car arrangements were not without annoyances. Passengers could reserve a lower berth, but they received no tangible evidence of their reservation. Clemens explained that "the word 'engaged' appears on the window, but it doesn't state who the compartment is engaged *for*. If your Satan and your Barney arrive before somebody else's servants, and spread the bedding on the two sofas and then stand guard till you come, all will be well; but if they step aside on an errand, they may find the beds promoted to the two shelves, and somebody else's demons standing guard over their masters' beds, which in the mean time have been spread upon your sofas." A small closet in each compartment contained washing facilities — Clemens mentioned a washbowl and a place to hang towels (brought by the traveler), but there was probably also a pitcher of water and a chamber pot or open hole.

The compartments Clemens described were more spacious than the sleeping cars found today, which substitute electric lights for oil lamps, air conditioning for a natural breeze, and unopenable windows, often opaque with grime, for blue-tinted windows that can be lowered and raised.

At seven in the morning, the light still gray, the Clemenses arrived in Baroda, where, according to Clara, they were met at the station by the "prince's carriage drawn by picture-book horses with glossy, arched necks" and staffed by three footmen. After breakfast the Clemenses were shown the town, with its ancient houses and crowded bazaars, and then the Gaeikwar's flamboyant, lavish new palace, which Clemens derided as "mixed modern American-European ... wholly foreign to India, and impudent and out of place," in contrast to the old palace, where Clemens performed, which was "Oriental and charming, and in consonance with the country." The Clemenses were also shown the elephant stables. In his journal, Clemens noted the elephants, their gold and silver ornaments, their insanely costly howdahs, and their closeness to a village of complete destitution.

He accepted an invitation to ride on an elephant. "I did not ask for it," he explained in *Following the Equator*, "and didn't want it; but I took it, because otherwise they would have thought I was afraid, which I was." Many years later, Clara wrote that she found the sight of her father atop an elephant irresistably funny. "Father, suspecting what I was giggling about, said, 'What are you laughing at, you sassmill?'" The Clemenses were shown two ceremonial cannon, one gold, the other silver, for firing salutes, but Clemens complained to his journal that his hosts had failed to show them the Jewel House, although it was only five minutes away. "It is claimed here that no monarch in the world can match this mass of magnificence."

Clemens performed in the great hall of the old palace before an audience of two or three hundred guests. Clemens found the hall unsuitable for public speaking "on account of the echoes, but it is a good place to hold durbars in and regulate the affairs of a kingdom, and that is what it is for. If I had it I would have a durbar [a ruler's public audience] every day, instead of once or twice a year." But he didn't need a lofty hall. He held court wherever he found ready listeners, from an immense auditorium with an audience of thousands to a hotel room with a single newspaper reporter.

The Gaekwar, according to Clemens, was fluent in English and "a fine and cultivated gentleman." At the time of their meeting, Sir

Sayaji Rao III was thirty-two years old. The ruler of a principality long famous, in Clemens's words, "for its barbaric pomps and splendors, and for the wealth of its princes," he was the son of a humble farmer when he was elevated to the throne at the age of twelve. His predecessor had been deposed by the Viceroy for gross mismanagement (in addition to oppressing his subjects, the deposed Gaekwar, who had been wisely kept in jail by his predecessor, was suspected of attempting to poison the British resident). With the throne now vacant, the widowed sister-in-law of the deposed ruler was permitted to adopt an heir from among the descendants of former Gaekwars. The heir, found in a mud village, was educated by an English tutor while a regent administered the state for eight years. The result, according to a contemporary British source, was a success: "the Gaekwar has shown himself a model prince, and his territories became as well governed and prosperous as a British district."

This model prince gave Clemens the impression, Clara reported, that India was dissatisfied with its British rulers and would never be content until it was wholly independent. The memoirs of Aga Khan III confirm this impression. For the Gaekwar, he said, "India always came first." In a conversation during the summer of 1908, the Gaekwar told him that "the first thing you'll have to do when the English are gone is to get rid of all these rubbishy States. I tell you, there'll never be an Indian nation until this so-called Princely Order disappears." And of course it did disappear. Lord Mountbatten, India's last viceroy, persuaded almost all the princes to sign deeds of accession, mainly with India, which promised to give them considerable autonomy as well as financial guarantees, promises that were broken within a few decades. The "rubbishy States" are gone, but thanks to those enterprising princes who have converted their palaces into hotels, you can glimpse the splendors if not the barbaric pomps of one hundred years ago.

Chapter Thirty

*C*LEMENS SLEPT ALL THE WAY from Baroda to Bombay, arriving at seven on Saturday morning, February 1, 1896. He then took himself to the Bombay Club, which had made him an honorary member. After drinking a cup of coffee and reading the paper in a small breakfast room there, he asked for the bill, only to be brought another cup of coffee. Each time he requested the bill, he was given more coffee. Failing to make the various waiters he approached understand what he wanted, it occurred to him that they mistook him for an intruder and were pacifying him with coffee until they could find a club officer to deal with him.

"It was a delicate situation," as he later described the episode, which Mrs. Clemens persuaded him to delete from his travel book. "It was embarrassing to stay, & it was embarrassing to try to go. On the whole, I thought I would try to go." Finally he learned that because the club president had ordered that he not be allowed to pay for anything, none of the waiters would present a bill. "It is wonderful, the grip that the natives have upon their solemnity. Without a doubt they would have seen me sit there & pray for the bill & drink coffee until it ran out of my ears, & never have betrayed by a smile that they were not used to that inhuman spectacle every day."

The Clemenses left Bombay that night for the two-and-a-half-day trip to Allahabad, about 750 miles northeast. They traveled through a great plain, "perfectly flat, dust-colored and brick-yardy," relieved by "scattering bunches of trees and mud villages," Clemens wrote in *Following the Equator*. He noted in his journal that "all the way yesterday was through parched land, sown thick with mud villages in all stages of crumbling decay. It is a sorrowful land — a land of unimaginable poverty and hardship." Although the Indian countryside is not beautiful, he wrote in his travel book, "there is an enchantment about it that is beguiling, and does not pall," because you sense its history, the millions who have been born, grown old, and died there, "the barren and meaningless process" that has repeated itself generation after generation, century after century, and "gives to this forlorn, uncomely land power to speak to the spirit and make friends with it; to speak to it with a voice bitter with satire, but eloquent with melancholy."

They arrived Monday morning, February 3, at Allahabad, where Clemens performed that evening to a sold-out house. Everyone seemed to arrive at the hall in a private carriage, each with its white-turbaned footmen and driver. According to Clemens, this was true of most Indian cities, where Europeans did not walk even short distances: "the vicinity of a lecture-hall looks like a snowstorm, and makes the lecturer feel like an opera." As for his performance, a reviewer wrote "that it is hardly fair to Mark Twain or his audiences that his remarks should have been so fully reported, and yet the charm of his delivery is so delightful that no one who hears him could wish to have been content with the report."

The next day, in the light of the early morning, the Clemenses drove about three miles to the huge fort built by the first Mogul emperor, Akbar, three hundred years earlier. Inside the fort they saw a polished stone pillar, thirty-four feet high, erected by the Emperor Asoka more than two hundred years before the current era, engraved with edicts promoting Buddhism. In Clemens's time as at present, a Hindu temple occupied an underground corner of the fort. "And now the Fort belongs to the English," he wrote in *Following the Equator*, "it contains a Christian Church. Insured in all the companies."

The Asokan pillar still stands inside the fort, now occupied by the Indian army, but it is difficult to see. Save for the area occupied by the underground Hindu temple, the fort is off-limits to visitors, although passes in theory can be obtained by those who are patient.

The fort stands at the confluence or *sangam* of three rivers, the blue Jamuna, the brown Ganges, and the unseen, mythical Saraswati, the river of enlightenment. Hindus regard river confluences as auspicious places, and none more so than the sacred sangam at Allahabad, where pilgrims in their hundreds of thousands come to its annual religious fair, the Magh Mela, from mid-January to mid-

February. As the Clemenses drove out to the fort, they found the road crowded with pilgrims, some of them months on the way, "plodding patiently along in the heat and dust, worn, poor, hungry, but supported and sustained by an unwavering faith and belief." Only a few great souls among "our kind of people, the cold whites," he wrote, would sacrifice themselves to the same extent. "Still, we all talk self-sacrifice, and this makes me hope that we are large enough to honor it in the Hindu." Clemens was, according to Clara, "amazed at the intense atmosphere of spirituality in all classes of people" that he found in India.

The entire 1,500-mile course of the Ganges, or Ganga, as it is properly called, is sacred to Hindus, from its source in the Himalayas to its delta at the Bay of Bengal. Hindus, who believe it fell from heaven to earth and who venerate it as goddess and mother, bathe in it and drink it, especially at such holy sites as Allahabad. They cup the water in their hands and pour it back as an offering to gods and ancestors. They decorate it with floating garlands. In the evening they float small oil-filled lamps upon it. They pour its water into brass vessels that they carry home, often miles away. They bathe in it as newlyweds after their long wedding rites. They consign to it the ashes of their dead.

From the fort, the Clemenses looked down upon "a mighty swarm of pilgrims" and upon the "towns of tents . . . with a multitude of fluttering pennons," which occupied a curving spit between the Ganges and the Jamuna. Below, crowds were buying from merchants' booths; devotees were bathing, praying, and drinking the waters; sick pilgrims were being carried in palanquins; ascetic mendicants, some naked and smeared with ash, were mortifying their bodies.

"If we had got to the Mele this morning," Clemens wrote in his journal, "we might have seen a man who hasn't sat down for years; another who has held his hands above his head for years and never trims his nails or hair, both very long; another who sits with his bare foot resting upon a lot of sharp spikes — and all for the glory of God. Human beings seem to be a poor invention. If they are the noblest work of God where is the ignoblest?" The annual fair continues to attract pilgrims in their hundreds of thousands, along with the impressive variety of religious ascetics for which the Magh Mela is especially known.

That afternoon, after their visit to the fort, the Clemenses boarded a train for an even holier city on the Ganges, Benares (now Varanasi), about eighty-five miles southeast. Later, a two-hour wait to change trains proved too short for Clemens. A long interval in a railroad station is usually a dull affair, he commented in *Following the Equator*, but not so in India, where "you have the monster crowd of bejeweled natives, the stir, the bustle, the confusion, the shifting splendors of the costumes — dear me, the delight of it, the charm of it are beyond speech." On the same day he noted in his journal that he had thought such sights would become commonplace after a week, but three weeks had only made them more fascinating. "I think I should always like to wait an hour for my train in India."

After they alighted from their railway carriage, the Clemenses drove through the outskirts of Benares to reach their hotel, through "a vision of dusty sterility, decaying temples, crumbling tombs, broken mud walls, shabby huts," as Clemens described the scene. "The whole region seems to ache with age and penury. It must take ten thousand years of want to produce such an aspect." Indeed, Benares is one of the oldest continuously inhabited cities in the world, not ten thousand years old, like Jericho, but as old as Athens, as old as Jerusalem.

The Clemenses drove to the British Civil Lines, where they found their hotel, today the slightly dilapidated Hotel de Paris, a gracious structure of high ceilings and arched colonnades. For some reason the Clemenses preferred its annex, about a mile away, a large compound with a great peepul tree in which a monkey lived, perhaps because they could take one of the bungalows there for themselves. The compound now offers budget accommodations to Western travelers. One bungalow in the compound, we are informed, is at least one hundred years old; it may have housed the Clemenses. They would, perhaps, be amused by its present incarnation as petrol station, car-repair works, astrologer-palmist's office, and perfume shop. Soaring above the compound is a nearby telecommunications tower, tapered like an enormous minaret, overshadowing the compound's great tree, which no longer houses a monkey.

"Benares is older than history," Clemens wrote, "older than tradition, older even than legend, and looks twice as old as all of them put together." It is old because its religious significance has kept it alive. Whereas Greeks no longer worship Zeus and Jews no longer make temple sacrifices, tens of thousands of Hindus dip themselves daily in the Ganges at Benares and light fires along its banks to Lord Shiva. Although Lord Shiva is present everywhere and in everyone, he is thought to live with special intensity in Benares.

Hindus call Benares *Kashi,* which means "luminous." At Benares, the City of Light, the world was created and time began. Those fortunate enough to die in Benares attain transcendance, liberation from an unending cycle of reincarnation. So holy is Benares that the fruit of any ritual action there is magnified: in Benares a modest offering to a priest matches a costly gift elsewhere; in Benares fasting for several nights is equal to the abstentions of several lifetimes elsewhere. When pilgrims arrive in Benares, they touch its dust to their foreheads in acknowledgment of the city's sanctity. "Religion," wrote Clemens, "is the *business* of Benares," a statement which is still true, for the town's economy continues to be dependent on pilgrimage and tourism.

"Benares is the sacredest of sacred cities," he wrote. "The moment you step across the sharply defined line which separates it from the rest of the globe, you stand upon ineffably and unspeakably holy ground." Hindus' veneration for Benares, he thought, "makes our own religious enthusiasm seem pale and cold."

Since he understood the religious significance of Benares, it is disconcerting to read his "little itinerary for the pilgrim," an ironic guide to the city, where "every conceivable earthly and heavenly good is procurable under one roof, so to speak — a sort of Army and Navy Stores, theologically stocked." Three examples convey the itinerary's flavor: to protect yourself from fever, you must walk halfway down a flight of steps to "a tank filled with sewage. Drink as much of it as you want"; or to regain your youth, you must visit a temple in which "you will find a shallow pool of stagnant sewage. It smells like the best limburger cheese, and is filthy with the washings of rotting lepers, but that is nothing, bathe in it; bathe in it gratefully and worshipfully"; or to record your five-day pilgrimage by foot around the sacred city, you must go to a temple, where "you will see a Brahman who will attend to the matter and take the money. If he should forget to collect the money, you can remind him."

Clemens's "little itinerary" provides an implicit contrast between the physical Benares — decaying, foul, and venal — and the spiritual Benares, where to the pilgrim every step is holy, but you squirm at its lack of respect for what is sacred to others. Were the Hindu to lose his religion, Clemens wrote, "he would gain much — release from his slavery to two million gods and twenty million priests, fakirs, holy mendicants, and other sacred bacilli." Of course, Clemens was not writing for an audience schooled in political correctness, an audience sensitive to the sensibilities of others, but to Eurocentric readers awash in the high tide of colonialism. For example, fifteen years later his biographer found the pilgrim's itinerary "about the best thing in the book." And it must be remembered that Clemens's view of Christianity was scarcely more flattering. His description of the Christian holy places in Palestine, in *The Innocents Abroad*, is as irreverent as his treatment of the holy places in Benares.

Clemens relied on conversations with the Reverend Mr. Arthur Parker, who may have accompanied the Clemenses for part of their time in Benares, and on Parker's *Guide to Benares* for information about the city and its holy places. Parker was one of a small group of Christian missionaries — Clemens mentioned five Protestant missions — who had gathered in Benares and opened schools and clinics there, perhaps in hopes that if they could convert the Benarsis, residents of that most holy of Hindu holy cities, other Hindus would surely follow the Benarsis' example. As one nineteenth-century missionary wrote, "the news would soon spread that Hinduism was drying up at its fountain, and that its power could not much longer be maintained." Is it too great a dream, he asked, that "the Brahmans of Benares, accepting Jesus as their Saviour, will go forth with His Gospel to diffuse it far and wide among the nations of India, and then, with their converts, make their way to the remotest East?" As a modern ethnographer of Benares has commented, little did the missionaries dream "that when the brahmins of Banaras went forth, it would be to the West, and they would teach Indian music, Vedanta philosophy, Ayurvedic medicine, Hindu meditation, and yogic exercises to the many millions in Europe and America who would appreciate their message."

Clemens mocked Hindu practices but not Hindu spirituality. Clara reported that when he saw the masses of worshipers at the Ganges, he cried out, "they spend hours like this while we in America are robbing and murdering."

He was moved by his meeting in Benares with a famous Hindu holy man, Sri Swami Bhaskara Nand Saraswati. "We went to see a recluse," Clemens later told a reporter in Calcutta, "a man who is worshiped for his holiness from one end of India to the other." Clemens showed the interviewer a photograph of the saint, sitting cross-legged and miminally clothed. "Yes," said Clemens, "that man started with a grand head on his shoulders, and after thinking and reading and improving upon his original advantages he came to the conclusion that the greatest object in life is — that." Clemens pointed to the photograph of the nearly naked ascetic, "but neither in mockery nor contempt," reported the interviewer. "It may surprise his many readers, but when Mark Twain is serious he is very serious."

Clemens stood at the hermit's hut and wondered why the swami was worshiped. "Suddenly a man came up who had travelled thousands of miles for this very object. As soon as he approached near enough he prostrated himself in the dust and kissed the saint's foot. I had never realised till then what it was to stand in the presence of a divinity. Because he is a divinity. Not even an angel. At the age of seventeen, I am told he renounced his family ties, and embraced the asceticism in which he has lived these forty years and over." The reporter asked him if the saint's austerities were reflected in his talk or in his visible behavior. Not at all, Clemens replied. "It is just as though you had taken a very fine, learned, intellectual man, say a member of the Indian Government, and unclothed him. There he is. He is minus the trappings of civilization. He hasn't a rag on his back. But he has perfect manners, a ready wit, and a turn for conversation through an interpreter . . . We traded autographs. I said I had heard of him, and he said he had heard of me. Gods lie sometimes, I expect."

In *Following the Equator*, Clemens transformed the holy man's hut into "a good house in a noble great garden" and the anonymous devotee into a raja. Possibly Clemens's regard for the dedicated religious life, which he stated in his travel book, was similarly inflated, but it rings true. He appeared to respect the swami's disciple, Mina Bahadur Rana, who had, according to Clemens, abandoned a distinguished career "to live in a hut and study the sacred writings and meditate upon virtue and holiness and seek to attain them." The disciple believed that "this was not an idle and foolish waste of his life, but a most worthy and honorable employment of it." Many who revere Christian scholars who are similarly employed, Clemens wrote, will view Mina Bahadur Rana as a crank. "But I shall not. He has my reverence. And I don't offer it as a common thing and poor, but as an unusual thing and of value." It costs nothing, he continued, to revere "one's own sacred things . . . But the reverence which is difficult, and which has personal merit in it, is the respect which you pay, without compulsion, to the political or religious attitude of a man whose beliefs are not yours. You can't revere his gods or his politics, and no one expects you to do that, but you could respect his belief in them if you tried hard enough; and you could respect *him*, too, if you tried hard enough. But it is very, very difficult; it is next to impossible, and so we hardly ever try."

On Wednesday, February 5, the day after they arrived in Benares, the Clemenses arose at six in order to see the sights of the city. It rises from the western bank of the Ganges and sweeps in a great northward curve for over three miles along the riverbank, fifty to seventy-five feet above the water. The bluff is magnificent, blanketed from top to bottom with palaces, temples, shrines, ashrams, pavilions, and hostels, "a splendid jumble of massive and picturesque masronry," Clemens wrote, "a bewildering and beautiful confusion." Long flights of stone steps lead from narrow lanes at the top of the bluff down to more than seventy landing platforms from which Hindus enter the water, a daily rite for the city's residents and the first act of the pilgrim.

"We made the usual trip up and down the river," Clemens reported, "seated in chairs under an awning on the deck of the usual commodious hand-propelled ark." Let us hope that they started their river trip in time to see the sunrise from the river, although if

Clemens's memory of rising at six was correct, they may have been too late.

Alice and I rose at five-thirty this morning to meet a taxi that, after a twenty-minute drive, has deposited us at a point within a five-minute walk of the landing platform where we are to meet our boatman. The driver leads us now on foot along lanes only wide enough for rickshaws. The narrow ways, lined by numerous temples and linga, simple stone shafts that are Shiva's symbol, are so absorbing that it's hard to watch your step along the broken surfaces, which are littered with sewage, refuse, and cow patties. Cattle saunter insouciantly, munching on garbage, their tails swishing against your trousers. When asked if he had to make way for the Brahmani bulls in Benares, Clemens responded, "Well, yes. I will make room for a bull any time."

As we step into our rowboat, the river is pearly pink. When the sun suddenly appears above the clouds at the horizon, the river turns to rose and the splendid jumble of massive and picturesque masonry along the bluff turns to dull gold, the City of Light glowing in reflected light.

We ask our boatman if the hand-propelled canopied boats of Clemens's day are still afloat, for we haven't seen any. Yes, he tells us, there are a few, but he prefers to supply his clients with umbrellas to protect them from the sun. Awnings impede photography, he says. As we approach one of the two main platforms on which corpses are cremated, foreign tourists in a riverboat are boldly and shamelessly videotaping, with long-distance lenses, the smoke rising from a funeral pyre and the praying mourners circling its fire. Unfortunately, none of the photographers falls into the river. After the wood has been consumed by fire, the ashes of the departed will be added to the water.

Each year about 40,000 traditional riverside funerals are held at Benares. The corpses of those too poor to afford a traditional funeral are simply thrown into the river, perhaps three thousand a year. To reduce this number, as well as the amount of bone and flesh incompletely consumed by traditional burning but nonetheless entrusted to the river, the government has introduced an electric crematorium on one of the two main burning platforms. These funerals, which cost about one-twentieth of a traditional funeral, have become popular.

Modern technology, however, is inadequate to the task of cleaning up the Ganges, into which more than one hundred cities dump their raw sewage and where, at Benares, the fecal-coliform count sometimes reaches 340,000 times the acceptable level. The expensive wastewater plants that the government has built along the river are unsuitable for Indian conditions, where the electricity supply is uncertain, where the plants are overwhelmed during the monsoon, and where many cities are unable to afford their maintenance. A more appropriate and less costly sustainable technology is now being considered: a system of ponds in which waste decomposes naturally through bacterial action and photosynthesis.

In an interview in Calcutta, Clemens commented upon the filthy state of the river, in the context of caste restrictions. "The subject of caste," he said, "seems to me a great mystery . . . When I am told that this man will not drink out of that man's *lota*, because if he does so he will be defiled — these are simply so many words to me. I can't grasp the idea. When, again, you say that the man with a special cord round his neck is a Brahmin, and twice born, and that because of the cord and what it implies he is to be grovelled before, I ask how is it? And I can't for the life of me imagine. When, too, I see a Hindu — the very man, perhaps, who fears defilement so much through the other man's *lota* — when I see him going down to the muddy, filthy Ganges, and washing himself in and drinking out of water only fifteen yards away from where a dead body is lying — I can't help thinking he is at least sincere."

Muddy and filthy as Clemens found the Ganges, it was cleaner than European rivers of comparable size. Experiments by Mr. E. H. Hankin, a Fellow of St. John's College, Cambridge, whom Clemens was to meet in Agra, had recently shown that in spite of the corpses thrown into the Ganges and the Jamuna and in spite of the sewage emptied there, those rivers were from one hundred to three hundred times safer than the Elbe at Hamburg. The Indian rivers were purer, he explained, because microbes were killed by intense sunlight acting at high temperatures and because of the small percentage of organic matter in the rivers, which were chiefly made up of melted snow from the Himalayas. He found that some Indian wells, in contrast, were hideously polluted. At Allahabad, for example, he found 90,000 microbes per centimeter in water distant from the Ganges, whereas in the river itself he found 360 microbes. Since one hundred microbes per centimeter was considered safe to drink, Ganges water was dangerous at Allahabad. But he found the Ganges safe at other locations, including Benares, with only six per centimeter. If his figures were correct, today's river pollution is many times greater than it was one hundred years ago, not surprising in view of India's great increase in population and industrialization. As for his comparison with European rivers, it is unlikely that residents of Hamburg, then as now, would have drunk from the Elbe.

As our boatman rows us down the river, Brahmins seated upon the platforms offer blessings to the faithful, while bathers — serene, eyes closed, reciting prayers — purify themselves. Men and women, old and young, well built and flabby, their wet skin glistening, all manage their ablutions with modesty. One older man, perhaps aware that the spiritually cleansing river is frighteningly unsafe, holds his nose as his head disappears beneath the water.

Chapter Thirty-one

CLEMENS WROTE TO ROGERS from Benares, "I have been barking around on the platform (troublesome cough), in Bombay, Poona, Baroda, etc., for a week or so, but now at last I've got my health and voice back in time for Calcutta — we leave for there to-morrow." During the seventeen-and-a-half-hour railway journey to Calcutta, about 430 miles southeast of Benares, he caught a severe cold.

On the day of his arrival, Friday, February 7, 1896, he wrote to his daughter Susy: "I caught cold last night, coming from Benares & am shut up in the hotel starving it out; and so, instead of river parties & dinners & things, all three of us must decline & stay at home. It is too bad — yes & too ridiculous. I am perfectly certain that the exasperating colds & the carbuncles come from a diseased mind, & that your mental science could drive them away." Susy, along with many other upper-class Americans of the day, believed that affirmative thinking promoted health and well-being, and that people could regulate their health by force of mind.

Too sick to go out that first day in Calcutta, he nonetheless received two reporters. "If I have seen anything like India anywhere before," he remarked, "it was years ago — perhaps in the Holy Land. But here there is so much life and colour; it is all on such a big scale; everything is so thoroughly alive." His interest in Calcutta, he said, was "chiefly historical — Clive, Warren Hastings, and the Black Hole. I mean to see as much as possible. Asked whether his travel book would require a year or two before it appeared, he replied, "Quite that. I am taking a heap of notes, but I have still a tour of several weeks in South Africa before I even go to England to begin it."

Speaking in connection with what he called "the obvious advantages which the British have conferred on India," Clemens

stated his belief that "the strongest race will by and by become para-
mount — the strongest physically and intellectually. Now if we look
round among the nations we find that the English seems to possess
both these qualifications. It has spread all over the earth. It is vigor-
ous, prolific, and enterprising." Clemens had said as much in
Australia and New Zealand. But now he added that "above all [the
English race] is composed of merciful people — the best kind of
people for colonising the globe." As an example of their benevo-
lence, he pointed to "the greater humanity with which the American
Indians are treated in Canada. In the States we shut them off into a
reservation, which we frequently encroached upon. Then ensued
trouble. The Red men killed settlers, and of course the Government
had to order out troops and put them down. If an Indian kills a white
man he is sure to lose his life, but if a white man kills a redskin he
never suffers according to law." Had Clemens momentarily forgotten the transportation of convicts to New South Wales, the extermination of Tasmanians, and the shanghaiing of South Seas
islanders to Queensland, among the British atrocities he was to condemn in *Following the Equator*? Or did he consider that the British —
rapacious, brutal, and heartless though they might be — were more
merciful than their competitors? Or, like most of us, was he inconsistent, holding two conflicting opinions at the same time?

The Negro question, he agreed, was somewhat allied to the
American Indian question, but he thought that the former would
eventually settle itself. "The negroes at present are merely freed
slaves, and you can't get rid of the effects of slavery in one or even
two generations. But things will right themselves. We have given
the negro the vote, and he must keep it." There was not, he said in
response to a question, the slightest likelihood of intermarriage.
"The white and the black populations, however, will in time learn
to tolerate each other and work harmoniously for the common good.
They will co-exist very much as the different races in India have
done for centuries."

The day after his interviews, Clemens dined with Sir
Alexander MacKenzie, lieutenant governor of Bengal, who had
taken up his post in December. Unlike his colleague in Bombay,
Lord Sandhurst, Sir Alexander was no stranger to the Indian service.
He had come out to Bengal more than thirty years before in the

junior position of assistant magistrate and, before his appointment to the lieutenant governancy of Bengal, the highest post of that province, he had risen through the ranks to become Chief Commissioner of Burma, where he suppressed the raids of hill tribes. His history of the relations between the government and the hill tribes of the northeast frontier of Bengal, criticized for its candor, had become the standard authority. He was considered one of the ablest men of his time in India.

Clemens may have been thinking of Sir Alexander when he wrote, in *Following the Equator,* about unsung British public servants. "Often a British official spends thirty or forty years in India, climbing from grade to grade by services which would make him celebrated anywhere else, and finishes as a vice-sovereign, governing a great realm and millions of subjects; then he goes home to England substantially unknown and unheard of, and settles down in some modest corner, and is as one extinguished. Ten years later there is a twenty-line obituary in the London papers, and the reader is paralyzed by the splendors of a career which he is not sure that he had ever heard of before."

This comment was occasioned by the great Calcutta monument to Boston-born Sir David Ochterlony, the conqueror of Nepal. Clemens expressed surprise that the most notable monument in the city — "a fluted candlestick two hundred and fifty feet high," as he described it — was dedicated to a man about whom he had never heard, instead of to Clive or Hastings. Ochterlony, he said, could not have expected such a memorial, for "if monuments were always given in India for high achievements, duty straightly performed, and smirchless records, the landscape would be monotonous with them." The monument still stands, a focal point for political rallies, but it is now known officially as the Shahid Minar, or Martyrs' Memorial.

Sir Alexander received the Clemenses at Belvedere, a palatial eighteenth-century house that passed through several hands before the government purchased it as the lieutenant governor's residence. It is now the National Library. As Alice and I approach it, an egret on the grass looks up at the decaying house, its discolored stucco flaking and peeling. The exterior is partially redeemed by potted flowering plants set out at the sides and center of the grand staircase leading from the garden to the main floor, where scholars work at tables under the reading room's forty-foot ceiling. A gallery, supported by Corinthian columns, runs around three sides of the room.

The next day, Sunday, February 9, Clemens drove out to the site of the Black Hole, the location of a notorious incident in 1756. After the East India Company's garrison at Calcutta surrendered to the Muslim ruler, the Nawab of Bengal, the surviving defenders were not slaughtered, as might have been expected, but placed for the night in the Company's lockup, a small room with little ventilation, which even then was known by soldiers as the Black Hole. According to the garrison's commander, John Z. Holwell, 146 people were confined to the tiny room on that hot June night, and only twenty-three emerged the next morning. The rest had suffocated. Holwell's report created a sensation in Britain, where the incident was interpreted as evidence of British bravery and the Nawab's cruelty, and where it contributed to the idealization of British imperialism in India. Clemens, who accepted Holwell's account at face value, devoted several pages in his travel book to the incident, including a lengthy extract from Holwell's report. Today most historians believe that Holwell was an unreliable witness, that the Nawab's contribution to the affair was negligence rather than malice, that the number entering the cell was much lower than Holwell reported, and that the percentage of survivors was much higher. The survivors were no dewy innocents: before the fall of Calcutta, some had been beheading their servants.

Clemens described the Black Hole as "the first brick, the Foundation Stone, upon which was reared a mighty Empire — the Indian Empire of Great Britain," for it was that episode that "maddened the British and brought Clive, that young military marvel, raging up from Madras"; it led to the Battle of Plassey, where Clive "laid deep and strong the foundations of England's colossal Indian sovereignty." Clemens was surprised to find that the structure housing the prison cell had been "torn down and thrown away as carelessly as if its bricks were common clay, not ingots of historic gold." He did see, however, an engraved plate. "I saw that; and better that than nothing." The plaque was removed from the site after Independence.

The lieutenant governor of Bengal and the Commander-in-

Chief of the Armies of India were among the fashionable house at Clemens's first, sold-out *At Home* in Calcutta, on Monday, February 10. The crowd cheered his appearance and then repeatedly punctuated his remarks with laughter, although it was clear that he had not fully recovered from his cold, his voice at times sinking to a stage whisper. In the words of one reviewer, the audience paid a "joyous tribute of laughter to the genius of the work-a-day Aristophanes of America." Another reviewer wrote that "the humour of the speaker was of such an infectious description that he had hardly opened his mouth and spoken half a dozen words before his audience felt on the very best of terms with him . . . The humour which sparkled from the old grey man who talked to us from the stage of the Theatre Royal is as youthful as ever."

Clemens gave two more performances in Calcutta that week, on Wednesday and Thursday, both to packed houses in which extra seats had been provided, before departing on Friday for Darjeeling. His ornithorhyncus poem, which he delivered on Wednesday, was an enormous success. "I wrote it in haste while traveling in Australia as I knew the poetlaureateship was vacant, but I have since found that I was too late. However, I am reconciled to having lost the laureateship, for it has been given to a good poet like me . . . The present Laureate is just the same kind of poet as I am." The appointment of Tennyson's successor as laureate, the inept Alfred Austin, was widely derided at the time, so Clemens's teasing generated vast amusement.

Most of the reviewers praised his performance, although the Calcutta correspondent for the *Madras Mail* was dissatisfied. "Mark Twain as a lecturer is rather disappointing. He has a sing song methodical kind of delivery that becomes monotonous as he proceeds. He draws out his stories to the last extremity, and it seems to me that he was trying to kill time; and he failed to give all the points that might have been given to his best jokes. Still, he is a very funny man and most interesting. He has a refined intellectual face beaming with kindness and good nature, though sometimes wearing an expression of sadness and weariness that was touching."

Perhaps that was the performance in which Clemens's servant had misunderstood what to do. "Barney was to put a glass of water on my stage table," Clemens noted in his journal. "He seemed to understand perfectly after I had explained, behind the scenes, four times and pointed to the stage. What he finally did was to put a vast empty glass on the stage and a full one behind the scenes."

The one unfavorable opinion notwithstanding, the demand for tickets was so great that Smythe planned a fourth performance for the following week — an appearance that, in the end, had to be cancelled due to scheduling conflicts.

"There was plenty to see in Calcutta, but there was not plenty of time for it," Clemens observed in *Following the Equator*, but in fact he did see a great deal. For example, on the day of his first *At Home* he watched an early-morning inspection of the Calcutta garrison and later attended a repeat performance of the Grand Military Tournament. It closed, he reported, "with the mimic storming of a native fort which was as good as the reality for thrilling and accurate detail, and better than the reality for security and comfort."

The tournament of 1896 was "the best and greatest military show that Calcutta has ever witnessed," according to a newspaper of the day. An editorial expressed gratification that the performances had "attracted all classes of the native community" and then related "an amusing incident [that] illustrates the irresistible force of the fascination which the show exercises on the Native mind. A swarm of Natives were seen, as they may be seen at any performance, peeping through the matting of the enclosure. Patiently they stuck to their peep-holes, rewarded by the occasional glimpse of a trooper in the outer circle. An hour and a half went past, and then began the storming of the mountain fortress. The effect of the fusilade on the peeping throng was electrical. In a moment all was excitement, and when Maxim and mule battery came into play, the outsiders cast thrift to the winds and made a rush for tickets. Eagerly they paid the full charge of eight annas for the final ten minutes of the show." When you read this editorial on its yellowing page, a page so brittle it crumbles at the edges, you are glad the writer is dead, because otherwise you would be tempted to shoot him. But then you wonder if you would have noted the cruelty and condescension of that column one hundred years ago, had you had been an English resident of Calcutta reading the paper as you sipped your breakfast tea. It is pleasant to consider ourselves superior to the people of that time.

Clemens visited a session of the Governor-General's Council

chaired by the viceroy, Lord Elgin (Calcutta was then the capital of British India), inspected the portraits at Government House, lunched with the lieutenant governor, and called on the commander-in-chief. In addition, according to *Following the Equator*, Clemens's sightseeing included the "fort that Clive built," the Indian Museum, "the great botanical gardens," and the site near Belvedere House at which Hastings, who created the outlines of British India as its first governor-general, shot his political tormentor Philip Francis in a duel. Today you must obtain special permission to enter the fort, which is still in use, but no permission is required to visit the Indian Museum or the Botanical Gardens. The high-ceilinged museum, built around a pleasant central courtyard, is the greatest in India. "One should," Clemens advised, "spend a month in the museum, an enchanted palace of Indian antiquities." The museum, however, needs no promotion. Its fossils, stuffed animals, superb ancient sculptures and carvings, archaeological finds, and nineteenth-century Indian paintings, among other exhibits, attract thousands of visitors from all over the country.

The Botanical Gardens lie in Howrah, Calcutta's twin city across the Hooghly River. The taxi that Alice and I have hired for the day takes us over the new suspension bridge, sleek and elegant, its cables forming ever-changing geometric patterns as we approach. On the other side of the river we share narrow lanes with bicycle rickshaws and two herds of goats. A man in spotless white trousers and smock passes a woman relieving herself in the gutter.

In an oblique reference in his journal, Clemens mentioned what was daily before his eyes: people relieving themselves in public, the human excrement on pathways. "You have noticed from the car windows that [Indians] publicly and without embarrassment indulge in various habits which to us are forbidden . . . Each race determines for itself what indecencies are. Nature knows no indecencies; man invents them." In a bow to Victorian sensibilities, *Following the Equator* did not mention these "various habits." Nor did it exploit Clemens's journal entries regarding the "pious cant" of not providing clean prostitutes for the 70,000 British soldiers in India, of whom there were constantly more than 3,000 in hospital from this cause.

We pass the leafy quadrangle of a college and then stop at the gates of the Botanical Gardens. It is a weekday, with only a few visitors enjoying the grounds. Most of the bicyclists and pedestrians here, some with briefcases, seem intent on their destinations, to which the park may be a shortcut. On one side of a long avenue, a scummy lake nourishes glorious water lilies, pale purple and white. The park's most notable feature, an enormous banyan tree, was about 140 years old at the time Clemens saw it. Almost one hundred feet tall and covering a circumference of over sixteen hundred feet, the aerial roots that drop from its branches and anchor themselves in the ground create the illusion of a small woods. Although it lost its central trunk to a fungus about thirty years after Clemens's visit, the tree continues to flourish.

After leaving the gardens, Alice and I enter another unexpected refuge, the South Park Street cemetery. At this peaceful, shaded, quiet spot, we wander among English tombs from the eighteenth and nineteenth centuries. The monuments and gravestones, often slightly askew on ground that has shifted, stand crowded together like guests at a reception. You are impressed by the grandeur of some of the monuments and saddened by the youth of many who lie buried here. Here lie Joseph Hatton, eight years old, his sister Elizabeth, five years old, and their father Henry, forty years old. All perished within fourteen months of one another, between 1839 and 1840. Here lies Rose Aylmer, who died in 1800 at the age of twenty. This daughter of a noble house was immortalized by Walter Savage Landor's brief poem, perhaps his most famous. It is engraved on the plinth of her monument, a tall, fluted, tapering column, its splendor sadly at variance with the simple elegance of Landor's elegy. Here lies Sir William Jones, whose monument, according to a list of notable tombs, is the tallest in the cemetery. He was one of the men brought out by Hastings, who wanted to create a corps of British officials that could speak the local languages and that would be respectful of local traditions. Sir William, a judge and legal writer, founded the Bengal Asiatic Society. Oddly, the list of notable tombs fails to mention his most significant achievement, the discovery that Greek, Latin, and Sanskrit, the holy language of the Hindus, sprang from a common ancestor. He was forty-seven when he died in 1794. Outside the cemetery walls, a long line of indigent people moves slowly forward. A charitable agency is distributing food.

Clemens did not visit the cemetery, which would have seemed less exotic in 1896 than it does one hundred years later, although it was little more than a mile from his hotel. It was at his hotel, in fact, that he later claimed to have encountered the past, not in the tombs of dead colonists, but in a long-forgotten personal episode. As he entered the hotel, he glimpsed in passing a lovely young woman going out. The glimpse shocked him. She looked exactly like a childhood friend. Later he found that the young woman was not a ghost but the granddaughter of that friend, now a gray-haired widow, who was staying in the same hotel and who invited him to call. "We sat down and talked. We steeped our thirsty souls in the reviving wine of the past, the pathetic past, the beautiful past, the dear and lamented past; we uttered the names that had been silent upon our lips for fifty years and it was as if they were made of music." They recalled story after story and laughed until tears flowed. Suddenly his childhood friend revealed that she had witnessed a boyhood scene in which he had capered naked, unaware that two girls were watching him behind a screen. Later, the boy Clemens was mortified to learn there had been female witnesses, although he did not know who they were. Finally, fifty years later in Calcutta, he learned the identity of one of them. An account of his meeting in Calcutta appears among Clemens's autobiographical jottings and dictations, some of which bear little resemblance to the facts. It is probably an invention, although it may have been psychologically true, based on an incident, perhaps in Calcutta, that reminded him of his youth.

Chapter Thirty-two

*F*ROM THE TERRACE you hear the peal of wind chimes, the lowing of a cow now and then, the muffled voices of occasional passersby on the path below, and, if you're not imagining it, a soft rustling from the feathery Japanese pines, beyond the garden bordered by budding azaleas. From the garden the ground slopes sharply away, yielding an unimpeded view of wooded hills at the other side of a steep valley. Sprays of blossoms — white, lavender, and violet, the petals of potted primroses or "powder plants" as they're called here — enliven the terrace. A stray wisp of coal smoke dilutes the purity of the cool mountain air, but you do not complain after the foulness of Calcutta. Here, 7,000 feet above the vast Bengal plain, you feel as if you have stumbled into Shangri-la.

This is Darjeeling, a town on a lower spur of the eastern Himalayas, the Clemenses' next stop after Calcutta. It was one of the so-called hill stations of the British Raj, a retreat from the baking, polluted, pullulating cities of the plains, a place where the sick might find health, where debilitated colonials might regain their strength, where children whose parents were unwilling or unable to send them to Britain attended school, and where the provincial administration worked during the summer months. Today rich Indians and foreign tourists enjoy the amenities established by the British, who left behind them hotels, clubs, country houses, churches, and a tradition of cosseting the visitor.

The Clemenses, who left Calcutta at four-thirty in the afternoon, on Friday, February 14, 1896, traveled to Darjeeling in style. Mr. Barclay, the railroad's chief of traffic south of the Ganges, reserved a special parlor car for them, with an attached car for their servants, and accompanied them part of the way. After an hour, tea was served, while two servants stood behind their chairs. In another three hours they reached the Ganges, where they left the train. In a letter to her youngest daughter, Jean, Mrs. Clemens wrote how she wished that Jean could have seen the Ganges station. "Natives in all the brilliant and picturesque costumes that one could imagine, standing about the station area all the way down to the boat." As guests of the railroad they dined "most sumptuously" on the ferry during their one-hour crossing of the river, at that point more than one mile wide. Mr. Holmes, the railroad's chief of traffic north of the Ganges, who had joined them at dinner on the ferry, saw them into their sleeping car, which took them to Siliguri, the railhead for Darjeeling.

"Up with the sun" the next day, wrote Clemens in *Following the Equator*. "The plain is perfectly level, and seems to stretch away and away and away, dimming and softening, to the uttermost bounds of nowhere." He noted the countless villages. He mentioned the naked men and boys plowing the fields, and the absence of women there, unlike European countries in which he remembered grandmothers pulling plows in harness with an ox. "Come," he wrote in his journal, "let us introduce Austrian, Bavarian and French civilization, and Christianity, right away." The adoption of Christianity seems not to have been necessary; in today's India you see women working not only in fields but also in road gangs and on construction sites.

That morning the Clemenses found "a dainty breakfast-table" spread for them, as Mrs. Clemens told Jean. Their host had left them by this time, she wrote, but his orders had been carried out so that "every thing was most delightfully arranged for us. Then up the mountain we came in the pleasant open car."

They ascended to Darjeeling on the narrrow-gauge, miniature railway whose toy train consisted, in Clemens's words, of "little canvas-sheltered cars that skimmed along within a foot of the ground and seemed to be going fifty miles an hour when they were really making about twenty." The train required eight or nine hours to travel forty miles, so steep was the climb and so frequent the loops and switchbacks, with the train sometimes passing above itself. The coaches, more than three times the width of the narrow track, often seemed to be passing over thin air, as the train ran close to horrifyingly deep and sheer chasms.

Before beginning its ascent, the train stopped at "a little

wooden coop of a station just within the curtain of the somber jungle," Clemens reported in *Following the Equator*. The royal Bengal tiger, he continued, inhabited the area in great force. "It was there that I had my first tiger-hunt. I killed thirteen." A few days later, as he was preparing to return to the plains, he wrote a letter to Charles Henry Webb, who had met Clemens years before in Nevada and who had published Mark Twain's first book, *The Celebrated Jumping Frog of Calaveras County*. Clemens informed Webb that in Darjeeling he had "met a man who conversed with a man who knows the man who saw a tiger come out of the jungle yesterday and eat a friend of his who had just put on his breech-clout and was starting out to pay calls. We expect to see that tiger to-day, for we have to pass right by that spot, and he will probably want some more."

Little more than one week later, about five hundred miles west of Calcutta, a tiger mauled an English sportsman, T. H. Butler, whose servants were reported to have acted improperly at the time. The incident created a sensation. Butler had wounded the tiger and set out the next day to finish it off, despite the pleas of his companion, who was confined to the camp with swollen feet and who said that, judging from the scant traces of blood, the animal had been only lightly wounded. Butler hunted his prey for two days, setting out from camp each morning with some bearers and a headman who held Butler's rifle. ("Why," asked *The Times of India*, "will people following dangerous quarry give the gun into the hands of a coolie.") On the second day, Butler confronted the tiger, took his rifle, and, according to the head bearer, told his men to run away, which they promptly did, without first shouting to frighten the animal. Butler shot but missed the tiger, which rushed at him and mauled him. When Butler reached for the revolver at his side, the motion frightened the tiger, which fled. After the men returned to find Butler still alive, they brought him back to camp, from which he was taken to a hospital, where he died. "It is well-known here," reported *The Times of India*, "that there was a spare gun with the natives with Mr. Butler; and yet no effort of any sort was made on their part at rescue; and a European life was thus sacrificed to their pusillanimity!"

Even without a tiger hunt, Clemens found the ascent to Darjeeling "so wild and interesting and exciting and enchanting that it ought to take a week." He enjoyed the sinuous track that wound around and under the towering cliffs, he was impressed by the variety and lushness of the vegetation, and he was fascinated by the men and women walking up and down the mountain, particularly the Gurkhas or Nepalese, whom he saw here for the first time. Finally he could look down upon the plains of India, "level as a floor, shimmering with heat." At 7,400 feet he reached Ghoom and then descended a few hundred feet to Darjeeling, where he arrived at about four-thirty in the afternoon on Saturday, February 15, twenty-four hours after leaving Calcutta, about 375 miles to the south.

The party rode to their hotel in dandies, rented from the railway company for a small sum. A dandy was a box chair, which Clemens called an "open coffin." Four strong men would place the horizontal cross-poles supporting the conveyance on their shoulders and trot to their destination, while their swaying passenger clutched a bar in front. In those days luggage followed on the backs of female porters, who supported their loads by a strap around the forehead.

You can no longer follow the Clemenses' railroad journey from Calcutta to Siliguri; the route has been changed to avoid traveling through Bangladesh, and the journey ends not at Siliguri but at its sister town, New Jalpaiguri, two or three miles away. Your train crosses a long bridge over the Ganges, obviating a ferry ride. The best train accommodation we could find was on the Kanchenjunga Express, named after one of the great Himalayan peaks visible from Darjeeling. The long train provided a single air-conditioned coach, whose dirty, crazed windows made objects outside look as if they were under water. The window nearest us had trapped between its inner and outer panes a small mouse.

Trying not to think of the special parlor car in which the Clemenses began their journey, we rode backwards in an uncompartmentalized coach on a bench with a bunk above us, facing another couple who sat on a bench with a bunk above them. If the four of us had wanted to sleep, we could have drawn a curtain between our four beds and the aisle, but it was unnecessary to do so, since we reached New Jalpaiguri an hour or so after dark. The whole journey took about thirteen hours, just a few hours shorter than the Clemenses' journey one hundred years ago.

The Clemenses stayed at the Woodlands Hotel, then the town's leading inn, a low wooden building below Auckland Road, now Gandhi Road. A local resident remembers taking Nepali lessons there in the 1940s, before it burned down. On its site stands Circuit House, a rest house for officers of the West Bengal civil service. During the Raj, the Woodlands did not accept Indian guests.

Clemens's *At Home* began at nine-thirty, about five hours after his arrival. The "fairly good house" included planters from outlying tea plantations. Clemens told his audience that Darjeeling had greatly impressed him and that the Himalayan Railway was "the most remarkable forty miles of railroad in the world." He had been told, he said, that Darjeeling would be cold. "No fewer than nine people in Calcutta advised me to put on specially warm clothes. I have taken their advice and am now wearing the whole nine suits."

He probably performed at the old Town Hall, an annex of the Amusement Club on Observatory Hill, then the hub of British social life in Darjeeling. The Town Hall, a venue for dances, public meetings, and amateur theatricals, was located between the club's lawn tennis ground and its covered tennis courts, more or less on the site of the present Gymkhana Club, founded early in the century. You can obtain a temporary membership and play tennis there still.

The next day, a Sunday, the main market day for the hill peoples of the region, Clemens watched the pageant of "swarthy strange tribes" on their way to the bazaar, streaming for hours "from their far homes in the Himalayas." Later the Clemenses ventured into the bazaar to see "that novel congress of the wild peoples."

Clemens's view of the hill peoples as exotic seems relatively benign at a time in which racial characterizations and rankings were common. An Englishman who lived in Darjeeling during the early years of the twentieth century quoted Milton to imply that the hill peoples were "a herd confused / a miscellaneous rabble." With the same degree of certainty with which he advised travelers to sit on the left-hand side of the toy train when ascending to Darjeeling, the author divided the dominant Nepali hill peoples into three physiognomic categories, Types A, B, and C, with A the most intelligent, B the most enterprising, and C the hardiest and most martial.

Then as now, Darjeeling's population reflected its position as a border region, about sixty miles from Tibet and even closer to Nepal, Bhutan, and Sikkim (which India annexed in 1975). The Lepcha and Bhutia peoples whom the British found in the early nineteenth century were soon engulfed by Nepali-speaking peoples, the Gurkhas, who came to work the tea plantations. More recently Tibetan refugees have enlarged the local Tibetan population.

Nepali speakers still form the majority of the people, and a Nepali nationalist movement controls the local council. That movement, backed by the Communist Party, fomented widespread riots and engaged in guerrilla warfare about ten years ago in support of an autonomous Gurkhaland. Hundreds lost their lives, thousands lost their homes, a rebel paramilitary unit occupied the Gymkhana Club's indoor skating rink, and tourism vanished. A compromise in 1988, whereby the local council received a considerable degree of autonomy, permitted the revival of tourism and the return of an uneasy version of normalcy, although as a legacy of the troubles no public life exists at night. While nationalist graffiti continue to salute a nonexistent Gurkhaland, the local council has done little to improve the town. Electricity, water, and fuel remain in short supply. "Yes," a town official told us, "the infrastructure is crumbling but the people are happier because they are free." He predicted renewed violence as the Gurkhas pursue independence.

Tea, of course, is Darjeeling's most famous export, so desired by the world that only a fraction of the product labeled Darjeeling is grown near Darjeeling; visitors come here not for the tea, however, but for the superb views of the Himalayas. The best viewing seasons are spring and fall, but even then a visitor can wait for days before the clouds and mists dissipate to reveal the stupendous peaks, about forty miles away. The Clemenses were out of season as far as viewing was concerned. Both on Saturday, the day they arrived, and on Sunday the mountains were obscured, although Clemens wrote that it would have been worth traveling to Darjeeling just to see the "wild peoples" there.

On Sunday, Clemens spent a few hours at the club, where, according to the *Darjeeling Standard*, he had a drink "and was genial and entertaining and kept the billiard-room so jolly that though it was full of members, no one could play." That night the club hosted him at dinner. "In every town and city in India," Clemens explained in *Following the Equator,* "the gentlemen of the British civil and military service have a club; sometimes it is a palatial one, always it is pleasant and homelike. The hotels are not always as good as they might be, and the stranger who has access to the Club is grateful for his privilege and knows how to value it." To this he might have added that in each town and city in India the club was a central symbol of imperial rule: only white men belonged to it, with the exception of a local Muslim or Hindu ruler, a nawab or rajah, if he wanted to join. It has been suggested that the exclusion of Indians was based not on racial snobbery but on the Indians' inferior rank, but this argument is weakened by the observation that membership was open to men who were neither in the civil nor the military service. In fact, the club in Darjeeling was established by planters and called the Planters Club until 1908, when it became the Darjeeling Club. Planters and officers attached to the military and civil services were entitled to membership; other Europeans were readily admitted "if properly vouched for." The club, a long, low wooden building with verandas on each of its two levels, still operates in the same structure, overlooking what was once Commercial Row and is now Nehru Road. The changed composition of its members is reflected in the names of its secretaries: Major E. Carew Hunt in 1896, Major S. K. Sobti one hundred years later. You can take a temporary membership and stay there, if you like, and for a daily fee you can play on the club's surviving billiards table. The club appears to be struggling: the library's newest book was probably first shelved fifty years ago; the public rooms are gloomy and dilapidated; and some of the upstairs bedrooms are in deplorable condition, although others have been remodeled, improving their comfort at the expense of their period charm. The plants on the downstairs veranda, however, are flourishing.

On Monday morning, the Clemenses' last day in Darjeeling, the fogs and clouds cleared long enough to reveal the peaks of the Himalayan massif. After arising at five-thirty, Mrs. Clemens, Clara, Smythe, and a male acquaintance set out to watch the mountaintops reflect the sunrise, while Clemens, clad in a dressing gown, wrapped a few blankets around his shoulders, lit a pipe, and viewed the mountains from a window inside his hotel. In *Following the Equator* he wrote that "my party rode away to a distant point where Kinchinjunga and Mount Everest show up best." This sounds like Tiger Hill, seven miles away, then as now a popular observation point. From there you can glimpse Mount Everest, if only as an unimpressive knob at the end of a spectacular chain. But it is unlikely that the party went to Tiger Hill. Accompanied by the male acquaintance and Clara on horseback, Mrs. Clemens traveled in a mountain rickshaw, pulled by two men and pushed by one, while Smythe walked. A fourteen-mile round trip is improbably long for a mountain rickshaw, and the walk in one direction requires two hours. Since they rose at five-thirty, they could not have gone far before the sun came up at about six o'clock. They probably traveled to the highest point of Darjeeling, Observatory Hill, or to an observation point on the Mall, which circles the hill.

The mountain view from Darjeeling is unrivaled in terms of the number and height and closeness of visible peaks, with distances from Darjeeling ranging from thirty-two to forty-five miles. Kanchenjunga, the third highest mountain in the world, rises to more than 28,000 feet, seven other mountains soar to at least 22,000 feet, and none of the remaining peaks that you see along the great snowy range is lower than 15,000 feet. At daybreak the Clemenses watched the peaks glimmer pink and orange in the reflected glory of the sunrise.

After breakfast, at which they sat as close to the fire as possible on that cold day, the Clemenses left for the train station, accompanied by some members of the club. Clemens informed them that he "had intended to tell the many people in Calcutta who had told him of the grandeur of the snows that he had seen them, whether he had or not, and he was glad to be saved the pain of telling a lie."

The Clemenses boarded the toy train for its first and highest stop, Ghoom, about five miles away. From the region of "eternal snow," as Clemens later told Rogers, they began their descent to "perpetual hellfire," thirty-five miles away and 7,400 feet below, in a six-seated, canvas-covered handcar. Propelled by gravity, it sped so close to the ground that it gave its passengers the illusion that they were flying down a crooked toboggan slide. Rounding crags and skirting precipices, shedding their rugs and furs as they descended, they left Darjeeling behind. Clemens wrote of their corkscrew descent: "For rousing, tingling, rapturous pleasure there is no holiday-trip that aproaches the bird-flight down the Himalayas in a hand-car." It was, he said, "the most enjoyable day I have spent in the earth."

Chapter Thirty-three

*T*HE PARTY RETURNED to Calcutta at eleven the next morning, Tuesday, February 18. Clemens spent less than half a day in Calcutta; at nine-thirty in the evening, he and Smythe boarded a private car for Muzaffarpur, about 320 miles northwest near the Nepalese border, where an *At Home* had been scheduled for the following evening. Writing to her daughter Jean from Calcutta that night, Mrs. Clemens explained that she and Clara would follow Clemens the next day. They were tired and had to repack, because two trunks were to be left behind. Presumably these contained their warmer clothing, to be placed on the steamer that would later carry the Clemenses to Ceylon and Mauritius.

The Clemenses reunited on Thursday, Clemens himself traveling southwest from Muzaffarpur and the women northwest from Calcutta. Together they continued to Benares, arriving at noon on February 20. Their return visit to "that strange and fascinating piety-hive" lasted just one day, spent largely in viewing bazaars and temples.

The next day found them traveling to Lucknow, about 170 miles northwest. "Hot as the nation," Clemens wrote in his journal, "the flat plains the color of pale dust, & the dust flying . . . No doubt all these native grayheads remember the Mutiny."

Both in Lucknow and in Cawnpore (now Kanpur) he visited sites connected to the great uprising of 1857. The uprising began among Britain's Indian troops, sparked by the introduction of the Enfield rifle. Before loading the rifles, soldiers were supposed to bite off the cartridge ends, but the paper cartridges were greased with cows' fat and pigs' fat, one forbidden to Hindus and the other to Muslims. As soon as the British realized their mistake, they withdrew the cartridges, but it was too late. The various reforms they had introduced over the past few decades — for example, the abolition of suttee, the suppression of infanticide, the expropriation of land whose holders could not show valid title, and the annexation of states to which there was no direct heir — and the brutal fashion with which they had imposed these reforms convinced the soldiers that the introduction of greased cartridges was part of a deliberate plot to overturn the traditional order. The uneasy and fearful chief representatives of that order, the landowners and princes, helped transform a military mutiny into a general revolt that raged across northern India.

The uprising shook British complacency, but not their confidence in the inherent strength and enduring nature of their rule. Determined to learn from the errors that the uprising exposed, they reorganized and reformed their administrative, financial, and military institutions, and changed their attitude toward their Indian subjects. The British resolved to stay in closer touch with Indian opinion, to enlist the support of the princes and the landed classes, and to avoid offending religious sensitivities. Those changes, practical and psychological, gave to British India the character which Clemens found during the apogee of Imperial rule. During this time, Indian traditionalists, who respected British power, and the newly modern Indian classes, who respected the new knowledge, conceded British superiority.

The military and civil service officers whom Clemens met in clubs throughout India were both efficient and devoted to their work. But they questioned Indian competence, opposed Indian advancement to the higher civil and military services, and regarded the British administration as wise and benevolent, a view that Clemens appeared not to challenge.

On Saturday, February 22, Clemens visited the ruins of the Residency, the palace of the British resident at the court of Oudh, the state whose annexation had contributed to the uprising. This is where the Siege of Lucknow took place. At the end of June 1858, the British residents of Lucknow, the small British garrison, and a smaller number of loyal Indian soldiers took refuge in the Residency complex after rebellious Indian troops had overrun the town. For over four months, until Sir Colin Campbell relieved the siege, the defenders and occupants of the Residency endured a relentless artillery barrage and constant efforts to mine the buildings. They also suffered from malnutrition, cholera, and infected wounds. In *Following the Equator*, Clemens devoted several pages to the Siege of Lucknow as part of his account of British valor during the uprising.

"The British were caught asleep and unprepared," he wrote. "They were a few thousands, swallowed up in an ocean of hostile populations. It would take months to inform England and get help, but they did not falter or stop to count the odds, but with English resolution and English devotion they took up their task, and went stubbornly on with it, through good fortune and bad, and fought the most unpromising fight that one may read of in fiction or out of it, and won it thoroughly."

Clemens described the Residency grounds as "sacred." He predicted that they would be maintained as a memorial as long as the British remained masters of India. The grounds are a memorial even today. In the shattered Residency itself you can walk down a circular staircase to the cellar, where many women and children slept, and you can see a model of the positions during the siege. Opposite the Residency stands a different memorial, one that honors the martyrs of India's struggle for independence. It was erected in 1957 to mark the centennial of the great uprising.

On Sunday, the day after their visit to the Residency, the Clemenses rode with Major and Mrs. Aylmer and Captain and Mrs. Dallas over the bloody route taken by Sir Colin Campbell and his relieving force as they fought their way to the Residency, thirty-nine years earlier. They also drove out to the great *imambara* (literally "imam's house," a mausoleum for a Shiite leader), built in 1784 by the reigning nawab. Lucknow, the capital of the nawabs of Oudh, became a center of Muslim power in the eighteenth century and it is still India's chief Shiite city. The great imambara, perhaps the principal monument to the Nawabs' rule, is open to the public.

Another monument, the Chattar Manzil palace, was the United Services Club during the Clemenses' visit. Major Aylmer's uniformed orderly, riding a caparisoned camel, brought Clemens an invitation to dine there. Clemens described the palace as "ancient and elegant" and "sumptuous," a far cry from the modest if comfortable club at Darjeeling. It was at the Chattar Manzil palace that Clemens met a survivor of the siege, who in 1857 "was perfecting his teething and learning to talk." The forty-one-year-old survivor was to Clemens "the most impressive object in Lucknow after the Residency ruins." The palace in which this meeting took place now stands empty, forlorn and neglected.

During one of his performances at Lucknow, he addressed his routine on moral regeneration mainly to a child who sat close to the platform. She was, according to Smythe, "a delightful little girl . . . conspicuous for her naive and evident enjoyment." Later, just before the club banquet in Clemens's honor, a guest told him of a difference of opinion between the child and her parents as to the number of possible sins that Clemens had mentioned. Clemens claimed that the number given by the child was right. Then and there he insisted on writing her a note confirming that her memory was correct, that there were only 354 possible sins in the world, and that none of the experts in jail had been able to invent any more.

After three days and two performances at Lucknow, the Clemenses left on Tuesday, February 25, for Cawnpore, about forty miles southwest, where Clemens performed that night and visited some of the sites associated with the uprising. He saw the site at which the besieged British garrison fought until promised a safe conduct by Nana Sahib, one of the leaders of the revolt. He saw the small temple on the shores of the Ganges where a bugle blew to signal the massacre of the garrison after it surrendered. He saw the palace in which, shortly before the arrival of a rescue party, Nana Sahib slaughtered the British women and children that had been rounded up and imprisoned. And he saw the infamous well into which the victims of the palace butchery had been thrown. One can imagine the lofty self-righteousness with which Clemens's guides described these atrocities. No Indian guide showed him the sites of British reprisals, which included blowing away captives spread-eagled to the mouths of cannons.

The Clemenses left Cawnpore at three on Thursday morning and reached Agra, about 150 miles northwest, seven and a half hours later. In a letter to her sister, Mrs. Clemens wrote that they were staying there with a high British functionary, Colonel Loch, who oversaw the local rulers of three states. "Nine months ago there was a Rajah deposed, and it has brought much extra work upon him."

Clemens noted in his journal that he offered to dethrone one or two princes for him, or, for the sake of change, drown some.

Five other guests were staying at the house, in addition to the Clemenses, so that when all went sightseeing, they required two carriages, each with a coachman and two footmen standing behind. The Clemenses saw the Taj Mahal twice, once during the day and once at night. After the *At Home* on February 28, the Clemenses reached the monument at eleven-thirty, under a clear sky and a full moon. To their surprise, a total eclipse began immediately upon their arrival. "Attempts were made to furnish an eclipse for the Prince of Wales in 1876," wrote Clemens in his journal, "and in recent years to 20 other princes of that house, but without success." The Clemenses' host, however, had "much more influence than any of his predecessors have had."

Clemens claimed to have been disappointed by the Taj Mahal. He knew all the time he saw it that it was a wonder of the world, but it was not the building he had imagined on the basis of the literary descriptions he had read. These had led him to expect transcendence, a monument "built of tinted mists upon jeweled arches of rainbows supported by colonnades of moonlight."

In 1896, photographic images of tourist icons were only beginning to become common property through their publication in newspapers and magazines. Today, before you have reached middle age, you have seen thousands of photographs of the Taj Mahal, taken at all hours of the day and night and from every imaginable vantage point. You have seen these pictures not only in newspapers and magazines, in articles and in advertisements, but also on television and in film. The Taj Mahal in your imagination is based not on written descriptions but on repeated visual images, and by the time you arrive in Agra you have seen so many of them that you half wonder why you are bothering to visit the original at all. And so, when you finally view it, you are shocked to discover that it is even more impressive than you had expected it to be. You return to it at night and you glimpse it from various parts of the town and you are surprised that successive sightings do not diminish your pleasure or wonder. What a pity that the main input to Clemens's imagined Taj Mahal had been written rather than visual.

On Saturday, February 29, following their night visit to the Taj Mahal, the Clemenses traveled 130 miles southwest to Jaipur, the capital of a princely state founded in the twelfth century. When they arrived the next morning, Clemens felt unwell. According to Mrs. Clemens, he had noticed for several weeks "a pricking sensation in his left hand & arm, which made us rather anxious." He was also suffering from diarrhea. "I am in the doctor's hands again," he wrote to Rogers from Jaipur five days after his arrival. "He made me cancel a week's engagements and shut myself in my room and rest. Said he would not be responsible for the consequences if I didn't." Smythe and Clara also fell ill; the stay in Jaipur lengthened to two weeks. Meanwhile, news of Clemens's illness, announced to explain the cancellation of several performances, spread swiftly and in exaggerated form so that the world thought he was seriously ill. Rogers wrote him that "we have been quite disturbed in regard to the newspaper reports concerning your illness ... Do try and take care of yourself."

The Clemenses' hotel in Jaipur was the Kaiser-i-Hind, which means Emperor of India, a grandiose name for the small, noisy establishment run by nine brothers. It stood, he reported in *Following the Equator*, "in a large empty compound which was surrounded by a mud wall as high as a man's head." The brothers lived with their families off to one side of the compound, in a building whose veranda was always "loosely stacked" with children, among whom was "a detachment of the parents wedged among them, smoking the hookah or the howdah, or whatever they call it."

The main structure, a smaller version of the Hotel de Paris in Benares, still operates as a hotel, but its verandas and scalloped arches now welcome budget travelers. When Alice and I visit, we find an old Indian lady reclining on floor cushions at the entrance to the central veranda. She appears to be one of the locals who occupy the smaller buildings inside the compound. The "mud wall as high as a man's head," which surrounded the compound in Clemens's day, has been replaced by a lower stone wall and by a building facing the street. An enormous water tank now rises behind the main house.

"The secluded and country air of the place," which Clemens mentioned, was destroyed when the town spread out to meet it.

Across the street stands a new luxury hotel, with a waterfall in its lobby, whose guest rooms are probably half the size of the original chambers at the Kaiser-i-Hind. If the Clemenses were to visit Jaipur today, they would probably choose not the new, glitzy hotel but the romantic Rambagh Palace Hotel, formerly the home of the Maharajah of Jaipur, where plashing fountains moisten the air and peacocks strut upon well-tended lawns.

During their two-week stay, the Clemenses ventured forth from their hotel. On their way to watch a religious procession, they passed what Clemens described as a "new and beautiful palace stocked with a museum of extraordinary interest and value." This was Albert Hall, "a beautiful construction of stone which shows arched colonnades, one above another, and receding, terrace-fashion, toward the sky." The terraces were crammed with Indians, who presumably had come to watch the procession. "One must try to imagine those solid masses of splendid color, one above another, up and up, against the blue sky, and the Indian sun turning them all to beds of fire and flame."

Mrs. Clemens visited the museum on a ladies' morning, when women who observed purdah would be safe from the gaze of men. Muslims introduced purdah, the seclusion of women from public view, but many Hindu families had adopted the custom and still practiced it in the Clemenses' time. When Clemens performed in Baroda, the Marahani and two court ladies watched him from behind a screen, and when the Clemenses called on the prince of Palitana, Mrs. Clemens and Clara made a separate visit to the Princess. Writing to her daughter Jean about her visit to the museum, Mrs. Clemens said she wanted to visit it on a ladies' morning in order to see the local women and their sumptuous costumes. The place, she wrote, was packed with gorgeously dressed women. "The only trouble was that I was as great a curiosity to them as they were to me."

The Albert Hall, with its arched verandas and domed pavilions, continues to serve the public, though Western visitors are no longer a curiosity. Some of the exhibits appear unchanged from one hundred years ago: a mummy, Egyptian statuary, stuffed animals, lifeless fabrics. A series of small terra cotta figures illustrate yoga positions, of which only one looks comfortable, lying prone upon one's back. Pigeons fly through the long, dark corridors lined with poorly labeled exhibits. Museums like this, common a few generations ago, can still be found in small American towns. This one attracts crowds of locals, including a few women garbed from head to toe in black, their faces covered, accompanied by a man.

The Clemenses visited the walled city, built in the eighteenth century by Maharajah Jai Singh, who named it after himself. A philosopher king and enthusiast of astronomy, he and his architect laid out the city according to ancient Hindu principles of city planning, with straight, spacious streets at right angles to one another, each street lined with houses, shops, temples, and mosques whose design had first to be approved by the city's architect. The straightness of the streets, in marked contrast to the winding alleys characteristic of Indian cities of the day, served as a foil to the embellishment of the buildings. "The blocks of houses," wrote Clemens in *Following the Equator*, "exhibit a long frontage of the most taking architectural quaintnesses, the straight lines being broken everywhere by pretty little balconies, pillared and highly ornamented, and other cunning and cozy and inviting perches and projections, and many of the fronts are curiously pictured by the brush, and the whole of them have the soft rich tint of strawberry ice-cream."

From a vantage point in the old city, the Clemenses watched a procession, bracketed at the front by "majestic elephants, clothed in their Sunday best of gaudinesses," as Clemens described them in *Following the Equator*, and at the rear by stately camels. In those days no great occasion was complete without a procession of gaily decorated elephants. Today's visitors to Jaipur can still see gaudily embellished elephants if they attend the Elephant Festival, held annually in the Chaugan Stadium.

"The paradoxical pachyderm known as elephant is coming toward you . . . dripping in radiant color," announces a female voice, whose English throughout the spectacle is as decorated as the beasts who are entering the grounds. The enormous animals are draped in velvet brocade, with great bracelets circling their ankles and scales of silver blanketing their foreheads. Tinsel chandeliers sprout from their brass-rimmed tusk-sheaths, gold and silver embroidered scarves hang from their ears and tusks, and chalk-drawn stylized flowers and bits of glittering paste festoon their bare skin. Even their toenails are painted. In addition to processions, the organizers of the event treat us to elephant races (the jockeys prod the poor beasts with a device that combines a spear with a hook), a tug-of-war between an elephant and twenty tourists (the elephant wins easily), and a bit of elephant polo, all of which are interspersed with marching bands and troupes of singers, as well as dancers in resplendent costumes, hips swaying and shoulders shrugging. When visitors leave this spectacle they feel as Clemens did, after he watched the procession, that "for color, and picturesqueness, and novelty, and outlandishiness, and sustained interest and fascination, it was the most satisfying show I had ever seen, and I suppose I shall not have the privilege of looking upon its like again."

Chapter Thirty-four

*I*WAS GOING to start last night for Lahore," Clemens wrote to
Rogers on Sunday, March 15, 1896, "but wasn't yet in condition;
but we all start to-night and lie over a day for rest in Delhi." They
reached Delhi, 150 miles northeast of Jaipur, at half past midnight,
and repaired to the mansion of the Burne family — Mr. Burne was
with the Bank of Bengal. The Clemenses saw little of the city
because they expected to return to it after several *At Home*s elsewhere. Also, as Mrs. Clemens later told her sister, a smallpox epidemic discouraged them from visiting places frequented by large
numbers of the local population. The Clemenses were staying in a
private house, she wrote, and naturally they wanted to avoid endan-
gering their hosts.

The private house, wrote Clemens, "was built by a rich
Englishman who had become orientalized — so much so that he
had a zenana [harem]. But he was a broad-minded man, and
remained so. To please his harem he built a mosque; to please himself he built an English church."

The "rich Englishman who had become orientalized" was
James Skinner, whose father was a Scottish officer in the East India
Company's army, and whose mother was the daughter of a Rajput
landowner. Because of British prejudice toward Anglo-Indians, he
could not follow in his father's footsteps as an officer in the East
India Company. So in 1796, at the age of eighteen, he became a
junior officer in the forces of one of the Company's rivals, Sindhia,
the Maharaja of Gwalior. As a result of Skinner's bravery, military
skill, and gifts of leadership, he advanced in rank, finally commanding two battalions of infantry. But when Sindhia decided to
attack the East India Company's forces, his French general sum-
marily dismissed all the British and Anglo-Indian officers, including
Skinner, who had served gallantly for seven years.

Impressed by Skinner's reputation, the British offered him the command of an irregular troop of horse, irregular in the sense that it was not part of the Company's regular army, which was still unprepared to accept an Anglo-Indian officer. Skinner raised, trained, and commanded a corps of 3,000 men, Skinner's Horse, a mounted guerrilla force that helped the East India Company subdue northern India's native princes. Skinner's Horse eventually joined the Company's army and survives today as an armored regiment in the Indian Army. Unfortunately his house, at which troupes of dancing girls entertained his guests at celebrated parties, and in which the Clemenses spent a night, no longer stands. But the handsome church he built across the way survives.

From Delhi the Clemenses traveled to Lahore, 270 miles northwest, in today's Pakistan. "Mark Twain at Last!" proclaimed a notice for two *At Homes* there. These were scheduled for Wednesday and Thursday, March 18 and 19, 1896. "On Wednesday night," reported Lahore's *Civil and Military Gazette,* "when he stepped on the platform, he was looking a trifle pale and worn after his recent illness: at the age to which the great humourist has attained, railway travelling is a fatiguing business, especially when added to the delights of our Indian climate. But though Mark Twain's hair now is nearly white and his cheeks are deeply lined, the fire in his eye testified to the still youthful and indominitable spirit which has made him undertake, in the evening of his life, this crusade in a cause so contrary to the tendencies of our modern age." In a local allusion, Clemens introduced himself as a friend of Kipling, who had once worked in Lahore.

After his second performance, a reviewer commented that "Mark Twain has come, has been seen, and has conquered the hearts of all Lahore." Even the lieutenant governor of the Punjab, with whom Clemens lunched, was captivated, if lending an elephant indicates esteem. Apparently it was accepted by the travelers of the day that the best way to see the city's antiquities was from a howdah. "I am used to being afraid of collisions when I ride or drive," wrote Clemens in *Following the Equator,* "but when one is on top of an elephant that feeling is absent. I could have ridden in comfort through a regiment of runaway teams."

Clemens performed but one more time in India, in Rawalpindi,

160 miles northwest of Lahore, on Friday, March 20. India was becoming too hot. "It was always summer in India," Clemens wrote Rogers a month later. "Of course we never saw any of the real summer; they do say that when that comes Satan himself has to knock off and go home and cool off." Clemens received letters from total strangers warning him to leave the country before the intense heat set in. Besides, the sailing date to Ceylon and Mauritius had been advanced by two days. So on Saturday, March 21, the Clemenses left Rawalpindi for Calcutta, a journey of more than 1,200 miles that lasted almost three full days.

At sunrise on Tuesday, March 24, they returned to Calcutta and the Continental Hotel, where a reporter found Clemens "comfortably ensconced in an easy chair and smoking a Meerschaum, black with age." Clemens was healthy now, he said, but Clara was suffering from a touch of malarial fever, although she was much better. He denied the rumor that he had sold the copyright for his forthcoming travel book for £10,000. It was unlikely, he said, that he would ever sell the copyright to one of his books when he could readily command royalties on sales. Publishing, he stated, is all a gamble. For instance, at the outset of his career he had refused to sell the copyright to *The Innocents Abroad* because he didn't know how well it would sell and didn't want the publisher to lose through him. (The claim was disingenuous. He insisted on a royalty after consulting Henry Ward Beecher, who was experienced in negotiating such contracts.) He had taken a multitude of notes during his tour of India, he said, but he had not had time to work them up because social and business engagements had kept him fully occupied. He would need more than six months, he thought, to prepare his manuscript, which he might begin in Cape Town, the last stop on his world tour. At the moment he was afraid to say anything about so vast and complex a country as India. He needed time to digest his impressions.

That afternoon the Clemenses boarded the British India Company's *Wardha* for the long voyage to Mauritius, via Madras and Colombo. The vessel remained at its anchorage on the Hooghly River all night. "When wind blew in, icy cold," Clemens noted in his journal, "the moment it stopped, blistering hot & mosquitoes. We all went up & slept on deck." At seven in the morning the next day, the *Wardha* dropped its moorings and started down the

Hooghly. "For six hours now," he wrote in his journal, "it has been impossible to realize that this is India and the Hoogli (river). No, every few miles we see a great white columned European house standing in front of the vast levels, with a forest away back — La. planter? And the thatched groups of native houses have turned themselves into the negro quarters, familiar to me near forty years ago — and so for six hours this has been the sugar coast of the Mississippi." On the following day they entered the Bay of Bengal, and sailed southwest along the coast.

During their voyage to Madras, Mrs. Clemens wrote a discouraged letter to her sister. Her Hartford home had been much in her thoughts, she said. But when she considered the long list of their creditors and the sums owed them, she felt that it would be a very long time before they could return to their home in Hartford. "Sometimes it comes over me like an overwhelming wave, that it is to be bitterness and disappointment to the end." Still, most of the time she managed to keep up her courage. Her husband was not as sanguine as she would like him to be, but he had been suffering from colds and other disabilities. Also the fact that he was now sixty years old depressed him. "Naturally I combat that idea all that I can, trying to make him rejoice that he is not *seventy*." They did not take much money out of India beyond their expenses, she said, because the halls and theaters tended to be small, typically seating no more than four hundred people. But, cheering up, she added that India had become extremely enjoyable. Her husband's reception there proved to be universally enthusiastic. Besides, India offered better material for his travel book than did Australia or Africa. Clara also relished India. In a letter to her cousin she wrote that their visit to India was "the most interesting by far we ever had or dreamed of having."

Four days after leaving Calcutta they reached Madras, early on the morning of March 31. The party went ashore for breakfast, intending to drive around the town, but Clemens, who had caught another cold, decided he wasn't up to sightseeing and returned to the ship while his family spent the day on land. A reporter found him reclining peacefully on deck, in a deep cane-bottomed chair, reading a Madras newspaper. "When this boat leaves Madras to-day," he said, "I suppose I will be leaving India quite behind me.

Let me see, I landed at Bombay in the middle of January and here is the 31st of March. It seems such a short time and India is such a large place to study." Did he find what he had expected? "Well, hardly . . . I came here like many others with only a very vague idea of the country, and I am bound to confess that I did not find it the immensely wealthy place it has been described as . . . A feature that has struck me very forcibly in India is the poverty of the country . . . Here the failure of the crops is universal at times and when a district can't be approached in time by railway, famine prevails and the mighty masses die of sheer starvation."

He had, he continued, noticed that most of the land between Bombay and Calcutta was diligently tilled wherever water was accessible. "As regards General Booth's scheme, I have read something of it, but I do not think he can hope to succeed if he means to sandwich the religion of the Salvation Army with his peasant-settlement scheme." William Booth, the founder and first general of the Salvation Army, had recently left India after a promotional tour on behalf of his population redistribution proposal. He hoped to set up colonies in India that would offer low-interest loans to peasants, the settlements to be administerd by zealous volunteers from the Salvation Army. The government rejected his proposal, which required grants of land as well as money, and his plan found no favor whatsoever among the Indian population, probably because they suspected, as did Clemens, that it was motivated by the desire to convert. In response to Booth's proposal, an Indian journal wrote that "India is already swarmed enough by various missionary bodies and it is time for all people of India to make a determined stand for the safety of their ancient religion."

Clemens asked the reporter about an equestrian statue he had seen in Madras. "Sir Thomas Munro, did you say? Ah, that takes one way back in your history to Clive. Yes, I recollect now, he was one of your early Governors." That reminded him of the last governor, Lord Wenlock. According to one paper Clemens had read, Wenlock was a failure. "I think it a mistake myself to send out your landed noblemen to administer this vast country. They are not cut out for administrative work and are better left on their wealthy estates. You want men who are born to govern and who have made statesmanship a life-long study. Your new Governor comes up to that mark, I am told."

When the conversation turned to inventive genius, Clemens remarked that it was a mistake to consider America "as *the* inventors of the world, but we do what is worth a great deal more; we take up an invention and work at it till it results in something perfect. 'Promoters of inventions' would be the proper way of describing us Americans."

As for the Anglo-American conflict over the Venezuelan border, Clemens was gratified to learn that the sides had agreed to arbitration, although he never doubted that the dispute would be resolved peacefully. "It was absolutely silly to think that America and England would ever fire a shot at each other."

Clemens concluded the interview by thanking the reporter for his kind wishes. "I have had nothing else all over India, and will carry the best recollections of this country home with me." Indeed, years later, when he was dictating his autobiography, he would say that India was "the only foreign land I ever daydream about or deeply long to see again."

Chapter Thirty-five

*T*HE CLEMENSES DOCKED at Colombo at about noon on Good Friday, April 3, 1896. Vast clouds piled up on the horizon, a harbinger of bad weather soon to come. The vessel arrived flying a yellow flag: the carrier of an infectious disease had been found on board. A passenger suffering from chicken pox was removed to a hospital ship before the flag was lowered. When Clemens learned that there was a strong probability of his ship's being quarantined at Port Louis, Mauritius, he asked for information about the quarantine accommodations there and advised the captain that if the Clemenses were not back on board fifteen minutes before departure time on the following day, he had "better up-anchor and get off and not wait" for them.

Along with the Clemenses, other arrivals included Harmston's Circus, which Clemens had watched embarking at Madras, where he admired its tigers. Now in Colombo a black panther was reported to have devoured a performing monkey who had come too close. "The menagerie section," commented the *Times of Ceylon,* "will amuse the natives largely no doubt."

Mrs. Clemens and Clara, leaving the menagerie and Clemens behind, went up to the hill country and spent the night in Kandy, capital of a kingdom which had resisted European domination for three hundred years. Clemens stayed in town, where he was the guest of Dr. and Mrs. Murray, a likable couple, if his notes are to be trusted, who lived in a large, cool home set in an attractive compound with many trees. The family lived on Brownrigg Road, today a leafy street of old houses and old trees, guarded at each end by soldiers at sandbagged positions to protect the high government officials who live there. The Murrays' house, with Dutch gables at each end and a long, arched veranda, is now the police officers' club.

Clemens performed that night at the Public Hall, where his

audience was small, due to the rainy weather and Good Friday — there had been a European exodus to the hills because of the long weekend. He looked better than he did when he arrived in January, thought one reporter, "but it is evident that age is beginning to tell on him, and that the vigour and energy which once characterised him are fast losing their power."

Apologizing for scheduling an *At Home* on Good Friday, Clemens claimed disarmingly to have forgotten all about it. In spite of a hacking cough that interrupted some of his routines, he kept his audience laughing throughout his performance, at the end of which he received a rapturous ovation. Nonetheless, one reporter criticized Clemens for not staying closely to the text of his stories, which "are spoiled by altering one word," changes that some of his admirers considered to be "almost profanity." The reporter thought the performance "ex tempore."

The Public Theatre is now a cinema, with a projectionist's tower built at one end. Part of the building's exterior has been plastered over, but the remainder shows the old columned arcade. The tower supports a lurid poster advertising a Sinhala film for adults only.

Apparently the intelligence Clemens received about the quarantine facilities at Port Louis was favorable. The party boarded the vessel on Saturday evening, immediately after the second *At Home*, which, like the first, was thinly attended but warmly received. They sailed out of Colombo under a cloudburst.

A few days later Clara wrote to her cousin that she and her mother were sleeping on deck every night because of the heat and the enormous cockroaches in their cabins. The creatures did not bother her father, who was resigned to insects on tropical voyages. According to a journal entry, he considered the vessel quite comfortable. In a subsequent entry he wrote that "seventeen days ago this ship sailed out of Calcutta and ever since barring a day or two in Ceylon there has been nothing in sight but a tranquil blue sea and a cloudless blue sky. All down the Bay of Bengal it was so; it was so on the equator, it is still so here in the vast solitudes of the Indian Ocean; 17 days of heaven, and in 11 more it will end. There will be one passenger who will be sorry."

The voyage to Mauritius was a welcome holiday, but it was not long enough for Clemens. "There *are* no sea-holidays any more," he complained to Rogers, "the voyages are all too short, unless you take a sailing-vessel." The speed of modern travel, he told his journal, had so shrunk the world that countries once thought remote had lost their mystery.

If no countries are remote, Mauritius, a Lilliputian volcanic island in the Indian Ocean, five hundred miles east of Madagascar, is the next best thing, at least to Europeans and Americans for whom the place is little more than a name. It was better known in Clemens's day because of the phenomenal success of the romance *Paul et Virginie* (1787), by Jacques-Henri Bernardin de St-Pierre, a disciple of Rousseau. The novel portrays a boy and girl of the same age brought up in a state of nature by their families in Mauritius. "It was that story," Clemens wrote in *Following the Equator,* "that made Mauritius known to the world, made the name familiar to everybody, the geographical position of it to nobody." The novel was read in Mauritius, too. "No other book is so popular here except the Bible. By many it is supposed to be a part of the Bible ... It is the greatest story that was ever written about Mauritius, and the only one."

The Clemenses anchored off Port Louis, the capital of Mauritius, on Wednesday, April 15. Clemens had expected to be quarantined. Not only had there been a passenger with chicken pox on board, but cholera had been raging in Calcutta when the ship sailed. Nonetheless, the authorities did not impose a quarantine, and the next day the Clemenses went ashore. They took a train ten miles southeast to the highland town of Curepipe, where they remained for almost two weeks. Smythe scheduled no *At Home*s in Mauritius, presumably to allow Clemens to rest.

After about ten days in Curepipe, Clemens wrote to Rogers that "this holiday comes very handy for me; I am very glad to have a resting spell; I was getting fagged with platform work." Clemens went on to tell Rogers about the place. Although it rained so much that "a match that will light on anything is a curiosity," the countryside was beautiful, "surrounded by sugar plantations and the greenest and brightest and richest of tropical vegetation." Sugar was the dominant crop, and it remains so one hundred years later, so that a drop in price, a poor harvest, or a bad cyclone can damage the economy, although the economy is not as vulnerable as it once was. The export of manufactured goods has risen, as has the proportion of land devoted to crops other than sugar.

The island, continued Clemens, was a British possession, "but there are few English people and many French; so the French have everything their own way — and the French way is seldom a good way in this world." Most of the population was not French, however, reported Clemens, but East Indian. When the British took over the island from the French in 1814, they permitted the French to keep their laws, language, and property. French was the chief European language, and French Creole the lingua franca. When slavery was abolished in the 1830s, the British imported Indian indentured laborers, mainly Hindus, to work the sugar plantations. They remain the majority, and because Mauritius is a democracy, Hindus dominate the government. If the Franco-Mauritians, now a minuscule if rich minority, no longer have everything their own way, French is still the dominant European language and French Creole the lingua franca.

After reporting that Clara was suffering from a large carbuncle, he concluded his letter by promising that "if I think of any more facts about Mauritius that will be valuable in Wall Street I will write again."

On April 28, the Clemenses sailed for South Africa in the *Arundel Castle*, which Clemens called "the finest boat I have seen in these seas," although it retained what he considered a universal and eternal maritime defect, poor beds. Soon they passed Ile de Bourbon (now Réunion), and by the first of May they were sailing past the southern end of Madagascar. Only six months before, the Queen of Madagascar, Ranavalona III, had signed a treaty recognizing and accepting the protection of the French, who had invaded the island, the fourth largest in the world, and occupied the capital. As the Clemenses were steaming by, the French were extending their occupation over the entire island, which it would annex in a few months. "All that I remember about Madagascar," Clemens joked in *Following the Equator*, "is that Thackeray's little Billee went up to the top of the mast and there knelt him upon his knee, saying, 'I see / Jerusalem and Madagascar, / and North and South Amerikee.' "

The next day they had reached the Mozambique Channel, which divides Madagascar from southeast Africa, and were sailing due west to Delagoa Bay. At the head of the bay stood the port of Lourenço Marques (now Maputo) in Mozambique. Although the Portuguese had controlled Mozambique in varying degrees for almost four hundred years, their "right" to Delagoa Bay had been established little more than twenty years before, in arbitration with two other armed robbers, Britain and Germany.

The Clemenses reached Lourenço Marques on May 4. Approaching the port, they saw "a bold headland — precipitous wall, one hundred and fifty feet high, very strong, red color, stretching a mile or so. A man said it was Portuguese blood — battle fought here with the natives last year. I think this doubtful." In 1894 the Portuguese had suppressed an uprising around Lourenço Marques.

A railroad ran seventy miles northwest from the port to the border of the landlocked South African Republic, one of the two Boer Republics. Clemens observed "thousands of tons of freight on the shore — no cover. This is Portuguese all over — indolence, piousness, poverty, impotence." Later he told a reporter in Durban that "Delagoa Bay at the time of the creation was intended for an important port in Africa — the most important port in South Africa — in energetic and intelligent hands; but to remember that it is in the hands of the Portuguese is to recognize that it is not in energetic and intelligent hands, and that its development to the importance which it ought to possess is never to be expected."

The Clemenses spent the afternoon on shore. Clemens didn't think much of it: "a small town — no sights. No carriages. Three 'rikishas, but we couldn't get them — apparently private." He noticed the "outrageously heavy bags of freight" that the African women stevedores carried on their heads. "The quiver of their leg as the foot was planted and the strain exhibited by their bodies showed what a tax upon their strength the load was."

The ship headed southwest along the coast. Clemens wrote that two days later, during the afternoon of May 6, "the ship slowed down, off the land, and thoughtfully and cautiously picked her way into the snug harbor of Durban, South Africa."

5

SOUTH AFRICA

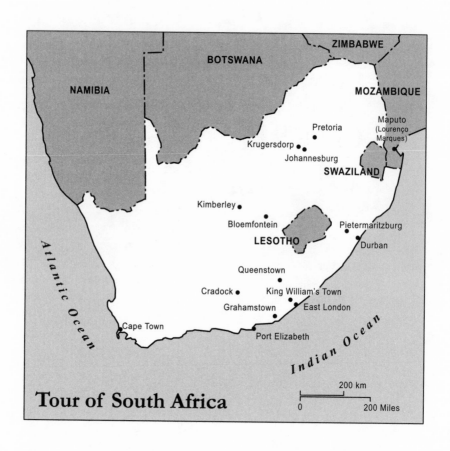

Tour of South Africa

Chapter Thirty-six

*O*NE WEEK AFTER the Clemens party left Mauritius, they landed at Durban. Two founding members of Durban's Savage Club welcomed the Clemens party at the pier, before the party drove off to the Royal Hotel. Then as now, Durban was the largest city of Natal, then a self-governing British colony, now the South African province of KwaZulu/Natal. Then as now, the English royal coat of arms hung over the hotel's entrance, but if the Clemenses were to find themselves in Durban today they would not recognize their accommodations. Two towers sheathed in ceramic brick have supplanted the miscellaneous collection of one- and two-story buildings that greeted them. In 1896 the hotel's bayside garden overlooked palm trees and an occasional sailboat. Today's guests will not see the bay from the hotel's lower floors because tall buildings intervene, nor will they be served by barefoot waiters with white turbans, nor will they find rickshaw pullers, Zulus adorned with beads and horned headresses, waiting for them outside.

"'Rikishas," wrote Clemens in *Following the Equator,* "drawn by splendidly built black Zulus, so overflowing with strength, seemingly, that it is a pleasure, not a pain, to see them snatch a 'rikisha along. They smile and laugh and show their teeth — a good-natured lot." Perhaps Clemens did not know that in nearby Pietermaritzburg, rickshaw pullers were throwing stones to defend themselves from whip-wielding cabdrivers, who resented the loss of business from the newly introduced conveyances. Today in Port Elizabeth, an industrial town farther down the coast, taxi companies feuding over routes are shooting and stabbing one another's drivers.

More serious is today's bloody conflict in KwaZulu/Natal between the Zulu-based Inkatha Freedom Party and the country's ruling African National Congress, dominated by Xhosas. In 1995 from sixty to eighty people in the province died each month from political violence. On Christmas Day, for example, hundreds of Inkatha partisans, armed with guns, spears, and clubs, entered a village south of Durban and set its thatched huts ablaze. When the inhabitants, supporters of the Congress, tried to flee, the mob shot or hacked at them. Eighteen people, including several children, died and many more were wounded.

The civil war in Natal has simmered for years, despoiling the province's lush, well-watered valleys with corpses and burned-out homes. Just as in Belfast, where there are "no-go" zones for Protestants and Catholics, here there are such zones for Zulus and Xhosas.

The root cause of the conflict is the reluctance of the Zulus, South Africa's largest ethnic group, to be ruled, as they see it, by Xhosas, the country's second-largest group. Chief Mangosuthu Buthelezi, the charismatic leader of the Inkatha Freedom Party, has stimulated a revival of Zulu nationalism and its associated martial tradition. He demands greater autonomy for the provinces, including the right to his own army, and he promotes the prerogatives of tribal chiefs.

One Afrikaner friend, who told me years ago that he would rather be a gardener in a majority-ruled South Africa than the beneficiary of a white-minority regime, now says jokingly that he wishes the old government would return for just ten minutes so that it could dispose of Buthelezi. He knows, of course, that the old regime encouraged the Inkatha, even training Inkatha members in guerrilla warfare, in a transparent effort to divide and rule. That our friend, a man who despises despotism, should make such a joke indicates his dismay at the current scene. It remains to be seen whether the Zulus will join the majority of South African peoples in supporting a unified country governed by elected officials, or whether violent Zulu nationalism will continue.

Whether by Zulu-drawn rickshaw or by cab, Clemens left the hotel to pick up his mail, probably at the Castle Mail Packets Company, where a clerk told him that no man could receive letters under two different names. Besides, *Mark Twain* was the name of a ship that occasionally tied up at Durban. When Clemens learned that the vessel was now shattered, its masts broken, he cried out "just my condition."

The day after his arrival, in an interview with *The Natal Mercury*, Clemens spoke of his visit to India, which he described as delightful. "I only wish my stay could have been extended two or three years longer; but the heat came and drove us out." Ever since leaving America in August, he said, he had been "knocking about," although he had never enjoyed extensive traveling.

Asked how he became a writer, Clemens replied that he had entered journalism without intending it. "It is just what happens in all frontier towns and in all new places. Half your time your vocation, if you have one, has no place there, and you must seek another; and you're apt to find it by accident. I found a vacancy in a newspaper office when I wasn't looking for one. That was in Nevada, in the silver mining days." This may have been psychologically true for Clemens, but the facts were more complicated. He had contributed occasional sketches and fillers to a few papers while working as a printer back East, before he became a riverboat pilot, and afterwards, during his disheartening attempts to become a mining magnate in Nevada, he wrote for various papers. His pieces for Virginia City's *Territorial Enterprise* had brought him to the attention of that paper's editor, who hired him as a full-time reporter. Clemens was wanted not only for his skills but also for his contacts: his brother, as Territorial Secretary, commissioned the government's printing contracts.

Two days after his arrival in Durban, Clemens wrote to Rogers that "we have been in the pitiless and uninterrupted blaze of summer from the time I saw you last until we reached this place — more than ten straight months of it . . . But here in Durban it is cool . . . The days are warm, but not too warm; coolness begins with sunset; an hour later you must put on an overcoat; and your bed must have several blankets on it."

On one of those warm winter days Clemens, accompanied by the two Savage Club members who had met him at the pier, took a two-hour drive to a Trappist monastery, where he marveled at the monks' "comfortless and forbidding" life. He saw the workshops and schoolrooms in which the monks were teaching literacy in both English and Zulu along with "wage-yielding mechanical trades" to African boys and girls. In those days, European expectations of Africans were not high. The town's leading paper, in an editorial published during Clemens's visit, commented that the development of the African "must not be forced — he must grow in the graces of civilisation slowly if it is to be surely, and if he be unduly urged or hastened . . . he will be unfit to occupy the position for which he strives, bringing disaster to himself and others."

On the drive to the monastery, Clemens noted "groups of negro men and women strolling along, dressed exactly like our darkies and with exactly the same faces — and I could imagine myself in Texas; then suddenly a gang of unmodified Zulus would appear, festooned with glass beads and with necklaces made of the vertebrae of snakes," and the illusion vanished.

Clemens described another drive, this one over the Berea, a ridge above Durban on which rich Europeans had built their homes. "Everything neat and trim and clean like the town," he wrote. "The loveliest trees and the greatest variety I have ever seen anywhere, except approaching Darjeeling."

The friends who took him on this outing were probably Dr. and Mrs. Samuel Campbell, who lived on Berea Road. Dr. Campbell, a physician, the founder and promoter of the first technical college in South Africa, a popular lecturer on women's suffrage, and a leading light in the Savage Club, was a beloved character, a man of such radiant personality that when he died in 1926 flags flew at half mast and meetings were canceled throughout the city. Too busy, or too diffident perhaps, to join his fellow Savage Club members in welcoming the Clemenses at the pier, and fearing to bother Clemens at the Royal Hotel, he conveyed through Smythe an offer to provide any needed assistance during the Clemenses' stay. Clemens asked to meet him, and the two liked each other. As a result, the Campbells opened their home to the Clemenses, took them on carriage drives, and provided Clemens with a retreat in their garden, where he would sit under an orange tree and, in Dr. Campbell's words, "spend quite a cheery time."

The Berea is still an upper-income enclave, although high-end apartment houses have replaced many of the old mansions. If you stroll through its sleek shopping mall, you will see few black customers. But in downtown Durban you will have no doubt you are in an African city. Crowds of black Africans throng the pavements, where street vendors sell produce unfamiliar to most European and

North American visitors. Despite the crowds, it is possible to find at Theatre Lane the site of the one-thousand-seat Theatre Royal, now on a block of nondescript warehouses opposite a cemetery.

On Tuesday, May 12, 1896, six days after his arrival in Durban, Clemens appeared at the theater, where his performance was so successful that extra rows had to be provided for his second and last appearance the following night. Clemens, probably the first world-class platform star to reach South Africa, managed the rare feat of filling the house two nights in a row.

After his first performance, the Savage Club entertained him at supper. Dr. Campbell, the evening's chairman, later recalled that "in a quite inadequate speech while proposing his health" he told of his indebtedness to Clemens, whose books he would recommend to his patients "as a tonic during their convalescence, — with the happiest results." In response Clemens said how "soothed" he was to learn that his books had helped Dr. Campbell in his medical practice. Had it never occurred to Dr. Campbell that the doctor was using Clemens's talent to acquire wealth and prestige? "It was surely evident to the simplest intelligence" that the doctor owed him something, and Clemens would be glad to receive a check from him before he left Durban.

On Thursday, May 14, Clemens and Smythe left on the 6:00 P.M. train for Pietermaritzburg, about forty miles northwest. Durban's *Natal Mercury* reported that "socially, the visit of Mark Twain has been the event of the week, and Durban has, to its credit made the most of it . . . So pleased are they with the town and climate that Mrs. and Miss Clemens are staying here a fortnight longer."

Clemens, who arrived in Pietermaritzburg the same night, wrote to Mrs. Clemens the next morning from his large and comfortable room, telling her he was lonely and missed her all the time. This was the first of the almost daily letters he sent her until they were reunited about five weeks later, letters in which he expressed his perpetual longing for her and his regret for having left her and Clara behind.

According to his good friend and literary mentor, William Dean Howells, Clemens's "beautiful and tender loyalty" to Mrs. Clemens was "the most moving quality of his most faithful soul," a devotion merited "by her surpassing force and beauty of character." Howells described her as "the loveliest person I have ever seen, the gentlest, the kindest, without a touch of weakness; she united wonderful tact with wonderful truth; and Clemens not only accepted her rule implicitly, but he rejoiced, he gloried in it." In this first letter to her during their South African separation, Clemens told her he was lying in bed, rehearsing for his performance that night, when he planned to try out a new ending to one of his routines. After ten months on tour, he was still tinkering with his material.

That night, Friday, May 15, the governor-general and his wife, Sir Walter and Lady Hely-Hutchinson, were among the audience who crammed the Theatre Royal for Clemens's first *At Home*. According to one report, people flocked in "from all parts of the country by road and rail to see and hear him."

On Saturday, regretting that his wife and daughter could not be with him "to join culture and beauty to talent and make the fambly show up fine," he lunched with the Hely-Hutchinsons at Government House.

Two of the problems facing the governor were the threat of a cattle disease, rinderpest, which had broken out in other parts of South Africa and might soon cross the border, and "franchise protection." The latter referred to the white population's efforts to prevent the Indian community from voting. Many former indentured laborers from India, imported to work the sugar plantations, had remained in South Africa after the expiration of their contracts, much as they had in Fiji. In a letter to the London *Times*, a British resident of Natal claimed that the Indian inhabitants of the province were equal in number to the whites and utterly unfit to vote. "While colonists do all that can be done to make life in Natal pleasant for the Indians, we are determined about one thing. We will not on any account allow the Indian to govern Natal ... The government of Natal must remain in the hands of the white men of Natal, because the colored population is unfitted for it." The writer resented the suggestion that colonists were cruel oppressors. On the contrary, they were "actuated by the spirit of justice and fairness towards inferiors which has made the name of Englishman respected throughout the world."

In 1894 the Natal parliament had passed a bill that would have

excluded Indians from the franchise, but Britain disallowed the leg-
islation, claiming that it was, in the words of the attorney general,
"too brutally blunt and rude" and that some other means had to be
found to "effect the same object" in a way that would be less offensive to Her Majesty's subjects in India. Accordingly, two months
before Clemens arrived in Pietermaritzburg, the Natal parliament
passed a bill that provided that natives of countries without representative institutions would require special permission to vote. As
another letter-writer to the *Times* put it, "Coolies have no votes in
India; why should they have votes here? If they are not fit to govern
themselves, are they qualified to govern us? . . . If the Disfranchise-
ment Bill is disallowed, it will be passed again and again until it is
accepted by the home government." (Actually, Indians and
Englishmen had the same franchise in India, with equal rights to
vote in the 750 municipalities.) At the moment, then, the white residents of Natal were worrying that Britain would veto the bill.

According to data published by the colonial government just a
few months before the new law was passed, about 9,300 Europeans
and about 250 British Indians were registered to vote. The twenty-
six-year-old Mohandas K. Gandhi, then living in Durban, pointed
out that these numbers scarcely offered a threat to European rule.
Indians were content, he said, with the existing franchise law, which
contained a property qualification, even though it would exclude
the great mass of the Indian community.

Gandhi, a London-trained barrister, had come to Natal a few
years before, to represent an Indian trading firm in a matter that was
to be heard before the Pretoria Supreme Court. After he landed in
Durban, the young man, dressed in the London barrister's uniform
of frock coat and patent-leather shoes, entered a first-class train
compartment for Pretoria, a first-class ticket in hand. Because only
white people were permitted to travel in first-class compartments,
the white conductor ordered him to leave. Gandhi refused. At the
first stop, Pietermaritzburg, a policeman threw him off the train.

As he wrote later, two alternatives confronted him. He could
either return to India, freeing himself from his contract on the
grounds that the local circumstances had not been fully disclosed to
him, or he could accept whatever hardships arose and fulfill his
engagement. "I was pushed out of the train by a police constable at

Maritzburg, and the train having left, was sitting in the waiting room, shivering in the bitter cold. I did not know where my luggage was, nor did I dare to inquire of anybody, lest I be insulted and assaulted once again. Sleep was out of the question. Doubt took possession of my mind. Late at night, I came to the conclusion that to run back to India would be cowardly. I must accomplish what I had undertaken. I must reach Pretoria, without minding insults and even assaults. Pretoria was my goal. The case was being fought out there. I made up my mind to take some steps, if that was possible, side by side with my work. This resolution somewhat pacified and strengthened me but I did not get any sleep."

He made up his mind to take some steps. The first was to wear a turban when he appeared before the Pretoria Supreme Court. Ordered to remove it, he appealed for acknowledgment of his right as an Indian to wear this symbol of his country. He won. Commenting on this case, Allister Sparks wrote that "it was the first time any person of colour had challenged authority in South Africa. There was a long, long road ahead . . . but this was the moment when resistance to white rule began."

Gandhi, who had intended to remain in South Africa only for the duration of the legal case for which he had been engaged, stayed on for twenty-one years. It was in South Africa that he developed his strategy of passive resistance. Although he carried out his South African campaigns on behalf of the Indian community alone, his work was an inspiration to black Africans. He was, according to Sparks, in some sense the parent of the African National Congress, the first black resistance movement in Africa, founded in 1912, two years before he returned to India.

A statue of Gandhi in downtown Pietermaritzburg commemorates the centenary of his expulsion from the train and the beginning of his political struggle. Here he is, the bald, middle-aged hero of the Salt March, striding forward, staff in hand, wearing the familiar dhoti. It would have been more appropriate, perhaps, to represent him as a shy, frock-coated young man, brooding on a bench in the Pietermaritzburg waiting room.

Although the survival of the theater in which Mark Twain performed is not clear, it is certain that at least two other buildings associated with him still stand: Government House, where the

Hely-Hutchinsons entertained him at lunch, and one of the old structures at Maritzburg College, a boys' school whose headmaster received him. Government House, a bit dilapidated, its great entrance hall broken up into smaller spaces, now houses the reception and library of the Natal College of Education.

Maritzburg College still operates, although only a few of the original buildings have been preserved. Robert Douglas Clark, its third headmaster, hosted Clemens's visit. "Fifty years experience of men and books," he recalled, "has taught me that some men are not so good as their books, while others are better. I found that [Max] O'Rell was in the former category and Mark Twain in the latter . . . Mark Twain is the most genial-hearted man I ever met. As he sat at my study window, looking towards Edindale, he said: 'Do you know, I could not do a stroke of work in this room of yours. I should always be looking out at this window. I have done all my best work at a desk facing a brick wall.' "

The handsome brick building that housed Clark's office, built in the 1880s with bay windows across the front, is now a dormitory. Dense foliage obscures the view from its windows. We can see enough, however, to judge that the lovely Edindale Valley would have been no more distracting than the valley and mountains seen from Quarry Farm's eight-windowed study, where Clemens wrote most of his best work.

The trees at Maritzburg College are taller and thicker now, but the boys we see there are still white. However, some subjects of formal learning are new: the boys now study computer science and the Zulu language, while a "co-curricular" program helps them explore such topics as alcohol, sex, and drugs.

Headmaster Clark and the barrister G. Bulkley, representing the Savage and Victoria Clubs respectively, presided over a joint club dinner in honor of Clemens after the latter's first *At Home* on May 15. Clemens, who could find in the briefest of introductions a handle for his remarks, was usually impatient with long preliminaries, which tended to be tedious. Bulkley's lengthy memorized address proved an exception to the rule, because it kept the Savages and Victorians in howls of laughter. Justifying his comments on the grounds of advanced age and local knowledge, Bulkley told Clemens what he should and should not write about Maritzburg, soberly enumerating the town's advantages, including some that it did not as yet possess. Clemens reported to his wife that in reply "I got up and said with a seriousness amounting to solemnity, 'I am the unwilling slave of an exacting vocation and' etc. It was a good long paragraph choicely worded ending 'and it would appear that through the inscrutable providence of God I am come to Maritzburg to be taught my trade by this hoary expert.' Then I took his speech to pieces and we had a roaring time."

Clemens was pleased by both Pietermaritzburg *At Home*s. He wrote to his wife about his first performance that "Last night . . . I was satisfied with myself & with the noise that was made. I kept myself entirely in hand & spoke deliberately." As for his second *At Home*, he reported to her that he "talked slowly. No use of any short an[nouncement] to get off stage before intermish. Ghost made 2/3 of the house yelp. Both houses crowded. Wonderful lot of pretty girls & young misses." His reviews were favorable, although one reporter noted that Clemens was "falling into the sere and yellow leaf."

Before Clemens and Smythe left for Johannesburg, a representative of *The Natal Witness* interviewed Smythe at the Imperial Hotel. The reporter characterized "Mark Twain's 'Man'" as "a well-informed man of the world, courteous and tactful, with business aptitude and literary tastes." Smythe remarked that people were vastly mistaken if they viewed Mark Twain simply as a humorist. "I think, if anything, he prefers writing serious matter, and I know he prefers reciting such matter to the ordinary humourous work. He is an omnivorous reader; takes up anything he can get hold of. He even reads the *Witness*."

The *Witness* still operates. Founded in 1849, it is South Africa's oldest daily newspaper. It is remarkable how many of the papers that reported on Clemens's tour are still in business, from the *Plain Dealer* of Cleveland, his first venue, to *The Cape Times* of Cape Town, his last.

Chapter Thirty-seven

A GRAND TORCHLIT RECEPTION had been planned for Clemens's nighttime arrival in Johannesburg on May 17, but was canceled as a result of an outpouring of public grief, prompted by a prisoner's suicide. Earlier that day, Fred Grey, a popular and prominent businessman and father of six, had been buried in Johannesburg after slitting his throat with a borrowed razor. His fellow prisoners in Pretoria Gaol sent an enormous wreath of flowers.

He had been one of the sixty-four members of the so-called Reform Committee — mine owners and managers, solicitors and barristers, company directors, physicians — all foreigners or "Uitlanders" as the Boers called them, who had been imprisoned by the Transvaal government and charged with plotting its overthrow.

The Transvaal (officially the South African Republic) and the Orange Free State were republics founded by the Boers, descendants of the Dutch and French who had emigrated to South Africa in the seventeenth century. After the British annexed their territory in the Cape, some trekked northward in search of fresh lands and renewed independence, and they did so again after the British annexed their territory in Natal.

The discovery of gold in 1886 transformed the Transvaal's poor and largely pastoral economy. From almost all parts of the world, thousands flocked to the goldfields on which, in a few short years, the glittering city of Johannesburg arose, created by the genie of enormous wealth. Buildings to rival the greatest in Melbourne and San Francisco were rising, creating a shortage of bricklayers, stonemasons, and carpenters. Social life among the expatriate white community — the bankers, businessmen, mining engineers, physicians, lawyers, and their families — was elegant and brilliant. To those familiar with gold-boom towns, Johannesburg was a wonder of the world. But like other gold-rush towns, it was wild and dissipated, with ninety-seven brothels serving a population of 25,000 white men, according to a survey carried out in 1895. One observer described the town as "Monte Carlo superimposed on Sodom and Gomorrah."

Great contrasts emerged between rich and poor. There might have been no young crossing-sweepers, as in London, but there were barefoot urchins hoping to earn a tip by holding the reins of your horse.

Although the Uitlanders soon made the Transvaal the richest of the four white South African states, and paid most of the state's taxes, they had no vote and received few services. Further, the government imposed unnecessary costs upon the mining companies in addition to the bribes exacted by government officials. The political and economic constraints under which the Uitlanders labored were exacerbated by a culture clash: the newcomers viewed the conservative, old-fashioned, and provincial Boers as uncouth, uneducated, and benighted, while the Boers saw the cosmopolitan, modernizing foreigners as a money-grubbing, soulless rabble.

Clemens, who socialized mainly with Uitlanders, adopted their view of the Boers, although he was influenced as well by the work of Olive Schreiner, who was born in the Cape Colony of a German missionary father and an English mother. Her *Story of an African Farm* (1883), based on her experiences as a young governess on remote Cape farms, became an immense success in America and England and won her many admirers abroad, including Clemens.

Although he viewed the Boer as a "white savage," Clemens understood the Boer point of view. The Afrikaner, Clemens wrote in *Following the Equator*, "has stood stock-still in South Africa for two centuries and a half, and would like to stand still till the end of time, for he has no sympathy with Uitlander notions of progress. He is hungry to be rich, for he is human; but his preference has been for riches in cattle, not in fine clothes and fine houses and gold and diamonds. The gold and the diamonds have brought the godless stranger within his gates, also contamination and broken repose, and he wishes that they had never been discovered."

The Uitlanders sought, in the words of one of their leaders, "those simple, democratic rights which had been denied alike to their respectful petitions and to their constitutional protests." Those simple rights, of course, belonged only to whites. Granting black Africans the vote occurred no more to the Uitlanders than it did to the Boers.

By the end of 1895 it was common knowledge that an Uitlander uprising was imminent. Guns and ammunition were being smuggled into Johannesburg in oil tanks and coal cars, and then hidden in disused mine shafts. Cecil Rhodes was centrally involved in the conspiracy. Self-made millionaire by the age of thirty, prime minister of the Cape Colony, and the richest and most powerful man in South Africa, he was an arch-imperialist, convinced that the English were supremely fitted to dominate the world. He viewed the Transvaal republic as a major barrier to his dream of a railroad from Cape Town to Cairo traveling entirely through British territory. Supporting Uitlander grievances to the point of revolt, he financed their weapons and, with the connivance of the British High Commissioner in Cape Town and the British Colonial Secretary in London, planned an armed intervention once the uprising began. He instructed his friend and right-hand man, Dr. Leander Starr Jameson, to wait with an armed, mounted force at Pitsani, a village in the Bechuanaland Protectorate, on the western Transvaal border. This mounted force was to come to the assistance of the Uitlanders once the insurrection began and the signal was given.

Jameson waited for the signal in vain. Some of the conspirators had begun to suspect that Rhodes was exploiting their grievances for his own purposes, namely to bring the Transvaal into a British-dominated South African federation, whereas most of the conspirators wanted to preserve the republic's independence. Others were rightly worried that they had not yet accumulated enough arms and ammunition. Further, word had arrived that Jameson's force was smaller than anticipated. Others pointed out that the invasion was planned for the end of the year, when large numbers of Afrikaner farmers, in town for Christmas, could be quickly mobilized against them. Besides, many Uitlanders hoped that the mere threat of force might be enough to extract concessions from the government. They ordered Jameson not to move, but, impetuous and fatally overconfident, he disregarded them. He himself would incite the uprising that they had been too timid or disorganized to mount. On December 29, 1895, he dashed across the border with his men.

A few days later, after skirmishes in which seventeen of his men were killed and fifty-five wounded (among fewer than five hundred men), Boer commandos surrounded Jameson and his raiders, fourteen miles from Johannesburg, and forced them to surrender. Three weeks later they were handed over to British representatives at the Natal border and packed off to England for trial. Meanwhile the British High Commissioner, who had come up to Cape Town to effect a settlement between the Transvaal government and the Uitlanders, persuaded the Uitlanders to give up their weapons as a condition for entering into negotiations. Members of the Reform Committee, which had been acting to promote Uitlander rights, soon found themselves in a Pretoria jail. Collectively representing millions of pounds sterling, these gentlemen were confined to a prison whose conditions were appalling even for the poor.

About a week before Clemens landed in Durban, the Reform Committee members were tried and convicted. Four leaders were condemned to the gallows, among them John Hays Hammond, an American mining engineer who stood at the head of South Africa's mining experts. Clemens had met him long ago, when Hammond was a senior at Yale. The remainder were sentenced to two years in jail, a fine of £2,000 each, and three years of banishment after their release. The next day the death sentences were commuted, but at the time Clemens arrived in Johannesburg, the terms to be served by the four leaders had not yet been announced.

A reporter joined Clemens and Smythe in the carriage that took them to the Grand National Hotel. On the way, Clemens spoke about their journey from Pietermaritzburg, about 280 miles to the southeast. He described the locusts he had seen clouding the sky. "At one place there were great silver-plated acres of veld, all due to the locusts. When you looked at them against the sun, each black silhouette was distinct. When the sun shone on their gauzy wings they made the best imitation of a snow-storm I have ever seen . . . Yes you have had a fearful time here lately, what with wars, revolutions, rinderpest, locusts, drought — and me! I guess you can go no further with plagues. Now that I've come you must take a change for the better."

Two travelers, he reported, invaded their compartment. "I tried to explain that the car was reserved for Royalties, but as they only saw two Princes, they refused to be impressed. First thing they asked was what my business was. I said writing books. They thought I said keeping books, so to encourage me they said: — 'Well, there's a countryman of yours here, one Hammond who's done well, he might manage to get you a job.' "

The next morning, another reporter found Clemens in "the best bedroom" of the Grand National Hotel, propped up against pillows at the foot of the bed. Dismissing the possibility of an Anglo-American war, Clemens said that England and America "were made to help and stand by each other," adding that if England had decided to fight for the sake of the Armenians, America would have come to her aid. At that time the bankrupt, tottering government of the Ottoman Sultan, disturbed by rising Armenian nationalism, was carrying out a campaign of ethnic cleansing. During the time of Clemens's tour, Turkish and Kurdish mobs, protected by soldiers, were butchering largely unarmed Armenians and plundering and destroying hundreds of their villages. Armenians in the scores of thousands were dying, from massacre or starvation, a forerunner of the massacres and expulsions of 1915, when Armenians in the hundreds of thousands died, and a precursor of the Holocaust, a generation later, when Hitler remembered that no one had helped the Armenians. "And these things are going on undisturbed," commented *The Times* of London at the end of 1895, while the most powerful fleet of modern times lies idle in the Aegean, and the six Great Powers of Europe are looking on in hopeless imbecility."

The reporter asked Clemens a standard question: What was his favorite among his own books? Clemens would vary his response to this query, naming different books at different times, perhaps to relieve the tedium. In this case he claimed not to be familiar with any of his books, and asked to be excused from answering. "He says he has only taken up one of his books to read, after writing them, and that was *Huckleberry Finn*. He read that once to a little girl in his family, and — he owns it shamefacedly — he laughed over it, whereupon his young critic sharply reproved him for laughing at what he had written himself. That experience, he says, was so discouraging that he never ran the risk of repeating it." He said that his most popular books, judging by sales, were *Roughing It, The Innocents Abroad,* and *The Prince and the Pauper.*

The talk turned to some of the authors Clemens knew, which led him to speak of Howells. "Howells is one of the very best literary men America has produced; there is no bludgeoning with him. His is the rapier method. You English don't like him because he once adversely criticised Dickens, and I believe even Thackeray! But we honour him as a man who delivers his verdicts after weighing the evidence most carefully; a man who despatches this aspirant or that not hurriedly or with passion, but slowly, deliberately, almost lovingly. Howells is a gentle, kindly, refined spirit; he is too good for this world. In my opinion there is never a trace of affectation or superiority in either the man or his books, though he is accused of both."

One of the century's most remarkable literary phenomena, Clemens said, was "the Bellamy 'boom.' " Edward Bellamy, a journalist and editor, is best known for his novel *Looking Backward,* set in Boston in the year 2000, when Americans worked until the age of forty-five in a national industrial army. Honor and prestige were the motivations for work, not material want, since a socialistic system provided for all. The book, published in 1888, sold more than a million copies and led to the organization of Bellamy Clubs to discuss its social implications. Clemens, who knew Bellamy, assured the reporter that no one was more surprised by the book's popularity than the author himself. The publishers didn't expect much from it either, "for the first edition was about as scrofulous-looking and mangy a volume as I have set eyes on."

In another interview, Clemens referred to the political situation that had arisen after Jameson's raid as "an inexpressible tangle." The first he had heard of the invasion, he said, was when he was in Albany, in Western Australia: "It was just the bare fact of the incursion having taken place. At Colombo we got nothing further that was definite beyond the fact of the defeat, and we were without any more news till we got to Bombay, although it was aggravating to reflect that particulars were passing under the sea along the wires we were passing over. From that day to this I have been getting more and more bewildered through missing weeks of news at a time. From Calcutta to Mauritius I was in a handsome state of suspense, until at last I heard that the leaders were all in gaol, and I could not for the life of me make out what it was for."

That Monday night he gave the first of four *At Home*s on four consecutive nights. The audience was so large that "it filled every available part and several strictly unavailable nooks and crooks of the Standard Theatre." Two or three semicircular rows of listeners sat behind him on the stage. When he first appeared, "he was so vociferously applauded that it was a full minute or two before he could proceed." The "gods," those seated in the upper balconies, whistled "Yankee Doodle," and when at last he began to speak, "auditors wiped tears from their eyes, mopped their brows, and threw one fit after another. Nuances were wasted, broad strokes alone were in order. The clamor wore down poor Mark, whose voice sank after the intermission. A man shouted, 'Speak up, old fellow!' and the offender won his audience back by saying, 'I have caught a succession of colds lately, and they do cripple me; but I suffer from them more than you do.' " A reporter from *The Star* wrote that the story of the golden arm was "well-known among the South African Dutch." He had heard the story from an old nurse when he was a boy, and she had heard it from her grandmother, who was born a slave. A reviewer for *The Johannesburg Times* wrote that "at all times the lecturer was eloquent; we, however, must not forget that the great American has come to us in person in the autumn of his life, and though we appreciate and applaud his eloquence and humour, we would fain have had the opportunity of listening to him when his talents sparkled with the freshness, crispness, and brilliance of middle age."

Clemens lunched on Tuesday, May 19, at the Rand Club, where many of the Reform Committee members had been arrested. For lunch on Wednesday he may have gotten himself into trouble. He suspected, as he wrote Mrs. Clemens that day, that he had engaged himself with two different groups for one o'clock, a problem that never would have arisen, he said, if she had been with him.

After Clemens's fourth *At Home*, on May 21, the Johannesburg correspondent of an out-of-town paper reported that Clemens had been received with tremendous enthusiasm. "The Standard Theatre was packed from 'gods' to stage, and not even standing room was available in any one of the four *At Homes* . . . Twain, who unconsciously carries on a crusade against pessimism, has done more for the salvation of the human family than ten score of priests."

The unconscious crusader dined with Natalie Hammond, the pregnant wife of John Hays Hammond, on Friday evening, the day after his fourth *At Home*. A few days before, the government had announced that her husband and the other three Reform leaders, whose death sentences had been commuted, were sentenced to fifteen years' imprisonment. At the same time, eight prisoners were released immediately upon the payment of their fines, and the jail terms of the remainder were reduced to a maximum of one year. The Transvaal, under the auspices of its formidable president, Paul Kruger, was demonstrating what came to be called "magnanimity by inches."

Clemens had met Mrs. Hammond on a crossing from Southampton to New York, but when he first saw her in Johannesburg he couldn't remember her name. He was, he asserted, "a wretched hand at remembering people's names," confiding that "I even forget my own at times, and I often have to give a fictitious name to the police." But his memory was jogged when he read her husband's name in the papers. Mrs. Hammond sent her carriage for him early, before her other guests were expected, which gave her a chance to tell him of the stirring events that followed Jameson's raid.

Among Mrs. Hammond's guests that night were the American consul, Robert Chapin, and his wife. Mrs. Chapin had taken Clemens on carriage rides and had entertained him at lunch. The morning after Mrs. Hammond's dinner party, Mrs. Chapin even packed his luggage, before she and her husband took him to the station. They accompanied him, Smythe, and Mrs. Hammond on the train to Pretoria, about forty miles northeast, where they hoped to visit the Reform prisoners and where Clemens would next perform.

Chapter Thirty-eight

*E*ARLY SATURDAY AFTERNOON, May 23, 1896, the party checked in at the Grand Hotel and then repaired to Pretoria Gaol. Hammond greeted Clemens. "Mr. Clemens, I'm certainly glad to see you again. How did you ever find your way into this God-forsaken hole?" Clemens replied, "Getting into jail is easy. I thought the difficulties arose when it came to getting out."

According to a newspaper account, based on notes that Smythe made from memory and gave the press, Clemens said he was delighted to see that there was only one journalist among the prisoners and that he was not at all surprised to find so many lawyers. "The dream of his life had been to get into gaol, but misfortune dogged his footsteps, for whenever he had committed anything, it had always happened that no witnesses were present except himself, and his reputation for veracity had not been sufficient to obtain conviction without corroborative evidence. There is no place where a man can secure such uninterrupted quiet as in gaol." He proposed taking the prisoners' place, serving as hostage for their good conduct and at the same time finding peace and quiet in which to write his book. Neither *Don Quixote* nor *Pilgrim's Progress* would ever have been written had their authors not been imprisoned. Yes, the longer the Reform Committee members remained in jail the more they would appreciate the "insidious charm of the life."

Clemens described his visit in a letter to his friend Joseph Twitchell. "A Boer guard was at my elbow all the time, but was courteous and polite, only he barred the way in the compound (quadrangle or big open court) and wouldn't let me cross a white mark that was on the ground — the 'death line' one of the prisoners called it. Not in earnest, though, I think . . . These prisoners are strong men, prominent men, and I believe they are all educated men. They are well off; some of them are wealthy. They have a lot of books to read, they play games and smoke, and for awhile they will be able to bear up in their captivity; but not for long, not for very long, I take it. I am told they have times of deadly brooding and depression. I made them a speech — sitting down. It just happened so, I don't prefer that attitude. Still, it has one advantage — it is only a *talk*, it doesn't take the form of a speech . . . I advised them at considerable length to stay where they were — they would get used to it and like it presently; if they got out they would only get in again somewhere else, by the look of their countenances; and I promised to go and see the President and do what I could to get him to double their jail-terms."

After declining Hammond's invitation to wait until the prisoners were ready to leave, Clemens returned to his hotel to prepare for the first of three *At Home*s at Pretoria's Caledonian Hall. Reviewers praised his performance but condemned the hall's acoustics. "The Caledonian Hall is excellent for dancing, but as a lecture hall it is hopeless. The alcove or platform is a grand retreat for an aggressive brass band but it is no place for a lecturer." Although it was impossible to hear him satisfactorily at the far end of the room, he elicited "a veritable boom of laughter." One critic chided those reviewers who related too much of the performer's material, which threatened to lessen its freshness. "It is not satisfactory to find that Mr. Clemens had previously given absolution in the apple incident — to Durban, Maritzburg, and Johannesburg — before he absolved Pretoria of the desire to eat forbidden fruit." Clemens found his largely Boer audience "promptly and abundantly responsive" once he had broken through their reserve.

The next day, at an interview in his hotel, Clemens spoke ironically about the filthy, overcrowded, vermin-ridden jail, with its grossly inadequate sanitary facilities. He was glad, he said, that the prisoners' comfort was so well looked after and that they fully appreciated the advantages of an outdoor life. He called it "an ideal rest cure for tired businessmen." The next day a humorless editorial writer, taking Clemens's comments literally, railed against the jail's leniency, pointing out that a prison was supposed to be a place of punishment. Hammond claimed that as a result of the editorial the prisoners' rations were reduced.

The following day, Sunday, Clemens again went to the prison, but according to his letter to the Reverend Twitchell, he was unable to enter because a minister was visiting the prisoners. The warden "[ex]plained that his orders wouldn't allow him to admit saint and sinner at the same time, particularly on a Sunday." Outside the jail, there was such stillness on the streets that Clemens felt as if the Puritan Sundays of the seventeenth century had returned.

Competition from a promenade concert given by the Pretoria Volunteer Cavalry Band at the cavernous Market Hall, where the Reform prisoners had been tried, may have accounted for the smaller assembly at his third performance, on Tuesday, May 26. Clemens told a new story, describing his reaction to the clock in the Government Buildings opposite his hotel, which chimed in the old Afrikaner style. After the half-hour signal, the number of the next hour would be chimed. Two strokes, for example, would indicate half past one. Unable to reconcile the chiming with his Waterbury watch, he claimed to have lost faith in his expensive timepiece and to have tossed it out the window. His audience greeted the local anecdote with "immense applause."

That day Clemens visited President Kruger, then seventy years old and serving the third of four consecutive five-year terms as president of the republic. As a child he had participated in the great northward migration of Afrikaner farmers from the Cape Colony. Eventually settling in what became the Transvaal, this God-fearing Calvinist of little formal education became a farmer and soldier. He fought the Matabele and the Zulus, struggled to establish an orderly government in what became the South African Republic, helped organize resistance to British rule after Britain annexed it, and, following a series of Boer victories in the first Anglo-Boer War of 1880–81, skillfully negotiated a peace convention that restored Boer independence, albeit under nominal British suzerainty.

After the restoration of the republic, a Boer farmer complained to him that the departure of the British occupiers had depressed the market for "mealies" (Indian corn). Kruger asked him how many bags of mealies he produced each year. About three hundred. And how many did he need for his own consumption? About 150. "There, that is what I always ask when I am asked these questions.

Here is a farmer who only needs 150 bags of mealies a year and he goes to the trouble of producing 300! I have no patience for such people."

When news reached Pretoria that Jameson and his forces were close to Krugersdorp, Kruger took out his rifle and ordered that his horse be saddled. This was a man who years earlier had severed his own thumb at the joint, when gangrene began to spread after a hunting accident. He might be old, but he was still brave. "Now that this Jameson's on the veld," he is reported to have said, "we'll soon see what he's worth." It took considerable skill to persuade him that he would be more useful to the state in Pretoria than on the veld.

At the time of his interview with Clemens, Kruger faced a cruel problem. On the one hand he wanted to placate the Uitlanders, who controlled the economy and, since most were British subjects, could appeal to Britain to support their claims. On the other he needed to maintain the support of his traditional constituency, who were probably already outnumbered by the Uitlanders and who were understandably alarmed at the prospect of losing political control. Jameson's raid convinced Kruger and his government that the British intended to subvert the republic's independence. From that time onward, the Transvaal prepared for war, which finally broke out three and a half years later. In the meantime his lenient treatment of the raiders and the conspirators bought him time. Severe punishment, although amply deserved, might have encouraged the British to intervene before the Boers felt ready for them. "If the heads of the Boer Government had not been wise men," wrote Clemens in *Following the Equator*, "they would have hanged Jameson, and thus turned a very commonplace pirate into a holy martyr."

Clemens, accompanied by the American consul Robert Chapin, visited Kruger on behalf of the American Reform prisoners. A translator mediated their conversation. Kruger was, Clemens noted, "in ordinary everyday clothes, and sat in an armchair, smoking Boer tobacco (the common black kind), his head and body bent forward. He had a bad cold and a very husky voice. He said he felt friendly toward America, and that it was his disposition to be lenient with the American captives." According to Hammond, prison conditions improved after Clemens's meeting with Kruger.

On Wednesday morning, May 27, Clemens and Smythe left Pretoria for Krugersdorp, about thirty-five miles southwest, where Clemens was to perform that evening. It was near Krugersdorp, at the edge of the Transvaal gold reef, that the Boers had ambushed Jameson's raiders, who had intended to take the town before continuing on to Johannesburg. The Boers killed, wounded, or captured sixty men in this encounter, while suffering only a few casualties themselves. The raiders then sought another route to Johannesburg, but they were surrounded the next day and forced to surrender.

Clemens's hostess in Krugersdorp, Mrs. Seymour, served as a volunteer nurse at the improvised field hospital, in a new store about to be opened, to which the wounded were brought after the ambush. She remained on duty for several days, until trained nurses could arrive. She and the other untrained nurses were commended by the district surgeon, who said that although attendance at operations imposed "a great strain" on them, they "worked splendidly, and better than I would ever have thought possible." He described Mrs. Seymour's work as "especially valuable."

She was now engaged in a more congenial activity, welcoming Clemens as an overnight guest and organizing a late supper for him after his performance. The *At Home* did not impose a financial sacrifice upon the committee that had guaranteed the house, since the hall was "crowded to utmost capacity," but the local critic was disappointed. "The yarns were rather too lengthy and too prosily told to evoke much enthusiasm ... But all the same the lecture was enjoyable and afforded a rich treat to most of those who were present." Perhaps inflated expectations caused the critic's disappointment. As Clemens noted in his journal during his South African tour, "the human imagination is much more capable than it gets credit for. This is why Niagara is always a disappointment when one sees it for the first time ... God will be a disappointment to most of us, at first ... St. Peter's, Vesuvius, Heaven, Hell, everything that is much described is bound to be a disappointment at first experience." Clemens was almost certainly tired. Aside from the interludes of sea voyages and those imposed by illness, he had been performing for ten months.

The morning after his Krugersdorp *At Home*, he traveled to Johannesburg. Mrs. Seymour drove him to the station "with a pair of horses over a rough & rocky & guttered road — drove like Satan; how she kept her seat I don't know; it would have been a hard drive for me, only I was in the air the main part of the time & the air at [Krugersdorp] is very thin & soft on account of the great altitude. Nothing else saved me from having my spine driven out at the back of my head like a flagstaff."

That night he performed for the fifth and last time in Johannesburg, before a packed and fashionable audience, who accorded him deafening applause for his sympathetic references to the Reform prisoners. It was a pity, he said, that men of such tremendous talent, intelligence, and energy were locked away for even a short time. He could not convince himself that they had deliberately set about to overturn the Transvaal Republic. As for the Americans involved, he continued, their training forbade such a thing. Love of republicanism was characteristically American; without it an American was like an "unclassified dog." To explain his allusion, he referred to an old minister who said that Presbyterianism without the doctrine of Infant Damnation would be like a dog that had lost its tag on a railroad journey and was therefore "unclassified." He hoped that the Reformers would soon be released from prison and that the Americans among them would still be wearing their tags.

Clemens's private opinion about the Reformers was less complimentary. To Mrs. Clemens he wrote that Rhodes and the principal Reformers had intended the government's overthrow. In his journal, he remarked that "Miss Rhodes, middle-aged sister of Cecil and the Colonel (one of the four) told Smythe in the hotel in Pretoria that the prisoners were furious because I praised their lodgings and comforts; Smythe said the Colonel said — either *he* was a damn fool or *I* was. He seems to be in doubt. I'm not. We are all fools at times; this is his time. The prisoners ought to have had a policy and stuck to it. But no — Butters and others were for conciliating the Boers (which was wise). Col. Rhodes and others were for *driving* them — which wasn't."

Clemens saw Rhodes not only as the fomentor of Jameson's raid, but also as an engine of rapacious and unscrupulous exploitation in Rhodesia, "a happy name for that land of piracy and pillage," as he wrote in *Following the Equator.* "That he is an extraordinary man, and not an accident of fortune, not even his dearest South African enemies were willing to deny . . . The whole South African world seemed to stand in a kind of shuddering awe of him, friend and enemy alike. It was as if he were deputy God on the one side, deputy Satan on the other . . . I admire him, I frankly confess it; and when his time comes I shall buy a piece of the rope for a keepsake."

But Rhodes, representing the British, was not the only highwayman. "There isn't a foot of land in the world," Clemens noted in his journal, "which doesn't represent the ousting and re-ousting of a long line of successive 'owners,' who each in turn, as 'patriots,' with proud swelling hearts defended it against the next gang of 'robbers' who came to steal it and *did* — and became swelling-hearted patriots in *their* turn. And this Transvaal, now, is full of patriots, who by the help of God, who is always interested in these things, stole the land from the feeble blacks, and then re-stole it from the English robber and has put up the monument — which the next robber will pull down and keep as a curiosity."

Since it is indeed the rule that new owners pull down their predecessors' symbols, it is astonishing that two years after all-race national elections, the old symbols by and large remain. True, a new flag waves from government buildings and citizens sing a new anthem, but government receptionists answer the phone in English and Afrikaans just as they did under the old regime. Inside the Voortrekker Monument, a monument to the Boer pioneers on the outskirts of Pretoria, a candle flame still burns to represent the civilization that the Boers believed they brought to Africa, although the sign forbidding admission to blacks has been removed. The site of Market Hall, where the Reform leaders were tried, is still named Strijdom Square, after one of the principal architects of apartheid. Even Kafferrivier, literally Nigger River, remains the name of a rural village in Afrikaner country.

A white acquaintance, who serves on a committee that chooses street names for Pretoria, tells us that black members, including the chairman, rarely attend committee meetings. White members are unwilling to choose street names for black areas without black participation, so that streets go for months without a name, which in turn holds up housing construction. Our informant thinks that black intergroup rivalries may explain black committee members' reluctance to choose names, an understandable aversion to being caught in crossfire.

An aversion to being caught in crossfire also explains Clemens's remarks about the Reform prisoners at the conclusion of his last performance in Johannesburg. By flattering the prisoners' abilities, he buttered up the English, and by asserting his disbelief in their intention to overturn Kruger's government, implying the immorality of such an act, he pleased the Afrikaners. After leaving the theater he accompanied a friend to the home of a German bachelor, where, as Clemens wrote in his journal, they had "supper and comfortable fire (cold night) and hot whiskey and cigars; and good talk."

The friend who took Clemens there was the forty-four-year-old Poultney Bigelow, an American adventurer, world traveler, and roving foreign correspondent for New York's *Herald*. In his autobiographical *Seventy Summers* (1925), Bigelow recalled that in Johannesburg, gold miners would rush forward to shake Clemens's hand at the end of each performance, referring to shared experiences in Nevada or California. "Put it there, old man! Don't you remember me? — don't you remember Bill Bloodgood that night in Jim Dusenbury's cabin? and that Chinaman who poured our whisky into the oilcan? Dear old Mark! those were happy days! Put it there, old hoss — I knew you'd know me again, etc. etc." Clemens would reply "Of course — why of course!" but later, alone with Bigelow, he dismissed them as "God damned liars."

Chapter Thirty-nine

*E*N ROUTE TO BLOEMFONTEIN, Clemens enjoyed looking at the veld. It was, he wrote his wife, "just as beautiful as Paradise — rolling, & swelling, & rising & subsiding, & sweeping on, & on, & on, like an ocean, toward the remote horizon, & changing its pale brown by delicate shades, to rich orange and finally to purple & crimson where it washes against the hills at the base of the sky."

On the night of his arrival, Saturday, May 30, Clemens performed at the Town Hall before a large audience. "Of course," wrote one reviewer, "most of his yarns were familiar to most of those present — everybody has read Mark Twain — but that could not rob them of their charm, as told by the inventor himself. Everything seemed as fresh as if told for the first time." That critic was equally enthusiastic about the second *At Home*, given on Monday evening: "Mark Twain was simply delightful last night, and anyone who went home without aching sides must have been either stone deaf or in a hopeless melancholy."

On the day of his second performance, with a letter of introduction from Poultney Bigelow in hand, he called on the newly elected president of the Orange Free State, the tall, bearded Martinus Theunis Steyn. Although only thirty-nine years old at the time, Steyn's bearing was such that he did not appear too young for his office. Born in Bloemfontein and educated in Holland and London, where he was called to the bar, Steyn worked as a lawyer, state attorney, and judge in the Orange Free State before his election as president. His country, which had sent a commando unit to its Vaal River border with the Transvaal at the time of Jameson's raid, was drawing closer to its sister republic, with which he was soon to renew a mutual defense pact. Although he urged conciliation with Britain and although Kruger later rejected his recommendation to give the Uitlanders the vote, Steyn stood by Kruger in the second Anglo-Boer War (1899–1902). "I would rather lose the independence of the Free State with honour," he said, "than preserve it with dishonour or disloyalty." After the British occupied Bloemfontein, Steyn took to the field as a guerrilla leader. The hour he spent with Clemens was doubtless among the more pleasant ones of his political career.

When Clemens ventured forth for a walk from his hotel on Market Square, he heard the voices of African women, which reminded him of the African slave women he had heard in his youth. In *Following the Equator* he reported that "I followed a couple of them all over the Orange Free State — no, over its capital, Bloemfontein — to hear their liquid voices and the happy ripple of their laughter." Market Square, where horses, cattle, and sheep were sold on Saturdays and farm produce on Mondays, has changed its name but not its function. These days more than a dozen vendors are present on the square, selling merchandise, mainly clothing, under gaily striped awnings.

On June 4, after another overnight journey, Clemens and Smythe arrived in Queenstown, Cape Colony, about two hundred miles southeast of Bloemfontein. That day Clemens wrote to his wife with the news that the four leading Reform prisoners were to be released from jail. A week later the four were free, after payment of an enormous fine, £25,000 each. They were offered the alternative of expulsion from the Transvaal or a fifteen-year ban on political activity there, with all but Colonel Rhodes choosing the latter.

In the meantime, all but two of the remaining prisoners had been released from jail after their fines had been paid and they had accepted a three-year political ban. Replying to their thanks, Kruger said "if my little dogs are naughty, I must whip them, but I am always sorry to do so. Next time I must get hold of the big dog." But there was no need to do so; the big dog had been chastised. The raid curtailed Rhodes's power: he was forced to resign as premier of the Cape Colony and as a director of the British South Africa Company, which had been charged with the exploitation of land north of the Transvaal. He also had to cough up the Reform prisoners' fines, which totaled about £200,000, or about $18,250,000 in today's terms. The two prisoners who remained in jail did so because, unlike the others, they refused to sign a petition for clemency. They stayed another year until Kruger, ostensibly in honor of the Queen's silver jubilee, released them unconditionally.

Clemens was to meet Hammond again. At a luncheon in New York, years later, Clemens told the gathering how his remarks about the prisoners' jail conditions in Pretoria had been misconstrued. According to Hammond, Clemens promised him compensation "by giving me a banquet whenever I cared to name the day."

On Friday, June 5, one day after his arrival in Queenstown, Clemens performed at the Town Hall, where he was greeted by loud and prolonged applause and, according to a reviewer, gave "an evening's entertainment, which for intellectual amusement, and refined enjoyment, will scarcely ever be equalled, and certainly not excelled in Queenstown."

Another local journalist looked forward to Clemens's travel book. "He'll have a lot to say about South Africa, and perhaps he'll find time and space to say something about Queenstown, which some people say has much the same characteristics as the village where he spent his boyhood." Clemens had described Hannibal as a place "where half the people were alive, the other half dead, and it took an expert to tell them apart."

Queenstown, named in honor of Queen Victoria, was established in 1853 as a frontier post, to defend settlers against hostile Africans. It was laid out as a hexagon, with streets radiating like the spokes of a wagon from a six-sided market square, enabling defenders to shoot down the streets from a central point. As it turned out, the hexagon was never used for this purpose. It is now the site of a small park, suspended above which a huge banner advertises a review called "Melodrama," to be performed at the Town Hall half a block away. Alice and I find our way to the hall, which appears much as it did in Clemens's day, except for the temporary scaffolding and the handsome clock tower added the year after his visit, in honor of Queen Victoria's silver jubilee. We walk upstairs, turn left, and find a door opening onto the gallery of an auditorium.

"Do you have a ticket?" asks a blond, thirtyish man with a grin. He's unpacking a crate containing lighting equipment, two expensive bulbs, which he is installing for the performance. The young man, who runs an electrical appliance shop in town, is a member of the Round Table, a service organization like Rotary and Lions, with branches all over the country and abroad. He tells us that Round Table is for men up to age forty, at which point "they get the chop." The review, sponsored by Round Table, opens tomorrow night for the first of six performances, the proceeds of which will be donated to charity. Had this young man been living here one hundred years ago, he would have been in some other business. Electricity had not yet reached Queenstown. A glorious gaslit chandelier illuminated Clemens's performance. After we leave the Town Hall, we find the Queenstown Club, whose building is too new to have been the one in which Clemens lunched the day after his performance. The old clubhouse, we learn, is still standing, although devoted to other purposes.

In Queenstown, Clemens stayed at Joplin's Commercial Hotel, on the corner of Joplin Street and Cathcart Road. Joplin Street has kept its name, but Joplin's Commercial Hotel is now the Windsor Hotel, its nineteenth-century structure masked by an art deco façade. Were Clemens to return to his hotel on this bright cloudless day, he might smile to see the sign posted on the glass door of one of its tenants, the Transkei Development Corporation: "Closed on account of weather." Through the glass door he could see a sole clerk typing listlessly. The civil service is nearing collapse in the East Cape, with pensioners not receiving their pensions nor teachers their salaries. Widespread corruption in the former homeland governments of Transkei and Siskei, which have been incorporated into the East Cape, have accustomed many of its civil servants to appear only on pay day. The employees that do appear are demoralized because they do not know who will be found redundant due to amalgamation. The Transkei Development Corporation, for example, is to become part of an Eastern Cape Development Agency.

From Queenstown, Clemens wrote to Rogers that if he had had $100,000 the week before and had known that the minor prisoners were to be released, he would have "dumped it into stocks," which soared upon news of their freedom. "The best stock in the lot jumped up 33 points when the news came."

In his previous letter to Rogers, written from Pretoria less than two weeks before, he appeared to be in a good mood: "We have been having in South Africa a repetition of the charming times we had in India and the other places. In truth I am sorry to remember that the lecture trip is drawing to a close. I would like to bum around these interesting countries another year and talk." But now, in Queenstown, he sounded depressed: "If I had the family in a comfortable poor-house I would kill myself." His mood is understandable: he longed for his wife ("It's no use, Livy dear," he wrote her, "I am homesick for you all the time"); the demands of performing and traveling remained inexorable; and perhaps he was bored, spending the weekend in a small provincial town, with nothing much to do, aside from his single performance, but play billiards with Smythe.

It was at about this time that Clemens considered taking Chapin's place as American consul in Johannesburg. Chapin had confided his desire to leave the post, and Clemens dreamed of the financial opportunities he might grasp should he take the job, which he was pretty sure would be his for the asking. Mrs. Clemens, who longed for home, nixed the proposal.

On Sunday morning, June 7, Clemens and Smythe boarded the train for King William's Town, about seventy-five miles southeast, which they reached in about ten hours. Writing to Mrs. Clemens at five in the afternoon, just after his arrival, Clemens told her about the beautiful scenery he had watched from the train. He mentioned seeing Africans dressed only in blankets, as well as Africans in European clothes.

King William's Town is a pleasant, leafy community with lots of nineteenth-century buildings, of which the auditorium in which Clemens performed is one of the less well maintained. The building remains a venue for amateur productions and visiting professional artists. It is considered, according to a municipal brochure, a "gem of a little theatre," but the structure's exterior is neglected. The locked front door exhibits broken glass panes. The side entrances, one of which smells of urine, appear derelict.

In that theater on Monday, June 8, the day after he arrived, Clemens gave the first of two performances before a packed and enthusiastic audience. "Never, we believe," wrote one critic, "in the history of the Hall, has so much laughing and clapping of hands been crowded into an hour and a half, and the strange thing was that the people did not laugh so much at what the lecturer said, as at the unique way in which he said it." Seventy years or so later, an old man, recalling one of Clemens's performances at King William's Town, mentioned the paraffin lamps and two candelabra that illuminated the theater. Clemens, he said, was "a handsome looking man, agile, with a shock of silvery hair."

On Sunday, the day of his arrival in King William's Town, Clemens spotted about twenty African women "mincing across the great barren square dressed — oh, in the last perfection of fashion, and newness, and expensiveness, and showy mixture of unrelated colors — all just as I had seen it so often at home; and in their faces and their gait was that languishing, aristocratic, divine delight in their finery which was so familiar to me." It seemed, he reported in *Following the Equator,* as if he were among old friends, friends of fifty years before, and he stopped to greet them. They laughed, "flashing their white teeth upon me, and all answered at once." He did not understand a word. "I was astonished; I was not dreaming that they would answer in anything but American."

Clemens left King William's Town on Wednesday morning, June 10, after his performance the night before, and traveled about twenty-five miles southeast to East London, at the mouth of the Buffalo River on the Indian Ocean. He checked into the Beach Hotel, built two years before and until 1920 the only hotel on the town's beach. It was next to the beach, as Clemens described it in his journal the day of his arrival. From our room at the Kennaway Hotel, built on the site of the Beach Hotel, we see fundamentally the scene described by Clemens: waves crashing onto nearby black rocks, an attractive beach curving off to the left for a mile or so, and ships at anchor offshore. The vessels have changed, though, from passenger liners to freighters.

A photograph, taken on a sunny Sunday morning in 1907, shows a throng of white women, most in long white dresses, and white men in suits strolling along a dirt road past the hotel. Many of the women shade themselves with white parasols. Now the road is paved and carries automobile traffic. Where grass once sloped from the road to the beach, pedestrians stroll along an esplanade, joined by joggers in shorts and wetsuited surfers with boards under their arms.

On Thursday, the day after his arrival, a downpour reduced attendance at Clemens's *At Home*, the first of three in East London's Mutual Hall. For this diminished audience, he prefaced his remarks by humorous references to other instances of bad weather encountered in his travels. In the "other London," he said, he once lectured before a house that was full, as the manager was to explain, of fog.

Mutual Hall stood on Market Square, next to the municipal market building. A photograph of the square, taken eleven years after Clemens's visit, shows numerous wagons drawn by teams of as many as twelve oxen. Some wagons are being driven, others have been left alone, with the lead oxen immobilized. In the same issue of the *East London Despatch* that reviewed Clemens's second performance, a letter written by a farmer complained about "the overzealous application" of local laws restricting the places and times oxen might be taken into town. "A farmer runs back into a shop to fetch a forgotten parcel and when he runs back" he sees "his oxen and wagon being driven up the street by a policeman," who will refuse to release them before the payment of a nine-shilling fine. It is hard for farmers, he wrote, to be treated so shabbily by the town in which they spend all their money. Today the square serves as a parking lot.

"We are having a lazy comfortable time here," Clemens wrote to Mrs. Clemens the day after his first performance, "billiards in the day time & cards at night." To his journal he complained that Smythe was beating him at billiards by accidentally making successful strokes or "flukes." "Now [that] I have ruled fluking out, neither beats the other more than five points in a hundred. We *count* a fluke, but retire. We make the same number of flukes in each game, but the trouble before was that he generally piled three flukes on top of the first, but I *never* could." According to his friend and biographer, Paine, who played many a game with the master, "It was his habit to make new rules driving billiards."

On Monday afternoon, June 15, Clemens and Smythe boarded the *Norham Castle* for their voyage to another coastal city, Port Elizabeth, about 150 miles to the southwest. The sea had been blustery and heavy over the weekend, and although the *Norham Castle* was due to sail on Tuesday afternoon, they boarded a day early, fearing that the sea might become so rough on the day of departure that they would be unable to cross the sandbar to reach the vessel, which was anchored offshore. From the ship on Tuesday, Clemens wrote that "there is a considerable sea today; it dashes itself against the big stone breakwater near the mouth of the river and bursts up in a vast white volume with laced edges, apparently 100 feet high."

Clemens and Smythe reached Port Elizabeth the next morning. They went to the Grand Hotel, where Mrs. Clemens and Clara had been staying for a week, after a three-day sea voyage from Durban. Shortly before she saw her husband again, Mrs. Clemens wrote to her sister that she felt as if he had been away a year.

The Grand Hotel, high on a hill among gardens overlooking the sea, offered a view that Mrs. Clemens called "*beautiful,* even *ravishing.*" The hotel, if not its elegance, has survived. A sign at the desk advises guests that the hotel accepts cash only. The pinging of electronic games can be heard from a room off the lobby, which was once hung with hunting trophies. A sign above the sink in the men's washroom, on the mezzanine, asks guests to "save water," needless advice: the spigots have been removed. The owner, a young man who bought the hotel two years ago, tells us that he hopes to refurbish the property and restore it to its former glory.

On Thursday, June 18, the day after Clemens's arrival at Port Elizabeth, news came by cable that the *Drummond Castle,* sister ship of the two Union Castle vessels on which he had sailed, had struck a rock near the French coast. All but three of the several hundred people on board had been drowned. The ship, sailing from Delagoa Bay to England, had picked up passengers at ports in Natal and the Cape Colony. Flags throughout South Africa flew at half mast.

From Port Elizabeth, Clemens sent to Rogers a letter of congratulations. Rogers, now a widower, had written him in February, announcing his engagement to marry Emilie Hart, but the letter had only recently reached Clemens, after being forwarded from India. "I would have chosen Mrs. Hart every time; and so it has cost me not a pang to praise you up, to her, a blame sight higher than you probably deserve; for I want her to be satisfied with you . . . and at the same time I was determined to earn the million you owe me if it cost the last rag of conscience I had in stock." He was, he said, sending a few wedding presents:

"Pair of elephants;

"Pair of rhinosceroses;

"Pair of giraffes;

"Pair of zebras;

"30 yards of anacondas;

"Flock of ostriches;

"Herd of niggers.

"The wedding-present business is expensive when you work it from Africa."

While the last item on Clemens's playful list is offensive to the modern reader, we should remember that norms have changed, that for his time Clemens was a progressive on racial issues, and that when it counted, in public forums, he enlisted his prestige and literary power on behalf of the dispossessed and persecuted. His ironic broadside, "King Leopold's Soliloquy" (1905), helped bring that monarch's malfeasance to public attention, leading Belgium to end the king's personal control of the Congo.

A few years after sending his letter of congratulations to Rogers, Clemens was to write, "I am quite sure that (bar one) [the French] I have no race prejudices, and I think I have no color prejudices nor caste prejudices. Indeed I know it. I can stand any society. All that I care to know is that a man is a human being — that is enough for me; he can't be any worse."

Chapter Forty

*O*N MONDAY, June 22, 1896, after five nights in Port Elizabeth, Clemens gave the first of three performances at the Town Hall. During the first, a woman in the audience began to laugh, and she continued to laugh so loudly and so often that she created a nuisance and had to be removed. It turned out that she was blind. Having learned that Clemens was the funniest man in the world, she persisted in thinking that everything he said was funny. According to a local reviewer, her hilarity disturbed the "venerable writer" and sometimes interrupted his points.

Town Hall, now City Hall, dominates Market Square, where farmers once unyoked their oxen. Today Market Square is a handsome, traffic-free plaza, enhanced by decorative brickwork and potted palms, an attractive oasis in a large, grim, industrial city. About twenty years ago a fire destroyed City Hall, which was gutted and rebuilt, its modern interior "all mohair and marble," in the words of one local who described it for us. But the original stately façade, with its arched windows and central clock tower, was reproduced. Indeed, the façade looks better now than it had for years before the fire, as, bit by bit, decorative elements had broken off or had worn away. Now it looks as grand as it did when Clemens performed there.

After his third *At Home* and eighth night in Port Elizabeth, Clemens and his party boarded the train for Grahamstown on Thursday, June 25. They reached their destination, about seventy-five miles to the northeast, after a seven-hour ride, during which they saw ostriches in the fields.

Grahamstown, with its broad, straight streets, library, and air of culture, impressed Clemens. The streets are still broad and straight, the library still stands, and the town is still cultured, as can be seen from the University Bookshop on High Street, which currently displays in its shop window *Tom Sawyer, Huckleberry Finn, The Prince and the Pauper,* and *A Connecticut Yankee in King Arthur's Court.* Grahamstown is the home of Rhodes University.

Grahamstown would feel like an English country town, with its pubs and churches, and with its high school students wearing blazers, ties, and straw boaters, were it not for the brilliant blue sky overhead and the preponderance of black pedestrians on the sidewalks. The university tower and the cathedral spire face each other down the length of a broad, tree-shaded street, divided by a grass median and lined by one- and two-story structures, many from the last century.

The Anglican Cathedral of St. Michael and St. George, parts of which date from 1824, dominates the town. When Alice and I step into the cathedral we are surprised by its lack of security. No church personnel seem to be present, although somebody gently ejects a madman who has shouted himself up the street and into the sacred place. Of the many memorial plaques found inside, one is sacred to the memory of an officer who fell in 1846 against "the Kaffirs." Another memorializes a man who perished in the same year in an effort to "repel the inroads of a barbarous enemy."

A notice appears below these markers: "There is a wide variety of memorial tablets and plaques in the Cathedral. Not all of them are written in language which would be used today. Some words are offensive to us all . . . But the Church has never hidden away its failures and its sins. The Church cannot and should not try to purify its history as if things never happened . . . So for the moment these plaques remain as part of our common history, and as a visible sign of our need for penitence."

Near the cathedral is the Albany Drill Hall, where Clemens performed the night after his arrival in Grahamstown. It is a beautiful two-story stone building, near the library that Clemens noted. The Drill Hall is the past and present headquarters of the prestigious First City Regiment, whose members wear kilts when in dress uniform. A plaque above the door to the hall in which Clemens performed marks the campaigns in which the regiment has fought, including Basutoland (1880–81), South Africa (1899–1902), and Cassino (1944). Black-painted silhouettes of tanks decorate the walls. There is no stage. Instead, a small platform, reached by stairs on each side, stands at one end of the room. The hall, used for festive affairs such as weddings, still accommodates audiences. It will be a venue for the ten-day Grahamstown Festival in July.

The lack of a conventional stage did not impair Clemens's ability to impersonate Mark Twain. A reviewer of his Grahamstown performance noted that "Mark Twain's method of approaching his audience is unstudied to a degree. It suggests the idea of a retiring man taking a quiet stroll and while most pre-occupied finding himself suddenly confronted by an animated crowd anxious to pay him homage. The assembly may have disturbed his cogitations, but the enthusiasm with which his popular presence is greeted is apparently very gratifying, and his acceptance of it seems to express the fact that he was indeed somewhat lonesome, before he met them a moment ago, but now, he was glad to see them there." Clemens's personality, he wrote, was one of "exceptional charm and distinction," and his manner is "chiefly conspicuous for its extreme simplicity, charm, and naturalness ... There is an entire absence of straining after effect." Whatever effort he makes "is wholly and admirably concealed."

Upstairs, above the Drill Hall, is the officers' lounge. It is done up in high colonial style, with trophies, photographs, and memorabilia displayed on shelves and a leopard skin draped over a chair. There is no record of Clemens's being invited for a drink here, but on the day of his performance he signed the Visitors' Book at the Grahamstown Club, where he played billiards with Smythe. Seven years later, Dr. Jameson, who had returned to South Africa and entered politics in the Cape Colony, after his trial and brief imprisonment in England, became a member. A member who joined considerably later, a mayor of Grahamstown, wrote an official letter ten years ago to congratulate the club upon the occasion of its centenary. Membership in the club, past and present, he wrote, "has always covered the broadest spectrum of our inhabitants."

The Clemenses and Smythe took the midday train for Kimberley on Sunday, June 28, and after ten hours broke their journey for a day at Cradock, Cape Colony, about one hundred miles northwest of Grahamstown. Their hotel stood "in a side of the vast bare dust-blown square," as Clemens noted in his journal. "Clouds of dust blowing along the powerful wind, like snow in New England on a raw March morning." For the first time since he was a boy, he saw a servant start a fire by bringing it on a shovel.

A reporter showed him the last telegram from Salisbury, reporting on the Matabele uprising, which had begun shortly after the failure of Jameson's raid. The papers in England and South Africa had been covering the "rebellion" and writing dismayed editorials urging that Rhodesia not be allowed to relapse into "barbarism." The Matabele had revolted once before, in 1893–94, after suffering brutal and large-scale confiscation of their land and cattle by Rhodes's British South Africa Company. That revolt was put down by Jameson, as the Company's administrator in the area. Now that Jameson was in jail, the Matabele — half starved as a result of the rinderpest, which was ravaging what was left of their cattle — rose again. Within a week of Jameson's raid, the Matabele had killed more than one hundred whites. Soon joined by the Shona farther north, they mounted what was probably the most serious resistance to colonialism in southern Africa at that time. The dispatch shown to Clemens reported that 2,000 "natives" met the fire of Maxim guns and that 2,000 black workers had deserted their railroad gangs. Clemens may have also seen a Reuters dispatch that mentioned a hostile force of "two thousand natives." "Strange," Clemens told the reporter, "how that number, 2,000 natives, recurs in every telegram. Never more — never less!"

The Clemens party left Cradock on a cold Tuesday evening for Kimberley, 240 miles northwest, with Clemens complaining that he had to wait ten hours before the train stopped at a place where he could relieve himself. They arrived shortly after noon on Tuesday and proceeded to their hotel, which had erected a triumphal arch and flew the American flag in Clemens's honor. "When the Great Yankee passed up the pathway," reported a journalist, "a gentle breeze stirred the bunting, and lo! it was a signal of distress — it was upside down."

Kimberley had begun as a shantytown twenty-five years earlier, when a diamond found by chance on the farm of an Afrikaner, Johannes Nicolaas de Beer, transformed the diamond rush that had begun the year before into a frenzy. Within four months of the discovery on de Beer's farm, thousands of prospectors had flocked to this remote, sparsely populated place and were digging an enormous hole that looked, according to one commentator, "like a block of gorgonzola with spoonfuls of cheese gouged out of it." Britain soon snatched the diamond fields from under the resentful noses of the Afrikaner republics, and before long speculators bought up the diggers' claims. Within a few years a handful of entrepreneurs, Rhodes foremost among them, controlled the diamond industry, and by 1889 Rhodes had bought up the claims and mines of most of his rivals. It was chiefly the diamond millionaires, with their capital and knowledge, who invested in the gold industry after the goldreefs of the Rand were found in 1886.

When news of spectacular diamond finds reached Clemens in 1870, he responded with manic enthusiasm; he would write a book about the diamond rush, a subject, he told his publisher, that was "brimful of fame and fortune for both author and publisher." Newly married, the father of a sickly newborn, and in his first year as partner in a Buffalo newspaper, Clemens could not go to the diamond fields himself. But he proposed to send a proxy, who would spend three months on the fields and take notes, which Clemens would then transform into another *Innocents Abroad*. He persuaded a journalist, former gold prospector, and old drinking buddy, John Henry Riley, to take the job. Clemens agreed to pay Riley's passage to and from South Africa, give him a monthly stipend in South Africa, and a salary and board when he returned to live with Clemens during their collaboration. Riley could keep whatever diamonds he excavated, up to a value of $5,000. Any diamonds unearthed beyond that value, Riley would have to share with Clemens.

Riley, perpetually broke and dreaming of a fortune to be made first in diamonds and then in lecturing about his experiences, left his work in Washington at the beginning of 1871 and sailed for London and Cape Town, from which he made his way to East London. There he auctioned off his excess possessions, including the copy of *The Innocents Abroad* that Clemens had given him as an example of the kind of impressions that were needed for the new book, and then embarked, via oxcart, on the long and difficult journey to the diamond fields.

Three months later he left the fields and the thousands of prospectors who were digging there, with nothing to show for his pains but his notes and some mining claims — worthless, as it turned out — to be shared with Clemens. By the time he returned to America in the fall, Clemens had lost interest in the book and kept postponing his collaboration with Riley who, by the following spring, was fighting a losing battle with cancer. He died in September of 1872.

Years later, when Clemens was in East London, he met the man who had bought Riley's copy of *The Innocents Abroad*. The day after that journal entry, during his first performance in Kimberley, he told his audience that "I was in Kimberley by proxy 20 years ago. On that occasion my representative bought a diamond mine from a man who did not own it. Before leaving Kimberley, I intend to take a look at it, and if it pleases me, I will buy it again."

During his next two days in Kimberley, Clemens did visit some diamond mines, including the Kimberley Crater or Big Hole, which, as he wrote in *Following the Equator*, "is roomy enough to admit the Roman Coliseum." The hole, one mile in circumference and 780 feet deep, is the largest hand-dug excavation in the world. It no longer yields diamonds, mining having stopped in 1914. Although partially filled with water now, it is still immensely impressive. Birds fly below its rim, dwarfed by the immense space. On one side you see the towers of Kimberley, which seem insignificant in comparison.

Once you have finished gawking, you can visit, on the west side of the hole, an open-air reconstruction of Kimberley in the 1880s. There you can visit a saloon (where you hear drunken, raucous singing), a church, a diamond buyer's office, a ballroom, etc. As you walk under the huge pepper trees, you do not see the squalor in which the early miners lived and worked nor the conditions of the Africans who replaced them. You can, however, see a machine that deloused the latters' clothing and blankets.

One of the most impressive displays is that of three small railroad cars, each holding a few bushels of brilliants. This is the volume of all the diamonds ever extracted from the hole, after they were sifted from the 22.5 million tons of earth and rock excavated along with them.

Clemens reported in his journal that the De Beers concern handled 8,000 carloads of excavated earth and rock a day, with each carload weighing 1,600 pounds. After passing these 12,800,000 pounds through successive processes, only three pounds of diamonds, "a big double handful" as he called them, would be extracted. He saw the tanks in which carloads of mud and water were stirred and churned and reduced to slush. He saw the slush reduced to sand. He saw men spread out the sand and seize the diamonds, and he saw young girls sort them. "Every day ducal incomes sift and sparkle through the fingers of those young girls," he commented in *Following the Equator,* "yet they go to bed at night as poor as they were when they got up in the morning."

Today all South African diamonds are sorted and graded at Kimberley's Oppenheimer House, a skyscraper ringed by a security fence. The building was designed to provide ideal lighting conditions for the delicate work inside. Its north side is bereft of windows, and the windows on its south side are slanted to prevent direct sunlight from entering.

The long two-story building with lacy wrought-iron balconies, in which Clemens saw the diamonds that De Beers had collected in one day, still stands. The uncut gems were worth about £10,000 or £12,000, or between $50,000 and $60,000. (In *Following the Equator* he increased the take to $70,000, equivalent to the debt that sent him around the world.) He was also shown the compound in which the African miners were confined. "They are a jolly and good-natured lot, and accommodating," he observed in his travel book. "They performed a war-dance for us, which was the wildest exhibition I have ever seen. They are not allowed outside of the compound during their term of service — three months, I think it is, as a rule."

On Friday evening, July 3, after two *At Home*s and three nights in Kimberley, the Clemens party boarded a train to Cape Town, about 560 miles southwest, for a journey of a day and a half. On July 6, a day after his arrival, Clemens told a reporter that in Kimberley he had found a diamond as big as the end of his finger, "but there were so many people watching me that I did not bring it away."

Chapter Forty-one

A T SEVEN ON SUNDAY MORNING, July 5, 1896, the Clemenses arrived at Cape Town, where they stopped at the last Grand Hotel of their world tour. During their stay in Cape Town, a stream of admirers trooped to the hotel to press handpainted ostrich eggs upon Clemens or to ask him for favors, from signing his autograph to serving as godfather.

Unlike the other towns Clemens had visited in South Africa, all of which were relatively young, Cape Town dated from the seventeenth century. The settlement began as a stopover for ships of the Dutch East India Company, and was seized by the British at the beginning of the nineteenth century. If Cape Town was older than other South African towns, it was also different in at least two other ways. First, the town was more heterogeneous racially. A relatively large proportion of "coloreds" lived there, the descendants of Boer men and nonwhite women. The town was home also to many Cape Muslims or Cape Malays, the descendants of Muslims brought by the Dutch to Cape Town as slaves or as political prisoners. Second, Cape Town was without question the most beautiful city in South Africa, among the most beautiful in the world, with its white, sandy beaches and its immense, dramatic, flat-topped Table Mountain, against which the town was built.

Cape Town is still exceptionally beautiful, but its racial diversity declined a generation ago. Breyton Bretenbach, the Afrikaner poet and painter, remembers the city in the late 1950s as "Alexandria in the southern Atlantic." This was before the Group Areas Act drove nonwhites from neighborhoods in which they had resided for years, forcing them to live far from their jobs, usually in poorer housing in dangerous districts.

A colored cabdriver tells Alice and me, as he takes us on a tour of the city, that in 1963 he was driven from a Cape Town neighborhood in which his family had owned land for generations. He lost his land, his cows, his sheep. "So unfair," he says. He took a job as an assistant to a young white guy, who sat around playing the guitar, while allowing him to do all the work. After learning that his young boss, who did virtually nothing, earned more than he did, he quit and joined the railroad. By virtue of acting humble and doing as good a job as he could, he eventually supervised seventy men, some of them white. The whites resented working under him, and the blacks viewed him as siding with the whites. Stink bombs were thrown into his office, and his life was threatened. Trusted by neither whites nor blacks, finding that his job had become intolerable, he left his employer after eighteen years and became a taxi driver. "Life is better now," he says. "Now anyone can go anywhere."

A black cabdriver, who works at night, agrees. During the afternoon he operates an after-school program for young people in his neighborhood, offering activies such as ballet, music, and sports. His wife began a day-care program, tending two neighboring children. Today she cares for forty children and employs several assistants. Now, he says, people's success is up to them.

A Hindu bartender, whose family has been here for generations, also says that life has changed for the better. As recently as six years ago, he tells us, certain stores were closed to nonwhites; other stores would allow nonwhites to enter, granting them a special entrance at the rear and restricting them to special counters. Jobs once confined to whites are now open to others as well. Black and colored shop assistants and hotel desk clerks, for example, work alongside their white colleagues, who are sometimes supervised by nonwhite managers. He used to think that blacks were unintelligent, but now that he sees them in responsible jobs, and now that he's seen black children at his son's multiracial school, he's changed his mind. He's optimistic about the future.

Clemens was optimistic too. The day after his arrival in Cape Town he told a reporter that one need not be a prophet to predict that the Uitlander population in the Transvaal would continue to increase so that eventually it would "carry its desires without any war." Three years later the second Anglo-Boer War began. Expected by both sides to last a few months, it proved to be, in the words of a South African historian, "the most extensive, costly and humiliating war fought by Britain between the defeat of Napoleon in 1815 and the outbreak of the First World War in 1914." After almost three years of fighting, after 450,000 British and Empire troops had been required to subdue a part-time army of 45,000 farmers, after the British had burned down 30,000 farms, and after ten percent of the Boer civilian population had died in British concentration camps, the British were forced to negotiate a settlement, which excluded blacks and coloreds from political participation in the Transvaal and the Orange Free State.

The interviewer asked Clemens his views about South African audiences. Not surprisingly, Clemens reported that they were "very delightful" and "exceedingly bright." Most of the audience were people who had traveled abroad, he said. "I have seldom met anybody who has been able to say that he has not been out of Africa. I played billiards with a man in Kimberley whom I met only once before and that was over a billiard table twenty-five years ago in America. The guard of a train reminded me that he crossed in the steamer with me twenty-five years ago. Captain Mein, one of the political prisoners, I knew very well thirty-two years ago, and John Hays Hammond I have known for many years."

On Thursday, July 9, three days after that interview, Clemens gave his first *At Home* in Cape Town's Opera House, where he was received enthusiastically by a crowded and fashionable audience, including the colony's chief administrator and his staff, the Speaker of the Assembly, and several members of Parliament. Fifteen minutes late, he apologized for his tardiness, explaining that he had lost his way on Table Mountain, which he thought provided a shortcut from his hotel to the Opera House. Clemens's hotel was a few blocks down the street.

The one-thousand-seat Opera House, which survived another half century, faced the Grand Parade, the town's oldest square. The Parade now serves as a combination of parking lot and flea market. A statue of Edward VII, robed and regal, surveys the pigeons and seagulls that flock about the square. Usually one of them has flown down to perch upon his head. A nearby monument memorializes soldiers from the Cape Colony who fell during the second Anglo-Boer War.

Clemens's three performances at the Opera House, on the

ninth, tenth, and eleventh of July, were successful enough to warrant a fourth performance. It could not be held at the Opera House,
however, because that venue was engaged. As a substitute, Smythe
hired the Town Hall in suburban Claremont, about six miles away,
for the last paid performance of Clemens's world tour.

Until the Group Areas Act destroyed it a generation ago,
Clarement was a racially mixed community. "Outsiders complain,"
wrote a resident in the fifties, "that the population of Claremont is
'so mixed,' not stopping to think how much the character of the
Village owes to this variety. The different races have learnt to live
together here in a civilised fashion: there is room for all in this Market
Place. There is no Colour Bar in the shops, and no one is scowled at
or jostled off the pavement because of the colour of his skin."

Clemens's last performance of his world tour was followed by
his last club supper, when about two hundred members and friends
of Cape Town's Owl Club entertained him. The club presented him
with an album of Cape views and drank to his health and to that of
Mrs. Clemens and Clara. In response, Clemens referred to that
night, July 13, as the anniversary of the first lecture of his tour. The
anniversary, he said, was "an occasion of parallels," for he hoped that
he had just given his last lecture on any stage. The first lecture of
his world tour, he said, was on July 13 (actually it was July 14) in
Elmira, New York, before a male audience. Like the present one,
they were "intelligent men who had done something to bring their
name before the world." But, he continued, he must not forget to
point out that his first audience was — in jail. Unlike those present,
the men in Elmira were paying for their crimes, whereas the
gentlemen before him had "not even commenced to repent of
theirs." He would, he said, remember with pleasure the evening he
spent with "this noble assembly of unclassified convicts."

The next afternoon he visited another assembly. Sitting in the
Distinguished Visitors' Gallery of the Cape Colony's House of
Assembly, Clemens listened to a tumultuous debate about whether
Rhodes, who had already resigned as Prime Minister, should be
granted a leave of absence from his seat. Would a leave be construed
as a vote of confidence, exonerating him from involvement in
Jameson's raid? Members cheered when references were made to
"combating barbarism in the north" (Rhodes was currently in

Rhodesia, helping to quell the revolt) and relatively few approved a reference to him as "the man who brought red ruin to the Transvaal." A member of the Assembly sat with Clemens and interpreted those speeches that were made in Afrikaans.

A journalist reported that "anyone who witnessed the last two days debate at the House would have been reminded of Huck Finn's description of a show in which every man who went in had his pockets bulging." After quoting Huck, "I shoved in there for a minute, but it was too various for me; I couldn't stand it!" the reporter noted that "Huck Finn's genial creator . . . 'shoved in for a minute' at the House of Assembly yesterday afternoon; and members could not have been much surprised if he had found the moral atmosphere almost too various. Speaker after speaker yesterday and the day before seemed to have come in with his pockets bulging with dead-cat charges and sickly-egg imputations against his fellows." In *Following the Equator*, Clemens recalled his visit to the Parliament: "they quarreled in two languages when I was there, and agreed in none." The handsome, red-and-white neoclassical building in which Clemens heard the debate is now a wing of the nation's parliamentary complex.

In addition to the Parliament, Clemens reported seeing Table Rock, Table Bay ("so named for its levelness"), the castle constructed by the Dutch East India Company, and St. Simon's Bay, the headquarters of the fleet. He drove along the mountain roads and saw "some of the fine old Dutch mansions."

In one of the Dutch mansions, Clemens saw "a quaint old picture . . . a picture of a pale, intellectual young man in a pink coat with a high black collar." It was a portrait of Dr. James Barry, a military surgeon who was born in London. Educated in Edinburgh and London, he started his army medical career as a hospital assistant in Cape Town in 1816, and ended it as the senior of Her Majesty's Inspectors-General of Army Hospitals, a rank equivalent to that of Major-General, when he retired in London in 1859.

Dr. Barry's life would be remarkable even without the romance associated with his name. He performed the first successful cesarean section in South Africa, years before this operation succeeded in Britain, and saved the lives of both mother and child. In lieu of a fee, he asked that the child be named after him, a name that has been handed down to the present day, held among others by James Barry Munnik Hertzog, founder of the Nationalist Party and a prime minister of the Union of South Africa, who was the godson of James Barry Munnik, the son of the child Barry saved. Highly regarded by his medical colleagues, Barry cured the Cape's governor, Lord Charles Somerset, of a nearly fatal attack of typhus and saved the life of Somerset's daughter after her case had been declared hopeless. When invited to treat a desperate case, he would throw out all the patient's medicines, open the windows, and order the patient to be bathed, often with wine because of its antiseptic properties. He would never ask for a second opinion. If the patient survived, Dr. Barry took all the credit. If the patient died, Dr. Barry had been summoned too late.

During the twelve or so years he spent at the Cape, he performed his official duties zealously, angering pharmacists by his insistence on examining their drugs, and offending officials by his outspoken criticism of their behavior. He regularly inspected government institutions such as the town jail, the leper colony, and the Somerset Hospital, and as regularly submitted indignant reports about the appalling conditions he found there. Of the hospital, for example, he wrote that the wards were as dirty as the patients.

Witty and brilliant but imperious, quarrelsome, strongly opinionated, and politically obtuse, he alienated many and created powerful enemies. Nonetheless, his inflexibility upon matters of principle and his outspoken criticisms helped lead to reforms in the prisons and hospitals of the Cape.

He left Cape Town in 1828, but so vivid was his personality that years after his death, nannies there would tell their wards that if they were not good, Dr. Barry's ghost, said to appear in the Georgian dress of a young officer, would come and get them.

Short and slight, he placed three-inch false soles in his boots and stuffed cotton wool into the shoulders of his jacket. Nonetheless, he looked slightly ridiculous when he wore his uniform, with its plumed cocked hat, long spurs, and large sword, the ordinary dress of a military doctor. He flirted with the prettiest girls and challenged Captain (later Sir) Josiah Cloete, the governor's aide-de-camp, to a duel. Cloete and Barry fought with pistols, both missing their mark and later becoming fast friends. After he left the

Cape, Barry served in other outposts of empire, conscientious and combative to the last.

The romance surrounding Barry began almost immediately after he died in 1865, at the age of about seventy, when the charwoman who had laid out his body claimed that Dr. Barry was a woman and had borne a child. Barry's body exhibited the striations that indicate motherhood, she said. "I am a married woman, and the mother of nine children. I ought to know."

Clemens told Barry's story as he heard or remembered it, which included a few misstatements of fact as well as some of the unsubstantiated legends which had become attached to Barry's name. The story is a great one and surely deserves its place in *Following the Equator*, but it may have been especially compelling to Clemens, who seemed fascinated by twinship and dual identity, a favorite topic in his books and stories. His interest is not surprising in view of the doubleness in his own life, in which Samuel L. Clemens and Mark Twain shared the same body, and in his own performances, in which the contrast between comic content and solemn demeanor was central.

James Barry's portrait still hangs in the home where Clemens saw it, the white, oak-shaded, eighteenth-century manor house of the Cloete family. They have recently converted it into an elegant hotel. The manager, Mr. Leaver, tells us that Dr. Barry and Sir Josiah fought their duel behind the house.

On July 15, soon after his visit to the Cloete mansion, and a year and a day after he left Elmira, Clemens sailed away from Cape Town and South Africa, his world lecture tour completed. He told readers of *Following the Equator* that "I seemed to have been lecturing a thousand years."

Chapter Forty-two

"A FRICA SEEMED A COLORLESS COUNTRY after India,"
wrote Clara years later, "and we were glad to embark on our last
voyage. Father luxuriated in cigars and books all the way from Africa
to England and we thought of nothing but the pleasure of seeing
Susy and Jean again." The Clemenses docked at Southampton on
July 31, 1896, sixteen days out of Cape Town.

A few days later Clemens wrote to Howells, "We hope to get a
house in some quiet English village away from the world and society, where I can sit down for six months or so and give myself up to
the luxury and rest of writing a book or two after this long fatigue
and turmoil of platform-work and gadding around by sea and land.
Susie and Jean sail from New York today, and a week hence we shall
all be together."

Susie did not join them. Less than three weeks after the
Clemenses arrived in England, she died of meningitis, aged twenty-
four. "In my despair and unassuageable misery, I upbraid myself for
ever parting with her," Clemens wrote the following month, "but
there is no use in that. Since it was to happen it would have happened."

The Clemenses leased a large brick corner town house, on a
quiet, leafy square in London's Chelsea, where Clemens composed
Following the Equator. Burdened by grief, indifferent to everything
but his work, he completed the book in May 1897. By January of the
following year, he had paid all his creditors in full, an accomplish-
ment that the world press heralded as a triumph. When Clemens
returned with his family to New York in 1900, he received a hero's
welcome.

The Clemenses never again lived in their Hartford house,
where reminders of Susy would have been too painful to bear. In
1904, at the age of fifty-eight, the ailing Mrs. Clemens died in

Florence, where the Clemenses had moved in hopes of restoring her health. The remaining Clemenses returned to the United States. Clemens took a house on lower Fifth Avenue in New York, where he lived until 1908, when he moved into the mansion he had built for himself in the Connecticut countryside. There, in 1909, Clara married the Russian-born pianist and conductor Ossip Gabrilowitsch. A few months later, Jean drowned there in her bath during an epileptic seizure. And, in 1910, Clemens died there at the age of seventy-four. *Following the Equator* was his last major book.

Appendix
Samuel L. Clemens's Itinerary, World Lecture Tour

Performances marked by asterisk

Sun	Jul	14, 1895	Leaves Elmira
Mon		15	Cleveland *
Tue		16	Cleveland
Wed		17	Sails on *Northland*
Thu		18	Sault Ste. Marie *
Fri		19	Mackinac Island *
Sat		20	Petoskey *
Sun		21	Sails on *Northwest*
Mon		22	Duluth *
Tue		23	Minneapolis *
Wed		24	St. Paul *
Thu		25	Train
Fri		26	Winnipeg *
Sat		27	Winnipeg *
Sun		28	Winnipeg
Mon		29	Crookston *
Tue		30	Train
Wed		31	Great Falls *
Thu	Aug	1	Butte *
Fri		2	Anaconda *
Sat		3	Helena *
Sun		4	Helena
Mon		5	Missoula *
Tue		6	Spokane
Wed		7	Spokane *
Thu		8	Spokane
Fri		9	Portland *
Sat		10	Olympia *

Sun	11	Olympia
Mon	12	Tacoma *
Tue	13	Seattle *
Wed	14	New Whatcom *
Thu	15	Vancouver *
Fri	16	Vancouver
Sat	17	Vancouver
Sun	18	Vancouver
Mon	19	Vancouver
Tue	20	Victoria
Wed	21	Victoria *
Thu	22	Victoria
Fri	23	Sails for Sydney on the *Warrimoo*
Fri	30	At anchor, Honolulu Roadstead
Sat	31	At anchor
Sun Sep 1		Sails at midnight
Tue	10	Half day in Suva
Thu	12(?)	Auckland
Sun	15	At anchor, Sydney
Mon	16	Sydney
Tue	17	Sydney
Wed	18	Sydney
Thu	19	Sydney *
Fri	20	Sydney
Sat	21	Sydney *
Sun	22	Sydney
Mon	23	Sydney *
Tue	24	Sydney *
Wed	25	Train
Thu	26	Melbourne
Fri	27	Melbourne *
Sat	28	Melbourne *
Sun	29	Melbourne
Mon	30	Melbourne *
Tue Oct 1		Melbourne *
Wed	2	Melbourne *
Thu	3	Melbourne

Fri		4	Melbourne
Sat		5	Melbourne
Sun		6	Melbourne
Mon		7	Melbourne
Tue		8	Melbourne
Wed		9	Melbourne
Thu		10	Melbourne
Fri		11	Train
Sat		12	Adelaide *
Sun		13	Adelaide
Mon		14	Adelaide *
Tue		15	Adelaide *
Wed		16	Adelaide *
Thu		17	Horsham *
Fri		18	Stawell *
Sat		19	Ballarat
Sun		20	Ballarat
Mon		21	Ballarat *
Tue		22	Ballarat *
Wed		23	Bendigo *
Thu		24	Bendigo *
Fri		25	Maryborough *
Sat		26	Melbourne *
Sun		27	Melbourne
Mon		28	Geelong *
Tue		29	Prahan *
Wed		30	Melbourne
Thu		31	Sails for Bluff on the *Mararoa*
Fri	Nov	1	At sea
Sat		2	Half day in Hobart

Tue		5	Bluff, Invercargill *
Wed		6	Dunedin *
Thu		7	Dunedin *
Fri		8	Dunedin *
Sat		9	Timaru *
Sun		10	Timaru
Mon		11	Oamaru *
Tue		12	Christchurch
Wed		13	Christchurch *
Thu		14	Christchurch *

Fri	15	Christchurch *
Sat	16	Sails for Wellington on the *Flora*
Sun	17	Lands in Wellington, sails for Auckland on the *Mahinapua*
Mon	18	Day in Nelson; sails to New Plymouth
Tue	19	Day in New Plymouth; sails to Auckland
Wed	20	Auckland
Thu	21	Auckland *
Fri	22	Auckland *
Sat	23	Auckland
Sun	24	Auckland
Mon	25	Auckland *
Tue	26	Sails for Gisborne and Napier on the *Rotomahana*
Wed	27	Heavy seas prevent landing at Gisborne
Thu	28	Napier *
Fri	29	Napier
Sat	30	Napier
Sun Dec	1	Napier
Mon	2	Palmerston North *
Tue	3	Wanganui *
Wed	4	Wanganui *
Thu	5	Hawera *
Fri	6	New Plymouth *
Sat	7	Wanganui
Sun	8	Wanganui
Mon	9	Wellington
Tue	10	Wellington *
Wed	11	Wellington *
Thu	12	Wellington
Fri	13	Sails for Sydney on the *Mararoa*
Sat	14	At sea
Sun	15	At sea
Mon	16	At sea
Tue	17	Sydney
Wed	18	Sydney
Thu	19	Scone *
Fri	20	Sydney *
Sat	21	Sydney *
Sun	22	Sydney

Mon	23		Sails for Ceylon on the *Oceana*
Tue	24		At sea
Wed	25		Melbourne
Thu	26		Melbourne *
Fri	27		Melbourne *
Sat	28		At sea
Sun	29		At sea
Mon	30		Adelaide
Tue	31		Adelaide
Wed Jan	1,	1896	At sea
Thu	2		At sea
Fri	3		At sea
Sat	4		Albany Roadstead
Sun	5		Passes Cape Leeuwin, turns NW for Ceylon

Mon	13	Colombo
Tue	14	Sails for Bombay on the *Rosetta*

Sat	18	Bombay
Sun	19	Bombay
Mon	20	Bombay
Tue	21	Bombay
Wed	22	Bombay
Thu	23	Bombay
Fri	24	Bombay *
Sat	25	Bombay
Sun	26	Bombay
Mon	27	Bombay *
Tue	28	Bombay *
Wed	29	Poona *
Thu	30	Train
Fri	31	Baroda *
Sat Feb	1	Train
Sun	2	Train
Mon	3	Allahabad *
Tue	4	Benares
Wed	5	Benares
Thu	6	Train
Fri	7	Calcutta
Sat	8	Calcutta

Sun	9	Calcutta
Mon	10	Calcutta *
Tue	11	Calcutta
Wed	12	Calcutta *
Thu	13	Calcutta *
Fri	14	Train
Sat	15	Darjeeling *
Sun	16	Darjeeling
Mon	17	Train
Tue	18	Train
Wed	19	Muzaffarpur *
Thu	20	Benares
Fri	21	Train
Sat	22	Lucknow *
Sun	23	Lucknow
Mon	24	Lucknow *
Tue	25	Cawnpore *
Wed	26	Cawnpore
Thu	27	Agra
Fri	28	Agra *
Sat	29	Train
Sun Mar	1	Jaipur
Mon	2	Jaipur
Tue	3	Jaipur
Wed	4	Jaipur
Thu	5	Jaipur
Fri	6	Jaipur
Sat	7	Jaipur
Sun	8	Jaipur
Mon	9	Jaipur
Tue	10	Jaipur
Wed	11	Jaipur
Thu	12	Jaipur
Fri	13	Jaipur
Sat	14	Jaipur
Sun	15	Train
Mon	16	Delhi
Tue	17	Train
Wed	18	Lahore *
Thu	19	Lahore *
Fri	20	Rawalpindi *

Sat	21	Train
Sun	22	Train
Mon	23	Train
Tue	24	Calcutta
Wed	25	Calcutta
Thu	26	Sails for Ceylon and Mauritius on the *Wardha*
Fri	27	At sea
Sat	28	At sea
Sun	29	At sea
Mon	30	At sea
Tue	31	Half day at Madras
Wed Apr	1	At sea
Thu	2	At sea
Fri	3	Colombo *
Sat	4	At sea

Wed	15	At anchor, Port Louis
Thu	16	Curepipe
Fri	17	Curepipe
Sat	18	Curepipe
Sun	19	Curepipe
Mon	20	Curepipe
Tue	21	Curepipe
Wed	22	Curepipe
Thu	23	Curepipe
Fri	24	Curepipe
Sat	25	Curepipe
Sun	26	Curepipe
Mon	27	Curepipe
Tue	28	Sails for Durban on the *Arundel Castle*

Mon May	4	Half day in Lourenço Marques
Tue	5	At sea
Wed	6	Durban
Thu	7	Durban
Fri	8	Durban
Sat	9	Durban
Sun	10	Durban
Mon	11	Durban
Tue	12	Durban *

Wed	13	Durban *
Thu	14	Pietermaritzburg
Fri	15	Pietermaritzburg *
Sat	16	Pietermaritzburg *
Sun	17	Johannesburg
Mon	18	Johannesburg *
Tue	19	Johannesburg *
Wed	20	Johannesburg *
Thu	21	Johannesburg *
Fri	22	Johannesburg
Sat	23	Pretoria *
Sun	24	Pretoria
Mon	25	Pretoria *
Tue	26	Pretoria *
Wed	27	Krugersdorp *
Thu	28	Johannesburg *
Fri	29	Johannesburg
Sat	30	Bloemfontein *
Sun	31	Bloemfontein
Mon Jun	1	Bloemfontein *
Tue	2	Bloemfontein
Wed	3	Train
Thu	4	Queenstown
Fri	5	Queenstown *
Sat	6	Queenstown
Sun	7	King William's Town
Mon	8	King William's Town *
Tue	9	King William's Town *
Wed	10	East London
Thu	11	East London *
Fri	12	East London *
Sat	13	East London *
Sun	14	East London
Mon	15	At anchor, *Norham Castle*
Tue	16	At sea
Wed	17	Port Elizabeth
Thu	18	Port Elizabeth
Fri	19	Port Elizabeth
Sat	20	Port Elizabeth
Sun	21	Port Elizabeth
Mon	22	Port Elizabeth *

Tue	23	Port Elizabeth *
Wed	24	Port Elizabeth *
Thu	25	Grahamstown
Fri	26	Grahamstown *
Sat	27	Grahamstown *
Sun	28	Cradock
Mon	29	Train
Tue	30	Kimberley *
Wed Jul	1	Kimberley *
Thu	2	Kimberley
Fri	3	Train
Sat	4	Train
Sun	5	Cape Town
Mon	6	Cape Town
Tue	7	Cape Town
Wed	8	Cape Town
Thu	9	Cape Town *
Fri	10	Cape Town *
Sat	11	Cape Town *
Sun	12	Cape Town
Mon	13	Cape Town (Claremont) *
Tue	14	Cape Town
Wed	15	Sails on *Norham Castle* for Southampton

Based principally on Ahluwalia (1996), Mark Twain Papers (Bancroft Library, University of California at Berkeley), Parsons (1975/6, 1977, 1978), Pond (1900), and Shillingsburg (1995).

Notes

Abbreviations:

FTE	=	*Following the Equator* (Twain, 1992, 1993)
HHR	=	Henry Huttleston Rogers
MTA	=	*More Tramps Abroad* (Twain, 1897)
MTL	=	*Mark Twain's Letters* (Paine, 1917)
MTN	=	*Mark Twain's Notebook* (Paine, 1935)
MTP	=	The Mark Twain Papers, Bancroft Library, University of California at Berkeley
NB	=	Mark Twain's Notebooks and Journals
NYT	=	*The New York Times*
OLC	=	Olivia Louise Clemens
SLC	=	Samuel Langhorne Clemens

Prologue

1 **an advanced age** In 1900, the life expectancy at birth of a white American male was 46.6 (U.S. Bureau of the Census,1975: Series B 107–15, page 55.) By 1990, white male life expectancy had risen to 72.7 (U.S. Bureau of the Census, 1996: no. 114, page 87).

1 **he felt he had failed as a father and husband** Kaplan (1966:333).

1 **business failure meant disgrace** Paine (1912:986–87).

1 **an author could afford to be poor** Neider (1959:260).

1 **the international celebrity** According to Hoffman (1997:x), Clemens was "the most interviewed, most photographed, and most recognizable figure in North America and Europe."

2 **In the introduction to a selection** Theroux (1990:xvi).

2 **My wife's grandmother once met Mark Twain** They probably met on January 20, 1901, when Clemens addressed supporters of the Hebrew Technical School for Girls, of which my wife's great-grandmother was headmistress. The school, located on Henry Street, was the only one in New York to offer a vocational education to Jewish girls. In his speech, Clemens argued that if women had the vote, corruption in the city would be swept away. NYT, January 21, 1901:5.

2 **"There was an awkward pause"** FTE:I,13–14.

Chapter One

9 **a window on each of its eight sides** In the 1880s, the window in the fireplace was bricked up to improve the fireplace draft. Jerome and Wisbey (1977:39).

10 **"It is a cozy nest"** SLC to Joseph and Harmony Twitchell, June 11, 1874. MTL:220.

10 **"a foretaste of Heaven"** Ibid.

10 **"The city in the valley is purple with shade"** SLC to Molly Clemens, 1874. Paine (1912:825).

10 **Clemens was a familiar figure in Elmira** My description of Elmira in the Clemenses' era relies on Cotton (1985) and Jerome and Wisbey (1977).

12 **a "church home"** Taylor (1981:17).

12 **"roaring success"** SLC to HHR, July 16, 1895. Leary (1969:171).

12 **"My project of preparing"** SLC to HHR, June 4, 1895. Ibid.:150.

12 **"My gracious"** SLC to HHR, June 25–26, 1895. Ibid.:156.

12 **"I'll go to Cleveland on a stretcher, sure"** SLC to HHR, June 26, 1895. Ibid.:158.

13 **"I shan't be able to stand"** SLC to HHR July 8, 1895. Ibid.:165.

13 **carbuncle** For contemporary views of carbuncles and their treatment, I relied on *Johnson's Universal Cyclopedia* (1894), *The New International Encyclopaedia* (1904), and the eleventh edition of *The Encyclopaedia Britannica* (1910).

13 **the Erie Railroad Depot** The description of the turn-of-the-century depot is based on a photograph taken about five years before the Clemenses' departure for Cleveland, reproduced in Cotton (1985:12).

13 **The last passenger train** Byrne (1976).

14 **Jervis Langdon was the first to do so** Taylor (1977:168).

Chapter Two

15 **"I have been asked that question several times"** *Plain Dealer* (Cleveland), July 16, 1895.

15–16 **"which made them . . . the most conspicuous object"** SLC to HHR, July 16, 1895. Leary (1969:171).

16 **"I got *started* magnificently"** Ibid.

16 **"4,200 people present"** Pond (1900:201).

16 **he introduced a scheme** My account of his performance is based on the *Plain Dealer* (Cleveland), July 16, 1895; NYT, July 23, 1895:3.

17 **"convulsed"** *Plain Dealer* (Cleveland), July 16, 1895.

17 **"the scuffling boys had the audience's maddened attention"** SLC to HHR, July 16, 1895. Leary (1969:171).

17 **"at Sault Ste. Marie and here"** SLC to HHR, July 20–22,1895. Ibid.:172.

17 **"I am getting into good platform condition at last"** SLC to HHR, July 24, 1895. Ibid.:174.

17 **he could segue** Fatout (1960:259–60).

17 **the story of a christening** Ibid.

18 **"The humorous story is strictly a work of art"** Twain (1917c:263).

18 **"From the time of his stepping out"** *Melbourne Punch*, October 3, 1895:214. Quoted in Shillingsburg (1988a:131).

19 **his wife's suggestion** Pond (1900:206).

19 **"The performer . . . must vary the length of the pause"** Neider (1959:182).

19 the "Golden Arm" Twain (1917c:268–70).

20 "you *must* get the pause right" Ibid.:270.

20 "I know the look of Uncle Dan'l's kitchen" Twain (1907:461).

20 Justin Kaplan For his discussion of the "Golden Arm," see Kaplan (1966:309–10).

20 a man willing "to risk his soul" SLC to Joel Chandler Harris, December 12, 1881. MTL:403. Quoted by Kaplan (1966:310).

20 it was presented to a museum Paine (1912:996).

20 "He could persuade a fish" MTN:232.

Chapter Three

22 Pond left a remarkable record The text published by Gribben and Karanovich (1992) represents a manuscript that Karanovich purchased in 1984. In it he found almost all the material published by Pond (1900) plus previously unpublished text.

22 "You press the button, we do the rest" Gribben (1992:iv).

22 Clemens, in a dark three-piece suit Photograph in Gribben and Karanovich (1992:25).

23 In another photo Photograph in Gribben and Karanovich (1992:24).

23 "ink-black hair" ... "large dark eyes" *Bulletin* (Sydney), September 28, 1895:12. Quoted in Shillingsburg (1988a:48).

23 the loveliest girl From Pond's journal. Gribben and Karanovich (1992:11).

23 Clemens was pleased On June 11 he wrote to Pond: "I like the approximate itinerary first rate. It is *lake*, all the way from Cleveland to Duluth." Pond (1900:200).

23 "I have seen no boat in Europe" MTN:244.

23–24 "A small, peculiar, fine-grained sandstone" Pond (1900:202).

24 "The Madam ... will have no cause to complain" Ibid.

24 "A man may, indeed, shave himself" *Elmira Telegram*, July 7, 1895.

24 "groups of summer-dressed young people" MTN:244.

24 the warm greeting was for himself Paine's editorial comment, MTN:245.

24–25 *The New-York Times* The hyphen in "New-York" remained on the paper's masthead until December of the following year, a few months after Adolph S. Ochs bought the paper.

25 The average annual wage Statistics from Schlereth (1991:52, 78).

25 In Elmira Prices from advertisements in *Elmira Telegram*, July 14, 1895; *Elmira Daily Advertiser*, July 13, 1895; *The Elmira Weekly Advertiser*, July 12, 1895; and *Elmira Daily Gazette and Free Press*, July 13, 1895.

25 to raise another $70,000 Paine (1912:985), citing interview with HHR in 1908.

25 "I need not dream of paying it" Ibid.

25 But . . . "he stuck to it" Ibid.

25 In 1995 dollars The U.S. Consumer Price Index was 18.27 times higher in 1995 than in 1895. It rose from 25 in 1895 to 116.3 in 1970, with 1967 = 100 (U.S. Bureau of the Census, 1975:210–11) and from 38.8 in 1970 to 152.4 in 1995, with 1982–84 = 100 (U.S. Bureau of the Census, 1996:483).

Chapter Four

27 a woman in the audience suffered a heart attack *The Sault Ste. Marie News*, July 20, 1895:1. The paper, which did not suggest laughing as having precipitated the heart attack, reported that the woman was carried to her room and that "no serious result" was anticipated. She had come all the way from Iron Mountain, about 185 miles west of Sault Ste. Marie.

27 One horse produces five tons of manure a year Spence (1978:29)

27 the hotel dining room McKee (1981:54–55) describes the dining room c. 1895. He does not specify the tunes played by the orchestra, but Victor Herbert was popular at the time.

28 many changes of clothing Petersen (1973:59).

28 buttercup satin, with cream lace . . . white figured silk *Sydney Mail*, September 28, 1895:636. Shillingsburg (1988a:50).

29 **One advantage of the large amount of clothing** Randall (1989:139–55), on which my description of the dirtying and cleaning of clothes is based.

29 **sixteen pieces of hand luggage** Pond (1900:208).

29 **"so thick as to be almost stifling"** Ibid.:204.

30 **"The scheme to get people to do reportorial work"** *The Daily Resorter,* July 21, 1895. Quoted by Reed (1970:19).

30 **"This is too bad"** SLC to Major James B. Pond, July 21, 1895. Published in Reed (1970).

30 *The Petoskey Record* According to Reed (1970), the note was published in the July 31, 1895 issue.

30 **hundreds of sailing boats and steamers** Gribben and Karanovich (1992:5).

30 **"I am very glad, indeed"** *The Statesman* (Duluth), July 23, 1895:6.

30 **reluctant to laugh** Fatout (1960:20).

30 **he felt secure about his first program** SLC to HHR, July 29, 1895. Leary (1969:177).

30 **He found it thirty-five minutes too long.** Ibid.

30 **"Thus far . . . I have had more people in three opera houses"** Ibid.

31 **the young Stephen Leacock** He told about his meeting with Clemens in Leacock (1935).

31 **Clemens added his name to a petition** *Daily World* (Vancouver), August 12, 1895.

31 **Maria Barbella** Sometimes referred to as Maria Barberi. Her story is based on NYT July 8, 1895:8; July 16, 1895:1; July 17, 1895:5; July 18, 1895:12; July 19, 1895:2; July 20, 1895:8; July 23, 1895:8; July 24, 1895:1, 4; July 31, 1895:3; August 1, 1895:3; August 3, 1895:14; August 8, 1895:3, 4; August 14, 1895:4; August 16, 1895:12; August 18, 1895:4; December 11, 1896:9.

31 **"I have read all about the case"** Ibid.

31 **"Only hogs marry"** NYT December 11, 1896:9.

32 **"the evidence produced"** NYT July 19, 1895:2.

32 **"because what she did"** NYT August 14, 1895:4. The minister was

the Rev. R. F. Michaels of the Lexington Avenue Baptist Church. His reasoning, commented *The New-York Times*, would justify lynching.

32 **"For Gov. Morton to pardon the murderess"** NYT July 24 1895:4.

32 **"All that is apparent"** NYT August 16, 1895:12.

32 **"as though it had been a pleasure"** NYT December 11, 1896.

33 **the finest in the Northwest** *Daily Times* (Crookston), July 24, 1895.

33 **"But I won't without their consent"** SLC to HHR, July 29, 1895. Leary (1969:177).

33 **"the servant girl and the hired man"** *Daily Times* (Crookston), July 25, 1895.

33 **As to municipal services** McCulla and Wright (1979:5).

34 **Its ladders were chained and padlocked** Ibid.:29.

34 **"this is the first and will probably be the last"** *Daily Times* (Crookston), July 22, 1895.

34 **a rave review** *Daily Times* (Crookston), July 25, 1895.

34 **"I'm stealing a moment"** SLC to HHR, July 29, 1895. Leary (1969:177).

34 **about twenty new items** Fatout (1960:246).

34 **not entirely reasonable** From Pond's journal. Gribben and Karanovich (1992:7).

34 **"He insisted on traveling"** Pond (1900:208).

34 **Clara snapped the scene** Photograph reproduced in Gribben and Karanovich (1992:42).

35 **the fields green with wheat** "The level prairies of North Dakota wheat just turning, and the whole country a lovely green." Pond (1900:208–9).

35 **"the extortions from porters"** Ibid.:210.

35 **changed his watch for the third time** MTP:NB35.

35 **sitting in front of a tarpaper shack** Photograph in Gribben and Karanovich (1992:53).

35–36 **a young cowboy** MTN:246.

36 **Clemens would likely not have been sorry** MTP:NB35. Paine

amended the entry so that Clemens appeared thankful the cowboy had not been killed (MTN:246).

36 **"escorted Mrs. Clemens and Clara"** Pond (1900:210).

36 **"intellectual and dressed in perfect taste"** MTN:246.

36 **"a fine club"** Pond (1900:210).

36 **probably the Silver Bow Club** According to Everett (1995), Clemens is reported to have drunk toddies at the Silver Bow Club until 4:30 in the morning. The venue is more likely than the time he left it.

36 **"hot Scotch, winter and summer"** Pond (1900:210).

36–37 **the rawness and bleakness of the town** My description of Butte and its mines in the 1890s is based on Davis (1921), Federal Writers Project (1939), and particularly Emmons (1989).

39 **"Mark Twain cigars"** *Anaconda Standard*, August 2, 1895:2.

39 **"that he could have had a hand in the fake holdup"** Shoebotham (1956).

40 **Clemens "wasn't a bit scared or excited"** From Paine's interview with Gillis in 1907. Paine (1912:299).

40 **His treasure . . . did not lie in heaven** Ibid.

40 **"mad clear through"** Ibid.:300.

40 **a necklace of diamonds and rubies** Worn by Mrs. William A. Clark. Kelly (1983:38).

40 **"The manager was short about sixty dollars"** Pond (1900:211).

40 **"And you took the last cent"** Ibid.

Chapter Five

41 **formal, stag affairs** Fatout (1976:xix).

41 **"Hold on a minute"** Pond (1900:212).

42 **"Let's see. That — was — before"** Ibid.

42 **"up quite a mountain"** Ibid.

42 "the first sign of the decadence of the horse" Ibid.:213.

42 Pond photographed the scene. The photograph is reproduced in Gribben and Karanovich (1992:59).

42 the death of the horse NYT July 14, 1895:17.

42 Merchants in Chicago *The Elmira Weekly Advertiser*, July 12, 1892.

42 "the cycle will stay" NYT August 14, 1895:17.

43 "Mr. Clemens . . . it's remarkable" Paine (1912:767).

43 "You will not regret it, if you live" Twain (1917d:296). According to Paine, who edited the collection in which the essay appears, Clemens wrote it in the mid-1880s.

43 A reporter from the *Argus* September 27, 1895:5.

43 two and a half million pounds of manure Schlereth (1991:20).

44 "too tired to express disgust" Pond (1900:215/5).

44 the Twenty-fifth U. S. Colored Regiment Not the 27th, as reported by Pond (Cohen, 1982; Coleman, 1953).

44 "one of the finest military bands in America" Pond (1900:215).

44 Clemens confessed to his journal MTP:NB35.

44 "colored soldiers were more subordinate" Pond (1900:215).

44 Clemens noted in his journal MTP:NB35.

44 an acceptable fact of life Logan (1965).

45 two black prisoners My account of their lynching is from NYT July 15, 1895:8.

45 more than 150 lynchings per year Statistics from the NAACP, as reported in *The Encyclopedia Americana*, International Edition (1994), entry on lynching.

45 "That's right" Schlereth (1991:15).

45 an encyclopedia of American lynching Clemens, fearing that the project would destroy the market for his books in the South, withdrew his proposal, but he was ashamed of doing so. Hoffman (1997:439).

45 "The United States of lyncherdom" Twain (1923b). According to

Paine, who edited the collection in which the essay appears, Clemens wrote it in 1901.

Chapter Six

46 **The settlers claimed** NYT July 28, 1895:2.

46 **The Bannocks interfered with their livelihood.** NYT August 14, 1895:9.

46 **A federal treaty** NYT July 25, 1895:1.

46 **"Among the laziest and most worthless redskins"** NYT July 30, 1895:2.

47 **Wyoming's governor** Madsen (1958).

47 **In pursuit of this scheme** My account of the shooting of the six Bannock Indians relies on Madsen (1958).

47 **One man, shot four times** His fate and that of the wounded youth are from NYT August 31, 1895:12.

47 **"not fit to kill anything"** Ibid.

47 **two infants** From Madsen (1958).

47 **Fears were expressed** NYT July 22, 1895:1.

47 **Indians were gathering near Jackson Hole** NYT July 23, 1895:5.

48 **the Bannocks had killed three settlers** NYT July 25, 1895:1.

48 **"the backward Bannocks"** NYT July 24, 1895:4.

48 **the Bannocks had murdered all the settlers** NYT July 27, 1895:1.

48 **the Indian scare was over** NYT August 3, 1895:3.

48 **eager to pick a fight with them** NYT July 30, 1895:2.

48 **in order to defend themselves** NYT August 3, 1895:3.

48 **failed to indict** NYT November 17, 1895:9.

48 **"far more important to maintain the faith of the Nation"** NYT May 26, 1896:4.

48 **the Bannocks agreed to relinquish** Madsen (1958).

49 In 1885 he wrote to President Cleveland Foner (1958:237).

49 "enjoying everything" Pond (1900:216).

49 One reporter observed *Spokane Daily Chronicle*, August 7, 1895.

50 An essay Clemens had just published Fenimore Cooper's literary offenses. *North American Review*, July 1895.

50 "asphalt streets, electric lights" Pond (1900:216).

50 "It seems to be about the only thriving industry" Ibid.

50 "Stealthily guests came in" Ibid.:217.

50 the largest theater stage in the United States. Kalez (1972).

50 brilliantly colored leaded glass Hyslop (1983).

51 "picking oakum" Hyde (1963). Wilde was not sent to Reading Gaol until November of 1895.

51 "Oh, how I do wish" Pond (1900:217–18).

51 "another overgrown metropolis" Ibid.

51 "Really, your scenery is wonderful" Burnet (1951:194).

51 "each time it seemed" Pond (1900:219).

51 "That story . . . lacks a good deal" *The Sunday Oregonian*, August 11, 1895.

52 "I am a perpetual smoker myself" Pond (1900:219).

52 he felt it a privilege to lecture again Burnet (1951:194).

52 Clemens had "found his friends" Pond (1900:220).

52 "vigorously puffing a cigar" Burnet (1951:196).

52 a successful run of *H.M.S. Pinafore* Burnet (1951:187).

52 "Haf you been to Heidelberg?" *Seattle Post-Intelligencer*, August 14, 1895.

52 "one of those strange medleys" Ibid.

52 "a fellow oughtn't to be too severe on a man" *Seattle Post-Intelligencer*, August 14, 1895. The paper printed "in a man," not "on a man," probably a typo.

53 forest fires were so close Burnet (1951:191).

53 "You'll never play a trick like this on me again" Pond (1900:220).

53 Cascade Club Anecdote from Burnet (1951:191–93).

54 "a stretch of 18 miles" MTN:248.

54 "electric light is only turned on at a certain hour" Burnet (1951:193).

54 "There is a rumor afloat" Pond (1900:221).

54 "He is . . . a thoroughred" Ibid.

54 "very English" Ibid.

54 "convulsed at times" Burnet (1951:200).

Chapter Seven

55 "The smoke is so dense" SLC to HHR, August 19, 1895. Leary (1969:186).

55 "I was very anxious about him" OLC to HHR, August 17, 1895. Ibid.:183.

55 "Mrs. Clemens is curing him" Pond (1900:221).

55 "made the fortune of my life" Neider (1959:174).

56 "Lecturing . . . is gymnastics" Pond (1900:225).

56 "I shall arrive next January" SLC to Kipling, August 16, 1895. Published in MTN:248.

56 A statement to *The New-York Times* NYT August 17, 1895:8.

57 Clemens had earned $5,000 Paine (1912:1004).

57 "very plain and unpious language" Pond (1900:222).

58 "Here ends one of the smoothest" Pond (1900:221).

58 "superannuated" SLC to HHR, September 13–15, 1895. Leary (1969:188).

58 "I mean to write my book" SLC to HHR, February 5, 1896. Leary (1969:192).

59 Clemens wished MTN:249.

59 a kitten walked across the stage Ibid.

59 the Canadian-Australian Royal Mail Hamilton (1956).

59 The accident The account is based on the report in the *Victoria Daily Colonist*, August 11, 1895.

60 A few fishermen *Victorian Daily Colonist*, August 11, 1895.

60 A maritime inquiry Its conclusions were reported in the *Daily World* (Vancouver), August 19, 1895.

60 the passengers' letter to him Reported in the *Daily World* (Vancouver), August 12, 1895.

61 "Our young captain" FTE:I,2–3.

61 the damage was found to be much greater *The Sydney Morning Herald*, September 12, 1895.

61 The money spent to repair the vessel Hamilton (1956).

61 Arundell was not on board *Victoria Daily Colonist*, November 13, 1895.

61 "If perpetual smoking" Pond (1900:224).

61 "came into the world asking for a light" Twain (1917a:275).

61 "never to smoke when asleep" Twain (1923a:258).

61 The manuscript I am indebted to my daughter, Lisa Philip, for pointing out the faint smell of smoke.

61 "brave it through" Pond (1900:224).

61 Pond photographed the three Clemenses Photograph in Gribben and Karanovich (1992:77).

62 A subsequent snapshot Photograph in Gribben and Karanovich (1992: 78).

Chapter Eight

65 **The small boat** OLC to Susy Clemens, August 30, 1895. Harnsberger (undated:127).

66 **without any help from longshoremen** SLC to HHR, September 13–15, 1895. Leary (1969:187).

66 **the consumption of poisoned fish** *The Morning Herald,* September 17, 1895; *The Sydney Mail,* September 21, 1895. A similar story appeared in London, based on a report cabled from Auckland on September 13. A steamer, just arrived from Hawaii, brought a report that the deaths were caused by poisoned food consumed at a luau. *The Times* (London), September 14, 1895:5.

66 **sixty-two victims had died of cholera** An official statement of the cholera outbreak communicated by the Hawaiian Consul-General in London. *The Times* (London), October 26, 1895:10.

66 **"just as silky and velvety"** MTN:249.

66 **Paine . . . likened Clemens's banishment** Ibid.:250.

66 **"If I might I would go ashore"** Ibid.:249.

66 **"The old imitation pomps"** FTE:I,32.

66 **"eternal monotonies"** Ibid.:40.

66–67 **"We had the whole Pacific Ocean"** Ibid.:2.

67 **Of the more than eighty officers and men** New South Wales State Archives, Sydney. Inwards Passenger Lists, 31 August–31 October 1895, Reel 529.

68 **the minimum of fourteen knots** Hamilton (1956).

68 **"easily ran"** Ibid.

68 **The British chief engineer** FTE:II,2.

69 **"A flight of silver fruit-knives"** Ibid.:I,39.

69 **"violent exercise"** SLC to HHR, September 14, 1895. Leary (1969:187).

69 **"It will take a century"** FTE:I,44.

69 **"Champion of the South Seas"** SLC to HHR, September 14, 1895.

Leary (1969:187). In FTE (I42), Clemens wrote that the game was to determine the "Champion of the Pacific."

69 **"charming"** SLC to HHR, September 13–15, 1895. Leary (1969:187).

69 **Clemens recorded numerous gripes** MTP:35; FTE:I,2.

69 **"furnished by the Deity"** Ibid.

70 **"pretty cheerful"** OLC to Susan L. Crane, September 5, 1895. Hoffman (1997:407).

70 **"we have come far from the snake liar"** FTE:I,10.

71 **"an enormously rich brewer"** Ibid.:47.

Chapter Nine

72 **"brilliant blue and green"** FTE:I,66.

72 **Suva's rain** The story of Louie is taken from Derrick (1957:218–19).

73 **sort of hermit-crab formality"** FTE:I,70.

73 **"a neat retort"** Ibid.

73 **Contemporary sources** Summarized by Howe (1984:261).

73 **He is said to have clubbed to death** These and the other cruelties cited are from Howe (984:261).

73 **"The whites who have come to Fiji"** Cakobau, quoted in Grattan (1963:476).

73 **"notable monument"** FTE:I,69.

74 **an editorial** *The Fiji Times*, September 9, 1995.

74 **"In order to protect themselves"** Sir John B. Thurston, Letter to the Editor, *The Times* (London), September 6, 1895:8.

74 **"noble and beautiful view"** FTE:I,68.

75 **red enough to make one blink** Ibid.

75 **"a fine race"** FTE:I,71.

75 **"only sixty years ago"** Ibid.:67.

75 **carved wooden club** Clara Clemens (1931:143).

76 **"a British substitute"** Grattan (1963:479).

77 **its carrying capacity** The *Warrimoo* was 3,528 gross tons (Hamilton 1956). Our vessel was 17,176 gross tons.

77 **"Atlantic seas on to-day"** SLC to HHR, September 15, 1895. Leary (1969:188).

78 **Many remedies were** Brinnin (1971:514–15).

78 **"the most time-honored method"** Brinnin (1971:515).

78 **"We all like to see people seasick"** Twain (1911:I,29).

78 **one hundred years to the day** The *Warrimoo* anchored at 11:00 P.M., September 15, but the Clemenses did not disembark until the next morning. We landed on September 16.

Chapter Ten

79 **The Clemenses were at breakfast** Shillingsburg (1988a:26).

79 **Clemens praised the harbor** Ibid.

79 **"the darling of Sydney"** FTE:I,84

79 **"towers and spires"** Ibid.:85.

79 **"I don't know"** *The Sydney Morning Herald*, September 16, 1895:5. Quoted in Shillingsburg (1988a:24).

80 **"settled his fortune on his wife"** O'Rell (1895:307).

80 **"I can disgrace myself nearer home"** *The Sydney Morning Herald*, September 16, 1895:5. Quoted in Shillingsburg (1988a:24).

80 **"twaddle"** *Evening News* (Sydney), September 16, 1895:4. Quoted in Shillingsburg (1988a:26–27).

80 **"a delicate hand"** Ibid. Quoted in Shillingsburg (1988a:51).

81 **"Don't forget my soulful eyes"** *The Sydney Mail*, September 21, 1895:590.

81 **"After a few attempts at questions"** Low (1908). Quoted in Shillingsburg (1988a:25).

81 **"I'll meet you at the Australia"** Ibid. Quoted in Shillingsburg (1988a:27).

81 **"display of glass unrivalled in the colonies"** Handbook published in 1893 by the Australia Hotel, page 21. Mitchell Library, Sydney.

81 **It is likely that the reporter . . . was Low.** Shillingsburg (1988a:28).

81 **"blocked by a veritable race of genteel cadgers"** Low (1908). Quoted in Shillingsburg (1988a:28).

82 **"Mr. Clemens was delighted"** *The Sydney Daily Telegraph*, September 17, 1895:5. Quoted in Shillingsburg (1988a:29).

82 **The contest was particularly bitter** *The Times* (London), July 20, 1895:7.

82 **"Surely it is wrong"** *The Sydney Daily Telegraph*, September 17, 1895:5. Quoted in Shillingsburg (1988a:29).

82 **Local icons** Friedman (1996).

83 **"The Australians did not seem to me"** FTE:I,99.

83 **"let the Government own the land"** *The Sydney Daily Telegraph*, September 17, 1895:5. Quoted in Shillingsburg (1988a:30).

83 **"he wants plenty of protection"** *Australian Star*, September 17, 1895:4. Quoted in Shillingsburg (1988a:31).

83 **"it is easy to see that they are able men"** *Sunday Times* (Sydney), September 22, 1895:4. Quoted in Shillingsburg (1988a:31).

83 **"His forte is pathos"** *The Argus* (Melbourne), September 17, 1895:5. Quoted in Shillingsburg (1988a:32).

84 **"Harte read all the MS"** SLC to Charles H. Webb, November 26, 1870. Fischer and Frank (1995:248).

84 **"trimmed & trained & schooled me"** SLC to Thomas Bailey Aldrich, January 27, 1871. Fischer and Frank (1995:316).

84 **"nearly blemishless"** Clemens's annotated copy of Harte's *The Luck of Roaring Camp, and Other Sketches* (1870). Quoted by Booth (1954:494).

84 **"I will 'top' Bret Harte again or bust"** SLC to Orion Clemens, March 11, 1871. Fischer and Frank (1995:351).

85 **literary doldrums** Duckett (1964:115).

85 **"Tell Mrs. Clemens"** Bret Harte to SLC, December 16, 1876. MTP. Quoted by Kaplan (1966:203).

85 **"The holy passion of Friendship"** Twain (1922:56).

86 **"I think it would be better"** *Sunday Times* (Sydney), September 22, 1895:4. Quoted in Shillingsburg (1988a:36).

86 **in Australia, Harte's work was popular** Shillingsburg (1988a:34).

86 **"a mild . . . form of advertising"** *The Argus* (Melbourne), September 20, 1895:6. Quoted in Shillingsburg (1988a:35).

86 **"crammed from floor to ceiling"** Ibid. Quoted in Shillingsburg (1988a:41).

87 **"an old friend — a personal friend"** *The Sydney Daily Telegraph*, September 20, 1895:5. Quoted in Shillingsburg (1988a:41).

87 **"such an ovation"** *Australian Star,* September 23, 1895:3. Quoted by Shillingsburg (1988a:41–42).

87 **"he made up his mind"** Lawton (1972:269).

88 **"I went out at the window"** Twain (1911:I,174).

88 **"lecture-doubles"** FTE:I,127.

88 **"if the people should say"** Ibid.

88 **The 1881 letter** Paine (1912:711).

88 **his splendid Elizabethan house** Salamo and Smith (1997:432).

88 **"Being dead I might be excused"** Paine (1912:711).

Chapter Eleven

90 **"day of public humiliation and prayer"** *The Argus* (Melbourne), September 20, 1895.

90 **"So far, however, [Man] hasn't learned them"** *The Bulletin* (Sydney), September 21, 1895.

90 **per capita beer consumption** Finley et al. (1992:62).

90 **Canon Taylor** *The Argus (*Melbourne), September 20, 1895.

90 **Pipes from the roof** *The Sydney Morning Herald*, September 17, 1895.

90 **"for the Scriptures tell us"** *The Argus* (Melbourne), September 20, 1895.

91 **"the brightest passenger in the ship"** FTE:I,4.

91 **In a journal entry from Melbourne** MTP:NB35.

92 **"Advance Australia"** Shillingsburg (1988a:40).

92 **his book of poems** *Sonnets and Other Verse*. London: Kegan Paul, Trench, Trubner, & Co., 1895. Ibid.:38.

92 **he had lost his second wife** OLC to Susan L. Crane, November 3, 1895. Quoted in Potts and Potts (1978:47).

92 **horrified many Australians** Shillingsburg (1988a:50).

92 **"He said he could have married"** OLC to Susan L. Crane, November 3, 1895. Quoted in Potts and Potts (1978:47).

92 **Parkes's career** Biographical details from *The Times* (London), April 27, 1896:11; April 28, 1896:13.

93 **"his whole time was so sacredly devoted"** J. Henniker Heaton, Letter to the Editor, *The Times* (London), April 28, 1896:13.

94 **"gaily decorated with flags and evergreens"** *Evening News* (Sydney), September 24, 1895:3. Quoted in Shillingsburg (1988a:49).

94 **Clara thought the bouquets** Clemens (1931:143).

94 **"I don't know what would become of me"** SLC to HHR, September 25, 1895. Leary (1969:188–89).

94 **"Land of the Ornithorhyncus"** Clemens's routine from Fatout (1960:253).

94 **composed while still in British Columbia** Scott (1966:111) gives the date as August 22, 1895, the day before the Clemenses boarded the *Warrimoo*.

94 **"Come forth from thy oozy couch"** FTE:I,78–79.

94 **He introduced this routine** Shillingsburg (1988a:45).

95 **"with what seems to be a new carbuncle"** SLC to HHR, September 25, 1895. Leary (1969:188).

95 **"We have had a darling time"** Ibid.

Chapter Twelve

96 **one of Australia's most experienced ... theatrical managers** Shillingsburg (1988a:60–61).

96 **signed with Smythe for a tour** SLC to J. H. Harper, April 23, 1895. Leary (1969:143).

96 **"I have to-day written his lecture-agent"** SLC to HHR, February 3, 1895. Ibid.:127.

96 **"More Mental Telegraphy"** SLC to HHR, February 12, 1895. Ibid.:130–31.

96 **The brief article** Shillingsburg (1988a:13).

97 **A blitz of posters** Ibid.:23.

97 **"clean and fine and new"** FTE:I,119.

97 **"They are of a blueness not to be paralleled"** *Evening News* (Melbourne), September 26, 1895:2. Quoted in Shillingsburg (1988a:58).

97 **"a wonderful color — just divine"** FTE:I,121.

97 **really piles of dead rabbits** This joke first appears in Clemens's journal entry for November 5, 1895, with respect to New Zealand's Southern Alps, which he saw from the train en route from Bluff to Invercargill. MTP:NB34.

97 **"Long exposure and the over-ripe condition of the rabbits"** FTE:I,121.

97 **"they might as well propose a Bill"** "The Rabbit War in Australia," *The Times* (London), December 28, 1895:12. This is the basis for my summary of governmental efforts to exterminate rabbits in New South Wales up to 1895.

98 **"the oddest thing, the strangest thing"** FTE:I,119–20.

98 **"I believe in early rising"** *Herald* (Melbourne), September 26, 1895:I (second edition). Quoted in Shillingsburg (1988a:54–57).

98 **possibly Herbert Low** Shillingsburg (1988a:54).

99 **The greeting party** Ibid.:59.

99 **Clemens may not have known** Ibid.:60.

100 greeted with special sympathy Ibid.:20.

100 "clouds of tobacco smoke" *The Age* (Melbourne), September 27, 1895:6. Quoted in Shillingsburg (1988a:62).

100 Clemens, who had not slept well Shillingsburg (1988a:62–63).

100 "to prevent crushing and inconvenience" *Evening News* (Melbourne), September 24, 1895:1. Quoted in Shillingsburg (1988a:63).

100 some people had to sit on the stage Shillingsburg (1988a:62–63).

100 a voice from the gallery *The Argus* (Melbourne), September 28, 1895:7. Shillingsburg (1988a:65).

100 "The doctor asks the questions, generally" Twain (1911:I,303).

100 "Is — is — he dead?" Ibid.:I,305.

100 "That gentleman in the higher stage-box" *The Argus* (Melbourne), September 28, 1895:7.

101 Some parishioners may have thought Shillingsburg (1988a:63).

101 "The young men of Australia" *Australian Weekly*, October 4, 1895:8. Quoted in Shillingsburg (1988a:63).

101 "a stolid Englishman" *The Advocate* (Melbourne), October 5, 1895:14. Quoted in Shillingsburg (1988a:69).

101 "with a storm of applause" *The Argus* (Melbourne), September 30, 1895:6. Quoted in Shillingsburg (1988a:66).

101 Changes in Australian immigration policy Horvath, Harrison, and Dowling (1989:78).

101 a language other than English Based on the 1986 census. Ibid.:80.

102 "reminds me of its company occasionally" *The Australasian* (Melbourne), October 5, 1896:615. Quoted in Shillingsburg (1988a:70).

102 compared favorably with those on Regent Street *The Ballarat Star*, October 19, 1895.

102 Smythe canceled the Bendigo performances Shillingsburg (1988a:71–72).

102 "tea and chatter party" *The Australasian* (Melbourne), October 5, 1895:663. Quoted in Shillingsburg (1988a:71).

102 "charmed everyone" Ibid.

103 "The study of wall-paper patterns" Parsons (1961:456).

103 He stayed out of public view. Shillingsburg (1988a:72).

103 "the table, table-ware & decorations beautiful" MTP:NB35. Quoted in Shillingsburg (1988a:72).

103 "who was going out on circuit" FTE:I,139.

103 "Adelaide threw a short railway" Ibid.:I,140.

Chapter Thirteen

104 an increase of public curiosity" *The Advertiser* (Adelaide), October 12, 1895:4. Quoted in Shillingsburg (1988a:74).

104 Adelaide's papers Shillingsburg (1988a:79–80).

104 "will hand him over" *Quiz and Lantern*, October 3, 1895:3. Quoted in Shillingsburg (1988a:80).

104 Shopkeepers displayed photographs Shillingsburg (1988a:80).

104 "Innocents at Home" *The Advertiser* (Adelaide), October 14, 1895.

104 The crowd that gathered *The Advertiser* (Adelaide), October 14, 1895.

104 "The trees, shrubs, plants, and flowers" *The Advertiser* (Adelaide), October 14, 1895.

105 he had smuggled his carbuncle *The South Australian Register* (Adelaide), October 14, 1895:6. Reprinted in Budd (1977:57).

105 "a constant protest" *The Advertiser* (Adelaide), October 14, 1895.

105 "There is a frankness" *The South Australian Register* (Adelaide), October 14, 1895:6. Reprinted in Budd (1977:58).

105 "religious and peaceable" *The Advertiser* (Adelaide), October 14, 1895.

105 the nation's highest murder rate Lane (1997:350).

105 "much of the talk is exaggerated" *The South Australian Register* (Adelaide), October 14, 1895:6. Reprinted in Budd (1977:63).

105 "poor, hardworking, industrious" Ibid.

105 "a lively, self-possessed, frank, chatty young lady" *The South Australian Register,* October 14, 1895.

105 "a great roar of applause" *The Advertiser* (Adelaide), October 14, 1895.

106 Such a greeting Ibid.

106 "The doctor says I am on the verge" Paine (1912:1010).

106 "presumed they were intended for him" *The Advertiser* (Adelaide), October 14, 1895.

106 "electric-lighting in the Streets of Adelaide" Ibid.

106 "bored poor Mark Twain almost to death" *Quiz and Lantern,* October 24, 1895:6. Quoted in Shillingsburg (1988a:82).

106 probably retained only the original walls. Fischer (1960:97).

106 The "South" Marsden, Stark, and Sumerling (1990).

106 the public clamored to buy its bricks Ibid.

107 three-story veranda The Clemenses did not see the veranda, which was added in 1900. Burden (1983:213).

Chapter Fourteen

108 forced Clemens to reverse his route Shillingsburg (1988a:92).

108 thirty-five pounds Ibid.:92.

108 The secretary . . . and another young man Ibid.:93.

108 known for its lofty ceilings Brooke and Finch (1982:108).

108–9 "a very handsome cottonwood" FTE:I,185.

109 "The air was fine and pure and exhilarating" Ibid.:186.

109 Like his brother Maunders and Jaggs (1989).

109 He took over the college in 1890 The early history of the college is based on Maunders and Jaggs (1989).

109 **candy . . . and flowers** OLC to Susy Clemens, October 20, 1895. Harnsberger (1960:155).

109 **"all manner of fruits"** FTE:I,188.

110 **"clipped off a sample of the sheep"** Ibid.:I,189.

110 **Most were sixteen years old** The composition of the student body and its implications are taken from Maunders and Jaggs (1989).

110 **"a strange thing"** FTE:I,188.

110 **the "real" Australia** Sherington (1989:xv).

110 **agriculture represents a smaller and smaller component** Reuters, *The Jerusalem Post,* July 15, 1998:8.

110 **impressive changes** McWaters (1989).

111 **"only the shear in the shed"** *The Stawell News and Pleasant Creek Chronicle*, September 19, 1895.

111 **"never talked to a more enthusiastic audience"** OLC to Susy Clemens, October 20, 1895. Harnsberger (1960:155).

Chapter Fifteen

112 **It was probably in Stawell** Shillingsburg (1988a:97fn7) plausibly locates the anecdote there.

112 **"toddled off, contented with the world"** Clemens (1931:148).

113 **an entourage like that of the Clemenses'** Shillingsburg (1988a:98).

114 **"marvelously interesting creatures"** FTE:I,183.

114 **The Aborigine's "place in art"** Ibid.:180–81 .

115 **feats of tracking** FTE:I,140–41.

115 **skill in throwing** Ibid.:158–59.

115 **"fat wooden cigar"** Ibid.:167.

115 **"such unapproachable trackers"** Ibid.:168.

115 **"race-aversion"** Ibid.:168–69.

115 "so smart and generally competent" *The Bulletin* (Sydney), September 21, 1895:13.

115 "those naked, skinny aboriginals" FTE:I,168.

115 "They were lazy — always lazy" Ibid.:I,169.

116 the story of a settler FTE:I,172. Clemens quoted from Mrs. Campbell Praed's *Sketches of Australian Life.*

Chapter Sixteen

117 "Until last week" *Evening Star* (Geelong), October 22, 1895:3. Quoted in Shillingsburg (1988a:120).

117 "that his lecturer did not travel" *Otago Daily Times* (Dunedin), November 9, 1895:2. Quoted in Shillingsburg (1988a:88–89).

117 Carlyle Greenwood Smythe Biographical data from Shillingsburg (1988a:99).

118 "the finest thing in Australasian history" FTE:I,195.

118 Three survivors Shillingsburg (1988a:102).

119 "stretched out at full length" *Courier* (Ballarat), October 21, 1895:4. Quoted in Shillingsburg (1988a:102).

119 an hour of drollery Shillingsburg (1988a:102–3).

119 "warm-hearted, genial, sympathetic, and appreciative" *The Ballarat Star,* October 21, 1895:8.

119 "Every kind of wall-paper you possess" *The Ballarat Courier,* October 21, 1895:4.

119 It was not nostalgia Frank Cusack, Bendigo historian, as reported in *The Bendigo Advertiser,* May 4, 1991:12.

119 according to legend Finlay et al. (1992:689).

120 Clemens complained to his journal MTP:NB34.

120 He groused Ibid.

120 "He was an Irishman" FTE:I,203. The story is given in FTE:I,202–9.

121 meeting the man from the Mark Twain Club of Ireland MTP:NB34.

121 Today's Shamrock Hotel Finlay et al. (1992:687).

121 "All Australia ... is simply bedamned" FTE:I,253.

122 "The prices of admission" *The Advertiser* (Bendigo), October 24, 1895:3. Quoted in Shillingsburg (1988a:107).

122 "one of the finest panoramas" Shillingsburg (1988a:108), who quotes a statement by the Edwardses' daughter, published in the Bendigo Branch of the Royal Historical Society's *News Letter,* May 1974.

122 Clemens looked at his hosts Ibid.:109.

123 "Any town that has a good many votes" FTE:I,253.

123 "It might be a little behind" *The Maryborough and Dunolly Advertiser,* October 25, 1895.

123 Clemens ... hoped it would be chimeless. *The Maryborough and Dunolly Advertiser,* October 28, 1895.

Chapter Seventeen

125 an entry in Clemens's journal. MTP:NB34.

125 "A man who was travelling with [Clemens]" *The Bulletin* (Sydney), April 28, 1910:9. Quoted in Shillingsburg (1988b:29)

126 Clemens vented his displeasure FTE:I,252–55.

126 Clemens was tired Shillingsburg (1988a:115).

126 in the early evening Ibid.:116.

126 "How I edited an agricultural paper" Twain (1917b).

126 "I recognize that in lifting Mr. Dow" *Otago Daily Times* (Dunedin), November 9, 1895.

127 "thoroughly well qualified" *The Age* (Melbourne), October 28, 1895:7. Quoted in Shillingsburg (1988a:116–17).

127 "I reckon hot saveloys" *Melbourne Punch,* October 31, 1895:278. Quoted in Shillingsburg (1988a:118).

127 "superb house looking on a most beautiful view" OLC to Susan L. Crane, November 3, 1895. Quoted in Potts and Potts (1978:47).

127 "Yesterday we had our four o'clock tea there" OLC to Susan L. Crane, December 26, 1895. Quoted in Potts and Potts (1978:49).

127 John Wagner Biographical details from Sturrock (1990).

128 his name never appearing Ibid.

128 offended some of the Germans in the audience Shillingsburg (1988a:121–22).

128 greeted by cannon salutes *The Times* (London), October 26, 1895:5.

128 "It was all very interesting" OLC to Susan L. Crane, November 3, 1895. Quoted in Potts and Potts (1978:47).

128 "inimitable drollery" *The Prahan Telegraph*, November 2, 1895. Quoted in Shillingsburg (1988a:123).

129 they were sorry to leave Melbourne OLC to Susan L. Crane, November 3, 1895. Quoted in Potts and Potts (1978:47).

129 "pleasant but altogether too short" Ibid.

129 an American woman OLC to Alice Day, April 13, 1896. Mark Twain Memorial, Hartford. MTP:typescript.

129 "a glass of wine" OLC to Susan L. Crane, November 3, 1895. Quoted in Potts and Potts (1978:47).

129 "a bower" Ibid.

129 "the oldest people I have ever seen" FTE:I,242.

129 "Seventy is old enough" Ibid.:243.

129 "and could have told stirring tales" Ibid.

129 "wanton slaughter" Ibid.:239.

129–130 "the neatest town that the sun shines on" Ibid.:241.

130 Friends and relatives of people OLC to Alice Day, April 11, 1896. MTP:typescript.

130 "downright sorry" *Mercury*, November 4, 1895:4. Quoted in Shillingsburg (1988a:126–27).

130 **prize kidney beans** Parsons (1962:53–54).

130 **"I had an idea"** *Mercury,* November 4, 1895:4. Quoted in Shillingsburg (1988a:127–28).

130 **The *Mararoa* left Hobart** Shillingsburg (1988:128).

130 **Malcolm Ross** His interview with Clemens appeared as "A chat with Mark Twain," in the *Otago Daily News* (Dunedin), November 6, 1895:4.

130 **was asked to entertain the passengers** Shillingsburg (1988a:128).

131 **"I shan't retire from the gratis-platform"** Quoted in Fatout (1960:272–73).

Chapter Eighteen

135 **traditional observances** For observances of Guy Fawkes Day in New Zealand at the turn of the century, I am indebted to Aldbridge (1996).

135 **continues to commemorate** For contemporary observance of Guy Fawkes Day in New Zealand, I am indebted to Albert Smith, Christchurch, personal communication.

136 **In his journal entry for that day** MTP:NB34.

136 **He regretted the change** Ibid.

136 **"15 minutes after Mark Twain closes his remarks"** Parsons (1962:55).

136 **A local speculator** *The Southland Daily News* (Invercargill), November 6, 1895.

136 **cast-iron façade** *The Southland Times* (Invercargill), February 4, 1983. The original façade was replaced with brick in 1926.

136 **"small English town"** Reed (1969:17).

137 **theatergoers rushed for places** "The moment the doors were opened a rush for places lasting till nearly eight o'clock set in." *The Southland Daily News* (Invercargill), November 5, 1895.

137 **"A lovely summer morning"** FTE:I,246.

137 **"the Australasian National Day"** Ibid.:130–31.

138 even from New Zealand MTP:NB34.

138 "the Australian journals contended" Smythe (1898:34).

138 "a spectacle such as is never to be seen" FTE:I,130.

138 "everybody bet on the wrong horse" MTP:NB34. Quoted in Shillingsburg (1988a:131).

138 a solicitor from Christchurch *The Southland Daily News* (Invercargill), November 6, 1895.

138 "The people are Scotch" FTE:I,246.

138 adopted as colophon George Griffiths, personal communication.

138 perhaps thirty percent Ibid.

138 page after page Nine in all. Of course, some of these names indicate Irish origin. Dunedin's population is slightly over 100,000, the second-largest city on the South Island after Christchurch.

138 as he wrote in his journal MTP:NB34.

138 "When men want drink" Interview with the *Licensing Guardian*, New South Wales, as excerpted in MTN:257–59.

139 about an hour before his performance *Otago Daily Times*, November 7, 1895.

139 "Whether this was a case of cause and effect" *Otago Daily Times*, November 7, 1895:3. Quoted in Shillingsburg (1988a:135).

139 Dr. . . . Thomas Moreland Hocken Biographical information from Anonymous (1972), *The Dictionary of New Zealand Biography*, and Griffiths (1995).

139 "My, how you've grown" Parsons (1975/6:3fn1).

140 "there is nothing of the savage in the faces" FTE:I,246.

140 Moko Barrow (1984:46–48, 81–83).

140 "unpleasant and ignoble" FTE:I,246.

140 Maori wood and jade carvings MTP:NB34.

140 "a ghastly curiosity" FTE:I,246.

141 "Nature's attitude toward all life" MTN:255–56.

141 **He amplifed this essay** FTE:I,247–48; MTA:199–200.

141 **claimed that he had been wandering about** *Otago Daily Times,* November 8, 1895.

141 **a new item** From "Mrs. McWilliams and the Lightning." In *The Stolen White Elephant* (Boston: James R. Osgood and Company, 1882), 206–16. The story first appeared in *The Atlantic Monthly* in September 1880.

142 **originally scheduled to be the last** *The Evening Star* (Dunedin), November 5, 1895:2, reported that on November 6 Clemens "will give the first of his two nights of wit and wisdom in the City Hall."

142 **Clemens wrote to his nephew** SLC to Sam Moffett, November 10, 1895. Shillingsburg (1995:23).

142 **"the author of 'The Innocents Abroad'"** *Otago Daily Times,* November 9, 1895:2.

142 **If he was not the father of New Zealand art** Entwisle (1984:16).

142 **In one of these sketches** Both sketches are at the Field-Hodgkins Collection of the Alexander Turnbull Library, Wellington.

142 **"suffering the agonies"** *Otago Witness,* November 7, 1895:37.

142 **"Think of a town like this"** FTE:I,248.

143 **"the moderate enjoyment of a reader"** *The Timaru Herald,* November 11, 1895.

143 **"such people must have been misinformed"** *The Timaru Herald,* November 11, 1895:3. Quoted in Shillingsburg (1988a:139).

143 **"The two are as often as not simultaneous"** *Sydney Morning Herald,* September 17, 1895:5–6.

143 **a magnificent new three-masted steamer** The SS *Elginshire,* which ran aground on March 9, 1892. *Otago Daily Times,* March 10, 1892; *The Timaru Herald,* March 11 and 21, 1892.

144 **"but it is fast enough"** FTE:I,249.

144 **Demand had been slack** Shillingsburg (1988a:143).

144 **Dogs attended** MTN:261.

145 **the Brydone** The hotel was named after a pioneer of the frozen meat industry.

145 "It was Junior England all the way" FTE:I,256.

146 "the most charming I have seen" *The Press* (Christchurch), November 13, 1895:5.

146 "the green fields and the trim hedges" Ibid.

146 surprised by the great cities of Australia Ibid.

146 "the negro problem" *The Lyttleton Times*, November 13, 1895.

146 "colonial audiences at once are friendly" *Evening Star* (Dunedin), November 14, 1895:3, excerpted from an interview with a Christchurch paper.

146 stamping and cheering Parsons (1962:61).

147 "he left the crops flourishing" *The Lyttleton Times*, November 16, 1895.

147 the menu Fatout (1976:302).

147 "as large as your great moa" Ibid.

147 "The man said, 'Where's the snake?'" Ibid.:303.

147 "Christchurch is an English town" FTE:I,256.

148 Joseph Kinsey Biographical details from *A Dictionary of New Zealand Biography*.

148 "disreputable" Clemens's inscription, inside front cover of May Kinsey's copy of *Tom Sawyer*. The book is owned by the Alexander Turnbull Library, National Library, Wellington.

148 On a rainy night OLC to Joseph Kinsey, November 21, 1895. Letter in the Alexander Turnbull Library, National Library, Wellington.

149 "He says it is his most treasured possession" Ibid.

149 This was Anniversary Day Kirk (1967).

149 removed from service OLC to Joseph Kinsey, November 21, 1895. Letter in the Alexander Turnbull Library, National Library, Wellington.

149 *Flora* had not been built to the same standard Personal communication from David Graham, Auckland, who served with the Union Company for forty-five years, of which thirty-five were in management positions. He retired as assistant managing director in 1988.

149 "The people who sailed in the *Flora*" FTE:I,260.

149 "I had a cattle-stall in the main stable" Ibid.:I,261.

149 "we comfort ourselves now" OLC to Joseph Kinsey, November 21, 1895. Letter in the William Turnbull Library, National Library, Wellington.

149 "When the vessel got out into the heavy seas" FTE:I,262.

150 The Union Company would remember Personal communication from David Graham.

Chapter Nineteen

151 The Clemenses and Smythe debarked MTP:NB34.

151 "a wee little bridal parlor of a boat" FTE:I,262.

151 The vessel's master . . . took special pains Kirk (1967).

151 Newton had demonstrated exceptional ability Ibid. Newton was sailing from Liverpool to Vera Cruz when he encountered the Havana-bound *Niagara* (NYT, July 14, 1883:1).

151 "as helpless as a cork on the water" Clemens (1931:151).

151 "But he couldn't stop to talk about it" Ibid.

152 "The current tore through there like a mill-race" FTE:I,262.

152 "noble vast eddies" Ibid.:262–63.

152 "was disgusted" Clemens (1931:152).

152 After about a half hour on the sandbank Local newspapers reported that the sandbanking lasted a half hour around four in the morning. Shillingsburg (1988a:152).

152 "most 'tarnashun' place" *Nelson Evening Mail*, November 18, 1895. Quoted in Shillingsburg (1988a:152).

152 an interviewer found him holding a report Grace (1924:3).

152 "Pass on" Ibid.:5.

153 "Any one who reads that confession" FTE:I,267.

153 **"faithful soldier of Christ"** Hill and others (1924:21). The "soldier" was presumably one of the ministers who visited Burgess in his cell.

153 **"prelude to Heaven"** Hill and others (1924:144).

153 **"was as jubilantly happy on the gallows"** FTE:I,267.

153 a **"fearful blasphemy"** Hill and others (1924:115).

153 **"if you have flattered yourself"** Ibid.:124.

154 **At least two books about them** These are Burton (1983) and Clune (1959).

154 **"I have ever been a faithful comrade in sin"** Burton (1983:143).

Chapter Twenty

156 **"fine large Briton"** MTP:NB34. Quoted in Shillingsburg (1988a:154).

156 **Clemens ended his brief service** Hoffman (1997:62).

156 **"I was once idiot enough"** *New Zealand Herald* (Auckland), November 21, 1895:5.

157 **"The grassy crater-summit"** FTE:I,268.

157 **"I am prepared to swear on oath"** Kirk (1967).

158 **"the name of Arundell"** Ibid.

158 **"pathetically out of place"** FTE:I,3.

158 **they visited the American firm** Shillingsburg (1988a:159).

158 **"felt a little burdened"** OLC to Susan L. Crane, November 24, 1895. Quoted in Potts and Potts (1978:48–49).

159 **"vast and beautiful harbor"** FTE:I,269.

159 **sketched its three humps** MTP:NB34.

Chapter Twenty-one

160 **"was an object of thrilling interest"** FTE:I,271.

160 **"I guess it ought to be shortened"** *The Poverty Bay Herald* (Gisborne), November 27, 1895. Quoted in Parsons (1962:70).

160 occasionally the basket landed upside down Clemens (1931:149).

160 "not here where we have flung out a day" MTN:257.

160 "I do not like it one single bit" Paine (1912:1011).

160 "but the equivalent of scratching a nail" MTP:NB34. Quoted in Shillingsburg (1988a:163).

160 "We should have preferred" Parsons (1962:71).

160 "for sacrificing himself" Ibid.

160 "At Napier" MTN:261.

160 "I wish I had been born with false teeth" FTE:I,273.

160 "one of the best of men" Quoted in Rasmussen (1995:493).

161 "the Church of the Holy Speculators" Kaplan (1966:141).

162 "I think it was a good stroke of luck" Paine (1912:1011–12).

163 "stunning Queen of Sheba style of barmaid" MTN:259.

163 the abundance of workingmen's holidays FTE:I,155.

163 Mrs. Clemens wrote her daughter Susy OLC to Susy Clemens, December 5, 1895. MTP:typescript (Harnsberger, no date:137–38).

163 "rationally devised" FTE:I,275.

163 "charming scenery" Ibid.

163 "lots of Maoris" Ibid.:275–76.

164 "a superior breed of savages" Ibid.:276.

164 "a couple of curious war-monuments" Ibid.:278–79.

164 Clemens remembered two monuments The background for the Moutoa Gardens monument is based on Maclean and Phillips (1990:22–24), Smart and Bates (1972:107), and *The Encyclopaedia Britannica* (1980:IV,950).

166 "the killing of strangers" Twain (1885:203).

Chapter Twenty-two

167 In a letter to Susy. OLC to Susy Clemens, November 5, 1895. MTP:typescript (Harnsberger, no date:127).

167 the information in small type Shillingsburg (1988a:173).

167 "gentle, albeit sometimes jolty, ride" *The Evening Post* (Wellington), December 10, 1895:3. Quoted in Shillingsburg (1988a:177).

167 "it was difficult to stay in your seat" MTP:NB34, Quoted in Shillingsburg (1988a:177).

167 "they ought to put the milk in the train" Ibid.

167 "with the urbanity of a journalist" *The New Zealand Mail* (Wellington), December 12, 1895:51. Quoted in Shillingsburg (1988a:174).

168 "for travel is reducing the world" The reporter's paraphrase of Clemens's observation. *The Evening Post* (Wellington), December 10, 1895:3.

168 "I was in Australasia" FTE:I,108.

168 "Didn't know it was custom" MTP:NB34. Quoted in Shillingsburg (1988a:178).

169 "quiet power of description" *The Evening Post* (Wellington), December 11, 1895:2. Quoted in Shillingsburg (1988a:178).

169 "Well, I didn't think much of it" *The New Zealand Times* (Wellington), December 11, 1895:2.

169 "Natives of their own volition" Ibid.

169 "spent the three days partly in walking about" FTE:I,279.

169 The garden For information about Mrs. Ross's garden, I am indebted to George Kaye, a local historian.

169 Today, on a portion of the site I am grateful to Ian and Hisako Ewing for tracking down the location of Mrs. Ross's gardens.

169 a hospice serves the terminally ill I am grateful to the staff of Te Omanga Hospice for allowing us to walk through its grounds.

170 "Our stay in New Zealand" FTE:I,279.

Chapter Twenty-three

171 "three days of paradise" FTE:I,281.

171 "swelling seas and cloudy skies" Parsons (1962:76)

171 "the damnest menagerie" MTN:262.

171 a "burster" Ibid.

171 "The interviewer" MTP:4. Quoted in Shillingsburg (1988a:184).

171 "These towns & people" Ibid. Quoted in Shillingsburg (1988a:184–85).

172 "I thought the people" *Sydney Daily Telegraph*, December 20, 1895:6. Quoted in Shillingsburg (1988a:184).

172 " 'home,' as they all call England" OLC to Susan L. Crane, December 20, 1895. Quoted in Potts and Potts (1978:49).

172 Justice William Wendeyer . . . invited the family Potts and Potts (1978:49).

172 "beautifully laid out" FTE:I,108.

172 "plenty of room" Ibid.

172 a shark had seized a boy *The New Zealand Mail* (Wellington), December 12, 1895, giving a Sydney dateline of December 8.

172 "I . . . caught [a shark] myself" MTP:5–6. Quoted in Shillingsburg (1988a:185).

172 "story of his fishing expedition" Palmer (1954:94). Quoted in Shillingsburg (1988a:185–86).

173 Clemens noted reports Shillingsburg (1988a:185).

173 his fish story FTE:I,109–17.

173 "to-day the United States is practically sovereign" From President Cleveland's message to Congress, December 17, 1895. Quoted in *The Encyclopedia Americana* (1953), 27:533.

173 "the American people will deal roughly" Editorial, the New York *Sun*, quoted in *The Times* (London), December 20, 1895:5.

174 "when all is said and done" *Australian* (Melbourne), October 3, 1895. Quoted in Fatout (1976:293).

174 "that he had just arrived in Sydney" *Sydney Morning Herald*, December 21, 1895:7. Quoted in Shillingsburg (1988a:187).

174 "Whew! it was sweltering" *Sydney Daily Telegraph*, December 21, 1895:10. Quoted in Shillingsburg (1988a:187).

174 "In bidding his audience good night" *Sydney Morning Herald*, December 21, 1895:7. Quoted in Shillingsburg (1988a:187–88).

175 "gently waved his hand" *Sydney Daily Telegraph*, December 23, 1895:6. Quoted in Shillingsburg (1988a:188).

175 "farewell appearances" Shillingsburg (1988a:189).

175 verses not yet reported by the press Ibid.

175 "He declares unmistakably" *Advertiser* (Adelaide), December 27, 1895:5. Quoted in Shillingsburg (1988a:191).

176 an official luncheon My account is based on Shillingsburg (1988a:192–95) and Fatout (1976:305–7).

176 "they showed signs of the blightings" FTE:I,155–56.

176 "for the absence of the Minister for War" *Advertiser* (Adelaide), December 31, 1895:6. Quoted in Shillingsburg (1988a:194).

177 "The Board of Trade" MTN:263.

177 that September's running of the America's Cup My account is based on articles and letters in *The Times* (London): September 16, 1895:7; September 17, 1895:10; September 20, 1895:8; September 24, 1895:8; October 7, 1895:7; November 9, 1895:5; November 12, 1895:5; November 20, 1895:5.

177 "any thought or suggestion of war" Fatout (1976:305).

178 On the last day of 1895 My account of Clemens's activities on that day relies on Shillingsburg (1988a:195–96).

178 Clemens reported seeing many ships FTE:II,3.

178 "a little pilot" Ibid.

178 "One must say it very softly" MTN:265.

179 "Australasia governs herself wholly" FTE:II,5.

179 "Australasia is the modern heaven" MTP:18. Quoted in Shillingsburg (1988a:196).

Chapter Twenty-four

183 in the shade of canvas awnings MTP:NB37.

183 "the flooding brilliancies of the electric light" FTE:II,6.

183 attributed the custom MTP:NB37.

183 "Peace, everlasting peace" MTN:266.

183 "roasting hot" Ibid.:267.

183 "some ungoverned children" Ibid.:266.

183 "the calm and holy dawn" Ibid.:268.

184 "I am shut up in my cabin" SLC to HHR, January 12, 1896. Leary (1969:190–91).

184 "you only see things like this" *The Times of Ceylon*, weekly edition, January 16, 1896:56.

184 "that he was in no urgent need" *The Overland Ceylon Observer*, weekly edition, January 16, 1896:44.

184 "with a tightly rolled umbrella" Parsons (1963).

184 Exhausted by four in the afternoon MTN:NB36.

184 "an alert, gentle, smiling, winning" FTE:II,6.

185 "I can see it to this day" Ibid.:8–9.

187 the dismissal of **Mr. LeMesurier** *The Times of Ceylon*, weekly edition, January 16, 1896:45; *The Overland Ceylon Observer*, January 16, 1896: 31; *The Moslem Chronicle* (Calcutta), April 11, 1896:162.

187 Clemens noted in his journal MTP:NB36.

187 Smythe hoped to arrange engagements *The Times of Ceylon*, weekly edition, January 16, 1896:53.

187 "to one who is as well known" Ibid.

188 tour of Colombo MTP:NB36.

188 "The most enchanting day" *The Times of India* (Bombay), January 23, 1896. Reprinted in Ahluwalia (1996:35).

Chapter Twenty-five

189 "a poor old ship" FTE:II,11.

189 a bad cough, which confined him to bed MTP:NB36

189 The heat of the cabins OLC to Susan L. Crane, January 17, 18, 24, 1896. MTP:typescript.

189 earlier than expected *The Times of India*, weekly edition, January 25, 1896:4.

189 "The great humourist is with us" *The Times of India*, weekly edition, January 25, 1896:12–13.

189 he did not think much of his. MTP:NB36.

189–90 "It seemed such a shame" FTE:II,16.

190 he sent him a polite note. MTP:NB36.

190 "infernal cough" MTN:270.

190 "Irish stew under 14 different French names" MTP:NB36. Quoted by Ahluwalia (1996:9).

190 "Hindu servants yelling orders" MTN:270.

190 "the *most* fascinating place" OLC to Susan L. Crane, January 24, 1896. Published in Ahluwalia (1996:43).

190 "lest my cough jump on me again" MTN:272.

190 He even postponed an invitation The invitation, for all three Clemenses, was for Thursday, January 23. MTP:NB36; *The Times of India* (Bombay), January 23, 1896, reprinted in Ahluwalia (1996:35).

190 a brilliant evening reception It was held Wednesday night, January 22. *The Times of India*, weekly edition, January 25, 1896:9.

191 "However, there may be some advantage" *The Bombay Gazette*, January 23, 1896:5. Reprinted in Budd (1977:64).

191 "I work very regularly when I work at all" *The Times of India* (Bombay), January 23, 1896. Reprinted in Ahluwalia (1996:34).

191 "Yes, I am not for one moment going to pretend" *The Bombay Gazette*, January 23, 1896. Reprinted in Budd (1977:65–66).

191 "mere fluff and foam" *The Times of India* (Bombay), January 23, 1896. Reprinted in Ahluwalia (1996:34).

192 "I haven't seen anything yet" Ibid.:35.

192 1,400 persons Mutalik (1978).

192 "by almost every prominent citizen of Bombay" *The Times of India*, weekly edition, February 1, 1896:5.

192 The audience was mainly European Ibid.

192 "Mark Twain was there not as a stranger" *The Bombay Gazette*, January 25, 1896:5.

Chapter Twenty-six

193 "*Bombay!* A bewitching place" FTE:II,11.

193 "barbaric gorgeousnesses" Ibid.:21.

193 "Father ... seemed like a young boy" Clemens (1931:153).

193 Gandhi reported Virchand R. Gandhi, "A peep into Oriental philosophy" Appendix C of Mutalik (1978:106–11).

194 The Jain community My account of the Jains' reception for the prince is based on *The Times of India*, weekly edition, February 1, 1896:18; *The Bombay Gazette*, January 27, 1896:3.

194 "By and by, there was a burst of shouts" FTE:II,45.

195 "perhaps you don't care" Quoted by Carter (1958:204).

195 "all right, I'll make it emeralds" Ibid.

195 The prince, an athlete Biographical details from the prince's obituary in *The Times of India*, weekly edition, September 2, 1905:16.

195 "bales of rich stuffs" Paine (1912:1014), quoting Clemens.

195 "was our first glimpse" SLC to H.H. the Thakur Saheb of Palitana, February 5, 1896. Reprinted in Paine (1912:1013).

196 "not a bad average" *The Times of India*, January 23, 1896. Reprinted in Ahluwalia (1996:35).

196 "Even in Lancashire" *The Times of India*, weekly edition, February 1, 1896:12.

196 "It is all color" FTE:II,13.

197 "manned by a driver and three footmen" Ibid.:12.

197 "rich-colored turbans" Ibid.

197 "turbaned big native *chuprassies*" Ibid.:13.

197 Towers of Silence My account of the Clemenses' visit to the Towers of Silence is based on *The Hindoo Patriot* (Calcutta), February 4, 1896:3; Mutalik (1978).

197 "One marvels to see here" Ibid.

197 "As a sanitary measure" FTE:II,39.

198 Bombay's Parsis are considering a change Abram et al. (1994:593).

198 "remote from the world" FTE:II,35.

Chapter Twenty-seven

199 A maid accompanied them SLC to HHR, September 25, 1895, written from Sydney: "Mrs. C. and the maid are packing the trunks." Leary (1969:188). A maid was reported landing with the Clemenses in Bluff (*The Evening Star*, Dunedin, November 6, 1895:3) and sailing with them from Wellington to Sydney (Parsons 1962:76). In a letter to Susy from Palmerston North, Mrs. Clemens wrote about their maid, giving her name as Helene. OLC to Susy Clemens, December 2, 1895. Harnsberger (no date:138).

199 When the family arrived at a station OLC to Susy Clemens, December 2, 1895. Harnsberger (no date:138).

199 "you hire him as soon as you touch Indian soil" FTE:II,23.

199 All three Clemenses commented FTE:II,29; OLC to Jean Clemens, February 18, 1896, published in Ahluwalia (1996:44); Clemens (1931:162–63).

199 British residents in India Vernede (1995:103).

199 "because as long as he is in your employ" FTE:II,23.

199 two servants Clemens (1931:163).

199 the first servant they engaged FTE:II,24–29.

199 "All my heart" FTE:II,29.

200 "out of character" Ibid.:30.

200 "He was always busy" Ibid.:235.

200 "in a swell hotel" Ibid.:237.

200 "then put his head out at a window" Ibid.:235–36.

200 "but the family detested him for it" Ibid.:236.

200 "I loved him" Ibid.

201 "competent and satisfactory" Ibid.:238.

201 "God want to see you" Ibid.:30.

201 **Aga Khan III** Biographical details from Greenwall (1952), Jackson (1952), and Ogden (1996).

201 "not forty, perhaps not above thirty-five" FTE:II,31.

201 "a most courteous and charming gentleman" Ibid.:31–32.

202 "He had a pleasant, utterly unassuming charm" Shah, Sultan Sir Mohammed, Aga Khan III (1952:32).

202 "Satan see God out?" FTE:II,32.

202 forty rupees a month OLC to Susan L. Crane, February 28, 1896, published in Ahluwalia (1996:45); FTE:II,23.

202 "live in a mud hut" FTE:II,24.

203 "had pierced deep into the native quarter" FTE:II,49–50.

203 "a prophetic dream, as it were" Ibid.:52.

203 the home of a rich Hindu cotton merchant Mutalik (1978).

203 "wrapped in a perfect conflagration" FTE:II,50.

203 Clemens was moved Clemens (1931:156).

204 "a turbaned giant" FTE:II,51.

204 "is the stunningest of the Indian princes" MTP:NB36. Quoted by Ahluwalia (1996:10).

204 "perfect flower-beds of brilliant color" FTE:II,12.

204 "shining and shifting spectacle" Ibid.

Chapter Twenty-eight

205 "The misfortune was that it wasn't the serpent" From a composite of newspaper reviews of Clemens's performances in India, compiled by Ahluwalia (1996:26).

205 The Bishop of Bombay left the hall Mutalik (1978).

205 in 1964, she told an interviewer Interview with Miss J. M. Cursetjee. Published in Ahluwalia (1996:42).

205 "a village tenanted by people" *The Times of India*, weekly edition, January 25, 1896:9.

206 "but a continuous and ever-increasing evil" Letter to the editor, S. Allen Kennedy, *The Times of India*, weekly edition, February 29, 1896:10.

206 endemic typhoid. *The Times of India*, weekly edition, February 29, 1896:2.

206 the eleventh annual meeting Account based on *The Times of India*, weekly edition, January 4, 1896:5; *The Times* (London), December 28, 1895:5.

206 The Congress had begun Details of the Congress's early history are based on Spear (1978:169–74).

206 "modest reforms" *The Times* (London), December 28, 1895:5.

206 "Well, I have read of it" *The Madras Standard*, April 1, 1896. Reprinted in Budd (1977:71).

207 No one . . . "can deny" *The Englishman* (Calcutta), February 8, 1896:5. Reprinted in Ahluwalia (1996:39).

207 "When one considers" FTE:II,267.

207 "We are obliged to believe" FTE:I,93.

208 "appealing to the British nation" Article in the *Indu Prakash* reprinted in *The Times of India*, weekly edition, January 4, 1896:6.

208 "In our day" FTE:II,266.

208 "Without an effort" Ibid.:267.

209 "live in a fever pitch" *The Moslem Chronicle* (Calcutta), January 4, 1896:7.

209 "If the Hindus" Ibid., January 11, 1896:20.

Chapter Twenty-nine

211 "as if the whole world was present" FTE:II,67.

211 "tides upon tides" Ibid.:67–68.

211 "We named him Barney for short" Ibid.:68.

212 "built of the plainest and cheapest" Ibid.:68–69.

212 "handsome, spacious, light, airy" Ibid.:70.

212 "the American sleeping-car" *The Statesman* (Calcutta), February 8, 1896:3. Reprinted in Ahluwalia (1996:40).

212 "the word 'engaged' appears" FTE:II,109.

213 "prince's carriage drawn by picture-book horses" Clemens (1931:159).

213 "mixed modern American-European" FTE:II,75–76.

213 their gold and silver ornaments MTP:NB36.

213 "I did not ask for it" FTE:II,74–75.

213 "Father, suspecting what I was giggling about" Clemens (1931:154).

213 "It is claimed here" MTN:273.

213 "on account of the echoes" FTE:II,76.

213 "a fine and cultivated gentleman" MTN:274.

214 "for its barbaric pomps and splendors" FTE:II,73.

214 "the Gaekwar has shown himself a model prince" *Encyclopaedia Britannica*, eleventh edition (1910), from which my account of the Gaekwar's accession is taken.

214 **India was dissatisfied** Clemens (1931:160).

214 **"India always came first"** Shah, Sultan Sir Mohammed, Aga Khan III (1954:301).

214 **"the first thing you'll have to do"** Ibid.

Chapter Thirty

215 **Clemens slept all the way** MTP:NB36

215 **"It was a delicate situation"** The episode, based on the manuscript of FTE, the Berg Collection, New York Public Library, is published in Carter (1958:204–5). According to Clemens's account of the incident, he arrived in the city "early one morning" after "a long journey up country" This journey must have been to Baroda, from which he returned to Bombay, according to his journal, at 7:00 A.M. (MTP:NB36). From his other upcountry destination, Poona, he arrived at eleven (Ahluwalia 1996:11).

215 **"perfectly flat"** FTE:II,120.

215 **"all the way yesterday"** MTN:275–76.

215–16 **"there is an enchantment about it"** FTE:II,120–21.

216 **a sold-out house** *The Englishman* (Calcutta), February 5, 1896, cited by Ahluwalia (1996:12).

216 **"the vicinity of a lecture-hall"** FTE:II,126.

216 **"that it is hardly fair to Mark Twain"** *The Pioneer* (Allahabad). Quoted in Agrawal (1973:105).

216 **"And now the Fort belongs to the English"** FTE:II,130.

217 **"plodding patiently along"** Ibid.:129.

217 **"amazed at the intense atmosphere"** Clemens (1931:158).

217 **the Ganges, or Ganga** Details from Eck (1993:3, 212–13, 314).

217 **"a mighty swarm of pilgrims"** FTE:II,130–31.

217 **"If we had got to the Mele"** MTN:276.

218 for which the Magh Mele is especially known Abram et al. (1995:289).

218 "you have the monster crowd" FTE:II,132.

218 "I think I should always like to wait" MTP:NB36. Quoted by Ahluwalia (1996:12).

218 "a vision of dusty sterility" FTE:II,134.

218 "Benares is older than history" Ibid.:II,136.

218 the fruit of any ritual action there Eck (1993:315).

218 they touch its dust to their foreheads Ibid.:303.

218 "Religion . . . is the *business* of Benares" FTE:II,139.

219 "Benares is the sacredest" Ibid.

219 "makes our own religious enthusiasm" Ibid.:140.

219 "little itinerary for the pilgrim" Ibid.:141.

219 "a tank filled with sewage" Ibid.:142.

219 "you will find a shallow pool" Ibid.:143.

219–220 "you will see a Brahman" Ibid.:145.

220 "he would gain much" Ibid.:148.

220 "about the best thing in the book" Paine (1912:1054).

220 Clemens relied on conversations FTE:II,141.

220 "the news would soon spread" James Kennedy, *Life and Work in Benares and Kumaon*. New York: Cassell and Company, 1885:86–87. Quoted by Eck (1993:92).

220 "that when the brahmins of Banaras went forth" Eck (1993:93).

221 "they spend hours like this" Clemens (1931:159).

221 went to see a recluse" *The Englishman* (Calcutta), February 8, 1896:5. Reprinted in Ahluwalia (1996:38).

222 "a good house in a noble great garden" FTE:II,163. Parsons (1963:85) pointed out the difference between the account given to the reporter and that supplied in FTE regarding Clemens's meeting with the holy man.

222 "to live in a hut" FTE:II,166.

222 "But I shall not" Ibid.:166–67.

222 the Clemenses arose at six SLC to HHR, February 8, 1896. Leary (1969:194).

222 "a splendid jumble" FTE:II,150.

223 "Well, yes. I will make room for a bull" *The Englishman* (Calcutta), February 8, 1896:5. Reprinted in Ahluwalia (1996:38).

223 Each year about 40,000 My account of the current state of the Ganges and of efforts to clean it up is based on Stille (1998).

224 "The subject of caste" *The Englishman* (Calcutta), February 8, 1896:5. Reprinted in Ahluwalia (1996:38–39).

224 Mr. E. H. Hankin. *The Times* (London), August 26, 1895:6, citing the annual report of the bacteriologist to the government of the North-Western Provinces.

Chapter Thirty-one

226 "I have been barking around" SLC to HHR, February 5, 1896. Leary (1969:192).

226 "I caught cold last night" SLC to Susy Clemens, February 7, 1896. Wecter (1949:316).

226 "If I have seen anything like India" *The Statesman* (Calcutta), February 8, 1896:3. Reprinted in Ahluwalia (1996:40–41).

226 "the obvious advantages" *The Englishman* (Calcutta), February 8, 1896:5. Reprinted in Ahluwalia (1996:39).

227 Sir Alexander MacKenzie Biographical details from *The Dictionary of National Biography*.

228 "Often a British official" FTE:II,172.

228 "a fluted candlestick" Ibid.:170.

228 "if monuments were always given" Ibid.:171.

229 the Black Hole Details from *The Encyclopaedia Britannica* (1980) and Moorhouse (1994:43–45).

229 "the first brick, the Foundation Stone" FTE:II,173.

230 "joyous tribute of laughter" *The Englishman* (Calcutta), February 11, 1896:5.

230 "the humour of the speaker" *The Indian Planters' Gazette and Sporting News* (Calcutta), February 15, 1896:172.

230 "I wrote it in haste" Quoted by Parsons (1963:87–88).

230 "Mark Twain as a lecturer" *Madras Mail*, February 21, 1896. Quoted by Ahluwalia (1996:15).

230 "Barney was to put a glass of water" MTN:277.

231 "There was plenty to see in Calcutta" FTE:II,176.

231 "with the mimic storming of a native fort" Ibid.

231 "the best and greatest military show" *The Englishman* (Calcutta), February 12, 1896:5.

231 An editorial Ibid, February 10, 1896:6.

232 Clemens's sightseeing FTE:II,176.

232 "You have noticed from the car windows" MTN:287–8.

232 "pious cant" Ibid.:280.

232 more than 3,000 in hospital *The Times* (London), March 18, 1896:5, citing the annual report of the Sanitary Commissioner to the government of India for 1894.

233 He was one of the men brought out Moorhouse (1994:51).

234 "We sat down and talked" Neider (1959:40).

Chapter Thirty-two

235 The Clemenses . . . traveled to Darjeeling in style. Details of their journey from MTP:NB36; FTE:II,178–85; OLC to Jean Clemens, February 16, 1896, published in Ahluwalia (1996:43–44).

236 "Natives in all the brilliant and picturesque costumes" OLC to Jean Clemens, February 16, 1896. Published in Ahluwalia (1996:44).

236 "Up with the sun" FTE:II,178.

236 "Come . . . let us introduce" MTN:278.

236 "a dainty breakfast-table" OLC to Jean Clemens, February 16, 1896, published in Ahluwalia (1996:44).

236 "little canvas-sheltered cars" FTE:II,183.

236–37 "a little wooden coop of a station" Ibid.

237 "met a man who conversed with a man" SLC to Charles Henry Webb, February 16, 1896. Published in *The Critic*, volume 25 (new series), no. 740:286.

237 "Why . . . will people following dangerous quarry" *The Times of India*, weekly edition, March 28, 1896:16. The mauling occurred on Feburary 25.

237 "It is well-known here" Ibid.

237 "so wild and interesting and exciting" FTE:II,183.

238 "level as a floor" Ibid.:184.

238 "open coffin" Ibid.:185.

238 Four strong men Dozey (1989:25).

238 luggage followed on the backs of female porters Ibid.:24.

239 Clemens's *At Home* began at nine-thirty Ahluwalia (1996:16).-

239 "fairly good house" *The Statesman* (Calcutta), February 25, 1896, citing *The Darjeeling Standard*, as reprinted in *100 Years of The Statesman*. Calcutta: The Statesman, 1975:88. Reprinted in Ahluwalia (1996:41).

239 "the most remarkable forty miles" *The Pioneer Mail and Indian Weekly News* (Allahabad), February 20, 1896:22.

239 "No fewer than nine people in Calcutta" Parsons (1963:89).

239 the old Town Hall. The Darjeeling and Himalayan Railway Company (1921:52); Dozey (1989:118).

239 the main market day. Darjeeling-Himalayan Railway Company (1921:48).

239 "swarthy strange tribes" FTE:II,186.

239 "that novel congress of the wild peoples" Ibid.:187.

239 "a herd confused / a miscellaneous rabble" Dozey (1989:39).

239 **three physiognomic categories.** Ibid.:40.

240 **"and was genial and entertaining"** *The Statesman* (Calcutta), February 25, 1896, citing *The Darjeeling Standard*, as reprinted in *100 Years of The Statesman*. Calcutta: The Statesman, 1975:88. Reprinted in Ahluwalia (1996:41).

240 **"In every town and city in India"** FTE:II,185.

241 **It has been suggested** Vernede (1995:70).

241 **"if properly vouched for"** Dozey (1989:88).

241 **On Monday morning** Clemens, writing about a year later, reported incorrectly, in FTE, that they left Darjeeling on Tuesday. His account of their visit is incorrect in other respects as well: he was entertained by the club on Sunday, not after his performance on Saturday; they saw the mountain peaks change color at sunrise on Monday, not Sunday. These alterations were perhaps deliberate, intended to improve narrative flow. Clemens was not, after all, testifying under oath.

241 **After arising at five-thirty** Details of the sunrise excursion from OLC to Jean Clemens, February 17 (mistakenly dated February 18), 1896. MTP:typescript.

241 **Clemens, clad in a dressing gown** Ibid; FTE:II,186.

241 **"my party rode away to a distant point"** Ibid.

242 **The mountain view from Darjeeling** Statistics from Darjeeling-Himalayan Railway Company (1983:44).

242 **accompanied by some members of the club** *The Statesman* (Calcutta), February 25, 1896, citing *The Darjeeling Standard*, as reprinted in *100 Years of The Statesman*. Calcutta: The Statesman, 1975:88. Reprinted in Ahluwalia (1996:41).

242 **"had intended to tell the many people"** Ibid.

242 **"eternal snow"** SLC to HHR, February 17, 1896. Leary (1969:195).

242 **shedding their rugs and furs** Ibid.

242 **"For rousing, tingling, rapturous pleasure"** FTE:II,194.

Chapter Thirty-three

243 the next morning Ahluwalia (1996:16).

243 a private car Ibid.

243 Mrs. Clemens explained OLC to Jean Clemens, February 17 [18], 1896. MTP:typescript.

243 "that strange and fascinating piety-hive" FTE:II,200.

243 "Hot as the nation" MTN:278.

243 the great uprising of 1857 For the antecedents and consequences of the revolt of 1857, I have relied on Spear (1978:139–57) and Edwardes (1967:149–52).

245 "The British were caught asleep" FTE:II,202–3.

245 "sacred" FTE:II,217.

245 the Clemenses rode with Major and Mrs. Aylmer MTN:II,278.

245 Major Aylmer's uniformed orderly Ibid.

245 "ancient and elegant" and "sumptuous" Ibid.

245–46 "was perfecting his teething" FTE:II,218.

246 "the most impressive object" Ibid.

246 "a delightful little girl" Smythe (1898:34).

246 he insisted on writing her a note Ibid.

246 at three on Thursday morning. Ahluwalia (1996:17).

246 "Nine months ago" OLC to Susan L. Crane, February 28, 1896. Published in Ahluwalia (1996:45).

247 he offered to dethrone one or two princes MTP:NB36.

247 two carriages, each with a coachman OLC to Susan L. Crane, February 28, 1896. MTP:typescript.

247 "Attempts were made to furnish an eclipse" MTN:279.

247 "built of tinted mists" FTE:II,226.

248 When they arrived the next morning MTP:NB36.

248 "a pricking sensation in his left hand" OLC to Susan L. Crane, March 30, 1896. Published in Ahluwalia (1996:46).

248 He was also suffering from diarrhea. SLC to HHR, April 2, 1896. Leary (1969:202).

248 "I am in the doctor's hands again" SLC to HHR, March 6, 1896. Ibid.:196.

248 Smythe and Clara also fell ill MTP:NB36.

248 "we have been quite disturbed" HHR to SLC, March 20, 1896. Leary (1969:201).

248 small, noisy establishment MTP:NB36.

248 "a large empty compound" FTE:II,233–34.

248 "The secluded and country air of the place" Ibid.:234.

249 "new and beautiful palace" Ibid.:238.

249 "a beautiful construction of stone" Ibid.:239.

249 "One must try to imagine" Ibid.:239–40.

249 she wanted to visit it on a ladies' morning OLC to Jean Clemens, March 12, 1896. Published in Ahluwalia (1996:46).

249 "The only trouble was" Ibid.

250 "The blocks of houses" FTE:II,239.

250 "majestic elephants" Ibid.:240.

251 "for color, and picturesqueness" Ibid.

Chapter Thirty-four

252 "I was going to start last night for Lahore" SLC to HHR, March 15, 1896. Leary (1969:199).

252 a smallpox epidemic discouraged them OLC to Susan L. Crane, March 30, 1896. Published in Ahluwalia (1996:47).

252 "was built by a rich Englishman" FTE:II,232.

252 **James Skinner** Biographical details from Fraser (1955).

253 **"Mark Twain at Last!"** Advertisement in the *Civil and Military Gazette* (Lahore), May 16, 1896:9.

253 **"On Wednesday night"** *Civil and Military Gazette* (Lahore), March 20, 1896:5.

253 **"Mark Twain has come"** Ibid.

253 **with whom Clemens lunched** Ahluwalia (1996:19).

253 **the best way to see the city's antiquities** Parsons (1963:92).

253 **"I am used to being afraid of collisions"** FTE:II,231.

254 **"It was always summer in India"** SLC to HHR, May 8, 1896. Leary (1969:212).

254 **Clemens received letters from total strangers** OLC to Susan L. Crane, MTP:typescript.

254 **a journey . . . that lasted almost three full days** They left Rawalpindi at 12:45 P.M., March 21, and arrived in Calcutta at sunrise, March 24. Ahulwalia (1996:19).

254 **"comfortably ensconced in an easy chair"** *The Madras Mail,* March 31, 1896:7, reprinted from the *Indian Daily News.*

254 **He insisted on a royalty** Hoffman (1997:136).

254 **"When wind blew in, icy cold"** MTP:NB36. Quoted by Ahluwalia (1996:19).

255 **"For six hours now"** MTN:280.

255 **"Sometimes it comes over me"** OLC to Susan L. Crane, March 30, 1896. Published in Ahluwalia (1996:46–47).

255 **"the most interesting by far"** Clara Clemens to Samuel E. Moffett, April 7, 1896. Published in Ahluwalia (1996:47).

255 **The party went ashore for breakfast** *The Madras Standard,* April 1, 1896. Reprinted in Budd (1977:69–72).

255 **"When this boat leaves Madras to-day"** Ibid.

256 **his population redistribution proposal** Details from *The Times* (London), February 24, 1896:5; May 25, 1896:10.

256 **"India is already swarmed enough"** *Mahratta* (Poona), January 26, 1896:6.

257 **"the only foreign land I ever daydream about"** Neider (1959:288).

Chapter Thirty-five

258 **Vast clouds piled up on the horizon** Ahluwalia (1996:20).

258 **"better up-anchor and get off"** *The Times of Ceylon*, weekly edition, April 9, 1896:480.

258 **where he admired its tigers** Ahluwalia (1996:20).

258 **devoured a performing monkey** *The Times of Ceylon* (Colombo), April 4, 1896.

258 **"The menagerie section"** Ibid.

258 **a likable couple** MTP:NB36.

258–59 **his audience was small** *The Times of Ceylon*, weekly edition, April 9, 1896:475; *The Overland Ceylon Observer*, April 8, 1896:350.

259 **"age is beginning to tell on him"** *The Ceylon Examiner* (Colombo), April 4, 1896:3.

259 **Clemens claimed . . . to have forgotten** *The Times of Ceylon*, weekly summary, April 9, 1896:480.

259 **"spoiled by altering one word"** *The Times of Ceylon*, weekly edition, April 9, 1896:480.

259 **immediately after the second** *At Home The Ceylon Examiner* (Colombo), April 6, 1896:3.

259 **under a cloudburst** Ahluwalia (1996:20).

259 **Clara wrote to her cousin** Clara Clemens to Samuel E. Moffett, April 7, 1896. Published in Ahluwalia (1966:47).

259 **resigned to insects on tropical voyages** MTP:NB37.

259 **he considered the vessel quite comfortable** Ibid.

259 **"seventeen days ago"** MTN:289.

260 "There *are* no sea-holidays any more" SLC to HHR, April 24, 1896. Leary (1969:210).

260 The speed of modern travel MTP:NB37.

260 "It was that story" FTE:II,260.

260 "No other book is so popular here" Ibid.:263.

260 The Clemenses anchored off Port Louis Ibid.:258.

260 Clemens had expected to be quarantined SLC to Franklin G. Whitmore, April 12, 1896. MTP:typescript.

260 the next day the Clemenses went ashore FTE:II,259.

260 "this holiday comes very handy for me" SLC to HHR, April 24, 1896. Leary (1969:209–11).

261 "the finest boat I have seen" FTE:II,272.

261 by the first of May MTP:NB38.

261 "All that I remember about Madagascar" FTE:II,274.

262 The Clemenses reached Lourenço Marques Ibid.:276.

262 "a bold headland — precipitous wall" Ibid.

262 "thousands of tons of freight" Ibid.

262 "a small town — no sights" Ibid.:277.

262 "outrageously heavy bags of freight" Ibid.

262 "the ship slowed down" Ibid.:281.

Chapter Thirty-six

265 Two founding members Parsons (1977:236).

265 "'Rikishas . . . drawn by splendidly built black Zulus" FTE:II,283.

265 rickshaw pullers were throwing stones Parsons (1975/6:6).

265 shooting and stabbing one another's drivers *East Province Herald* (Port Elizabeth), May 21, 1996.

265 **bloody conflict in KwaZulu/Natal** My chief sources are Daley (1996) and Mostert (1996).

266 **Clemens left the hotel to pick up his mail** Parsons (1975/6:7).

266 **"just my condition"** *The Natal Mercury* (Durban), May 9, 1896. Quoted by Parsons (1975/6:7).

267 **"I only wish my stay"** *The Natal Mercury* (Durban), May 8, 1896:3. Reprinted in Budd (1977:72–73).

267 **His pieces for Virginia City's** *Territorial Enterprise* Hoffman (1997:71).

267 **commissioned the government's printing contracts** Ibid.

267 **"the pitiless and uninterrupted blaze"** SLC to HHR, May 8, 1896. Leary (1969:212).

267 **"comfortless and forbidding"** FTE:II,287.

267 **literacy in both English and Zulu** MTP:38.

267 **"wage-yielding mechanical trades"** FTE:II,288.

268 **"must not be forced"** *The Natal Mercury* (Durban), May 8, 1896:4.

268 **"groups of negro men and women"** MTN:292.

268 **"Everything neat and trim and clean"** FTE:II,284.

268 **who lived on Berea Road** Parsons (1975/6:8).

268 **Dr. Campbell** Biographical details from the *Dictionary of South African Biography*, 3:129; *The Natal Mercury* (Durban), obituary, March 13, 1926.

268 **"spend quite a cheery time"** Quoted by Parsons (1975/6:8).

269 **1,000-seat Theatre Royal** Parsons (1978:2).

269 **extra rows had to be provided** Ibid.

269 **probably the first world-class platform star** Rosenthal (1968:170).

269 **managed the rare feat** *The Natal Mercury* (Durban), May 14, 1896:4.

269 **the evening's chairman** Ibid.

269 **"in a quite inadequate speech"** "Story about Mark Twain, written by his friend Dr. Sam Campbell," Ethel Campbell Notes, Killie Campbell Africana Library. Quoted by Parsons (1977:237).

269 **"socially, the visit of Mark Twain"** *The Natal Mercury*, May 11, 1896. Quoted by Parsons (1975/6:9).

269 **telling her he was lonely** SLC to OLC, May 15, 1896. MTP:typescript.

269 **"beautiful and tender loyalty"** Howells (1910:10).

270 **"from all parts of the country"** Quoted by Parsons (1978:3).

270 **"to join culture and beauty to talent"** SLC to OLC, May 16, 1896. Published in Clemens (1931:168).

270 **"While colonists do all that can be done"** F. S. Tatham, letter to the editor, *The Times* (London), November 4, 1895:12.

271 **"too brutally blunt and rude"** *The Natal Mercury* (Durban), May 8, 1896:3.

271 **"Coolies have no votes in India"** Letter to the Editor from T. Hyslop, *The Times* (London), November 27, 1895:12.

271 **According to data published** *The Times* (London), January 27, 1896:4.

271 **Gandhi . . . pointed out** Ibid.

271 **"I was pushed out of the train"** M. K. Gandhi, *The Selected Works of Mahatma Gandhi*, vol. 3: *Satyagraha in South Africa*. Ahmedabad, 1968:56. Quoted by Sparks (1991:88–89).

272 **"it was the first time any person of colour"** Sparks (1991:89).

273 **"Fifty years experience of men and books"** Clark (1908:76). I am indebted to Margaret von Klemperer of *The Natal Witness* (Pietermaritzburg) for this reference.

273 **Headmaster Clark and the barrister G. Bulkley** *The Natal Witness* (Pietermaritzburg), May 18, 1896:3.

273 **Bulkley's lengthy memorized address** SLC to OLC, May 16, 1896. Published in Clemens (1931:168–69).

273 **Justifying his comments** *The Natal Witness* (Pietermaritzburg), May 18, 1896:3.

274 **"I got up and said"** SLC to OLC, May 16, 1896. Published in Clemens (1931:168–69).

274 **"Last night . . . I was satisfied with myself"** Quoted by Parsons (1978:3).

274 "falling into the sere and yellow leaf" *The Times of Natal* (Pietermaritzburg), May 16, 1896.

274 "Mark Twain's 'Man'" *The Natal Witness* (Pietermaritzburg), May 18, 1896:3.

Chapter Thirty-seven

275 **A grand torchlit reception** SLC to Clara Clemens, May 22, 1896. MTP:typescript.

275 **an outpouring of public grief** *The Critic* (Johannesburg and Pretoria), May 22, 1896:803.

275 **with a borrowed razor** Pakenham (1960:111).

275 **His fellow prisoners** *The Critic* (Johannesburg and Pretoria), May 22, 1896:803.

275 **Buildings to rival the greatest** Arthur Fell, letter to the editor, *The Times* (London), October 17, 1895:12. Fell, a resident of Cape Town, had just returned from Johannesburg.

275 **Social life among the expatriate white community** Hammond (1918:13).

275 **Johannesburg was a wonder of the world** Hattersley (1969:238).

276 **ninety-seven brothels** Sparks (1991:123).

276 **"Monte Carlo superimposed"** Ibid.

276 **barefoot urchins** Hattersley (1969:184).

276 **he was influenced . . . by the work of Olive Schreiner** FTE:II,316.

276 **"white savage"** MTN:298.

276 **"has stood stock-still in South Africa"** FTE:II,315–16.

276 **"those simple, democratic rights"** Hammond (1918:7).

277 **By the end of 1895** My account of Jameson's raid and its immediate aftermath, in this and subsequent chapters, is based on Pakenham (1960) and Smith (1996).

278 at the head of South Africa's mining experts *Standard and Diggers' News* (Johannesburg), weekly edition, May 30, 1896:21.

278 **Clemens had met him long ago** SLC to OLC, May 23, 1896. Microfilm, Elmira College Library. Clemens met Hammond at the home of William Buel Franklin, a Union general during the Civil War, who lived in Hartford.

278 **"great silver-plated acres of veld"** *Standard and Diggers' News* (Johannesburg), May 18, 1896. Quoted by Parsons (1975/6:15).

279 **"I tried to explain"** Ibid.

279 **"the best bedroom"** *The Star* (Johannesburg), May 18, 1896:4. Reprinted in Budd (1977:75–76).

279 **"And these things are going on undisturbed"** *The Times* (London), December 30, 1895:8.

280 **"an inexpressible tangle"** *The Johannesburg Times*, May 18, 1896:5.

281 **"it filled every available part"** *The Critic* (Johannesburg and Pretoria), May 22, 1896:821.

281 **"he was so vociferously applauded"** Ibid.

281 **"auditors wiped tears from their eyes"** Parsons (1978:3).

281 **"well-known among the South African Dutch"** *The Star* (Johannesburg), May 19, 1896.

281 **"at all times the lecturer was eloquent"** *The Johannesburg Times*, May 19, 1896.

281 **he may have gotten himself into trouble** SLC to OLC, May 20, 1896. MTP:typescript.

282 **"a wretched hand at remembering"** *The Johannesburg Times*, May 18, 1896. Quoted in Parsons (1975/6:16).

282 **gave her a chance to tell him** SLC to Clara Clemens, May 22, 1896. MTP:typescript.

282 **Mrs. Chapin had taken Clemens on carriage rides** Parsons (1975/6:16–17).

282 **even packed his luggage** SLC to Clara Clemens, May 22, 1896. MTP:typescript.

Chapter Thirty-eight

283 "Mr. Clemens, I'm certainly glad to see you" Hammond (1918:398).

283 based on notes that Smythe made from memory MTP:NB38.

283 "The dream of his life" *The Press* (Pretoria), May 25, 1896:3.

283 "A Boer guard was at my elbow" SLC to Joseph Twitchell, May 24, 1896. MTL:631–32.

284 After declining Hammond's invitation Hammond (1935:399).

284 "The Caledonian Hall is excellent" *The Press* (Pretoria), May 25, 1896:3.

284 it was impossible to hear him satisfactorily *The Transvaal Advertiser* (Pretoria), May 25, 1896:3.

284 "a veritable boom of laughter" *The Press* (Pretoria), May 25, 1896:3.

284 "It is not satisfactory" *The Transvaal Advertiser* (Pretoria), May 25, 1896.

284 "promptly and abundantly responsive" MTN:293.

284 He was glad *The Press* (Pretoria), May 25, 1896:3.

284 "an ideal rest cure" Hammond (1935:399).

284 Hammond claimed Ibid.:400.

285 "his orders wouldn't allow him" SLC to Joseph H. Twitchell, May 24, 1896. MTL:632–33.

285 such stillness on the streets MTP:NB38.

285 Competition from a promenade concert *The Press* (Pretoria), May 27, 1896:3.

285 the half-hour signal Parsons (1975/6:18).

285 "immense applause" *The Transvaal Advertiser* (Pretoria), May 28, 1896:3.

285 Clemens visited President Kruger *The Press* (Pretoria), May 27, 1896:3.

285 "There, that is what I always ask" Taylor (1939:88–89).

286 "Now that this Jameson's on the veld" *The Express and Orange Free State Advertiser* (Bloemfontein), May 26, 1896:4.

286 "If the heads of the Boer Government" FTE:II,316.

286 A translator mediated their conversation *The Press* (Pretoria), May 27, 1896:3.

286 "in ordinary everyday clothes" MTN:295.

286 According to Hammond Hammond (1935:400).

287 "A great strain" *The Krugersdorp Times*, February 1, 1896:6.

287 "crowded to utmost capacity" Ibid., May 30, 1896:3.

287 "The yarns were rather too lengthy" Ibid.

287 "the human imagination" MTN:299–300.

287–88 "with a pair of horses" Parsons (1975/6:20).

288 his sympathetic references *Standard and Diggers' News* (Johannesburg), weekly edition, May 30, 1896:1.

288 Rhodes and the principal Reformers SLC to OLC, May 25, 1896. Microfilm, Elmira College Library.

288 "Miss Rhodes, middle-aged sister of Cecil" MTN:297.

288 "a happy name" FTE:II,319.

288–89 "That he is an extraordinary man" FTE:II,332–34.

289 "There isn't a foot of land in the world" MTN:295–96.

290 "supper and comfortable fire" Ibid.:296.

290 "Put it there, old man!" Poultney Bigelow, *Seventy Summers* (1925), quoted by Parsons (1978:10).

Chapter Thirty-nine

291 "just as beautiful as Paradise" SLC to OLC, June 1, 1896. Quoted by Parsons (1975/6:21).

291 "most of his yarns were familiar" *The Friend of the Free State and Bloemfontein Gazette*, June 2, 1896:3.

291 "Mark Twain was simply delightful" Ibid.

291 with a letter of introduction Parsons (1977:248).

292 "I would rather lose" *Standard Encyclopaedia of South Africa*, X:285–89.

292 "I followed a couple of them all over" FTE:II,320.

292 where horses, cattle, and sheep were sold Parsons (1975/6:22).

292 "if my little dogs are naughty" *The Times* (London), June 12, 1896:5.

292 £200,000 *The Times* (London), June 12, 1896:9.

293 "by giving me a banquet" Hammond (1935:400).

293 "an evening's entertainment" *Queenstown Free Press*, June 9, 1896:3.

293 "He'll have a lot to say" *Queenstown Representative*, June 8, 1896. Quoted by Parsons (1975/6:25).

293 "where half the people were alive" Ibid.

294 A glorious gaslit chandelier Mr. Edric Russell, personal communication.

294 "dumped it into stocks" SLC to HHR, June 6, 1896. Leary (1969:216).

294–95 "We have been having in South Africa" SLC to HHR, May 26, 1896. Ibid.:215.

295 "If I had the family in a comfortable poor-house SLC to HHR, June 6, 1896. Ibid.:216.

295 "It's no use, Livy dear" SLC to OLC, June 10, 1896. Quoted by Clemens (1931:169).

295 Clemens considered taking Chapin's place SLC to OLC, June 8 (?), 1896. Microfilm, Elmira College Library.

295 Mrs. Clemens . . . nixed the proposal Kaplan (1966:335).

295 Writing to Mrs. Clemens at five SLC to OLC, June 7, 1896. Microfilm, Elmira College Library.

295 "Never, we believe" *The Cape Mercury* (King William's Town), June 9, 1896:3.

296 "a handsome looking man" Alfred William Burton, quoted by Coleman O. Parsons, who interviewed him. Parsons (1978:6).

296 "mincing across the great barren square" FTE:II,320.

296 built two years before Denfield (1965:65).

296 the scene described by Clemens MTP:NB38.

296 A photograph, taken on a sunny Sunday The photograph appears in Denfield (1965:115).

297 a downpour reduced attendance *East London Standard and Border Gazette*, June 12, 1896.

297 In the "other London" Parsons (1978:7).

297 A photograph of the square The photograph appears in Denfield (1965:99).

297 "overzealous application" *The East London Despatch*, June 13, 1896.

297 "We are having a lazy comfortable time here" SLC to OLC, June 12, 1896. Quoted by Parsons (1975/6:27).

297 "Now [that] I have ruled fluking out" MTN:298.

297 "It was his habit" Ibid.

297 The sea had been blustery and heavy Parsons (1975/6:27).

297 fearing that the sea might become so rough MTN:300.

298 "there is a considerable sea today" Ibid.

298 she felt as if he had been away a year OLC to Susan L. Crane, June 16, 1896. MTP:typescript.

298 *"beautiful,* even *ravishing"* OLC to Mrs. Samuel Campbell, June 9, 1896. Killie Campbell Africana Library, Durban. Quoted by Parsons (1975/6:28).

298 All but three *The Times* (London), June 18, 1896:10.

298 Flags throughout South Africa Parsons (1975/6:28).

298 "I would have chosen Mrs. Hart every time" SLC to HHR, June 18, 1896. Leary (1969:217).

299 "I am quite sure that (bar one)" Twain (1925c:264).

Chapter Forty

300 **a woman in the audience began to laugh** Smythe (1898:3).

300 **"venerable writer"** *The Eastern Province Herald and Port Elizabeth Commercial News*, June 24, 1896:6.

300 **ostriches in the fields** MTP:NB38.

300 **Grahamstown . . . impressed Clemens.** MTP:NB38.

302 **"Mark Twain's method"** *The Cape Argus* (Cape Town), July 8, 1896:3. From a review by Edward Vincent, who saw Clemens perform in Grahamstown.

302 **he signed the Visitors' Book** Parsons (1975/6:30).

302 **he played billiards with Smythe** Parsons (1977:251).

302 **"has always covered the broadest spectrum"** B. E. Latrobe, Mayor of Grahamstown, to T. G. Wiblin, Chairman of the Grahamstown Club, July 7, 1986. In Griffiths (1986).

302 **"in a side of the vast dust-blown square"** MTN:302.

303 **For the first time since he was a boy** Ibid.

303 **The dispatch shown to Clemens** Parsons (1977:251–52).

303 **a Reuters dispatch** *The Midland News and Karoo Farmer* (Cradock), June 30, 1896:12.

303 **"Strange . . . how that number"** Ibid.:4.

303 **complaining that he had to wait ten hours** MTP:NB38.

303 **shortly after noon on Tuesday** Parsons (1975/6:32).

303 **"When the Great Yankee"** *Diamond Fields Advertiser* (Kimberley), July 2, 1896. Quoted by Parsons (1975/6:33).

304 **"like a block of gorgonzola"** Sparks (1991:120).

304 **"brimful of fame and fortune"** SLC to Elisha Bliss, November 28, 1870. Quoted by Kaplan (1966:124).

304 **But he proposed to send a proxy** My account of Clemens's scheme to send John Henry Riley to South Africa relies primarily on Kaplan (1966:124–29).

305 he met the man who had bought **Riley's copy** Parsons (1978:8).

305 **"I was in Kimberley by proxy"** Parsons (1978:8).

305 **"roomy enough to admit the Roman Coliseum"** FTE:II,326–27.

305–6 **"a big double handful"** MTN:303.

306 **He saw the tanks** FTE:II,327–28.

306 **"Every day ducal incomes sift and sparkle"** FTE:II,331.

306 **about £10,000 or £12,000** MTN:303.

306 **He increased the take to $70,000** FTE:II,331.

306 **"They are a jolly and good-natured lot"** FTE:II,329.

306 **"but there were so many people watching me"** *The Cape Times* (Cape Town), July 7, 1896:7.

Chapter Forty-one

307 **At seven on Sunday morning** MTP:NB38.

307 **a stream of admirers** Masson (1950:180); Parsons (1975/6:37).

307 **"Alexandria in the southern Atlantic"** Breyton Bretenbach, *Return to Paradise* (1993), quoted by Weschler (1993:81).

308 **"carry its desires without any war"** *The Cape Times* (Cape Town), July 7, 1896:7.

308–9 **"the most extensive, costly and humiliating war"** Smith (1996:1).

309 **"very delightful"** *The Cape Times* (Cape Town), July 7, 1896:7.

309 **he was received enthusiastically** *The Cape Argus* (Cape Town), July 10, 1896:5; July 11, 1896:5.

309 **explaining that he had lost his way** Masson (1950:179).

310 **"Outsiders complain"** Murray (1958:64).

310 **his last club supper** Details of the supper from *The South African Review* (Cape Town), July 17, 1896:14.

310 **"an occasion of parallels"** Parsons (1977:253–54).

310 **Clemens listened to a tumultuous debate** Details of the debate from Parsons (1975/6:38–39).

311 **"anyone who witnessed the last two days debate"** *The Cape Times* (Cape Town), July 15, 1896.

311 **"they quarreled in two languages"** FTE:II,335.

311 **"so named for its levelness"** Ibid.

311 **"a quaint old picture"** Ibid.:335–36.

311 **Dr. James Barry** Biographical details from Burrows (1958:80–85); Rae (1958).

313 **"I am a married woman."** Rae (1958:116).

313 **Clemens told Barry's story** FTE:II,335–37.

313 **"I seemed to have been lecturing a thousand years"** Ibid.:337.

Chapter Forty-two

314 **"Africa seemed a colorless country"** Clemens (1931:170).

314 **"We hope to get a house"** SLC to William Dean Howells, August 5, 1896. Mildred Howells (1928:II,71).

314 **"In my despair and unassuageable misery"** SLC to Henry C. Robinson, September 28, 1896. MTL:636.

References

Abram, David, Harriet Podger, Devdan Sen, and Gareth John Williams. *India: The Rough Guide*. London: Rough Guides, 1994.

Agrawal, I. N. Mark Twain's visit to Allahabad. *Indian Journal of American Studies* 3, no. 1 (June 1973):104–8.

Ahluwalia, Harsharan Singh. Mark Twain's lecture-tour in India. *Mark Twain Journal* 34, no. 1 (1996).

Aldridge, Val. Celebrating a fizzer with a lot of bangs. *The Dominion*, November 5, 1996 (edition 2):7.

Anderson, Chris. Mark Twain in New Zealand. *New Zealand's Heritage* 5, no. 61 (1972):1702–5.

Anderson, Frederick, ed. *"Ah Sin": A Dramatic Work by Mark Twain and Bret Harte*. San Francisco: The Book Club of California, 1961.

Anonymous. Hocken and his library. *New Zealand's Heritage* 5, part 64 (1972):1794.

Barrow, Terence. *An Illustrated Guide to Maori Art*. Auckland: Reed Books, 1984.

Booth, Bradford A. Mark Twain's comments on Bret Harte's stories. *American Literature* XXV (May 1954):492–95.

Brinnin, John Malcolm. *The Sway of the Grand Saloon: A Social History of the North Atlantic*. New York: Delacorte, 1971.

Brooke, Brian, and Alan Finch. *A Story of Horsham: A Municipal Century*. Horsham: City of Horsham, 1982.

Budd, Louis J., ed. A listing of and selection from newspaper and magazine interviews with Samuel L. Clemens 1874–1910. *American Literary Realism 1870–1910* 10, no. 1 (Winter 1977).

Burden, Michael. *Lost Adelaide: A Photographic Record*. Melbourne: Oxford University Press, 1983.

Burnet, Ruth A. Mark Twain in the Northwest. *Pacific Northwest Quarterly* 42 (1951):187–202.

Burroughs, Edmund H. *History of Medicine in South Africa up to the End of the Nineteenth Century*. Cape Town: A. A. Balkema, 1958.

Burton, David, ed. *Confessions of Richard Burgess: the Maungatapu Murders and Other Grisly Crimes*. Wellington: A. H. & A. W. Reed, 1983.

Byrne, Thomas E. *Chemung County, 1890–1975*. Elmira, N.Y.: Chemung County Historical Society, Inc., 1976.

Carter, Paul J. Jr. Olivia Clemens edits *Following the Equator. American Literature* 30, no. 2 (1958):194–209.

Clark, R. D. *Anecdotes: Or Random Recollections of the Maritzburg High School and College*. Durban, South Africa: P. Davis and Sons, 1908.

Clemens, Clara. *My Father, Mark Twain*. New York: Harper & Brothers, 1931.

Clune, Frank. *Murders on Maunga-tapu*. Sydney: Angus & Robertson, 1959.

Cohen, Stan. *Missoula County Images*. Missoula, Mont.: Pictorial Histories Publishing Co., 1982.

Coleman, Rufus A. Mark Twain in Montana, 1895. *Montana Magazine of History*, Spring 1953, 9–16.

Cotton, Michelle L. *Mark Twain's Elmira, 1870–1910*. Elmira, N.Y.: The Chemung County Historical Society, 1985.

Crossette, Barbara. *The Great Hill Stations of Asia*. Boulder, Col.: Westview Press, 1998.

Daley, Suzanne. Where terror reigns in South Africa. *The New York Times*, June 26, 1996:A8.

Dalrymple, William. *City of Djinns: A Year in Delhi*. London: Flamingo, 1994 (first published 1993).

Darjeeling and Himalayan Railway Co., Ltd. *The Darjeeling and Himalayan Railway Illustrated Guide for Tourists*. London: The Darjeeling and Himalayan Railway Co., Ltd., 1896.

Darjeeling and Himalayan Railway Co., Ltd. *Darjeeling and Its Mountain Railway*. Darjeeling: Jetsum Publishing House, 1983. Reprint of first edition, 1921.

Davis, George Wesley. *Sketches of Butte from Vigilante Days to Prohibition*. Boston: Cornhill, 1921.

Denfield, Joseph. *Pioneer Past: The Illustrated History of East London*. Cape Town: Howard Timmins, 1965.

Derrick, D. A. *A History of Fiji*. Vol. 1. Suva: Government Press, Colony of Fiji. Third edition. 1957.

Dozey, E. C. *A Concise History of the Darjeeling District Since 1835 with a Complete Itinerary of Tours in Sikkim and the District*. Calcutta: Jetson Publishing House, 1989 (reprint of the second edition, the preface to which was dated 1922; the preface to the first edition was dated 1916).

Dwivedi, Sharad, and Rahul Mehrotra. *Bombay: The Cities Within*. Bombay: India Book House, 1995.

Eck, Diana L. *Banaras: City of Light*. New Delhi: Penguin Books India, 1993. (first published in London by Routledge & Kegan Paul, 1983).

Edwardes, Michael. *British India 1772–1947*. New Delhi: Rupa & Co., by arrangement with Pan Macmillan Ltd., London.

Emmons, David M. *The Butte Irish: Class and Ethnicity in an American Mining Town, 1875–1923*. Urbana: University of Illinois Press, 1989.

Entwisle, Peter. *William Mathew Hodgkins and His Circle: An Exhibition to Mark the Centenary of the Dunedin Public Art Gallery, October 1984*. Dunedin, N.Z.: Dunedin Public Art Gallery, 1984.

Everett, George. *Champagne in a Tin Cup: Uptown Butte and the Stories Behind the Façades*. Butte, Mont.: Outback Ventures, 1995.

Fatout, Paul. *Mark Twain on the Lecture Circuit*. Bloomington: Indiana University Press, 1960.

Fatout, Paul, ed. *Mark Twain Speaking*. Iowa City: University of Iowa Press, 1976.

Federal Writers' Project of the Work Projects Administration. *Montana: A State Guide Book*. New York: Viking, 1939.

Finlay, Hugh, Jon Murray, Alan Tiller, Charlotte Hindle, Tony Wheeler, John Noble, and Susan Forsyth. *Australia: A Travel Survival Kit*. Hawthorn, Victoria: Lonely Planet Publications, 1992.

Fischer, Gerald. The professional theatre in South Australia, 1838–1922. *Australian Letters* (Adelaide Festival of Arts Special Issue) 2, no. 4 (1970):79–97.

Fischer, Victor, and Michael B. Frank, eds. *Mark Twain's Letters, Volume 4, 1870–1871*. Berkeley: University of California Press, 1995.

Foner, Philip S. *Mark Twain: Social Critic*. New York: International Publishers, 1958.

Fraser, J. Baillie. *Military Memoir of Lieut.-Col. James Skinner, C.B.* Delhi: St. James Church (first published in 1856 in two volumes).

Friedman, Thomas L. Politics in the age of NAFTA. *The New York Times Weekly Review*, April 7, 1996:7.

Grace, A. A. Preface to Richard Hill and others, defendants. *The Maungatapu Mountain Murders: A Narrative of the Murder of Five Men between the Wakamarina River and Nelson by Burgess, Levy, Kelly and Sullivan*. Nelson, N.Z.: R. W. Stiles & Company.

Grattan, C. Hartley. *The Southwest Pacific to 1900: A Modern History*. Ann Arbor: University of Michigan Press, 1963.

Greenwall, Harry J. *His Highness the Aga Khan: Imam of the Ismailis*. London: Cresset Press, 1952.

Gribben, Alan. Introduction to Gribben and Karanovich (1992), iii–xi.

Gribben, Alan, and Nick Karanovich, eds. *Overland with Mark Twain: James B. Pond's Photographs and Journal of the North American Lecture Tour of 1895*. Elmira, N.Y.: Center for Mark Twain Studies at Quarry Farm, Elmira College, 1992.

Griffiths, George J. Unpublished notes for pre-dinner talk, Hocken Friends dinner on Mark Twain theme, September 2, 1895.

Griffiths, Reginald. *The Grahamstown Club, 1886–1986*. Grahamstown, S. Africa: The Grahamstown Club, 1986.

Hamilton, J. H. The "All-Red Route," 1893–1953: A history of the Trans-Pacific mail service between British Columbia, Australia, and New Zealand. *British Columbia Historical Quarterly*, January–April 1956.

Hammond, John Hays (as related to Alleyne Ireland). *The Truth about the Jameson Raid*. Boston: Marshall Jones Company, 1918 (first published in the *North American Review*, August and September 1918).

Hammond, John Hays. *The Autobiography of John Hays Hammond*. New York: Farrar & Rinehart, 1935.

Harnsberger, Caroline T. *Mark Twain, Family Man*. New York: Citadel Press, 1960.

———. *The Family Letters of Mark Twain*. Unpublished typescript copy in the Mark Twain Papers, Bancroft Library, University of California, Berkeley. No date.

Harte, Bret. *San Francisco in 1866. Being Letters to the Springfield Republican*. Edited by George R. Stewart and Edwin S. Fussell. San Francisco: Grabhorn Press, 1951.

Hattersley, Alan F. *An Illustrated Social History of South Africa*. Cape Town: A. A. Balkema, 1969.

Hirst, Robert H. "The Making of *The Innocents Abroad*: 1867–1872." Unpublished doctoral dissertation, University of California, Berkeley, 1975.

Hoffman, Andrew. *Inventing Mark Twain: The Lives of Samuel Langhorne Clemens*. New York: William Morrow and Co., 1997.

Howe, K. R. *Where the Waves Fall: A New South Sea Islands History from First Settlement to Colonial Rule*. Pacific Islands Monograph Series, no. 2. Honolulu: University of Hawaii Press, 1984.

Howells, Mildred, ed. *Life in Letters of William Dean Howells*. New York: Doubleday, Doran and Company, 1928.

Howells, William Dean. *My Mark Twain*. New York: Harper and Brothers, 1910.

Horvath, Ronald J., Graham E. Harrison, and Robyn M. Dowling. *Sydney: A Social Atlas*. Sydney: Sydney University Press in association with Oxford University Press Australia, 1989.

Hyde, H. Montgomery. *Oscar Wilde: The Aftermath*. London: Methuen, 1963.

Hyslop, Robert B. *Spokane's Building Blocks*. Spokane, Wash.: privately published, 1983.

Jerome, Robert D., and Herbert A. Wisbey Jr., eds. *Mark Twain in Elmira*. Elmira, N.Y.: Mark Twain Society, Inc., 1977.

Jackson, Stanley. *The Aga Khan: Prince, Prophet, and Sportsman*. London: Odhams Press, 1952.

Kalez, Jay J. *Saga of a Western Town . . . Spokane*. Spokane, Wash.: Lawton Printing, 1972.

Kaplan, Justin. *Mr. Clemens and Mark Twain: A Biography*. New York: Simon and Schuster, 1966.

Kelly, Matt J. *Anaconda, Montana's Copper City*. Anaconda, Mont.: Soroptimist Club of Anaconda, 1983.

Knight, Hardwicke, and Niel Wales. *Buildings of Dunedin*. Dunedin, N.Z.: John McIndoe, 1988.

Lane, Roger. *Murder in America*. Columbus: Ohio State University Press, 1997.

Lawton, Mary. *A Lifetime with Mark Twain: The Memories of Katy Leary, for Thirty Years His Faithful and Devoted Servant*. New York: Haskell House Publishers, 1972.

Leacock, Stephen. "A.L.O.W.," More of Mark Twain in Canada: 1895; a note from Winnipeg. *Queen's Quarterly* 42, no. 2 (1935):272–74.

Leary, Lewis, ed. *Mark Twain's Correspondence with Henry Huttleston Rogers, 1893–1909*. Berkeley and Los Angeles: University of California Press, 1969.

Logan, Rayford W. *The Betrayal of the Negro, from Rutherford B. Hayes to Woodrow Wilson*. New York: Collier Books, 1965 (originally published in 1954 as *The Negro in American Life and Thought: The Nadir, 1877–1901*).

Low, Herbert. Australian press reminiscences. *Worker* (Sydney), April 2, 1908:11.

Maclean, Chris, and Jock Phillips. *The Sorrow and the Pride: New Zealand War Memorials*. Historical Branch, New Zealand Department of Internal Affairs, 1990.

Marsden, Susan, Paul Stark, and Patricia Sumerling, eds. *Heritage of the City of Adelaide*. Adelaide: Corporation of the City of Adelaide, 1990.

McCulla, Dorothy, and Cathy Wright. *Footprints of Yesterday: Centennial, 1879–1979*. Crookston: Crookston Centennial Committee, 1979.

McKee, Russell, ed. *Mackinac: The Gathering Place*. Lansing, Mich.: Michigan Natural Resources Magazine, 1981.

Madsen, Brigham D. *The Bannock of Idaho*. Caldwell, Idaho: The Caxton Printers, 1958.

Masson, Madeleine. *Birds of Passage*. London: George Allen and Unwin, 1950.

Maunders, David, and Donella Jaggs. *An Asset to the State: Longerenong Agricultural College 1889–1989*. Melbourne: Victorian College of Agriculture and Horticulture, 1989.

McWaters, Vivian. *Daily Life at Longerenong 1889–1989*. Dooen, Victoria, Australia: Victorian College of Agriculture and Horticulture, 1989.

Moorhouse, Geoffrey, *Calcutta: The City Revealed*. New Delhi: Penguin Books India, 1994 (first published by Weidenfeld and Nicolson, 1971).

Mostert, Noel. Descendants of the Black Napoleon. Review of Stephen Taylor's *Shaka's Children*. *The New York Times Book Review*, July 21, 1996:24.

Murray, Joyce. *Claremont Album*. Cape Town: A. A. Balkema, 1958.

Mutalik, Keshav. *Mark Twain in India*. Bombay: Noble Publishing House, 1978.

Neider, Charles, ed. *The Autobiography of Mark Twain*. New York: Harper & Brothers, 1959.

Ogden, Christopher. *Throne of Gold: The Lives of the Aga Khans*. New York: William Morrow, 1996.

O'Rell, Max. Mark Twain and Paul Bourget. *North American Review*, March 1895:302–310.

Pakenham, Elizabeth. *Jameson's Raid*. London: Weidenfeld and Nicolson, 1960.

Paine, Albert Bigelow. *Mark Twain: A Biography*. New York: Harper and Brothers, 1912.

Paine, Albert Bigelow, ed. *Mark Twain's Letters*. New York: Harper and Brothers, 1917.

———. *Mark Twain's Notebook*. New York: Harper and Brothers, 1935.

Parsons, Coleman O. Mark Twain in Australia. *The Antioch Review* 21, no. 4 (1961):455–68.

———. Mark Twain in New Zealand. *The South Atlantic Quarterly* 61, no. 1 (1962):51–76.

————. Mark Twain in Ceylon. *The Twainian* 22, no. 1:4; no. 2:3–4 (1963).

————. Mark Twain: Traveler in South Africa. *The Mississippi Quarterly* 29, no. 1 (1975/6):3–41.

————. Mark Twain: Clubman in South Africa. *The New England Quarterly* 50, no. 2 (1977):234–54.

————. Mark Twain: Paid Performer in South Africa. *Mark Twain Journal* 19, no. 2 (1978):2–11.

Petersen, Eugene T. *Mackinac Island: Its History in Pictures.* Mackinac (Mich.) State Park Commission, 1973.

Pond, J. B. *Eccentricities of Genius: Memories of Famous Men and Women of the Platform and Stage.* New York: G. W. Dillingham, 1900.

Potts, E. Daniel, and Annette Potts. The Mark Twain Family in Australia. *Overland* (Melbourne) 70 (1978):46–50.

Rae, Isobel. *The Strange Story of Dr. James Barry.* London: Longmans, Green and Company, 1958.

Randall, Rona. *The Model Wife, Nineteenth-Century Style.* London: Herbert Press, 1989.

Rasmussen, R. Kent. *Mark Twain A to Z: the Essential Reference to His Life and Writings.* New York: Oxford University Press, 1995.

Reed, A. H., ed. *With Anthony Trollope in New Zealand.* Wellington: A. H. and A. W. Reed for the Dunedin Public Library, 1969.

Reed, Kenneth T. Mirth and misquotation: Mark Twain in Petoskey, Michigan. *The Mark Twain Journal* 15, no. 2 (1970):19–20.

Salamo, Lin, and Harriet Elinor Smith, eds. *Mark Twain's Letters, Volume 5, 1872–1873.* Berkeley: University of California Press, 1997.

Schlereth, Thomas J. *Victorian America: Transformation in Everyday Life, 1876–1915.* New York: HarperCollins, 1991.

Scott, Arthur L. *On the Poetry of Mark Twain: With Selections from His Verse.* Urbana: University of Illinois Press, 1966.

Shah, Sultan Sir Mohammed (Aga Khan III). *The Memoirs of Aga Khan: World Enough and Time.* London: Cassell, 1954.

Sherington, Geoffrey. Preface to Maunders and Jaggs (1989).

Shillingsburg, Miriam Jones. *At Home Abroad: Mark Twain in Australasia.* Jackson: University Press of Mississippi, 1988a.

———. Additional antipodean anecdotes, apocryphal adventures. *Mark Twain Journal* 26, no. 2 (Fall 1988b):28–29.

———. Down under day by day with Mark Twain. *Mark Twain Journal* 33, no. 2 (1995).

Shoebotham, H. Minar. *Anaconda: Life of Marcus Daly the Copper King.* Harrisburg, Mont.: Stockpole Co., 1956.

Smart, Maxwell J. G., and Arthur P. Bates. *The Wanganui Story.* Wanganui Newspapers, 1972.

Smith, Henry Nash, and William M. Gibson, eds. *Mark Twain–Howells Letters: The Correspondence of Samuel L. Clemens and William D. Howells, 1872–1910.* Cambridge, Mass.: Harvard University Press, 1960.

Smith, Iain R. *The Origins of the South African War, 1899–1902.* London: Longman, 1996.

Smythe, Carlyle. The real 'Mark Twain.' *The Pall Mall Magazine* 16, no. 65 (September 1898):29–36.

Sparks, Allister. *The Mind of South Africa: The Story of the Rise and Fall of Apartheid.* London: Mandarin Paperbacks, 1991 (originally published by William Heinemann, 1990).

Spear, Percival. *A History of India.* Volume 2. Harmondsworth: Penguin Books, 1978.

Spence, Clark C. *Montana: A Bicentennial History.* New York: Norton, 1978.

Steinbrink, Jeffrey. *Getting to Be Mark Twain.* Berkeley: University of California Press, 1991.

Stille, Alexander. The Ganges' next life. *The New Yorker,* January 19, 1998: 58–67.

Sturrock, Morna. *Stonnington: A Centenary History.* Burwood, Victoria: Victoria College Press, 1990.

Taylor, Eva. Langdon-Clemens plot in Woodlawn. In Jerome and Wisbey (1977):160–71.

———. *A History of the Park Church, 1846–1981.* Elmira, N.Y.: The Park Church, 1981.

Taylor, J. B. *A Pioneer Looks Back*. London: Hutchinson, 1939.

Theroux, Paul. Introduction to *To the Ends of the Earth: The Selected Travels of Paul Theroux*. New York: Random House, 1990:xv-xxi.

Twain, Mark. The private history of a campaign that failed. *The Century Magazine*, December 1885:194–204.

———. *More Tramps Abroad*. London: Chatto & Windus, 1897.

———. Chapters from my autobiography–XIII. *North American Review*, March 1, 1907:449–63.

———. *The Innocents Abroad*. Vol. 2 of *The Complete Works of Mark Twain*. New York: Harper & Brothers, 1911.

———. Concerning tobacco. In *What is Man?* Vol. 12 of *The Complete Works of Mark Twain*. New York: Harper & Brothers, 1917a:275–79.

———. How I edited an agricultural paper. In *Sketches New and Old*. Vol. 19 of *The Complete Works of Mark Twain*. New York: Harper & Brothers, 1917b:280–87.

———. How to tell a story. In *The $30,000 Bequest*. Vol. 18 of *The Complete Works of Mark Twain*. New York: Harper & Brothers, 1917c:263–70.

———. Taming the bicycle. In *What is Man?* Vol. 12 of *The Complete Works of Mark Twain*. New York: Harper & Brothers, 1917d:285–96.

———. *Pudd'nhead Wilson*. Vol. 3 of *The Complete Works of Mark Twain*. New York: Harper & Brothers, 1922.

———. Seventieth birthday speech. In *Mark Twain's Speeches*. Vol. 24 of *The Complete Works of Mark Twain*. New York: Harper & Brothers, 1923a:254–62.

———. The United States of lyncherdom. In *Europe and Elsewhere*. Vol. 20 of *The Complete Works of Mark Twain*. New York: Harper & Brothers, 1923b.:239–49.

———. A little note to M. Paul Bourget. In *In Defense of Harriet Shelley*. Vol. 16 of *The Complete Works of Mark Twain*. New York: Harper & Brothers, 1925a:171–86.

———. What Paul Bourget thinks of us. In *In Defense of Harriet Shelley*. Vol. 16 of *The Complete Works of Mark Twain*. New York: Harper & Brothers, 1925b:148–70.

————. Concerning the Jews. In *In Defense of Harriet Shelley*. Vol. 16 of *The Complete Works of Mark Twain*. New York: Harper & Brothers, 1925c:263–87.

————. *Following the Equator: A Journey Around the World*. 2 vols. Hopewell: Ecco Press, 1992, 1993 (first published by the American Publishing Company, 1897).

U.S. Bureau of the Census. *Historical Statistics of the United States, Colonial Times to 1970*. Part I. Washington, D.C.: 1975.

————. *Statistical Abstract of the United States 1996*. Washington, D.C.: 1996.

Vernede, R. V., ed. *British Life in India*. Delhi: Oxford University Press, 1995.

Weschler, Lawrence. An Afrikaner Dante. *The New Yorker*, November 8, 1993:78–100.

Wecter, Dixon, ed. *The Love Letters of Mark Twain*. New York: Harper & Brothers, 1949.

Acknowledgments

Samuel L. Clemens traveled around the world to pay his creditors, while I created my own by following him. If I cannot repay my debts, I can at least acknowledge them. Some of these will be clear to readers who consult my endnotes, in particular my obligations to Harsharan Singh Ahluwalia, Coleman O. Parsons, and Miriam Jones Shillingsburg, whose writings on one or more segments of Clemens's world tour were indispensable. The endnotes also include acknowledgment of personal communications, but because these are scattered and might be missed, I gather them here, with thanks to David Graham (Auckland), Albert Smith (Christchurch), George Griffiths (Dunedin), Margaret von Klemperer (Pietermaritzburg), Edric Russell (Queenstown), Lisa Philip (New York), and Hisako and Ian Ewing (Wellington). Although in the text itself I have acknowledged my indebtedness to Gretchen Sharlow (Center for Mark Twain Studies at Quarry Farm), I do so again here. She provided both encouragement and enlightenment at the beginning of my journey.

To Robert and Eleanor November I owe my serendipitous introduction to *Following the Equator*, Clemens's account of his world lecture tour. Serendipity, however, had little to do with the help I received in scores of libraries, museums, and archives along his route. Still, even though help was expected, special thanks are due to Sally Routledge, Bendigo Public Library (Bendigo); Brenda Bailey and David Briggs, Mark Twain Project (Berkeley); Dux van der Walt, City Librarian (Bloemfontein); Jackie Loos, South African Reference Library (Cape Town); Nandika Seneyiratne, Colombo Public Library (Colombo); Ed Melby, Polk County Historical Society (Crookston); Anthony Harris, Otago Museum, and David McDonald, The Hocken Library (Dunedin); Joan Simpson, Killie Campbell Africana Library (Durban); Alexandra de Sas Kropiwnicka and Gillian Vernon, East London Museum (East London); Alan

Gribbens, Elmira College (Elmira); William Jervois, Albany History
Museum (Grahamstown); Kathy McDonald, Longerenong College
(Horsham); Russell Beck and Karl Gillies, Southland Museum and
Art Gallery (Invercargill); Kokkie Duminy and Lynette van
Greunen, Africana Library (Kimberley); Noel Fields, Maryborough
Municipal Library (Maryborough); Kathleen Stringer, North Otago
Museum (Oamaru); David Buckley, Patrick McKenzie, and John
Morrison, Natal Society Library, and Marjorie Nicholson Hutchin-
son, Maritzburg College Museum (Pietermaritzburg); Margaret
Herradine, Port Elizabeth Library (Port Elizabeth); Helen Sparks,
Queenstown Public Library (Queenstown); and Penny Allen,
Wanganui District Council, and Lynley Fowler, Wanganui District
Library (Wanganui).

In addition, for useful background information I thank Erin
Broacha and Espi Moddie (Bombay); Allay Harendra Bikram, D. D.
Pradhan, and Evelyn Shah (Darjeeling); Jan Vorster (Durban);
Rhoda Hoft (Grahamstown); Colin D. Kerr (Invercargill); Neil
Plunket (Oamaru); Adrian Koopman (Pietermaritzburg); Anton
Jansen and Gerard Schuring (Pretoria); Leslie Tucker (Queens-
town); Donald Rickard and Graham Rickard (Stawell); Temple
Hauptfleisch (Stellenbosch); and Kemp Bailey (Wanganui).

All these and others helped provide the content of this book.
They cannot be blamed for whatever errors have crept into it. Nor
can the text's infelicities and obscurities be blamed on those who
did their best to expunge them. Readers and critics of the manuscript in various stages of its development include Jane Camhi, Paul
Cooper, Miriam Cooper, Cordelia Edvardson, Barbara Horvath, and
Ronald Horvath.

Exceptional thanks are due to my friend Ronald Horvath and
his colleague Peter Johnson, both at the Department of Geography,
University of Sydney, for providing the elegant maps that accompany this volume; to my agents Beth Elon and Deborah Harris, for
encouraging me to believe that I am a writer and for advising me to
keep Mark Twain on stage; to my editor, Webster Younce, for his
tact in persuading me to delete passages that impeded the narrative's flow; and to my brother Paul for long-term mentoring. It was
my great good fortune that my wife Alice not only accompanied me
on this around-the-world venture, but also helped carry out the

fieldwork and criticized each chapter as it was written and rewritten. In addition, she resigned herself with good grace to living with a man who would talk of little else save this project. In grateful recognition of her participation, support, and encouragement, I dedicate this book to her.

Index